CW01471731

Psittacine Birds

New Edition

General Editor

Peter H Beynon
BVSc MRCVS

Scientific Editors

Neil A Forbes
BVetMed MRCVS

and

Martin P C Lawton
BVetMed CertVOphthal CertLAS CBiol MIBiol FRCVS

Published by:
British Small Animal Veterinary Association,
Kingsley House, Church Lane,
Shurdington, Cheltenham,
Gloucestershire GL51 5TQ

A Company Limited by Guarantee in England
Registered Company No. 2837793
Registered as a Charity

Typeset by J Looker Printers Limited, Poole, England
Printed by Grafos SA, Barcelona, Spain

First Published 1996

ISBN 0 905214 30 7

Contents

Contributors

Brian H Coles BVSc MRCVS
17 Cross Green
Upton Chester
Cheshire CH2 1QR

John E Cooper BVSc CertLAS DTVM MRCPath CBiol FIBiol FRCVS
Durrell Institute for Conservation and Ecology
University of Kent
Canterbury Kent CT2 7PD

Margaret E Cooper LLB FLS
Durrell Institute for Conservation and Ecology
University of Kent
Canterbury Kent CT2 7PD

Gerry M Dorrestein DVM PhD
Department of Veterinary Pathology
Utrecht University Yalelaan
3548 CL Utrecht The Netherlands

Neil A Forbes BVetMed MRCVS
Clockhouse Veterinary Hospital
Wallbridge Stroud
Gloucestershire GL5 3JD

Christopher J Hall BVetMed MRCVS
346 Acton Lane Acton
London W3 8NX

Nigel H Harcourt-Brown BVSc FRCVS
30 Crab Lane Bilton
Harrogate
North Yorkshire HG1 3BE

Susanne Hendrich-Schuster DVM
Clinic for Avian Medicine
Justus-Liebig University
Frankfurterstra. 87
35392 Giessen Germany

Marie-Elisabeth Krautwald-Junghanns DVM
Clinic for Avian Medicine
Justus-Liebig University
Frankfurterstra. 87
35392 Giessen Germany

Martin P C Lawton BVetMed CertVOphthal CertLAS CBiol MIBiol FRCVS
12 Fitzilian Avenue
Harold Wood Romford
Essex RM3 0QS

A Dermod Malley BA MVB MRCVS
South Beech Veterinary Hospital
40 Southend Road Wickford
Essex SS11 8DU

Anne P McLoughlin BVSc MRCVS
Anwell Veterinary Centre
41 Brighton Road Coulsden
Surrey CR3 2BF

Peter W Scott MSc BVSc MIBiol MRCVS
Zoo and Aquatic Veterinary Group
Keanter
Stoke Charity Road
Kings Worthy Winchester
Hampshire SO23 7LS

Greg N Simpson BVSc(Pret) MRCVS
Clockhouse Veterinary Hospital
Wallbridge Stroud
Gloucestershire GL5 3JD

Victor R Simpson BVSc DTVM MRCVS
Veterinary Investigation Centre
Polwhele Truro
Cornwall TR4 9AD

John Stoodley
Down House Old Mill Lane
Lovedean Waterlooville
Hampshire PO8 0SW

Johanna Storm MRCVS
International Zoo Veterinary Group
Keighley Business Centre
South Street Keighley
West Yorkshire BD21 1AG

Foreword

The BSAVA manual series has a worldwide reputation for excellence. The predecessor to this manual, *The Manual of Parrots, Budgerigars and Other Psittacine Birds*, very rapidly established itself as an essential addition to the library of practitioners who wished to improve the quality of treatment provided for the parrots, budgerigars and other psittacine species which were presented to them.

The arrival of a vociferous psittacine patient in the veterinary surgeon's waiting room used to fill many practitioners' hearts with dread. However, easy access to an authoritative text helped them to overcome this feeling and to provide the level of service and treatment expected and demanded by today's clients. Many practitioners went on to develop an interest in these wonderful creatures which would otherwise have been virtually impossible.

This new edition has, quite rightly, been given a new title, *The Manual of Psittacine Birds*. It is not, as is often the case in the BSAVA manual series, a revised edition. There are fundamental changes to the style, content and authors, and so it is, in reality, a totally new book. As such it will be welcomed by veterinary practices and, I am sure, by many aviculturists.

Under the general editorship of Peter Beynon (who as President of the day wrote the Foreword in the original manual), the scientific editors, Neil Forbes and Martin Lawton, have marshalled the skills and knowledge of the seventeen authors to ensure that this title maintains the high standards and traditions of the BSAVA manuals.

John Robert Dalton BVMS MRCVS
President BSAVA 1995-96

CHAPTER ONE

Introduction

Neil A Forbes and Martin P C Lawton

Birds form a unique group that can be traced back some 150 million years ago to *Archaeopteryx lithographica* which is considered to be the link between birds and reptiles. There are many similarities between birds and reptiles, not least egg laying and the production of nitrogenous wastes in the form of various urates. The possession of feathers and flight in the majority of avian Families sets them apart from other animals. The major modifications of the forelimbs into wings are the basic reason for their success, allowing them more easily to seek out appropriate environments and fresh sources of food, and to escape the attention of predators. The Class Aves encompasses a wide range of Orders comprising over 9,000 species (see Table 1.1). Many are kept for food, eg. Galiformes, Struthioniformes and some Anseriformes; sport, eg. Falconiformes, Columbiformes and Strigiformes; or companionship, eg. Passeriformes and Psittaciformes. The Class is diverse with members differing in many significant aspects.

Table 1.1. Orders of the Class Aves.

Order	Type of bird
Anseriformes	Ducks, geese, swans.
Apodiformes	Swifts, humming-birds.
Apterygiformes	Kiwi.
Caprimulgiformes	Nightjars.
Casuariformes	Emus and cassowaries.
Charadriiformes	Waders, gulls, auks.
Ciconiformes	Herons, storks.
Coliformes	Colies.
Columbiformes	Pigeons, doves.
Coraciiformes	Kingfishers, hoopoes.
Cuculiformes	Cuckoos, turacos.
Falconiformes	Falcons.
Galiformes	Game birds.
Gaviformes	Divers.
Gruiformes	Cranes, rails.
Passeriformes	Perching birds.
Pelecaniformes	Pelicans.
Phoenicopteriformes	Flamingoes.
Piciformes	Woodpeckers.
Podicipediformes	Grebes.
Procellariformes	Albatrosses, petrels.
Psittaciformes	Parrots, parakeets.
Rheiformes	Rheas.
Sphenisciformes	Penguins.
Strigiformes	Owls.
Struthioniformes	Ostriches.
Tinamiformes	Tinamous.
Trogoniformes	Trogons

Table 1.2. Common and scientific names.

Common name	Scientific name
African Grey (Grey Parrot)* Timneh Grey	*Psittacus erithacus erithacus* *Psittacus e. timneh*
Amazon Parrots Blue-fronted Amazon Cuban Amazon Yellow-headed Amazon Mealy Amazon Orange-winged Amazon Red-lored Amazon White-fronted Amazon Yellow-crowned Amazon Yellow-naped Amazon	*Amazona* spp. *Amazona aestiva* *Amazona leucocephala* *Amazona oratrix* *Amazona farinosa* *Amazona amazonica* *Amazona autumnalis* *Amazona albifrons* *Amazona ochrocephala* *Amazona ochrocephala auropalliata*
Budgerigar	*Melopsittacus undulatus*
Cockatiel	*Nymphicus hollandicus*
Cockatoos Galah Cockatoo Goffin's Cockatoo Lesser Sulphur-crested Cockatoo Moluccan (Salmon-crested) Cockatoo Palm Cockatoo White Cockatoo	*Cacatua* spp.; *Eolophus* spp.; *Probosciger* spp. *Eolophus roseicapilla* *Cacatua goffini* *Cacatua sulphurea* *Cacatua moluccensis* *Probosciger aterimus* *Cacatua alba*
Conures Maroon-bellied Conure Red-masked Conure Sun Conure	*Aratinga* spp.; *Pyrrhura* spp. *Pyrrhura frontalis* *Aratinga erthrogenys* *Aratinga solstitialis*
Eclectus Parrots Eclectus Parrot Vosmaeri Eclectus	*Eclectus* spp. *Eclectus roratus* *Eclectus r. vosmaeri*
Amboina King Parrot	*Alisterus amboiensis*
Lorikeets	*Eos* spp.
Lories Chattering Lorie Rainbow Lorie	*Lorius* spp.; *Trichoglossus* spp. *Lorius garrulus* *Trichoglossus haematodus*
Lovebirds Fischer's Lovebird Masked Lovebird Peach-faced Lovebird	*Agapornis* spp. *Agapornis fischeri* *Agapornis personata* *Agapornis roseicollis*

* Although the correct common name is Grey Parrot, the editors have decided to use the more commonly recognised name, African Grey.

Table 1.2. Continued.

Common name	Scientific name
Macaws	*Ara* spp.
Blue and Gold (Blue and Yellow) Macaw	*Ara ararauna*
Chestnut-fronted (Severe) Macaw	*Ara severa*
Green-winged Macaw	*Ara chloroptera*
Hyacinth Macaw	*Andorhynchus hyacinthus*
Red-fronted Macaw	*Ara rubrogenys*
Red-shouldered (Hahn's) Macaw	*Ara nobilis nobilis*
Scarlet Macaw	*Ara macao*
Muller's Parrot	*Tanygnathus sumatranus*
Pionus Parrots	*Pionus* spp.
Blue-headed Parrot	*Pionus menstruus*
Dusky Parrot	*Pionus fuscus*
Maximilian's (Scaly-headed) Parrot	*Pionus maximiliana*
Parakeets	*Brotogeris* spp.; *Polytelis* spp.; *Psittacula* spp. *Myiopsitta* spp.; *Cyanoramphus* spp.; *Neophema* spp.
Alexandrine Parakeet	*Psittacula eupatria*
Canary-winged Parakeet	*Brotogeris versicolorus*
Lord Derby Parakeet	*Psittacula derbiana*
Moustached Parakeet	*Psittacula alexandri*
Plum-headed Parakeet	*Psittacula cyanocephala*
Princess (of Wales) Parakeet	*Polytelis alexandrae*
Quaker (Monk) Parakeet	*Myiopsitta monachus*
Red-fronted (Kakariki) Parakeet	*Cyanoramphus novaezelandiae*
Slaty-headed Parakeet	*Psittacula krameri*
Splendid (Scarlet-chested) Parakeet	*Neophema splendida*
Turquoise (Turquoisine) Parakeet	*Neophema pulchella*
Rosellas	*Platycercus* spp.
Eastern Rosella	*Platycercus eximius*
Golden-mantled Rosella	*Platycercus e. ceciliae*
Pale-headed Rosella	*Platycercus adscitus*
Senegal Parrot	*Poicephalus senegalus*
Vasa Parrot	*Coraopsis* spp.

This manual sets out to deal only with members of the Family Psittacidae belonging to the Order Psittaciformes, the group of birds commonly referred to as 'psittacines'. Although its use is not always grammatically correct, the term psittacine is generally accepted and widely used to refer to any of the 330 species in some 82 genera which make up the Family Psittacidae. For this reason, psittacine has been used throughout this manual.

The scientific names and Family names of psittacines, like all other taxa, are prone to change based on new information which affects previous classification. Throughout the manual the editors have opted to use common names in the text to prevent unnecessary repetition of scientific names. The scientific names of a number of psittacines, including all the species mentioned in this manual, are listed in Table 1.2.

Psittacines are companions, pets and exhibits. Because of their intelligence and ability to mimic and be trained, they have been popular for many centuries. It is difficult to obtain figures on the numbers of psittacines that are kept in captivity in the United Kingdom (UK). Some information is provided on those species which are covered by legislation, ie. that introduced as a result of the Convention on International Trade in Endangered Species of Wild Fauna and Flora (The Washington Convention or CITES). Data relating to the importation of psittacines into the UK is available from HM Customs and Excise; the Ministry of Agriculture, Fisheries and Food (MAFF) has data on quarantine returns. The breeding of many species is challenging but essential for the continuation of supplies both for captivity and, hopefully in the future, for the reintroduction of rare species back into the wild.

The veterinary profession does not have a good reputation when it comes to dealing with birds. However, as more veterinary surgeons are becoming involved in avian medicine and surgery, and the level of knowledge is increasing, advice is being sort more frequently on the health, welfare and breeding of psittacines. It is important that veterinary surgeons are willing to learn about and contribute to the knowledge on welfare, conservation, breeding and nutritional requirements, as well as investigating and treating causes of disease.

In order for the veterinary surgeon to deal adequately with psittacines, an understanding of their basic biology is required. There are many organisations which encourage and educate in the art and science of aviculture. In addition, there are veterinary associations, such as the Association of Avian Veterinarians, which provide continuing education, advice and literature. Even inexperienced veterinary surgeons can assimilate at least the basic knowledge necessary for them to deal with an avian case. Offering 'the orange powder' (tetracyclines) to be put into the water, often without even examining the patient or attempting to establish a possible diagnosis, is no longer acceptable.

There are many books, manuals and atlases available on birds in general and psittacines in particular. Reference has been made to papers, articles or books within the chapters so that more detailed information may be obtained. The veterinary surgeon who requires information on psittacines has no excuse for pleading total ignorance. Searches on specific subjects are available as a service by the Royal College of Veterinary Surgeons (RCVS) Wellcome Library which is also able to obtain copies of all relevant publications.

The aim of this manual is to provide an easily accessible source of information on the clinical aspects of psittacine medicine that are most likely to be required by the veterinary surgeon in general practice. The manual does not try to compete with the many authoritative texts, such as Ritchie, Harrison and Harrison (1994), but has attempted to bring together readily available information in a small volume that is easily referred to while the patient may be at the practice or even in the consulting room.

The format of the chapters in this manual was considered at length by the editors. It was decided that the manual should have a mixed layout with the initial chapters dealing with disciplines (Husbandry, Nutrition, Radiography, Anaesthesia, *Post-Mortem* Examination) leading onto some problem orientated headings (Nursing the Sick Bird, Polydipsia/Polyuria, Diarrhoea/Vomiting, Fits/Incoordination/Coma) as well as organ systems (Head Problems, Foot/Leg Problems, Wing Problems). The aim at all times has been to assist the practitioner when faced with a clinical problem or situation.

The Appendix lists the generic drugs mentioned in the manual together with an example(s) of the trade name(s) and manufacturer(s) current at the time of publication. In the case of drugs which are produced by several companies, eg. some of the antibiotics, the trade name and manufacturer favoured by the author is shown. The editors stress that the list is not a comprehensive list of all the trade names and manufacturers of drugs mentioned in this manual.

The Index should also be consulted as, with this format, a disease may be dealt with in several chapters. It may be necessary to read the references at the end of each chapter in order to obtain more detailed information or, indeed, to consult the author(s) of that chapter.

REFERENCES

Ritchie BW, Harrison GJ and Harrison LR (1994) Eds *Avian Medicine: Principles and Application.* Wingers, Lake Worth.

CHAPTER TWO

Husbandry

Johanna Storm

INTRODUCTION

Psittacines are maintained in captivity as pets in the home, as breeding birds in aviculture, in zoos and in conservation projects. All of these forms of husbandry have variations and generate their own veterinary problems. Although a large proportion of psittacines purchased in the UK nowadays are captive bred, importation of wild birds and captive-bred specimens from other countries still takes place. Indeed, the proposed relaxation of quarantine rules between the UK and the other countries of the European Union (EU) is likely to increase considerably the flow of captive-bred specimens and those already quarantined in Europe via this route.

INTERNATIONAL QUARANTINE

Present importation requirements for psittacines entering the UK are likely to be replaced or removed within the very near future. Currently (April 1995), birds or eggs entering from a non-EU country are restricted to certain ports of entry. Birds and eggs from EU and non-EU countries require import licensing by the Ministry of Agriculture, Fisheries and Food (MAFF) and they must undergo a 35-day quarantine in licensed premises. Domestic accommodation may be licensed for quarantine of small numbers of pet birds. During this period, they undergo inspection by a Local Veterinary Inspector (LVI), including within 24 hours of arrival, on the day of clearance and, for commercial imports, at regular intervals in between.

The duties of the LVI supervising the quarantine premises are summarised in the licence document issued to importers. For commercial importation sentinel birds are required: these are Newcastle disease virus (NDV)-free chickens which share the same air space and which have to be blood sampled at the beginning and end of the quarantine period to demonstrate that they have not seroconverted on the haemagglutination inhibition (HI) test for Newcastle disease (paramyxovirus type 1). Birds dying during the early stages of quarantine must be submitted to a MAFF Veterinary Investigation Centre (VIC) for *post-mortem* examination. Further submissions are at the

discretion of the supervising LVI. All submissions are investigated for NDV, which is the only current requirement. However, most VICs are now aware of the other significant psittacine diseases which may occur in quarantine and will alert the LVI to their presence. Submission of dead birds after the first three weeks of quarantine, which is not mandatory, may delay the clearance of the shipment because of the time needed to screen for NDV.

An exemption is granted for family pet birds: two birds per person (up to six per family) may be quarantined at the owner's home or other similar approved premises, provided there are no domestic poultry nearby. Sentinel birds are not required and LVI inspection is limited to the first and last days of the 35-day period. Import licensing is still required and import permits under the Convention on International Trade in Endangered Species (CITES) are required from the Department of the Environment (DoE) for most species, whatever the scale of the importation. Relaxation of Customs controls at ports of entry from the EU has already lead to the uncontrolled importation of unlicensed birds.

There is no onus on the LVI to have any special knowledge of psittacines or other wild birds under his/her care, but membership of the appropriate panel for bird import/export is necessary. This regrettable situation has often meant that shipments of birds which have developed disease other than NDV have not received adequate care, and most post-import deaths have been due to disease, much of which is preventable or treatable with the appropriate expertise.

EXPORT REQUIREMENTS

Veterinarians may be asked by psittacine owners to provide export health certificates for birds travelling to various countries, including Northern Ireland. Some countries require serological testing of birds for NDV, and it is important that blood samples are taken in sufficient time to allow the tests to be completed before departure. Clients should be questioned closely as to any health certification and testing requirements on their licence and reminded that they may need CITES export certification from the DoE.

PET BIRDS

The vast majority of psittacines which the practitioner will see in the surgery will be household pets. Although any species may be kept in this way, from the budgerigar to the Hyacinth Macaw, most pet birds will be budgerigars and cockatiels, which are domesticated species. Nevertheless, there are increasing numbers of larger parrots in private care. Pet birds may be kept in cages, with or without access to the owner's house; on stands, sometimes permanently chained by the leg; or even free in the house or at semi- or permanent liberty in the garden. All of these systems have their own risks and drawbacks, but clearly the best option for an active bird is to have the maximum liberty possible. It is the veterinarian's duty to encourage this option, though under controlled conditions. The worst scenario is for a solitary large parrot to be kept confined to a small cage by owners who are out all day, and to receive a poor quality, high fat diet (see Chapter 3).

Choice of Bird

The veterinarian should be able to advise a client on a suitable choice of species to keep as a companion, as well as the best source, age and sex. It is important to emphasise the distinction between the domesticated species and those which are within one or two generations from the wild. The following characteristics should act as a guide:

Budgerigars - domesticated birds available in a large variety of colours and types, some of them rare and valuable. Budgerigars are easy to tame, train and house, requiring only a simple cage with two or more perches, feeding bowls and toys. These birds can become finger-tame quite easily and be allowed limited liberty in the house, provided they are protected from doors and windows, poisonous metals, plants and chemicals. Their disadvantages are that they are relatively short-lived, often only reaching five or six years of age before succumbing to some breed-related disease, and many of the commercial breeding flocks are affected by chlamydiosis, trichomoniasis and *Megabacterium* sp.

Cockatiels - domesticated birds available as the normal grey (wild-type) colour or in a limited variety of colour mutations, some of which appear to have shorter life spans. Cockatiels are larger and more active than budgerigars, but are capable of being housed and managed similarly, though in a slightly bigger cage. Talking abilities are not as good as budgerigars or other parrots. Cockatiels are frequently infected with chlamydiosis, giardiasis and mycoplasmosis, and are probably the source of most human chlamydial infection acquired from birds. Chewing and biting abilities are considerably greater than for the budgerigar. Females kept alone may become persistent egg layers (see Chapter 11); therefore, male birds make better pets.

Lovebirds - quiet birds, but difficult to tame unless hand reared, when they make good individual pets. The commonest way for households to keep these birds is as a pair in a large cage. Unfortunately, visual sex determination in lovebirds is unreliable, and incompatibility between same sex birds can be serious. Nevertheless, an active pair will live and breed under 'pet' conditions. Lovebirds are not good talkers.

African Greys - this is the best pet among the larger parrots, although not the best talker. Many hand-reared birds are now available and clients should be strongly encouraged to pay the extra price for such birds, rather than buying an imported specimen, many of which will never become hand tame. Wild-caught birds can be distinguished by their crudely cropped flight feathers and a loud growling response when approached. Many are terrified of the human hand. This is not a bird for the beginner - it has a formidable bite and is highly intelligent, requiring a lot of stimulation and companionship from the owner. People who are out at work all day should not contemplate keeping this type of bird. If acquired as a hand-reared young bird, it will make an easily tamed pet, but may become aggressive and jealous as it reaches maturity, especially if male. A large cage is needed, although the bird will climb rather than fly in confinement. If the house is not suitable for the bird to fly free, the wings will have to be feather-clipped.

Amazons - these birds have the same housing requirements as African Greys, but are less demanding. Some, such as the Yellow-naped Amazon, are the best talkers among the parrots. Male birds can become very aggressive at maturity and Amazons are inclined to be one-person birds. Amazons are easier to adapt to novel foods than African Greys, which can be very conservative.

Cockatoos - white cockatoos make very demanding pets and should only be considered by owners with parrot experience and a great deal of time and patience. These birds are highly strung and very intelligent and destructive, yet they are the parrots most amenable to training and problem-solving. They are very easily upset and may begin feather-plucking and self-mutilation after even the most minor stresses or changes in their environment and routine. The Galah or Rose-breasted Cockatoo is becoming available as a hand-reared pet and, although expensive, seems more manageable than its larger relatives.

Parakeets, conures and lories - among the smaller species of wild psittacines, only the conures make good pets. They become extremely tame and friendly and are easy to feed and house; their call, however, can be extremely irritating and loud. Australian parakeets do not tame well and are best suited to aviaries, as are the Afro-Asian parakeets like the Ring-necked Parakeet. Lories would make superb pets, perhaps the best of all, if something could be done about their complex liquid diet and equally liquid faeces. Owners need to provide cages with protective surrounds for these birds.

Macaws - these very large birds are only suitable for large homes, with owners prepared to put up with their highly destructive nature. The practice of keeping them chained to stands is unsuitable - they need spacious cages and opportunity for exercise. Some species, eg. the Hyacinth and Green-winged Macaws, are very tame and confiding if hand reared, but others, like the Scarlet Macaw, can become spiteful as adults.

Housing

A wide variety of parrot cages is available. Most now have plastic bases and chromed or bronzed wire tops: these pose no risk to the birds and are easily cleaned. Cages for the larger species must be more substantial. Typical dimensions of commercially produced cages are given below:

Budgerigar cage	40 x 24 x 36cm
Medium parrot cages	48 x 48 x 68cm
	60 x 40 x 65cm
Macaw cage	100 x 75 x 166cm

Note should be made of Section 8(1) of the Wildlife and Countryside Act 1981 which deals with the keeping or confining of any bird in any cage or other receptacle which is not sufficient in height, length or breadth to permit the bird to stretch its wings freely.

Many owners like to construct their own cages, often of considerable size. The main risks involved are that they may leave sharp, unfinished edges and may use newly galvanised wire which can lead to zinc poisoning (see Aviary Design).

Perches should be made of wood; plastic and metal perches may seem to be easier to clean and more durable, but they do not provide a good surface for the bird's feet or allow chewing, which is a valuable source of occupation. Appropriately sized tree branches can be used, provided exotic and toxic plants are avoided. Oak, fruit woods and willow are suitable. Natural perches provide a variety of shapes and diameters for the feet. Standard diameters of commercial perches are 1.5, 2 and 3cm for small to medium sized birds.

Cages should be positioned in the home to avoid severe fluctuations in temperature. Exposure to constant direct sunlight should be avoided. Covering psittacines at night is not strictly necessary, but it allows the owner to regulate the bird's behaviour and photoperiod to some extent. Excessive artificial daylength may play a part in feather, behavioural and reproductive disorders in pet psittacines, as may the low humidity of centrally heated environments. Constant high temperatures are unnecessary for healthy birds. Toys play an important part in providing amusement and occupation for intelligent birds. Many purpose designed parrot toys made from heavy acrylic and metal chain are now available; these are expensive but virtually indestructible. Other toys may be dangerous to birds, especially those with weak chain links, toxic metal content or small, easily swallowed parts. Owners should always be questioned closely about possible ingestion of toys by their bird and asked to bring any toys to the surgery. Natural items, such as pine cones, large nuts, corn cobs or chop bones, occupy birds equally well, as do wooden clothes pegs, fibre ropes and cardboard boxes. Plastic and metal items should be avoided unless specially manufactured for psittacines.

AVIARY BIRDS

Parrot aviculture has a long history and has been widespread in the UK for at least a century. Recent years, however, have seen a substantial change in emphasis from the keeping of budgerigars, lovebirds and Australian parakeets towards the breeding of larger parrots in aviaries, often for profit. Much of this change has been brought about by the availability of large numbers of imported birds during the last three decades, coupled with a constant threat of import bans. More successful breeding of monomorphic species has followed the advent of surgical sexing in the late 1970s. Aviculturists are often very sophisticated in their approach to the care and breeding of their birds, and the veterinarian needs to spend time studying their aims and methods, as well as their medical problems, if he/she is to be of significant help. There are also many beginners in aviculture, especially those 'trading up' from small domesticated species to larger parrots, who need help and advice; the inexperienced veterinarian would do well to cultivate an experienced breeder to whom he can refer clients for discussion of management problems.

Aviculture medicine differs considerably from clinic-based avian practice, although it still needs good hospital and clinic support to deal with the individual bird. In a way, aviculture medicine resembles poultry medicine in that it deals with flock problems, nutrition, incubation, etc., yet goes forward from poultry medicine in that it must also deal with the individual bird needing a high level of veterinary care. Small animal practitioners interested in this field must, therefore, re-expand their horizons to serve the interests of a minor agricultural industry. Many may find this incompatible with their clinic-based approach.

Housing

There are many texts available covering aviary care of the different psittacine species, including all types of aviary design and structure, some of which are listed at the end of this chapter. However, there are two basic types of housing for breeding birds: intensive systems and extensive systems.

Intensive systems are indoors and thus benefit from temperature and light control, and ease of cleaning and management. Examples would be the typical birdroom for small species where a garden shed or garage, or even a room or cellar in the house, is lined with small breeding cages housing budgerigars or cockatiels, extending to large purpose-built buildings with suspended wire flights housing birds as large as macaws. These systems have the disadvantages of all intensive agriculture in that the concentration of birds leads to a high risk of infectious disease outbreaks and the requirements for ventilation and hygiene are high. Few aviculturists understand that essentially the intensive poultry industry has vaccinated or medicated its way out of many of the disease problems, an option not open to keepers of psittacines at present. Consequently, unless they operate a very careful, virtually closed-flock collection, intensive aviculturists may expect their birds to suffer major disease problems sooner or later.

Extensive systems are preferable in many ways, being outdoor collections (with appropriate weather protection) of larger flights which provide the birds with the benefits of fresh air, exercise and the disinfecting effects of the weather. The major disadvantages of open aviaries are risks from pests and predators, eg. mice and wild birds, an inability to control the environment for breeding purposes (light and temperature) and security. Whereas, a few years ago, intensification of production was the main reason for indoor systems, protection of the birds from theft is now the major concern.

Aviary Design

The standard outdoor parrot aviary, whatever the size, consists of a covered shelter, which may be constructed of wood or other building materials, and an outdoor flight of wire mesh with metal framework. All woodwork has to be protected from parrots, or they will demolish it. Floors may be planted soil, sand, bark, pebbles or impervious concrete. The larger the flight the less need there is for a disinfectable floor, and species vary in the amount of time they spend on the ground. Australian parakeets, for example, are ground feeders and will forage constantly, leading to a high risk of parasitic worm infestation on earth floors. Some aviculturists, copying the North American pattern, have raised their aviaries off the ground, allowing the droppings to fall through a wire floor away from the birds and providing greater protection from pests. Others have enclosed the roof and often much of the sides of their flights in an effort to keep out wild birds or their

droppings and provide greater weather protection, especially in the early spring when birds may begin to breed in cold weather.

Indoor accommodation may simply be large cages, with solid sides and back for small species, or all wire suspended flights for larger birds. Others may be solidly constructed within a building, with birds being visually separated from each other. Obvious safety features, such as the division of a house into separate sections, increased ventilation and effective drainage, may result from informed veterinary advice. Lighting may be natural, through roof lights, or totally artificial on a time-controlled regime designed to increase the breeding season. Either way, the lack of natural sunlight, which is important for vitamin D_3 metabolism, should be taken into account and the diet adjusted accordingly. Flights are usually of wire construction; it is important that the gauge and type of wire selected is strong enough. For larger species, dip-galvanised weldmesh is commonly used, but owners need to be aware of the severe risks to birds of zinc poisoning. Typically, drips of galvanising solution may be left on the wire and the birds may bite these off and swallow them. Treatment of new wire with metal brushes to remove drips, followed by washing in dilute acetic acid to 'age' the new zinc surface, is effective prevention. Using the American term 'new wire disease' for this problem is effective in alerting owners for the future.

Natural branches are preferred for perching and these should be spread around the flight to maximise exercise. Food should be presented in stainless steel dishes which can be protected from contamination by the birds and pests by careful siting. Attaching wire-mounted dishes to a large steel plate will prevent mice climbing into them, as will raising them off the floor on a smooth-sided plinth or pole. Frequent changes of food and dishes are required for some species, especially liquid feeders.

Beyond these generalisations, specific shapes and sizes of aviaries which suit the birds are a matter of experience and constant dispute. Undoubtedly, some birds will breed better in small, dark enclosures – African parrots, for example – whilst others benefit from long open flights. Space for moderate, unhindered flight would seem to be a minimum welfare requirement, and beyond this should be left to the aviculturist. The veterinarian need only apply his general knowledge of animal housing and hygiene, and his instinct for animal welfare, to assist in this area.

BREEDING

The main aim of psittacine aviculture is breeding, and all birds, other than single pets, should be given this opportunity. Many psittacines are monomorphic and sexing procedures (by laparoscopy, chromosomes or DNA) (see Chapter 22) are available to ensure that birds are properly paired. Single sex pairs will often indulge in very convincing homosexual behaviour, and any fertility investigation should start with the simple question of reliable sex determination. Laboratory-based sex diagnosis has suffered from the disadvantage that the individual bird cannot easily be connected with the report, and the veterinarian should be aware that fraud is extremely common.

Most birds are kept in pairs for breeding, although some will breed happily in groups, eg. cockatiels, budgerigars and lovebirds. Keeping larger parrots in groups may not necessarily prevent all breeding, but dominance often means that only one pair is successful. Some species, especially conures and Amazons, do well when pairs are kept within sight and sound of each other, whilst macaws seem to need visual separation. Aviaries are often constructed in rows with one internal service corridor, enabling several pairs to be kept efficiently, usually with a double wire partition between them. A more recent system houses all birds together in the non-breeding season in a large flight, and then later separates them into breeding aviaries. This has the advantage of increasing exercise and social interaction, but will magnify any disease problems. Obviously, the birds need to be individually identified to avoid inadvertent homosexual pairing. Similarly, and most typically with Australian parakeets, breeders will take all the young of the year from each breeding aviary and concentrate them in one group before dispersal. When coupled with regular use of the same flight without disinfection year after year, this system spreads and perpetuates disease extremely effectively.

Almost all psittacines are hole nesters, usually using natural holes in trees, rocks and even the earth, which they may excavate further with their powerful beaks. The common exception is the Quaker (or Monk) Parakeet, which builds a large communal nest of twigs. It follows, therefore, that in captivity they will need some similar opportunity, especially as the discovery, selection and preparation of the nest site plays such an important role in stimulating hormonal activity. It is usual to provide a nestbox, usually of vertical shape, with a round entrance hole of appropriate size. Nestboxes and entrance holes often appear very small for the birds, but this seems to mimic their natural choice. Recent studies have demonstrated much greater breeding success in Orange-winged Amazons when they were required to partially excavate the nest hole for themselves. Construction should be of natural tree or joinery wood, with enough surplus to allow the birds to chew and destroy much of the structure and form a woodchip lining for the nest. An inspection hatch is usual to monitor progress, often from outside the aviary, the nestbox being attached to the wire. Some aviculturists leave nestboxes in the aviary all year round, which may lead to repeated laying in some species. Aviculturists should be encouraged to give the

birds a break of some months; removal and replacement of their box can act as a powerful stimulus to breeding in non-productive pairs. Nesting material is not required for most species, although some will add chewed up branches and leaves to the wood which they remove from the inside of the box. This may be essential for the Palm Cockatoo. Occasionally, the nest will become heavily fouled during the breeding season and it may be advisable to replace it with clean litter; this should certainly be done at the end of the season and the boxes thoroughly cleaned, disinfected and treated for arthropod parasites. Infestations during the breeding season can be dealt with by adding a spoonful of 5% carbaryl dust to the nest material.

Egg Laying and Incubation

Avian veterinarians need to familiarise themselves with the normal processes of egg laying and development. Most small species lay eggs at daily intervals, whilst the larger birds lay at 2-3 day intervals. In species which have 2-3 egg clutches, eg. Amazons, there is often a prolonged delay of 4-5 days between the second and third eggs. Incubation starts with the first egg, leading to staggered hatching times; total incubation periods vary from 18-30 days over the whole species range (see Chapter 20). Females reach sexual maturity at ages ranging from a few months in conures to 5-6 years in larger macaws. These ages are often lower in captive-bred birds. Males usually mature slightly later, resulting in a high incidence of infertility in the first season. Removal of clutches immediately after laying will often lead to birds recycling after a short period ('double clutching'). Some species will breed all year round, whilst others have quite closely defined seasons which can be extended to a limited extent by photoperiod manipulation. Infertility is a common reason for removing a clutch and this can be determined by 'candling' the eggs at a few days of age (see Chapter 20). It is always wise to place such clutches in an artificial incubator for a few days, in case development was simply suspended because the female was not sitting on the eggs. Commercially available egg candlers can be used if the aperture is modified to take the smaller eggs of psittacines; alternatively, a simple pen light or fibre optic light source in a darkened box will suffice. Development of the air cell and a corona of blood vessels will indicate the presence of a viable embryo, although it requires around two weeks of incubation before clearly defined vessels are seen. Cracks in eggs can also be recognised and repaired with nail varnish or cyanoacrylate glues.

Artificial Incubation

Many aviculturists routinely incubate eggs artificially, either because they need to be rescued from incompetent parents, or to increase production by inducing the parents to recycle. Eggs that have been partially incubated by the parents do much better than those taken at day one; nevertheless, very good success rates have been achieved.

There are many different incubators available. Ideally, they should be forced-air type, fitted with rollers to turn the eggs and with a very accurate thermometer and sensitive thermostat. Most breeders use the Fahrenheit scale as it allows more precise settings over a very narrow range. Psittacine eggs will develop over the range 97-102°F (36.1-38.9°C), but the best results are obtained over a narrower range of 98.5-99.7°F (37-37.6°C). Relative humidity (RH) in the incubator is measured with a wet bulb thermometer (or hydrometer) and a conversion chart which relates the difference between the wet bulb thermometer reading and the dry bulb reading. Wet bulb settings are usually 80-82°F (27-28°C), equivalent to an RH of about 50%, but humidity may need to be manipulated to maintain eggweight loss at a steady rate. Eggweight loss over the whole incubation period should be around 15% of laying weight. Eggs are turned by hand or by rollers, although some aviculturists believe that the vibration caused by mechanical turning is detrimental to psittacine eggs. Turning usually takes place every two hours through 45°, with an additional hand turn of 180° once a day.

Hatching of eggs is a two part process and requires a substantial increase in humidity and a drop in temperature to around 98.5°F (37°C). A separate incubator is used as a hatcher, with its wet bulb reading set at 92-94°F (33.5-34.5°C) and an RH of about 80%. The first part of the process involves the chick breaking through the membrane into the air space at the blunt end of the egg, so-called internal pipping. This process is clearly visible if the egg is candled at the appropriate incubation date. This may occur 2-3 days before the expected hatching date and at this point the egg is moved into the hatcher and turning stops. External pipping begins some 24-48 hours later as the chick starts to chip its way out of the egg in a circular motion. Hatching assistance may be required if the chick has made no progress 48 hours after pipping the eggshell, although much experience is required to make this judgement.

After hatching, chicks are left in the incubator for 24 hours and then transferred to a brooder, where the process of hand rearing begins. Alternatively, newly hatched chicks can be fostered into other nests which have chicks of the same age, to be fed by adult birds. The benefits of this procedure need to be weighed against the possibility of transfer of disease between the foster parents and the chicks. The process of and problems associated with hand rearing will be covered in a later chapter (see Chapter 21).

Veterinary assistance, by the application of basic principles of hygiene, can be valuable in improving success with artificial incubation. Many problems are, however, not related to the infection of eggs, but rather to poor nutrition or transmissible disease in the parents (vitamin and mineral deficiencies, chlamydiosis and polyomavirus infection) and technical problems with incubation. Checking incubation equipment in a systematic way when failures have occurred is essential; frequently, measurements and readings prove to be inaccurate or misleading, and the distribution of heat and humidity within the incubator can be faulty. Small incubators have difficulty controlling their internal environment when subjected to extremes of external temperature and humidity. The incubator room itself should be as stable an environment as possible and capable of fumigation. Manufacturers are generally helpful and many have had considerable experience with breeding techniques. Owners should be instructed in the safe and effective disinfection of their equipment at the end of the season, and encouraged to operate all-in, all-out systems as far as possible.

RECORD KEEPING

Good record keeping is essential for successful aviculture. Owners should be encouraged to keep current and historical records of individual pairs, including the following information:
- Parentage (if known).
- Laying and hatching dates.
- Percentage fertility.
- Chick rearing and survival.
- Veterinary attention.

Incubation records, including temperatures and humidity, should also be kept. A daily diary is satisfactory for incubation, unless this is done on a large scale, in which case individual clutch cards will be necessary. Automatic continuous recording of incubator temperatures and humidity would be very valuable, but is rarely employed.

RECOMMENDED READING

Jordan R (1989) *Parrot Incubation Procedures*. Mattacchione, Ontario.

Low R (1986) *Parrots, Their Care and Breeding*. Blandford Press, Poole.

Schubot RM, Clubb KJ and Clubb SL (1992) *Psittacine Aviculture*. Avicultural Breeding and Research Center, Loxahatchee.

Stoodley J and Stoodley P (1983) *Parrot Production*. Bezels Publications, Lovedean.

INSTRUCTIONAL VIDEOS

Liddell-Taylor M (1993) *Self Raising Baby Parrots*. Pollywood, Beeston.

Liddell-Taylor M (1994) *Care and Breeding of Macaws, I & II*. Pollywood, Beeston.

Martin S (1983) *Parrot Care and Training*. Parrot Video, Escondido, California.

CHAPTER THREE

Nutrition

Peter W Scott

INTRODUCTION

In their natural environment, birds, like most animals, eat to meet their energy requirement. However, captive birds may become obese, often simply by overeating because of greater availability of food or to relieve boredom, or in a physiological drive to attempt to balance other nutrients which may be deficient.

There are a number of actual and potential problems encountered when assessing diets for psittacines, starting with a lack of basic knowledge of the requirements of even one species. Such information as there is stems mainly from work on cockatiels. The situation is made more difficult by the lack of reference data on the analysis of some of the ingredients frequently used in the diet.

The benefits of providing a good balanced diet are obvious. If the ratio of energy to protein is correct, and the amino acid profile and mineral and vitamin levels are suitable, birds do not become obese. Such 'well fed' birds look good, have good plumage and good disease resistance, and spend a reasonable part of the day in normal feeding activities. The rest, hopefully preparing for breeding, will live to a ripe old age.

Consideration given to providing the right foods to provide the essential nutrients is vital in any captive breeding project. More information is needed to improve the understanding of some of these areas. For the moment, assumptions are made on extrapolated information.

Deficiencies occur when birds are fed a restricted diet; they then often develop 'fads' and further restrict their own diet. Pet psittacines are often kept indoors and denied access to natural light. This causes vitamin D_3 deficiency, unless additional dietary vitamin D_3 is provided.

The basic diet types of many of the commonly kept species are summarised in Table 3.1. Table 3.2 gives information on the nutrient balance of various dietary items. The two Tables can be used together for improving a diet.

Non-nutritional 'food' items are very important. Cockatoos like to strip wood - any fruit branches are suitable provided that they have not been sprayed with garden chemicals. It is sensible to give them a good scrub with an antiseptic such as Ark-Klens (Vetark) to avoid introduction of infection from wild birds. Hide dog chews can be drilled and hung from chains etc.

PRACTICAL DIETS

This is not an exact science, as the necessary data is not available. There are various observations relating to particular species. Many psittacines, such as macaws and cockatiels, perform well on approximately 20% protein for growth; macaws seem to require a higher fat level than cockatiels. Quite low levels of protein seem to be sufficient to maintain bodyweight in adult cockatiels.

Diets for Larger Psittacines

Commonly used diets used by aviculturists are often along the lines of:
- One third: carrots, apples and beetroot in equal amounts.
- One third: soya beans, chick peas, field/garden peas, maize (corn), maple peas.
- One third: pearl barley (hulled), whole sunflower, wheat.
- Plus: sprinkling of small high quality pine nuts in the afternoon/evening.
- Plus: an appropriate vitamin/mineral supplement such as Avimix (Vetark).

The legumes and grains are soaked overnight to allow some germination. The pearl barley does not sprout but soaking loosens the hulls which can then be washed off. Sunflower does seem to show some activity. During the summer, sprouted components are best fed in the morning when the temperature is cool; this avoids rapid spoilage. A comparison with a basic seed diet shows that the aviculturist's diet is better balanced (see Table 3.3).

In practical terms a bird eating to a particular energy intake ingests more protein and has a better calcium:phosphorus ratio when fed the aviculturist's diet than the seed (high protein/high energy) diet. As an additional benefit it is also taking in a wider range of micronutrients. Appropriate supplementation is still important.

Table 3.1. Summary of dietary requirements of some commonly kept psittacines.

Main groups	Commonly kept species	Notes on diet
Australian parakeets	Budgerigars	Small seeds, eg. hemp, canary seed, millet.
	Cockatiels	As for budgerigars, plus some larger seeds. Fruit, especially apples, pears, oranges, grapes. Groats, wheat, lettuce, carrots, chickweed. Sprouted pulses.
Kakariki		Sunflower seed, larger parrot mix (sunflower, safflower, pumpkin seeds, etc.). Look out for selective feeding.
Lovebirds		Large seeds, small nuts, berries, apples and carrots. Green foods are popular. Soft fruits.
Ring-necked Parrots	Moustached Parakeets, Slaty-headed Parakeets, Alexandrines, Indian Ringnecks.	Large seeds, small nuts, berries, apples and carrots. Green foods are popular. Soft fruit.
Cockatoos	Moluccan, Goffin and the various Sulphur-crested Cockatoos.	Large seeds (Roseate Cockatoos are prone to obesity, so it is better to use small seeds with these birds). Fruit, greens, soaked pulses. Provide wood to 'strip'.
Conures	Sun Conures, Green-cheeked and Maroon-bellied Conures.	Mixed seeds. Enjoy fruit. Like to bathe in large water bowls.
Brush-tongued Parrots	Lorikeets. These have a long extensible tongue which is covered in papillae to collect pollen. They often crush flowers and lick nectar.	Nectar, pollen, soft foods, seeds, berries. Commercial lory diets.
Macaws	Scarlet Macaws, Blue and Gold Macaws, Green-winged (Red and Green) Macaws, Dwarf Macaws such as Hahns, Severes and Illigars.	Large seeds, nuts in moderation, small pine nuts for 'interest'. Enjoy soft fruit.
Amazons and Pionus Parrots	Amazons, eg. Blue-fronted, Red-lored, Yellow-headed and Cuban; Pionus, eg. Blue-headed and Dusky.	Large seeds, nuts in moderation, small pine nuts for 'interest'. Mixed pulses. fruit, vegetables. Enjoy soft fruit.
Eclectus Parrots	Vosmaeri.	As for Amazons, but with more fruit.
African Greys	Congo and Silver Greys, Timneh Greys.	As for Amazons, taking particular care to keep the diet balanced and avoiding fads. In particular, avoid exclusively sunflower seed diets.

Table 3.2. Information on dietary items.

Dietary classes	Typical ingredients	Comments
Small seeds	Hemp, millet, canary seed. Millet sprays when birds have reduced appetite, or when young are fledging.	Lower fat and higher carbohydrate than the larger seeds.
Large seeds	Sunflower, safflower, pumpkin. Grains - wheat, oats, buckwheat, groats.	Cereals are fairly low in protein (corn and wheat have 9-10%; oats and barley contain 11-12%) but have a high energy value due to their starch stores. Vitamins A, D_3, B_6 and B_{12} are quite low or absent; sweet corn is the only grain which contributes towards Vitamin A requirements. Cereals are also low in calcium, and their phosphorus is mainly in the form of phytate. These mixtures are of very variable quality, some being extremly poor. Check seeds between the hull and kernal for fungal growth; 'webby' seeds need to be avoided. *Aspergillus flavus* can grow on such food and can produce aflatoxin which may cause chronic hepatitis and other problems. Oil seeds need to be rationed; birds develop fads and often will eat nothing but sunflower seed.
Nuts	Brazil nuts are generally popular with macaws. Most psittacines enjoy pine nuts, from the giant Chinese ones to the tiny ones.	Fed in moderation, tiny pine nuts are ideal therapy; birds enjoy spending time opening them for the high fat taste, but actually get relatively little nutritionally from them. Batches of nuts should be examined by opening a few prior to using them. Harvesting followed by storage while damp encourages fungal growth. Peanuts in shell often harbour *Aspergillus* spp.; these are best avoided.
Fruit	Apples are popular with most psittacines. Soft fruit from berries to grapes are also usually well received, as in pomegranite.	Must be fresh, or will not be eaten, and if left will encourage growth of *Aspergillus* spp. In general the fruit is not eaten; it is squeezed to release pulp and juice. Oranges are enjoyed and orange juice can be used to flavour new foods or medicines.
Vegetables	Any fresh vegetables can be given. Grated carrots, sweet corn and celery are popular.	Frozen mixed vegetable is a very useful standby. Beetroot is enjoyed but will stain the faeces red.

Table 3.2. Continued.

Dietary classes	Typical ingredients	Comments
Sprouted and soaked pulses	Various beans such as haricot, soya mung, black eyed and maple, chick peas and green peas, and lentils.	Legumes (peas, beans and pulses are concentrate feeds with protein levels in the range 22-31%, fat 1-6% and carbohydrate 58-68%). Oil-seeds may have even higher protein levels, such as soya beans at 41%; they can be up to 55% fat. Soya beans are also the best balanced in terms of amino acids. Sprouting is a very important way of improving palatability and digestibility. Nutritional value improves a little.
Animal protein	Cooked bones, such as chicken or lamb.	These are always enjoyed, but the fatty remnants should be removed as high blood cholesterol levels and atherosclerosis may result.

Table 3.3. Comparison between an aviculturist's diet and a typical pet bird seed diet.

	Aviculturist's diet	Seed diet
Crude protein	18-19%	20%
Fat	7.5%	40%
Energy	3.8kcal/g	4.4kcal/g
Crude protein nutrient density index	49g/1000kcal	46.6g/1000kcal
Ca:P ratio	1:3.6	1:7

Processing/Treatment of Food

Sprouting of legumes and pulses raises the digestibility. Some of the relatively indigestible carbohydrate, such as starch, is converted into more digestible dextrins etc., and even into proteins as the sprout grows. The vitamin levels also rise slightly, especially vitamin C, although not enough to be relied on as a major source. Germination also makes the seeds of legumes safer, by reducing some of the toxic or antinutritive factors present in them. Soya beans, for instance, contain a trypsin inhibitor which reduces the digestion of proteins. The simple act of soaking also makes it easier for birds to break up the seed for digestion. Water used for sprouting/soaking of seeds should be changed every couple of hours as some of the nutrients will enter solution and encourage bacterial growth. For the same reason, seeds should be rinsed and drained before feeding.

The nutritional content of some common foods in their ungerminated and germinated states is shown in Table 3.6.

Complete Pelleted Diets

Several of these are now available in the UK, eg. Hagen, Kaytee, Pretty Bird, Roudybush. Most are well researched products which appear nutritionally adequate, certainly better on a purely nutritional level than many diets fed to psittacines. They should generally be supplemented with restricted amounts of fresh food.

In the USA there has been a greater acceptance by bird keepers of ready-made complete diets than there has in Europe, although this may change. Many European aviculturists feel strongly that birds look, behave and breed better on a natural type diet than those fed an artificial diet.

Many birds are offered nothing but seed simply because it is more convenient for the owner. For these birds, when owner convenience is a major factor, there is sound justification for converting them to pelleted diets. A pelleted diet will almost always be better than the purely seed diet fed to many pet psittacines. Experience suggests that seeds are used mainly because owners think that is what psittacines eat and because that is what pet shops sell to them. The main problem seems to be one of education. The major disadvantages with pelleted diets appear to be cost (which is balanced by convenience), that they appear to perform not as well as a balanced natural diet and perhaps, most importantly, that they are eaten too quickly - they totally ignore the bird's relatively high intelligence and inquisitive nature.

Converting 'Seed Junkies'

'Seed junkies' is the term used to describe birds which have become fixated on a particular dietary component, normally sunflower seed. It is important to realise that often these are presented as 'sick birds'. At this stage they should be allowed to eat whatever they like (within reason). The diet should be considered after treating any secondary problems, eg. vitamin A deficiency manifesting with aspergillosis, or run-down birds developing chlamydiosis. The basic routine used is:

● Estimate the amount of seed actually eaten in a day and present half of it to the bird. Monitor the bird's condition whilst trying the following: 'weed' the mixture, changing the balance of seeds away from sunflower seed.

● Use a top quality mix. The hulled blends available, such as Ultra Mix and Tidy Mix, are ideal. Importantly, they are fresh and palatable and can be top dressed with vitamins, using a little peanut oil or orange juice.

● Use non-threatening forms of food. Shredded carrot is less suspicious to a bird than a whole one.

● Try introducing new items in amongst the seed.

● Sprout seeds and pulses - they taste much better.

● Introduce a soft food, baby cereal, fruit pulp or proprietary mixes (CeDE or EMP). Again, this will give a vehicle for vitamins.

● Consider interval feeding. Instead of leaving food in the cage all day, try introducing meal times; 30-60 minutes access three times a day.

● Move the cage; place new food items such as corn on the cob close to favourite toys.

● 'Monkey see, monkey do.' Birds will often take and investigate titbits which they see the owner eating. Being able to see other birds eating a better diet may also help.

● Change the photoperiod. The natural photoperiod for many birds is 12 hours light, 12 hours dark. In captivity this is extended in the home by early risers and late night television. Covering the cage from 9pm till 9am can change a bird's behaviour and sometimes help with establishing new feeding patterns.

● Consider hospitalisation or boarding out. A new regime may be more acceptable under new management where everything else is new.

Remember - owners have starved birds to death trying to change their diet.

Hand Rearing Mixes

This is an area where ready-made diets have become extremely useful. There are a number of diets available (Aviplus, Pretty Bird, Hagen) which all appear to perform well. The person carrying out the hand feeding can greatly influence performance, but changing diets can still cause problems. It is not unusual for an experienced hand rearer using a home-made blend to experience serious problems when changing to a prepared diet. This is not a poor reflection on the diet. Changes to hand rearing diets should only be made very cautiously.

A general analysis of 18-20% protein and 5% fat seems to be acceptable and produces good results. At a basic level, a mixture of chick crumbs and approximately one third boiled round rice has proved successful. Another popular blend is monkey chow plus 25% boiled rice. This brings the protein level down to the 18-19% region. The mixture should be ground in a blender.

A practical home-made diet has been developed by aviculturist John Heath (Heath, 1993). This is probably the most widely used formula, with various modifications by other hand rearers. It consists of:

● 250g John E. Haiths Nectarblend rearing food.

● 250g of PTX budgie soft food.

● 150g of Milupa infant dessert - mixed fruit variety.

● 120g of Milupa infant dinner - spring vegetable variety.

● 3.25 level teaspoons of Avipro Paediatric (Vetark).

● One level teaspoon of ACE-High (Vetark) .

● One level teaspoon of Nutrobal (Vetark).

At two weeks of age the diet is modified by the addition of:

● 125g hulled sunflower, 125g sesame seed, 62.5g pumpkin seed.

At all stages the mixture is ground to a powder before being mixed with water. This is initially fed very runny. The crop should empty in 3-4 hours; within 3-4 days the consistency is gradually thickened until it is yoghurt-like.

Home-made diets, using children's packet foods as a major component, may lead to energy deficiencies since they often contain corn starch or other thickeners. These give the food the appearance of more 'body' than its nutritional content actually provides, ie. it looks more of a meal than it is.

It is essential to make up fresh food for neonatal psittacines for each feeding time (see Chapter 21). Bacterial blooms occur within 30 minutes even in the refrigerator.

Water for Chicks

Chlorinated tap water, either due to added chlorine or from chloramines, is reputed to cause upsets in some birds. Although this may be a regional problem depending on potable supplies and water supply practices, care needs to be taken, especially with chicks being hand reared. A link with non-specific poor growth, colic and deaths has been suggested. Activated carbon filters are becoming popular for removing such chemical additives from the water, but these are themselves not without problems. There is concern that some brands of filters are encouraging the growth of *Pseudomonas* spp. Potentially, this can cause very serious problems or even death, especially for chicks being hand reared on contaminated water.

Nectar Feeding Psittacines

In the wild, psittacines consuming nectar take in fairly large amounts of pollen. There is evidence, however, that much of this passes through the psittacine gut undigested. Some digestion occurs in the nestling bird, and in adults overnight. Some species may be better than others at digesting pollen. Pollen is a rich source of protein (typically 15-20%), carbohydrate (20-35%) and oils (1-3%). Some limited analytical information is available (see Table 3.5).

Calcium and Phosphorus

The Ca:P ratio for the whole diet should be in the region of 1.5-2:1, with a calcium level of approximately 1% of the dry matter content of the diet. This appears to be virtually universal for all vertebrates. Psittacines do not seem to require the higher calcium levels needed by production poultry - cockatiels manage to maintain egg production on 0.3% calcium. It is likely that calcium requirements are intimately related to growth rate; birds which achieve a rapid weight gain probably require the standard level.

Phytates within the food effectively bind the calcium and phosphorus and so lower the availability of both calcium and phosphorus. Adult birds may well be able to use some of the phosphorus locked up by phytates, but they will still be deficient in calcium. This means that, although foods may have a high phosphorus level on analysis, if it is bound in phytates it will not contribute towards the Ca:P ratio. Allowance needs to be made for this when considering the Ca:P balance. Phytates can also reduce the availability of other minerals which may be present, such as zinc and iron.

SPECIFIC NUTRITIONAL PROBLEMS

Protein and Essential Amino Acid (EAA) Deficiency

Protein required for growth is limited by the availability of the various EAAs. To obtain sufficient amounts of the limiting amino acids, the bird on a poor diet is forced to overeat and then eliminate the excess nitrogen. Protein levels in excess of what can be used are broken down as an energy source and may result in obesity, or in gout due to the formation of urates. The pathogenesis of gout is not clear. Water deprivation and nephrosis, even very short term, may have a considerable effect.

The levels of lysine in legumes are often high, making up for the relatively low levels in cereals. The lysine level is important (1-1.5% in chicks). In the majority of psittacine diets this is the limiting amino acid, lack of which prevents optimal use of others, such as methionine, arginine, tryptophan and threonine. Cereals, on the other hand, tend to provide good levels of the sulphur-containing amino acids methionine and cystine, which are low in legumes.

The energy:protein ratio (kcal/kg:CP%) needs to be considered in just the same way as the Ca:P ratio. This ratio changes through life. In domestic poultry the figure of approximately 143:1 for a chick changes as the bird matures to approximately 190:1, ie. for a given bodyweight a chick requires a higher protein level.

Although birds can manage on low protein levels, this does not apply to periods of special need. When birds are producing eggs, a low protein diet will stop production and can also inhibit new feather growth. Choline, lysine and tyrosine deficiency all lead to colour abnormalities. Methionine deficiency has been linked with stress lines in feathers. Lysine levels are low in seeds, therefore purely seed-fed birds often develop poor feathering. The requirement for lysine is estimated at between 1-2% (high percentage of a low protein diet). Poor matrices within the bones are another result of protein or amino acid deficiencies. EAA deficiencies in general will lead to fatty liver problems. These are compounded due to the high fat diets often fed.

Problems associated with excess protein are often also linked with calcium. In diets where both are high, stunting is reported. Renal or articular gout may also be seen. If calcium levels are low and growth is rapid due to high protein levels, leg deformities are often seen.

Table 3.4. Nutritional analysis of certain pollens (dry matter %).

Pollens	Protein	Carbohydrate	Ash	Fat	Ca	P	Ca:P ratio
Cyptomeria japonica	5.89		2.14	1.85			
Pinus sabiniana	11.36	13.15	2.59	2.73	0.0007	0.01	1.14
Zea mays	20.32	36.59	2.55	1.48			

Vitamin A Deficiency

This is the most common vitamin deficiency seen in psittacines. The pathogenesis includes squamous cell metaplasia of the epithelial surfaces of the oropharynx, renal tubules, reproductive tract and air sacs. Poor condition or chronic upper respiratory problems are the commonest presenting signs, although nephrosis is also linked to the renal tubule changes (see Chapters 12 and 15). Feather colour changes, hyperkeratosis of the feet and general poor feathering are also involved.

Supply of vitamin A relies on the bird converting ß-carotene (in the fruit or vegetables) into vitamin A. The efficiency of this conversion is uncertain in psittacines, but it is likely that due to the over-abundance of carotenes in their normal diet, conversion is not very efficient. The relatively high requirement of vitamin A by psittacines may be met by ß-carotene in fresh vegetables, carrot, corn on the cob, iceberg lettuce, green beans, celery, apricots, oranges, papaya, etc. Supplementation is generally required, eg. ACE-High (Vetark) or Avimix (Vetark). This is particularly important once signs of deficiency have been seen.

Metabolic Bone Disease (Calcium, Phosphorus and Vitamin D_3 Problems)

Calcium deficiency in adult birds can result in the production of soft-shelled eggs, eggbinding due to poor muscular function, or a cessation in breeding. African Greys are particularly prone to hypocalcaemic problems. The reason for this is unknown, although they are perhaps more likely than many species to develop a total addiction to sunflower seeds and be difficult to supplement. Signs of incoordination may be seen or hens may simply lay thin-shelled or soft-shelled eggs. Chicks showing a range of severities of metabolic bone disease may hatch from deficient eggs from deficient hens.

Calcium absorption requires the presence of vitamin D_3. Various precursors of vitamin D are converted to D_3 in the skin. These may be secreted from the skin or be within the secretions from the uropygial gland. Conversion into vitamin D_3 requires exposure to sunlight. It may be this factor which is most important in deficiencies seen in captive birds. African Greys, particularly in breeding establishments, are normally bred indoors and often spend most of their time in the nestbox, perhaps only coming out for food. Birds kept indoors need regular supplementation, particularly breeding birds. Nutrobal (Vetark) provides an appropriate balance of calcium and vitamin D_3. In African Greys it is often also necessary to supplement using calcium lactate in drinking water. Marginally hypocalcaemic birds may show clinical disease during or following medication with oxytetracycline or other binding agents.

Hypervitaminosis D_3 has been reported in several species in the USA; macaws appear particularly fea-tured. Cases are associated with gross oversupplementation of already supplemented commercial diets.

Vitamin E Deficiency

Deficiency of vitamin E may occur with rancid food. Commonly fed seed mixes may contain seeds which have been stored for far too long and in which levels of vitamin E have fallen and fats have become rancid. Signs of disease (especially myopathies) are seen particularly in birds which are also deficient in selenium or sulphur-containing amino acids. Vitamin E deficiency is seen commonly in cockatiels. Supplementation of these poor diets is essential, eg. ACE-High (Vetark). Vitamin E also has an important part in disease resistance.

Fat and Essential Fatty Acids

Fat related problems, often associated with vitamin E deficiency, are common among pet birds. These are often the result simply of overeating on a high calorie, low quality diet. In birds the liver is very active in lipogenesis. Linoleic and arachidonic acids are essential: when they are lacking, a fatty liver can develop due to impaired fat metabolism. Any hepatic pathology which inhibits proper fat metabolism may also lead to a fatty liver.

Diets high in saturated fats can lead to atherosclerosis and fatty liver syndrome, and are usually linked with a hypercholesterolaemia. Excessive amounts of cheese or animal fat, eg. frequent lamb bones, have both been seen to lead to these problems.

B Vitamin Deficiencies

The high fat diets of pet psittacines are normally low in B vitamins. Deficiency syndromes are poorly understood but poor growth, general unthriftiness and poor feathering are major features. They may be quite important. Classic single B vitamin deficiencies are associated with:

- Thiamine (B_1) - opisthotonus, fits.
- Riboflavin (B_2) - curled toes, dry skin, poor feather pigmentation, fatty livers.
- Pyridoxine (B_6) - perosis, jerky movements, convulsions.
- Pantothenic acid - dermatitis around eyes and mouth, wiry down, ataxia.
- Biotin - brittle feathers, swollen feet, ataxia, chondrodysplasia, fatty liver.
- Folic acid - poor feathering, white or brittle feathers, beak deformities.
- Choline - perosis.

Vitamin C Deficiency

Any form of stress, or physical, nutritional, toxic or infectious disease tends to deplete endogenous stores of vitamin C (McDowell, 1989). Supplementation

Table 3.6. Nutritional analysis of selected food items as fed (per 100g).

Food item	Kcal %	Prot %	Carb %	Ash %	Fat %	Water %	Ca g	P g	Vit A mg	Vit C mg	Vit D$_3$ mg	Vit E mg	Lysine %	Methio-nine %
Nuts														
Peanuts	567	25.6	16.1		49.1	6.6	58	383	nd	0			0.992	0.263
Brazil	656	14.3	12.8		66.2	3.3	176	600	0	0.7			0.541	1.014
Walnut	642	14.2	18.3		61.8	3.6	94	317	124	3.2			0.388	0.28
Pinyon (Pine)	568	11.5	19.3		60.9	5.9	8	35	nd	nd			0.434	0.207
Coconut flesh	354	3.3	15.2		33.4	46.9	14	113	0	3.3			0.147	0.062
Pecan	667	7.7	18.2		67.6	4.8	36	291	128	2			0.292	0.186
Acrocromia palm fruit		4	9	1	28	50	0.12	0.21						
Acrocromia palm nut		13	7	2	67	4	0.08	0.42						
Seeds														
Canary seed		17	57.5		8.4									
Hemp		19	18		32									
Linseed		21	24		34									
Millet		11	62		4									
Pumpkin	541	24.5	17.8		45.8	6.9	43	1174	380	0			1.833	0.551
Rape		19	10		40									
Safflower	517	16.1	34.2		38.4	5.6	78	644		0			0.534	0.284
Sunflower	570	22.7	18.7		49.5	5.3	116	705	50				0.937	0.494
Fresh Fruit														
Apple	57	0.15	14.84		0.31	84.46	4		44	4			0.009	0.002
Apricot	28	0.6	6.7			86.6	17	21	1380*	7				
Banana	92	1.03	13.43		0.48	74.26	6	20	81	9.1			0.048	0.011
Blackberry	52	0.72	12.76		nd	85.64	32	21	165	21			nd	nd
Grapes	63	0.63	17.15		0.35	81.3	14	10	100	4			0.014	0.021
Honeydew Melon	35	0.46	9.18		0.1	89.66	6	10	40	24.8			nd	nd
Orange	47	0.94	11.75		0.12	86.75	40	14	205	53.2			0.047	0.02
Peach	43	0.7	11.1		0.09	87/66	5	12	535	6.6			0.023	0.017
Pear	59	0.39	15.11		0.4	83.81	11	11	20	4			0.14	0.005
Plum	55	0.79	13.01		0.62	85.2	4	10	323	9.5			0.006	0.004
Pomegranite	68	0.95	17.17		0.3	80.97	3	6	nd	6.1			nd	nd
Vegetables														
Raw beetroot	28	1.3	6			87.1	25	32	0	6		0		
Green peppers	1	0.9	2.2		0.4	93.5	9	25	200*	100		0.8		
Maize/sweet corn	127	4.1	23.7		2.4	65.2	4	130	240*	12		0.8		
Tomatoes	14	0.9	2.8			93.4	13	21	600*	1.2		1.2		
Commercial Foods														
EMP		16.5		4.5	7.5				1950					
Haiths PTX		32		8.7	21.2		0.47	0.32	1000		250	1.25		
Haiths Nectarblend		14.3		2.9	4.8		0.47	0.32	1000		250	1.25		
Baby Dinners														
Robinsons Mixed Vegetable	360	16	61		6		1.2	0.7	750	50	9			
Robinsons Baby Rice	363	15	70		3		1.1	0.7	750	50	9			
Milupa 7 Cereal Breakfast	429	13.2	70.5		10.5		0.5	0.4	230	20	3.4	2.3		
Spring Vegetable Dinner	416	19	64.3		9.2		0.4	0.4	330	28	4.8	2.3		
Other Items Used														
Spirulina		63	14.5	10	6.5	6	120	830				199		
Eggs (boiled) including shell	147	12.3			10.9	74.8	52	220	140	0	1.75	1.6		

Table 3.6. Continued.

Food item	Kcal %	Prot %	Carb %	Ash %	Fat %	Water %	Ca g	P g	Vit A mg	Vit C mg	Vit D$_3$ mg	Vit E mg	Lysine %	Methio-nine %
Cheddar cheese	406	26			33.5	37	800	520		0		0.8		
Roast leg of lamb	266	26.1			17.9	55.3	8	200		0		0.11		
Molasses		4.7	69	69										
Soaking and Sprouting														
Peas														
Seed		23.2		3	3.3	7.1	61	300						
Germinated seed		7.3		1	0.9	71.5								
Sprout		4.1		0.4	0.5	92.7								
Mung Beans														
Seed	334	22.9		3.4	1.4	10.1	83							
Germinated seed	53	4.3		0.6	0.2	85.9	13			20				
Alfalfa														
Seed	389	35.1		3.1	12.6	7.4	136			26				
Germinated seed	41	41		0.4	0.6	88.3	28			16				
White Navy Beans														
Seed		22.4		3.5	2.2	16.3								
Germinated seed		8.7		1.3	1	65.7								
Sprout		3.6		0.6	0.4	92.6								
Soya Beans														
Seed	8.4	38.2		4.6	20.1	8.4	220							
Germinated seed	73.2	105		3	2.6	73.2	75			12				
Wheat														
Seed														
Germinated seed		7.52		1.01	1.34	44.43	0.29	0.21		2.83				

* in the Vitamin A column indicates that the figure is expressed in terms of carotene.

The data shown in this table is drawn from various sources and some is calculated. Figures should not be viewed as definitive but as illustrative of trends.

produces positive effects on egg quality. Although a specific deficiency syndrome is not reported in psittacines, there is good reason for including vitamin C in general supplements, especially those used when birds are under stress. ACE-High (Vetark) is particularly useful in this regard.

USE OF SUPPLEMENTS

The value of vitamin/mineral additives is the subject of debate. However, they are certainly widely used (see Table 3.7). Even when provided with the best balanced diet, birds may not eat all of it and so may develop a deficiency in one or more essential nutrients. Wild birds will balance their own diet over a long period, but in captivity this may not occur so readily. Observations of Red-fronted Macaws in the wild suggests that farming has caused maize to become one of their preferred foods. The potential consequences of this are not yet understood. As has already been mentioned, birds kept indoors lack natural light and may develop vitamin D$_3$ deficiency problems unless supplemented.

In general, supplementation is more effective given via the feed rather than in the water. The reasons for this are:
● Rapid vitamin oxidisation can occur in the aqueous phase.
● Calcium in hard water can interfere with the absorption of various vitamins. Also, there can be interactions involving any other minerals present. This restricts what can be included.
● Psittacines generally drink very little. They are also suspicious and will avoid drinking for days.

For general use in young and non-breeding birds, Avimix (Vetark) can be sprinkled on soft or fresh food three times a week. For breeding birds the extra calcium and vitamin D$_3$ present in Nutrobal (Vetark) is of value in egg production and establishing reserves which must be drawn upon. For birds which are particularly difficult to supplement, such as African Greys, BSP Vitamin Drops (Vetark) via the drinking water is a suitable means of achieving meaningful levels of dietary vitamins if in-feed methods cannot be used.

Table 3.7. Some veterinary supplements commonly used in psittacines.

	Vionate (Ciba-Geigy)/g	Coolo-Cal D(c-Vete)/ml	Nutrobol (Vetark)/g	Ace-High (Vetark)/g	Avimix (Vetark)/g
Vitamin A (IU)	220	-	500	2530	1177
Vitamin C (mg)	-	-	2.5	250	85
Vitamin E (IU)	0.12	-	20	122	54
Vitamin D3 (IU)	22	70	150	20	118
Calcium (mg)	94.5	0.5	208	9.9	142
Phosphorous (mg)	63.6	-	4.5	4.9	4.65
Ca:P ratio	1.48:1	no P	46.1	2.1	30.1

This can be done when birds first present with clinical problems.

REFERENCES AND FURTHER READING

Bauck L (1995) Nutritional problems in pet birds. In: *Seminars in Avian and Exotic Pet Medicine. Vol. 4, No. 1*. Ed AM Fudge. WB Saunders, Philadelphia.

Hagen M (1992) Nutritional observations, hand rearing formulae, and digestion in exotic birds. In: *Seminars in Avian and Exotic Pet Medicine. Vol. 1, No. 1*. Ed AM Fudge. WB Saunders, Philadelphia.

Heath J (1993) Hand rearing mixture. *Parrot Society Magazine* 26(January), 15.

Low R (1987) *Hand Rearing Parrots and Other Birds*. Blandford, Poole.

McDowell LR (1989) *Vitamins in Animal Nutrition. Comparative Aspects to Human Nutrition*. Academic Press, New York.

Nott HMR and Taylor EJ (1993) Nutrition of pet birds. In: *The Waltham Book of Companion Animal Nutrition*. Ed I Burger. Pergamon Press, Oxford.

Scott PW (1990) Nutrition of psittacines. In: *Genus Amazona*. Eds J Stoodley and P Stoodley. Bezel Publications, Portsmouth.

Speer BL (1995) Stunting in large macaws. In: *Seminars in Avian and Exotic Pet Medicine. Vol. 4, No. 1*. Ed AM Fudge. WB Saunders, Philapdelphia.

Voren H and Jordan R (1992) *Parrots. Hand Feeding and Nursery Management*. Silvertop Publishers, Rowley.

CHAPTER FOUR

Examination, Basic Investigation and Principles of Therapy

Neil A Forbes and Martin P C Lawton

INTRODUCTION

Frequently, birds who appear clinically healthy are in fact harbouring a number of subclinical diseases. Birds may be clinically divided into:
● Healthy.
● Healthy but subclinically infected.
● Diseased and showing clinical signs.

When apparently healthy but subclinically infected birds are stressed or exposed to other infections, the subclinical illness may become significant and life threatening.

This balance between health and disease is more delicate in birds than in other groups of animals. As birds are accustomed to being prey, they rarely show illness until they are severely debilitated by disease,

often to the extent of being beyond treatment. This ability to hide clinical signs is a natural defence mechanism, as any predator will naturally single out a sick or weak individual to attack first. A number of factors may influence the health status of a bird within this pyramid (see Figure 4.1).

Host Factors:
● The bird's immune status.
● The bird's inherent genetic resistance.
● Age.
● Sex.

Environmental Factors:
● Composition of diet.
● Feeding regime.
● Accommodation.

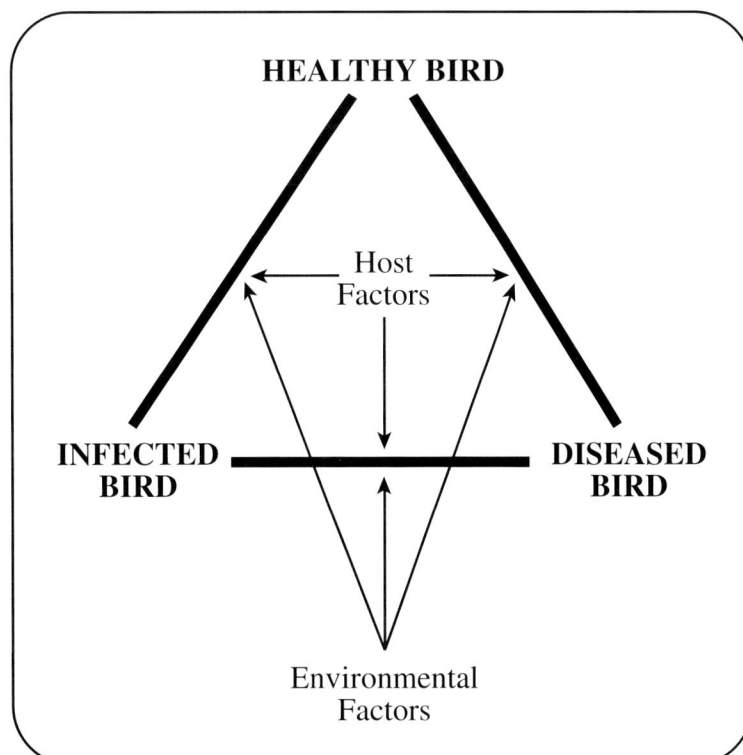

Figure 4.1: *Factors affecting the health status of a bird.*

- Hygiene.
- Interference from other birds (same or other species) or predators, eg. cats.
- Interference from keeper/trainer.
- Climatic conditions.

If the infected but apparently healthy bird can be distinguished from the healthy bird, subclinical disease or infection can be minimised, treated or eradicated. In the same way, if the host and environmental factors can be controlled, the chance of clinical disease will be reduced.

AVIAN CONSULTATIONS

Before a physical examination is undertaken, it is essential that a full background history is obtained from the owner on the source of the bird, length of time owned, any other in-contact birds, diet and environmental conditions. Three basic types of bird patients may be presented.

Newly Acquired Sick Birds
These birds may have been mixed with many others at the place of origin or purchase. They may have been carrying subclinical disease which has now become overt. Infectious or stress related diseases should always be considered.

Ill Birds from an Established Collection
A different approach is required for these cases. First, one should consider how good is the breeder's management protocol, especially in relation to quarantine (of imported birds) and isolation (of newly purchased birds). Second, how recently has the present bird been mixed with other new arrivals or existing birds on the premises. As one is dealing with a collection, a very full diagnostic work-up, including *post-mortem* examination, should always be carried out. It is imperative to discover immediately whether the condition is infectious. The bird and any in-contacts should be isolated. If an infection of unknown aetiology is suspected, it may be prudent to cull a sick bird for *post-mortem* examination and sampling. This will facilitate a more rapid complete diagnosis.

Individual Sick Birds
These are most commonly pet birds which have been in the current ownership for a considerable period and which have not recently been in contact with other birds. Such birds are more likely to be affected by malnutrition or chronic diseases, although it should be remembered that some psittacine diseases can be transmitted readily by fomites (including human clothing etc.), eg. Pacheco's disease and chlamydiosis. It is also important in terms of differential diagnosis to consider any diseases which can remain dormant or involve the carrier state, eg. chlamydiosis, psittacine

beak and feather disease (PBFD) or polyomavirus.

RECOGNITION OF ILL HEALTH BY THE CLIENT

Avian veterinarians should assist their clients by educating them in the recognition of ill health. The presence of carrier status should be stressed so that not only is the bird presented when unwell, but also for routine screening at other times. Client education is of prime importance. Client leaflets may be prepared. These may detail the subtle as well as the obvious signs of ill health, in order to allow their more rapid recognition. Owners should be encouraged to carry out thorough daily inspections of their birds and their birds' environment. The owner should be fully conversant with the signs of good health in each of the species kept; only then will minor deviations from the normal be recognised. At the first sign of ill health, the client should be encouraged to seek immediate veterinary attention; delay may result in rapid deterioration or even death. The clinician should be equally aware that an apparently healthy looking bird when described by its owner as being 'not quite right', does require further investigation and appropriate treatment.

NEW BIRD AND WELL BIRD EXAMINATIONS

In view of the rapid progression of pathogenesis of many avian diseases, together with the high incidence of carrier and subclinically affected birds, the avian clinician should encourage all new birds to be examined as soon after purchase as possible or at the start of their quarantine period. No new bird should be mixed with existing birds until it has completed 6-8 weeks of isolation. All birds should have a full clinical examination and be tested for parasites and chlamydiosis at least annually. The aim is to detect infection prior to clinical disease becoming established. A consultation will give time for discussion of the husbandry and dietary requirements in addition to allowing a full clinical examination (see later) to establish any signs of illness, damage or abnormalities. In addition to the basic clinical examination, a range of screening tests should be made available to the owner. Cost may be a factor in determing which, if any, tests are carried out.

A basic bird screen should include haematology and biochemistry profiles, Gram-stained smears of cloaca and choana, and chlamydiosis testing. It is important to emphasis to all clients that there is no foolproof method of testing for chlamydiosis and some other pathogens due to the intermittent shedding of the organisms. The authors suggest to owners that they pool faecal samples over a period of 14 days. This may then be tested by ELISA (enzyme linked immunosorbant assay) and/or PCR (polymerase chain reaction) test for the presence of antigen. A blood sample may also be tested for the presence of antibodies. The latter method is more reliable for establishing past exposure to *Chlamydia psittaci*, but gives no evidence of current or recent infection unless two samples are taken to demonstrate a changing titre. Every owner should be given a client advice sheet regarding the risks of chlamydiosis and the possible clinical signs in both the bird and in any human contacts. A more advanced screen should include the testing of a blood sample for PBFD and polyomavirus. More concerned owners may wish also to have radiographs and endoscopy performed to rule out certain diseases and allow an individual base line to be established for future reference, should that be required.

CONSIDERATIONS PRIOR TO AVIAN EXAMINATION

Timing of Consultation

Avian cases, with the exception of minor simple procedures such as nail clipping, should not be examined during a normal small animal clinic. Most birds will view a dog, cat or bird of prey as a predator, thereby further increasing the stress of the visit. Birds generally require more time than the average small animal case. Attempting to deal with such a case when rushed will probably not do justice to the clinician or the bird. In view of the extra time required, a realistic practice policy should be sought on the charging for such appointments. Generally, most parrot owners are prepared to pay for a thorough examination and comprehensive therapy, whilst keepers of small cagebirds seem to believe that they are doing the clinician a favour by bringing the bird in to see him/her, and resent any form of charge at all. The quoting of realistic fees in advance (especially possible diagnostic tests) is strongly recommended as this can avoid many misunderstandings.

When clients request an appointment, the receptionist should be trained to assess correctly the urgency of the case and to be able to advise on travelling and collection of any samples (of food and droppings) required. A sick bird should always be considered as serious and urgent, as opposed to a budgerigar needing its nails clipped or a chronic feather plucker. Where possible (depending on species) the bird should be transported to the clinic in its normal cage. This should not be cleaned out prior to the visit. The cage should be wrapped with a towel (or equivalent) in order to darken the environment, reduce stress and prevent drafts.

Relevant History

A full detailed history must be taken. A simple history form is often beneficial - an example is shown in Table 4.1. Taking of the history not only allows the clinician to assess the health status and possible causes of ill health, but also informs the clinician as to the owner's level of knowledge. The time taken for 'clerking' gives the patient time to settle, so that a more realistic assessment of behaviour can be made. Observation of the cage itself is invaluable. The nature and build up of faeces should be noted, and the water and food supply assessed. The age, type, condition and manufacture of the cage and contents may in itself indicate possible problems, eg. flaking old paint or chewed solder joints, either of which could lead to lead poisoning.

The following key points should be noted prior to physical examination:

● The bird's attitude and demeanour.
● Body conformation and contour.
● Condition of feathers, beak, cere and feet.
● Appearance of the eye (round and bright or ovoid and slit-like).
● Rate, depth and nature of breathing.

Environment

A great deal of information can be obtained from a thorough examination of the bird's cage. One can form an impression of the level of hygiene, knowledge of the owner, diet and water availability. Having already discussed the patient's diet with the owner, one can often glean further information and confirmation from the cage. Many owners believe that a bird's diet is exactly what they give the bird as opposed to what the bird actually eats. There is a clear distinction, as many birds are selective feeders even when given what appears to be a perfectly adequate diet.

Droppings

Many important aspects of a bird's health can be assessed from a thorough inspection of the droppings. Smaller birds defecate more frequently (budgerigars 25-50 times/day compared with macaws 8-15 times/day) (Harrison and Ritchie, 1994). Droppings are comprised of three portions. These are best visualised by placing an impervious sheet in the cage under the patient for a 3-4 hour period. Excrement should comprise faeces, urates (white to creamy white) and urine (clear and watery). The colour and consistency of the faeces will vary with species, but more importantly with dietary content and composition. Other factors, such as age, reproductive status, state of health, stress and medication, will all have an influence. A great deal of time may be usefully spent studying normal avian faeces, taking into account all these variables. Only when recognition of all the normal states has been mastered can the aetiological interpretation of abnormalities be made. These include endoparasites, bacterial imbalance, chlamydiosis, fungal and viral infections, or toxic causes. The first challenge is to be able to differentiate between the three portions of the excrement. Table 4.2 lists the main findings and possible differential diagnosis.

Table 4.1. Avian history form.

Owner's Name and Address:

Telephone Number:

Species .... **Age** .... **Sex** ....
Colour .... **Name/Identification No** ....

Has the bird been examined or treated by another veterinarian?   Yes/No
How long in current ownership? ....
Source (if acquired within last year)? ....
Any other in-contact birds? ....
Any previous disease history with this or other birds? ....
Presenting problem? ....
Duration of problem? ....
Any other birds/pets (own or friends) affected/ill?   Yes/No
Any new birds introduced within the last six months?   Yes/No
Any change of food or water (type or source)? ....
Have the birds had any medication at all? ....
Is the bird confined to cage/flight/free flight (inside/outside)? ....
Has any thing changed in the birds environment?   Yes/No
    If Yes, what...
Any change of appetite or diet?   Yes/No
What diet is fed (are other birds on the same diet)? ....
Any change in birds behaviour?   Yes/No
    If Yes what ....
Any supplements, additives, tonics, etc.?   Yes/No
    If Yes what ....
Any change in water consumption?   Yes/No
    If Yes what ....
What is the bird's reproductive status? ....
Has the bird's plumage changed at all in previous six months? ....
Has the appearance of the bird's droppings changed at all?   Yes/No
    If Yes, is it the coloured (faeces) or the white (urate) part which has altered ....
Observe from a distance, assess clinically, and tick the following:

	Yes	No		Yes	No
Normal activity			Lameness		
Normal flight			Ruffled feathers		
Normal walking			Mouth breathing or dyspnoeic		
Normal perching			Tail bobbing		
Alteration in voice			Any nervous signs		
Normal position of wings			Weight change		
Closed eyes			More time on the cage floor		

Table 4.2. Evaluation of birds' droppings (see also Chapter 17).

Appearance of the droppings	Possible aetiologies
Reduced volume	Decreased food intake; decreased gastrointestinal transit time; food deprivation.
Small dry faeces	Water deprivation; liver disease.
Dark discolouration	Meleana. Food stains, eg. blackberries.
Evidence of food	Gastrointestinal disease (enteritis, neoplasia, etc.); renal disease; testicular or ovarian tumours; coagulopathies; cloacal papilloma; calculus; cloacitis or other cloacal pathology; oviduct abnormalities (pre- or post-laying); liver disease; heavy metal toxicity; malnutrition. Acute haemorrhagic syndrome should be considered in Amazons.
Voluminous	High vegetable/fluid content in diet. Malabsorption, eg. gastrointestinal disease, pancreatitis, parasitism, peritonitis, diabetes, renal disease or neoplasia, liver disease.
Bright green or yellow/brown faeces or green urates	Indicates possible haemolysis or hepatitis caused by malnutrition or toxic damage, or by chlamydial, bacterial or viral infections
Clay coloured faeces	Maldigestion, malabsorption. Kaolin medication may also cause this appearance.
Undigested food (to be differentiated from regurgitation)	Malabsorption, maldigestion, hypermobility (due to inflammation, infection or parasitism), pancreatitis, proventriculitis ventriculitis, PPDS.
Excess urine	Renal failure (infection, neoplasia, immune mediated, toxic); any cause of polydipsia (diabetes mellitus or insipidus; pituitary disease or neoplasia; adrenal disorders or neoplasia; hyperthyroidism; iatrogenic, eg. corticosteroid, aminoglycoside, progestogens); hyper or hypocalcaemia; Vitamin A deficiency; excess dietary protein; hypervitaminosis D_3; excess dietary salt.

Undigested food in faeces must be differentiated from regurgitation (from the crop it is a neutral pH or alkaline; from the proventriculus it is acidic).

All birds should have a faecal sample examined under a microscope:
● A wet preparation should be examined for motile protozoa, fluke, etc.
● A flotation technique used for the identification of parasite ova.
● A Gram-stained sample should be examined for bacteria, fungi and anti-inflammatory cells (see Chapter 17 for further interpretation of enteric Gram stains).

Urine should be examined from an impervious surface as soon as possible after voiding. It should be tested for pH, glucose, sediment, ketones, colour and specific gravity using a standard dip stick test.

RESTRAINT AND HANDLING

A professional breeder, handler or keeper of psittacines should be approached by any prospective veterinarian wishing to specialise in avian medicine and surgery. They are usually only too happy to encourage further avian interest and knowledge. Spending time with these people allows the opportunity to learn the important aspects of handling, feeding and restraining, as well as the finer points of aviculture. Whilst such experienced keepers can advise, help and teach aspects of handling, the majority of pet owners often never handle their birds (more is the pity). As such they are no help to the veterinarian and are often a hindrance, despite having great expectations of you, the professional.

Psittacines have an excellent memory and will often bear grudges against any persons who they feel have invaded their privacy, caught them or in any way inflicted pain upon them. If the owner is present at the time a bird is restrained, that bird may well consider the owner responsible. For this reason it is best to advise (or offer the oportunity for) any owners to leave the room prior to handling, examination, medicating, etc.

Birds must be caught and removed from their cage before being examined. The first advice is to know your species and to appreciate their specific weaknesses and dangers. Psittacines are best approached or handled in a darkened room or in a dull room with only a blue or red light. Avian clinicians must have access to a darkened room. Before any bird is handled, one must ensure that all windows and doors are shut and extractor fans turned off. No member of staff should open the door unannounced; having 'peep hole' devices fitted into the doors is an advantage. All equipment for restraint and treatment must be available prior to attempting to catch the bird. A cloth or paper towel of varying thickness is the best form of protection when catching a bird. Gloves are of little value, as they are too thick to feel or manipulate through, and yet often not strong enough to give true protection. In view of the risk of disease transmission, a cloth should only be used for handling one bird, before being disinfected and washed thoroughly.

Budgerigars

These small birds must be handled with care. Furniture should be removed from the cage. A paper towel or clean cloth should be placed over the hand and advanced towards the bird against one side or corner of the cage. The bird should be caught between fingers and palm. Once held, the thumb and forefinger are placed either side of head, or the head can be placed between the first and second finger. The body, wings and feet are restrained gently in the palm of the hand whilst the other hand is free to examine the bird or administer medication. Care must be taken when handling birds not to compress the chest. This may lead to respiratory arrest and death.

Parrots, Cockatoos and Macaws

The clinician must remember that these birds are professional nut openers, and fingers are much more delicate than the average nut. Although they may grab you with their feet, only minor discomfort or injury will be caused. Handling is best carried out with a towel, doubled over if necessary. The bird should be taken into a darkened room, as previously described. If the bird is caged, the bottom of the cage should be removed as the standard door opening is often too small to remove bird, towel and hand. As much furniture as possible should be removed and the cage turned on its side. A member of staff should steady the cage so that it is stationary, whilst the bird is caught from the bottom opening. The bird is grasped firmly around the head with fingers and thumb either side of the head. Once gripped the head must not be let go on any account. Squashing or damaging the head is highly unlikely. However, if not held tight, the bird will pull away and is more likely to bite. Having caught the bird, it should be removed from the cage. A reliable assistant should hold the head whilst it is being examined or treated. Alternatively, the bird's head can be held in one hand, with the bird's body clamped between the forearm and chest, leaving the other hand free to examine and medicate. Crop tubing of psittacines is best accomplished with a metal cannula introduced at the left corner of the mouth (if done from the front, the bird may damage its beak on the cannula).

EXAMINATION OF THE SICK BIRD

Before embarking on a full clinical examination, the clinician should first consider if any of the serious infectious diseases or zoonoses are a possible differential diagnosis. Consulting or examination areas should be easily cleaned and fomites which might spread disease should be eliminated or discarded after each case. Particular caution should be taken when chlamydiosis is a possibility, bearing in mind the potential for airborne spread and zoonotic implications (see Chapters 22 and 23). Birds showing signs of ocular or nasal discharge, respiratory distress, fluffed up miserable appearance, bright green faeces or green discolouration of the urates should be considered as a potential case of chlamydiosis and should be screened prior to further examination, handling or mixing with other birds (see Chapter 23). A history of long-term isolation from other birds should not be relied upon to exclude the possibility of chlamydiosis.

There is no secret to the successful examination, recognition and diagnosis of diseases or injury in birds. The clinical examination should be carried out in exactly the same way as one would approach a cat or dog. A methodical approach must be employed, starting with the head and working down the body. Once the clinician is experienced at examining birds, it should take no more than 3-4 minutes. All parts of the body should, where relevant, be symmetrical; one side should always be compared with the other.

A brief description of the particular areas to be examined are menioned. In each case the relevant chapter should be referred to for a fuller description.

Head

Eyes, sinuses and rhinarium are all anatomically interrelated, hence infection of any one may lead to, or be indicative of, infection in all three. The eyes should be clear, round, centrally placed, moist and shining, with no epiphora or other discharges. Periorbital areas may show swellings, which are indicative of primary sinusitis or are secondary to hypovitaminosis A (see Chapter 12).

The ear consists of an aural canal situated ventrocaudal to the lateral canthus. Clinical problems are usually polyps, neoplasia or infections.

The nares should be clear, round and open, with a centrally placed shiny operculum. Discharge, occlusion or rhinolith may be present (chlamydiosis is a differential diagnosis).

The beak and cere should be healthy and shiny (white powder down present in cockatoos). The maxillary and mandibular portions of the beak should meet evenly. Poor beak condition may be indicative of a poor diet (hypovitaminosis A), lack of moisture, poor management or systemic disease. Aspergillosis and candidiasis of the beak are not uncommon, frequently secondary to vitamin A deficiency.

The oral cavity is easiest examined with the assistance of an auroscope operculum or mouth gag. All areas of the mouth, especially the tongue, sublinginal tissues, choana, oral membrane and glottis, should be visualised. A choanal swab should be taken in all cases. If any abnormalities are evident, swabs should be cultured and impression smears prepared.

Auscultation and Examination of the Respiratory System

As mentioned earlier, the nature and rate of a bird's respiration should be recorded prior to handling. Once the bird is handled the heart and respiratory rates will increase. Expected rates are shown in Table 4.3. If the bird is permitted to exercise, eg. fly around the cage prior to capture, respiratory rates will increase further but should return to normal within two minutes of the end of exercise (Harrison and Ritchie, 1994) (see Chapter 15 for further information on the examination and collection of samples from the respiratory system). Birds showing respiratory signs should always be screened for chlamydiosis. In-house laboratory faecal or air sac (swab or biopsy) ELISA tests can be used.

Auscultation is relatively unrewarding in avian patients. The heart rate is too fast to count reliably and is better assessed by an electrocardiogram (ECG) (100mm/sec paper speed is required) or heart monitor. As described in Chapter 15, the lung field is small and fixed compared with that of mammals. It is often

possible to hear a faint short inspiratory noise in the normal bird. If other noises are heard they are likely to be associated with diseases of the nares or sinuses, restriction to air flow in the trachea, eg. syringeal aspergilloma, or severe air sac disease (suspect chlamydiosis). Upper respiratory disease should be clinically differentiable from air sac disease. If the latter is suspected, radiography and endoscopy are indicated. If air sacculitis is present and endoscopy performed, an air sac swab or biopsy should be taken for bacteriology, histopathology, cytology or ELISA.

Neck

The neck should be examined systematically. The oesophagus should be palpated and the mucosal thickness assessed. In cases of doubt, the overlying skin should be wetted with surgical spirit and, if necessary, transilluminated. Alternatively, endoscopy should be carried out. The crop lining is better visualised if the crop is inflated with air or saline whilst the bird is anaesthetised and an endotracheal tube is in place.

Plumage

The condition of the plumage (see Chapter 10) may give clues as to the overall health of the bird or if there is evidence of disease, eg. PBFD or nutritional deficiencies (essential amino acids or vitamin A).

Body Condition

Different species will normally have varying degrees of pectoral covering over their sternum (keel) (see Figure 4.2). The clinician should be familiar with expected degrees of pectoral mass. Loss of condition will give some indication of severity and chronicity of the disease. All patients should be routinely weighed and recorded at each consultation, as this provides base line data for that individual.

Cloaca

Examination of the cloaca can often reveal signs not evident on examination of the droppings. Chronic soiling of the vent plumage may be caused by cloacitis, cloacal uroliths, cloacal papillomata, diarrhoea, polydipsia, etc. Following gentle eversion, the cloacal

Table 4.3. Normal physiological data for birds (after Harrison and Ritchie, 1994).

Weight (g)	Resting heart rate (bpm)	Restrained heart rate (bpm)	Resting Respiratory rate (rpm)	Restrained respiratory rate (rpm)
25	274	400-600	60-70	80-120
100	206	500-600	40-52	60-80
200	178	300-500	35-50	55-65
500	147	160-300	20-30	30-50
1000	127	150-350	15-20	25-40
1500	117	120-200	20-32	25-30
2000	110	110-175	19-28	20-30

0

2

1

3

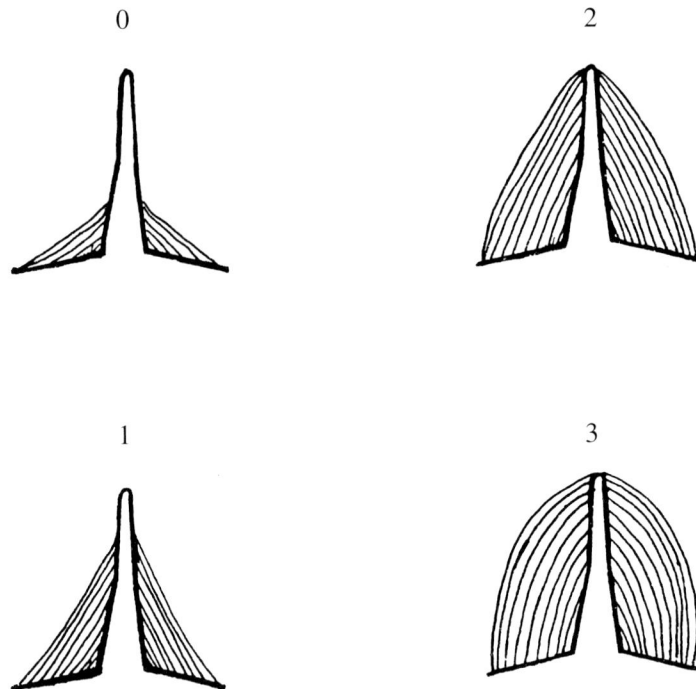

Figure 4.2: Cross sections of sternum illustrating condition scores – 0 (very low) - 3(fat).

mucosa can be examined for signs of papillomata. *Per cloacam* examinations may also be useful, especially in larger birds, for palpation of the kidneys.

Uropygial Gland

The uropygial gland (see Chapter 10), otherwise known as the preen gland, is situated on the rostral body wall, immediately anterior to the insertion of the central tail feathers. The gland is responsible for oil production, used during preening to assist with feather condition and waterproofing. The gland is present and well developed in most species, but absent in some others, eg. Amazons. When present it should be symmetrical and smooth; one should be able to express a small volume of oily secretion. Birds can suffer from dysfunction, abscessation or neoplasia of the gland.

Wings

The long bones, joints and soft tissue of the wings are examined in the same thorough manner (see Chapter 14).

NAIL AND BEAK CLIPPING

Nail and beak clipping is the commonest reason for psittacines being presented to small animal clinicians as opposed to avian veterinarians. The task is simple, easy and straightforward. First, the veterinarian should assess if indeed the claws or beak need to be clipped. Psittacines are meant to have sharp claws and beak, so scratching or biting of the owner is not a reason in itself for clipping. The length of the maxillary beak must be assessed in relation to the lower part of the mandible, and the degree of curling or length of the claws to the bird's ability to grip its perch. Attempting to clip claws or beaks which are of the correct length will not only upset the bird but also the client because of the bleeding which ensues. The clinician should be well prepared in advance. Clippers, cotton wool and silver nitrate pencil (or other caustic haemostatic agent) should be close by before handling the bird. The caged bird should be taken into a darkened room where it can easily be caught without injury to the veterinarian or upset to the bird (see earlier - Handling). In the authors' opinion it is preferable to ask the owner to wait outside the consulting room so that the bird does not bear a grudge against the owner. More importantly, the authors are wary of allowing owners of pet psittacines to hold onto the head or stroke the bird during this procedure as they, or the veterinarian, may be bitten. The procedure is made easier if the bird is held by a veterinary nurse trained in holding psittacines correctly; this allows each individual claw and the head to be positioned for clipping. The sensitive quick may be visible on some nails unless they are dark in colour. The cutting procedure is identical to that used in dogs. A pair of clippers or a power burr may be employed. The bird should not be released until the veterinarian is certain that the nails are not bleeding. If they are, a haemostatic agent should be applied.

COLLECTION OF DIAGNOSTIC SAMPLES

In view of their size, presence of air sacs, lack of a diaphragm and accessibility of most parts of the avian anatomy, birds are well adapted to the collection of all manner of samples for diagnostic tests. Clinical signs presented in the classical 'sick bird' scenario are usually unhelpful. Time is against the clinician, so therapy must often be instigated after sufficient samples have been taken to make a definitive diagnosis, but before one has been reached. It is for this reason that clinicians who become involved in avian work believe that there is a greater diagnostic challenge involved in this field than with many other fields of veterinary medicine.

Dependent on the species and origin of the patient, a mild sedative or short anaesthetic may aid a full, rapid and stress-free examination, at which time appropriate samples may also be taken. Clinicians interested in avian work must be capable of extensive in-house clinical pathology. Blood samples are often indicated for haematology and biochemistry. Swabs and aspirates from oesophagus, crop, choana, trachea, air sacs and cloaca can be extremely useful on occasions. Such samples must be processed immediately. Often, there is not time to send the samples away to outside laboratories. The clinician should be confident with haematology, biochemistry, parasitology, the preparation and interpretation of impression smears (a technique which might also revolutionise his/her clinical work in other species), Gram stains, etc.

Haematology

The authors generally use a 23-27G needle. The sample may clot if there is any delay or the sample is slow to draw out due to vein collapse when suction is applied. To prevent clotting, the authors advise that the syringe and needle are flushed with dilute heparin (1:100) prior to use; this is particularly helpful for novices sampling smaller species.

Blood Volumes

The total blood volume is approximately 6-13% of the bird's bodyweight (greater in smaller birds); 10% of this volume may be taken without any untoward effect, ie. for a 300g parrot one can safely take 0.6-1.3% of the bodyweight (1.8-3.9ml blood). A simple estimation is 1% of bodyweight.

Sampling Sites

There are a number of sites from which blood samples may be taken. The choice of site depends on personal experience and the amount of blood that is required. Having collected the blood sample, a blood smear should be made immediately.

Basilic (Brachial) Vein

This vein is found distal to the elbow on the ventral aspect of the wing. Venepuncture of the basilic vein is easily performed in all species over 150g, unless the patient is anaemic or has a collapsed circulation. For the right-handed operator, it is easier to use the right wing. The bird is cast on its back on a soft padded surface. The wing is extended and restrained by the operator who places the first and second finger of his left hand on the mid/distal humerus, with the proximal part of the palm placed onto the carpus. This manner of handling keeps the wing extended and restrained. The vein is raised with the thumb of the left hand, leaving the right hand free for sample collection. There is a risk of haematoma formation at this site, although digital pressure for 2-3 minutes will usually prevent this occurring.

Medial Metatarsal (Caudal Tibial) Vein

This vein is located on the medial aspect of the proximal metatarsus. It is not as readily visualised as the basilic vein. However, it can be easily accessed in larger species, without need to cast the bird. It is not so prone to haematoma formation.

Right Jugular

Samples may be taken from this vein with or without anaesthesia or assistance in restraint, depending on the species. This is the easiest vein to access in small birds. The neck is extended and the vein is readily visualised. No feathers need to be removed. If the feather tracts are parted (such as by wetting with surgical spirit), a featherless (apterium) section of skin can be moved directly over the jugular. Haematoma can be an occasional problem in small species. It is difficult to apply pressure at this site to control haemorrhage.

Toenail Clip

Short clipping a toenail can be used for collection of small samples of blood, such as for DNA sexing etc. However, it may yield abnormal cell distributions or cellular artefacts if relied upon for haematology (Campbell, 1994). It is therefore not recommended for the collection of samples for haematology. Samples taken by this method are also not suitable for uric acid assay, due to the risk of contamination from urates on the toes and feet.

Biochemistry

Normal values are not available for all species. It is important to check with the veterinary laboratory with respect to sample type, volume, critical time between sampling and testing, and the time between sampling and any previous meal, exercise, etc. If biochemistry is not performed in-house immediately after collection, it is usually preferable to harvest the plasma from the heparinised sample by centrifugation immediately after collection. The plasma should be refrigerated prior to testing or sending to an outside laboratory.

Swabs

Swabs may be taken from many parts of the body, eg. mouth, choana, crop, trachea, cloaca, skin feathers, etc. Samples are best examined as impression smears with stains such as 'Diff Quik', so that rapid diagnosis or confirmation of diagnosis may be made.

Aspirates

Aspirates are useful. They may be taken from any fluid or soft tissue swellings as well as from sinuses, joints, wounds, trachea, crop and body cavities, eg. air sacs.

Endoscopy

No avian clinician should be without a good quality endoscope. Most practitioners use a small (2.7mm) rigid scope, with either a 0° (straight) or a 30° lens. The ideal is a 30° lens with a piggyback cannula for the passage of biopsy forceps, grasping forceps, aspiration nozzle, etc. In this way these instruments can be clearly seen by the operator via the scope. Endoscopy is invaluable for examination of the crop, proventriculus, trachea, all air sac cavities and cloaca. A 0° (straight) endoscope is preferable for examination of the trachea.

Radiology

Radiology is also invaluable (see Chapter 7). Some practitioners will have radiographic equipment which is too powerful for most bird tissue, as the latter has such a low focal depth. Fine grain, intensifying screens or rare earth screens will increase the exposure requirements, and hence bring the exposures within the scope of most machines. High quality pictures are required and are easily attained by most practitioners. In view of the great variability of normal anatomy and hence radiological anatomy between even closely related species, it is imperative to radiograph the normal as well as the abnormal, for comparison. An extra joint in a toe can easily be confused with a fracture, if one is not aware of what is normal. As with any radiology, two views at right angles should always be taken. On occasions this can prove both surprising and very informative. Contrast studies can be useful; they are employed for visualisation of the crop, proventriculus, ventriculus, small and large intestine, cloaca and abdominal masses. Excretory urograms and arteriograms can also be used (see Chapter 7).

THERAPEUTICS

An understanding not just of the choice of drugs and their pharmokinetics, but also the best route of administration, is necessary. The distribution of drugs from one site within the body to another is more rapid in well perfused tissues, although there are significantly varying rates of perfusion within tissue and dependence upon lipid solubility and the degree of ionisation (Grauer and Maziasz, 1988). If poorly perfused tissues require therapeutic concentrations, an alternative route of administration may be required. The choice of route of medication may not be based solely on the most appropriate route, but also on the ability of the owner or veterinarian to manage that route, often on a repeated basis.

The aim of antimicrobial therapy is to aid the elimination of the infecting organism but at the same time allow the host's immune system to resolve the infection (Flammer, 1994). The overuse of antibiotics may also cause problems associated with side-effects (diarrhoea, secondary infections or renal damage), immunosuppression (protein synthesis is affected; some antiobitics may be catabolic if long-term therapy is given), and development of resistance. Often, supportive therapy (see Chapter 9) may have a greater effect on the recovery of a sick bird than purely the choice of antibiotic. The choice of antibiotic should be made on sensitivity testing whenever possible.

Methods of Administration

In Drinking Water

This is the least reliable method. Birds are less likely to drink water which has had its taste, smell or colour affected by the addition of medication. Calculating an acurate dose is difficult due to dependence upon the water intake of the bird. This route of treatment should be reserved for the treatment of flock problems only; it has no place in the treatment of the single pet bird. If a bird reduces its water intake because of the addition of medicines, this could lead to a deterioration in the bird's condition due to dehydration. Some drugs may also be affected by the pH of the water and its mineral content.

In Food

If this method of medication is used, it is essential that the medication is well mixed and that the patient is prepared to eat a soft diet. This is often a problem with psittacines, as they are usually only prepared to eat their own normal food. This is a very good reason for training birds to accept soft mix diets at all times. It is possible that intestinal absorption of some drugs may be affected by being mixed with food. If the food is given a strange taste, it is also possible that the bird may refuse to eat, even if it has previously been trained to accept soft mix diets. The addition of honey or orange juice to food may improve palatability and acceptance. Sick birds are also likely to be eating less and this will affect the amount of the drug ingested.

Crop Tube

This is an effective method of medication, as a calculated dose is known to be given to the bird. However, it can be stressful to the patient, especially if frequent medication is required. Some owners may be reluctant to perform this procedure themselves, although it is simple and easily taught. The tube should be chosen so that the diameter is bigger than the opening of the glottis. Plastic tubing is liable to be bitten through and its use should be avoided.

Parenteral

This is the best method for achieving rapid concentrations of therapeutic agents, especially in the critically ill bird. There are a number of routes for the administration of medication by this method.

Intramuscular injection (i/m). This is the most reliable route for absorption; ideally the pectoral muscles should be used. Because of the existence of the renal portal system, injections into the pelvic limb muscles may not result in therapeutic concentrations being reached as the drug may be excreted immediately via the kidneys.

Subcutaneous injection (s/c). S/c injections are generally poorly absorbed, especially if the bird is dehydrated. There is no advantage in using this route compared with the i/m route, although it can be used for irritating drugs to avoid the risk of muscle necrosis.

Intravenous injection (i/v). I/v injections are effective but safety is limited to certain types of drugs or fluids. This technique is easily achieved if one is using an indwelling venous catheter, but otherwise the frequency of therapy may lead to practical problems.

Intraosseous injection (i/o). I/o injections are mainly reserved for the administration of fluid replacement, although they may also be used for administration of drugs that are suitable for the i/v route. With an indwelling i/o cannula, this may be more practical than repeated i/v dosing.

Local infusion and infiltration. These routes are particularly useful when dealing with localised infections such as sinusitis, where sinus flushing has the advantage of providing an appropriate antibiotic to the site which requires the greatest concentration, but also serves to remove infected material. Drugs mixed with dimethylsulphoxide (DMSO) may be used for percutaneous absorption.

Intratracheal injection. This can be performed via the oropharynx or by direct injection in between tracheal cartilage rings. This technique is well tolerated in the conscious bird (see Chapter 15).

Nebulisation (see also Chapter 15)
This technique requires a nebuliser, which produces small droplets (less than 5μm) of a vehicle fluid (saline or DMSO) to produce a mist containing the therapeutic agent, and allows the bird to inhale this mixture. This method of medication is particularly useful for cases of pneumonia or air sacculitis. Nebulisation allows the use of drugs which are toxic when used systemically but which are not absorbed from the respiratory tissues, eg. gentamicin, and hence are not toxic when used in this manner. Nebulisation should be considered as a supplement to systemic medication (Bauck, 1993).

Topical
This is useful for localised infections such as conjunctivitis or dermatitis, or for areas of skin trauma which do not warrant systemic injections. There are limitiations with this choice of treatment. Creams and ointments are not often suitable as they may cause damage to the feather structure. Eye drops are preferable to ointmnets as this will limit damage to feathers. Powders can be used for the treatment of ectoparasites.

Calculation of Dosages
The appropriate dose of a drug will depend on its pharmacokinetics, ie. its route of absorption, metabolism and clearance. The dosages quoted for dogs and cats are often not appropriate for birds. The most important single factor is the surface area to volume ratio of the individual patient and the metabolic rate of the patient (Kirkwood, 1983). Smaller birds require higher levels of drug than larger birds. Allometric scaling of dosages is advised in all birds. This may be performed by using the following formula:

$$E = \left(\frac{W}{1000}\right)^{0.75} \times D$$

E = dose of drug in milligrams for a bird of a specific weight (W)
W = weight of bird in grams
D = dose of drug recommended for cat/dog (mg/kg)

REFERENCES

Bauck L (1993) *A Practitioner's Guide to Avian Medicine*. American Animal Hospital Association, Colorado.

Campbell TW (1994) Hematology. In: *Avian Medicine: Principles and Application*. Eds BW Ritchie, GJ Harrison and LR Harrison. Wingers, Lake Worth.

Flammer K (1994) Antimicrobial therapy. In: *Avian Medicine: Principles and Application*. Eds BW Ritchie, GJ Harrison and LR Harrison. Wingers, Lake Worth.

Grauer GF and Maziasz TJ (1988) The toxicokinetic approach to antidotal therapy: toxicant absorption and distribution. *Compendium on Continuing Education for the Practicing Veterinarian* **10(9)**, 1057.

Harrison GJ and Ritchie BW (1994) Making distinctions in the physical examination. In: *Avian Medicine: Principles and Application*. Eds BW Ritchie, GJ Harrison and LR Harrison. Wingers, Lake Worth.

Kirkwood JK (1983) Influence of body size on animals in health and disease. *Veterinary Record* **113**, 287.

CHAPTER FIVE

Cytology and Haemocytology

Gerry M Dorrestein

INTRODUCTION

Haemocytology and diagnostic cytology in psittacine medicine provide a means for better disease definition, which allows for a more specific therapeutic regimen. Haemocytology is a diagnostic tool in the clinical patient and cytology can provide microscopic information of many different disease processes. At necropsy, cytology is an invaluable tool for defining the presumptive diagnosis and to starting treatment in the flock situation. It is important that cytological specimens are taken from fresh sources, since cells degenerate rapidly following the death of the bird or removal of the tissue. Cytological evaluation is always an adjunct to other diagnostic procedures. A definitive diagnosis often requires information from the clinical history, physical examination, evaluation of samples obtained from the bird, radiographs, surgical investigations, necropsy and histopathology. Table 5.1 lists some psittacine diseases where cytology can provide important information.

The avian patient often does not lend itself to all of the diagnostic aids that are available for mammals. The small body size and blood volume of many birds often limits the use of extensive biochemical and serodiagnostic evaluation.

Table 5.1. List of diseases where cytology gives important information.

Disease	Organs to be examined
Bacterial infections	
Salmonella spp.	Liver, spleen, lung, gut.
Pseudomonas spp.	Lung, gut.
Clostridium spp.	Gut.
Mycobacterium spp.	All organs (tongue).
Megabacteria.	Stomach, gut.
Mycotic infections	
Candida spp.	Crop, gut.
Aspergillus spp.	Lung, air sac, syrinx.
Protozoal infections	
Plasmodium spp.	Blood, lung.
Haemoproteus sp.	Blood, lung.
Trichomonas spp.	Oesophagus, crop.
Giardia spp.	Cloaca, duodenum.
Leucocytozoon spp.	Muscle, heart.
Microsporidia spp.	Gut, brains, organs (lovebirds).
Miscellaneous	
Choking after forced feeding.	Lung, air sac.
Metaplasia.	Mucus glands, tongue, nostrils, syrinx.
Microfilaria spp.	Blood, lung, liver.
Chlamydia spp.	All organs.
Trypanosoma spp.	Lung, liver.
Anthracosis.	Lung.

There has been little controlled study involving correlation of the pathophysiology of diseased birds with their haematological response. In spite of these limitations, haemocytology can be a useful tool in the diagnosis of avian diseases.

In the clinic a cytological examination of swellings, discharges of eyes, nostrils and wounds, fluids, crop and cloacal swabs, and faecal smears can give much additional information about the nature and aetiology of a process or symptom. Cytological samples of the alimentary tract of live birds can be obtained by using a cotton swab or crop aspiration. At necropsy, samples are obtained by scraping any lesions with a cotton swab or spatula blade. The material can also be used for microbiological culture and microscopic examination.

At necropsy, cytology is an indispensable tool for a rapid investigation of possible bacterial, mycotic or yeast infections. The diagnosis of many protozoal infections, eg. *(A)toxoplasma* spp., *Plasmodium* spp., depends on demonstrating these organisms in impression smears of a selection of organs. For a quick differentiation between tumour and inflammation, this technique is an invaluable aid.

Haemocytology and cytology are both techniques based on the study of individual cells. In disease situations they can give information about pathophysiological changes caused by the disease. Both techniques provide a simple, rapid, inexpensive method of diagnosis that can be performed in the veterinary practice. Frequently, the aetiological agent causing the lesion can be identified. However, the veterinarian should be aware of the limitations of diagnostic cytology. Cytology does not always provide a definitive diagnosis. It does not give information concerning the architecture of the tissue (cells in the same smear may have originated from different areas of the organ or lesion), the size of the lesion or the invasiveness of a malignant lesion. The cells observed may not necessarily represent the true nature of the lesion. An example of this is the imprinting of the ulcerated surface of a neoplastic mass that reveals the cytological features of inflammation and infection only.

Cytopathology should not compete with histopathology; the two should complement each other in achieving a final diagnosis. It is important to note that occasionally one is unable to characterise the cells in a specimen and that a repeat smear or biopsy for histopathological evaluation may be required to define the lesion.

SAMPLING TECHNIQUES AND SAMPLE PREPARATION

Blood for haematological evaluation can be obtained by several methods as described in Chapter 4.

Blood smears should be made with fresh, non-heparinised blood (heparin interferes with the proper staining of the blood cells). Fresh, non-heparinised blood can be obtained from either the needle used to obtain the sample or from blood collected directly into a non-heparinised microhaematocrit tube. EDTA-treated blood can also be used. The smear can be made using the standard two-slide wedge technique or by using the slide and coverslip method. After spreading the blood the smear is air dried.

A successful cytological examination is only possible if these four conditions are achieved:
● Representative sample.
● Good quality smear.
● Good staining technique.
● Correct evaluation of the cytological findings.

Fine-needle aspiration biopsy often provides a good cytological sample for a rapid presumptive diagnosis without radical tissue removal, and this can be performed in the examination room. For more detailed information see Campbell (1984, 1988, 1994a), Fudge (1988), Hawkey and Gulland (1989) and Ingh and Vos (1989).

Contact smears are made by imprinting the removed mass or the tissue obtained from the scraping of an exposed lesion *in situ* or at necropsy. At a standard necropsy, impression smears are made from the cut surfaces of liver, spleen and lungs, and also from an endgut scraping. All this material can be collected onto one slide. Extra impressions are made from macroscopically altered organs. Impressions of organs should be made from a freshly cut surface, which should be fairly dry and free of blood. This can be achieved by gently blotting the surface onto a clean paper towel. Imprint slides can then be made by gently touching the glass or by touching the microscope slide onto the surface of the mass. It is important not to use too much pressure and to air-dry the slide quickly. Several imprints of the same organ should be made on each slide.

If the imprints show poor cellularity, more cells may be obtained by scraping the mass with a scalpel blade to improve exfoliation of the cells. The imprinting procedure can be repeated, or imprints can be made from the material remaining on the scalpel blade.

Direct smears should be made from aspirated fluids, eg. ascites or cyst contents. They can be made using the wedge method or the coverslip method commonly used for making blood smears. A 'squash-prep' procedure should be used to make smears from thick tenacious fluid or from fluid that contains solid tissue fragments. Fluids that have low cellularity require concentration methods to increase the smear cellularity. Sediment smears made after slow-speed centrifugation (500rmp for five minutes) of the fluid or smear made with cytocentrifuge equipment will usually provide adequate cytological specimens.

Once a sample has been collected and a smear has

been made, the specimen must be properly fixed on the slide. If smears are to be sent to a diagnostic laboratory, they must be air dried, properly packed (broken slides are fairly common) and accompanied by a distinct identification and case history.

The method of fixation depends upon which staining procedure is to be used. Fresh air-dried blood smears and cytology slides are adequate for Romanowsky stains, eg. Giemsa stain and many quick-stains.

A variety of stains and staining methods, eg. acid-fast (*Mycobacterium* spp.), Giemsa (cells), Gram (microorganisms), modified Giminez (*Chlamydia* spp.), Stamp (*Chlamydia* spp.) and Sudan III (fat globules), are used by cytologists (Campbell, 1984, 1986, 1988, 1994b). Proper fixation must be applied if specific stains are used. To obtain this information the diagnostic service should be contacted.

The cytological descriptions in this text are based primarily on slides stained with a modified quick Wright's stain (Hemacolor®, Merck). The great advantage of the quick stains is a short staining time (usually 20 seconds) which allows rapid examination of the specimen and provides satisfactory staining quality. These stains are suitable for use in veterinary practice where a simple staining procedure is desirable. Many quick stains also provide permanent reference smears for comparison with other cytological specimens.

Once the smears have been stained and dried they are ready for microscopic examination. For a reliable evaluation of the haematological or cytological changes in the sample it will often be necessary to consult a haematologist or cytopathologist. The recognition of many aetiological agents is often easier and can give a presumptive diagnosis.

Scanning and low magnifications (x100 or x250) are used initially to obtain a general impression of the smear quality. At these magnifications, the examiner is able to estimate the smear cellularity, identify tissue structures or large infectious agents (ie. microfilariae or fungal elements), and determine the best locations for more detailed cellular examination. Oil immersion (x1000) magnification is used to examine cell structure, bacteria and other small objects.

In addition to viewing cellular structure, the cytologist should also determine background characteristics, the amount of peripheral blood or stain precipitation present, the thickness of different areas in the smear, and the distribution of the cells. The background characteristics may be useful in defining the nature of the material being examined. Protein aggregates create a granular background with the quick stains. Bacteria, crystals, nuclear material from ruptured cells and exogenous material (eg. plant fibres, pollen and talcum or starch crystals from examination gloves) may be seen in the non-cellular background of the smear. Excessive peripheral blood contamination of a specimen will dilute and mask diagnostic cells; this will make interpretation difficult.

Stain precipitate on the smear should not be confused with bacteria or cellular inclusions. Stain precipitate varies in size and shape and will be more refractive than bacteria or most cellular inclusions. The thickness of the smear will affect the appearance of the cells and the quality of the smear. Thick areas do not allow the cells to expand on the slide, so they appear smaller and more dense when compared with the same cell type on thinner areas of the smear. Therefore, examination of cells in thick smears should be avoided. The cellular distribution should also be noted.

GENERAL PRINCIPLES OF HAEMOCYTOLOGICAL INTERPRETATION

The following blood cells are recognised in avian blood smears: erythrocytes, leucocytes and thrombocytes. Some characteristics and pathophysiological conditions will be described.

Avian Erythrocytes

The mature avian erythrocyte is an elliptical cell with an oval nucleus (see Figure 5.1). The cytoplasm is red-orange with most stains. The erythroblast (= rubriblast) is a large, round cell with much basophilic cytoplasm and a round nucleus with coarse, clumped chromatin and a large nucleolus. During its maturing process via polychromatic erythrocytes (= rubricytes) and reticulocytes the cytoplasmic RNA disappears and the cytoplasm becomes more bluish with dark clumps within the cytoplasm. These clumps disappear and the cytoplasm becomes orange-pink with an uniform texture. The nucleus changes via an oval-round shape with a fine nuclear chromatin pattern into an oval, centrally placed nucleus. The nuclear appearance varies with the age of the cell, becoming more condensed and staining darker with age.

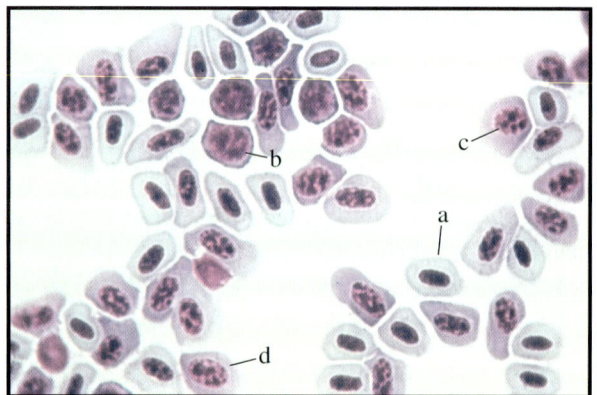

Figure 5.1: *Lung: erythropoesis. (Hemacolor® - Oil Immersion x1000.) a. mature erythrocyte; b. erythroblast; c. polychromatic erythrocyte; d. reticulocyte.*

Atypical and abnormal erythrocytes in peripheral blood may be found. Erythroplastids - enucleated cytoplasmic fragments - are common. Nuclear abnormalities include achromatic bands and chromophobic streaks. Smudge cells and cell debris are common in avian blood smears and are a result of cellular rupture at the time of making the blood smear.

An increase in red cell polychromasia is indicative of red cell regeneration. In normal birds the number of polychromatic erythrocytes (or reticulocytes) found in the peripheral blood film ranges between 1-5% of the erythrocytes. An anaemic bird with 5% or less degree of polychromasia is responding poorly to the anaemia. An anaemic bird showing a 10% or greater degree of polychromasia is exhibiting a significant regenerative response. The presence of immature erythrocytes in the peripheral blood, along with an increase in polychromasia, is indicative of a marked regenerative response.

Some causes of anaemia in birds are:
● Blood-loss anaemia - traumatic injury; parasitism; toxicity (aflatoxicosis, coumarin); organic disease.
● Haemolytic anaemia (regenerative) - red blood cell parasites, eg. *Plasmodium* spp.; bacterial septicaemia, eg. salmonellosis; toxicity.
● Depression anaemia (non-regenerative) - chronic disease, eg. tuberculosis, chlamydiosis, aspergillosis, neoplasia; hypothyroidism; toxicity (lead, aflatoxicosis); nutritional deficiencies; leukaemia (lymphoid or erythroblastosis).

Avian Granulocytic Leucocytes

Helpful references to the identification of avian leucocytes, together with beautiful illustrations, are found in more extensive handbooks (Lucas and Jamroz, 1961; Campbell, 1994b).

The granulocytic leucocytes of birds are heterophils, eosinophils and basophils.

Heterophils (or pseudo-eosinophils)

These are round cells with partially lobed basophilic nuclei. The cytoplasm is clear and contains a variable number of eosinophilic rod- or ellipse-shaped granules (see Figure 5.2).

Mature heterophils appear to show toxic changes. Signs of toxicity include increased cytoplasmic basophilia, vacuolisation, abnormal granules, degranulation and degeneration of the nucleus. The number of toxic heterophils present is an indication of severity and is suggestive of the duration of an inflammatory response (Campbell, 1994b).

A marked leucocytosis and heterophilia are often associated with chlamydiosis, avian tuberculosis and aspergillosis.

Eosinophils

These resemble heterophils, but usually have a blue cytoplasm with round eosinophilic granules. There is

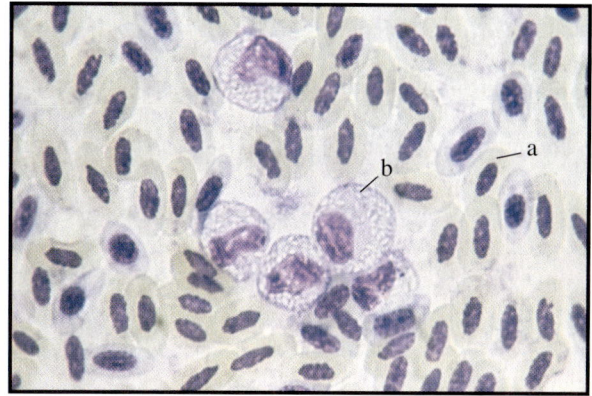

Figure 5.2: Lung: chlamydiosis (Muller Amazon). (Hemacolor® - Oil Immersion x1000.) a. erythrocyte; b. heterophil.

variation in the morphologic appearance of the eosinophils of avian species.

Basophils

Avian basophils resemble mammalian basophils, except that the avian nucleus is either partially lobed or non-segmented.

Avian Mononuclear Leucocytes

The mononuclear leucocytes found in the peripheral blood of birds are lymphocytes and monocytes.

Lymphocytes

Avian lymphocytes resemble mammalian lymphocytes, but are more variable in size and shape (see Figure 5.3). The small and medium mature lymphocytes are more common in peripheral blood. Immature lymphocytes are large, have basophilic cytoplasm and a round nucleus with smooth chromatin and, occasionally, have a prominent nucleolus (lymphoblasts).

Cytological indications for reactivity in lymphocytes include increased cell size, increased cytoplasmic basophilia, the presence of azurophilic cytoplasmic granules and smooth nuclear chromatin (Campbell, 1994a). The presence of many reactive lymphocytes is suggestive of antigenic stimulation.

A marked lymphocytosis, with the majority of cells appearing as small mature lymphocytes with scalloped cytoplasmic margins, is suggestive of lymphoid neoplasia.

Monocytes

Avian monocytes resemble mammalian monocytes. In general they are the largest cells found in peripheral blood and have abundant blue cytoplasm. The cytoplasm frequently contains vacuoles or fine eosinophilic granulation. The nucleus is eccentrically located in the cell, which can be round, bean-shaped or lobed, and contains a delicate basophilic chromatin.

Avian Thrombocytes

Thrombocytes are nucleated cells that tend to clump

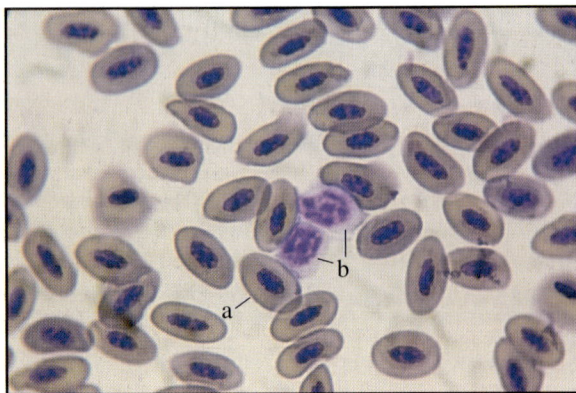

Figure 5.3: *Blood smear: normal (African Grey). (Hemacolor® - Oil Immersion x1000.) a. erythrocyte; b. lymphocyte.*

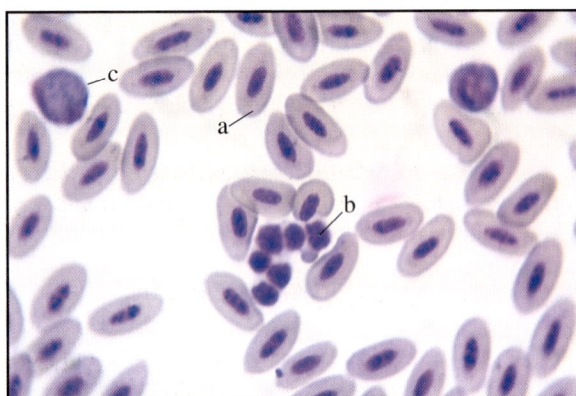

Figure 5.4: *Blood smear: normal (African Grey). (Hemacolor® - Oil Immersion x1000.) a. erythrocyte; b. thrombocyte; c. heterophil.*

in a blood smear. The cytoplasm is pale blue and the nucleus contains basophilic chromatin clumps (see Figure 5.4). The cytoplasm may contain eosinophilic granules.

Abnormal thrombocyte cytology includes the presence of reactive and immature thrombocytes. Reactive thrombocytes tend to be more spindle-shaped than non-reactive thrombocytes.

Common Blood Parasites
The most common blood parasites found in psittacines are:
● *Haemoproteus* spp. - only the gametocyte stage with yellow to brown pigment is found in the peripheral blood.
● *Leucocytozoon* spp. - the large round-to-elongated gametocytes cause the host cell (usually immature erythrocytes) to enlarge and appear to have two nuclei.
● *Plasmodium* spp. - has schizonts in the peripheral blood; gametocytes or schizonts appear in other blood cells as well as in erythrocytes. The nucleus appears eccentric.
● Microfilarial larvae are frequently found in the peripheral blood of psittacines.

GENERAL PRINCIPLES OF CYTOLOGICAL INTERPRETATION

The cytological appearance of many cells obtained from avian tissues and fluids is similar to that described for mammalian species. A cytological classification divides body tissue into four groups: haemic, epithelial-glandular, connective and nervous.

Haemic Tissue (Blood and Blood-forming Tissue)
Haemic tissue is composed of cells that are found in the peripheral blood, bone marrow and ectopic haemopoietic sites. Peripheral blood primarily contains the mature cells that are derived from cell lines located in the haemopoietic tissues.

Epithelial (including Glandular) Tissue
Epithelial tissue cells tend to exfoliate in clumps or sheets. Epithelial cells (except mature squamous epithelium) are usually round or oval with abundant cytoplasm and have round or oval nuclei. The nuclear chromatin is generally smooth and a prominent nucleolus may be visible. The cytoplasmic borders of epithelial cells are usually distinct, except for the liver. Normal epithelial cells are uniform in appearance.

Connective Tissue
Connective tissue cells tend to exfoliate poorly and provide cytological specimens with few cells. Often, traumatic exfoliation is required to obtain significant numbers of cells for evaluation. Depending on their origin, connective tissue cells tend to vary in the amount of cytoplasm and nuclear shape.

Nervous Tissue
Nervous tissue cells are rarely seen unless the cytological specimen was made from central or peripheral nervous tissue. Nervous tissue cells may be present in smears from other tissues, but are of little significance.

The goal of cytology is to identify the cellular message and classify the cellular response into one of the basic cytodiagnostic groups. These groups include inflammation, tissue hyperplasia or benign neoplasia, malignant neoplasia and normal cellularity. The smears or impressions will also give information about the possible aetiology of the pathological changes.

Inflammation
Inflammation may be caused by living agents (microorganisms) or non-living agents (traumatic, thermal, toxic or chemical agents). The cytology of inflammatory lesions may be classified into purulent or proliferative (including granulomatous) inflammatory reactions. Inflammatory cells include heterophils, eosinophils, macrophages, lymphocytes, plasma cells and (angio)fibroblasts.

Purulent Inflammation

Purulent reaction is characterised by a predominance of heterophilic granulocytes. Overwhelming bacterial infections commonly cause degenerative changes to the heterophils, eg. pyknosis, karyolysis, karyorrhexis, basophilic cytoplasm with phagocytic vacuolisation. The agent may be phagocytised within the cytoplasm.

Proliferative Inflammation

The cytology of proliferative inflammation shows many lymphocytes mixed with various numbers of plasma cells and macrophages. Occasionally, heterophils tend to be non-degenerate in appearance. This reaction becomes more granulomatous as evidenced by a predominance of mononuclear cells (macrophages and lymphocytes). A granulomatous reaction can also be represented by giant cell formation or by macrophages coalescing into net-like sheets.

The inflammatory response can also be classified as either heterophilic inflammation (acute inflammatory response), mixed-cell inflammation (an established, active inflammation) or macrophagic inflammation (common in avian tuberculosis, chlamydiosis, foreign body reaction, mycotic infections and cutaneous xanthomatosis).

(Malignant) Neoplasia

Certain criteria are required for the cytological diagnosis of neoplasia. In many cases, however, the differentiation between inflammation, hypertrophy and neoplasia is not so clear cut. The main cytopathological criteria for the diagnosis of neoplasia can be divided into several categories: general cellular, nuclear or cytoplasmic.

General Cellular

The general cellular features refer to the cell population on the smear. The neoplastic cells may appear related (have common origin) but can exhibit pleomorphism (variation in shape).

Nuclear

Sometimes, the nuclei are different from the nuclei of normal tissue cells. Changes in the nucleus include nuclear hypertrophy, variations in size and shape of the nuclei and in the ratio of nuclei to cytoplasm, changes in the nucleoli, multinucleation, irregularity of the chromatin and nuclear membrane, and abnormal mitotic figures (see Figure 5.5).

Cytoplasmic

The cytoplasm can also be different, eg. a different cytoplasmic volume, variations in the shape of the cytoplasmic borders, basophilia, vacuolation and inclusions bodies. Based on cytology only it will be very difficult, and often impossible, to classify the neoplasm as a carcinoma (= epithelial), sarcoma (= mesothelial)

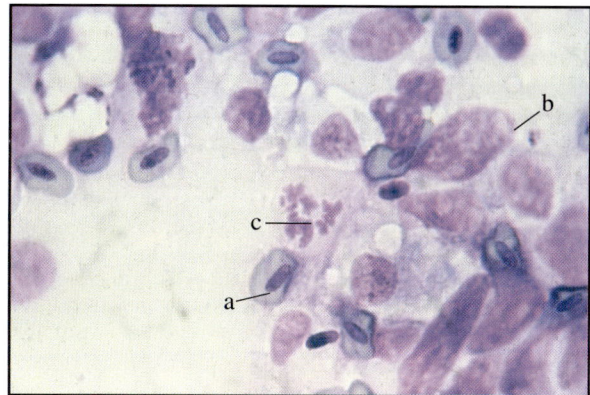

Figure 5.5: Sarcoma (Peach-faced Lovebird). (Hemacolor® - Oil Immersion x1000.) a. erythrocyte; b. tumour cells; c. mitotic figure.

or discrete cell (eg. lymphoid leucosis) tumour. The presence of cell types that are foreign to the tissue being examined (ectopic cells) may indicate a metastatic neoplasm.

In the practical situation, cytodiagnosis of swellings should differentiate between inflammation and neoplasms.

CONJUNCTIVA AND CORNEA

Samples can be obtained using a sterile moist swab or a metal or plastic spatula and gently scraping the margins of the cornea or conjunctiva. Local ophthalmic anaesthetic agents should not be used; they are toxic to cells. Normal conjunctival cytology shows a few epithelial cells occurring singly or in sheets, often with brown or black pigmented granules in the cytoplasm. These granules should not be confused with bacteria. Corneal cells are non-keratinised squamous epithelial cells with a central vesicular nucleus. A few extracellular bacteria are present on normal smears. Many inflammatory cells and cell debris can be seen with bacterial conjunctivitis and corneal infections. Chlamydial or mycoplasmal infections of the eye may show inflammatory cells, cell debris and epithelial cells or macrophages containing intracytoplasmic inclusions.

SKIN AND SUBCUTIS

The skin is composed of keratinised, stratified squamous epithelium and exfoliation produces primary cornified squamous epithelial cells. Bacterial infections are represented by large numbers of inflammatory cells, cell debris and bacteria. Fungal infections may reveal fungal elements on cytological examination. Foreign bodies produce granulomatous reactions with macrophages, giant-cell formation and a variable number of heterophils.

Cutaneous and subcutaneous masses should be examined cytologically. Pox lesions frequently produce cytological features of inflammation and swollen epithelial cells with small, round, pale eosinophilic inclusions (Borrel and Bollinger bodies) when stained with Wright's stain. Subcutaneous lipomata are common in budgerigars, and a needle aspirate reveals numerous background fat droplets and a variable number of fat cells. Subcutaneous lymphosarcoma (lymphoid leucosis) is characterised by a marked number of immature lymphocytes with variable nucleus size.

FLUIDS

Accumulation of fluid in avian species is confined mainly to the abdominal cavity (ascites, peritonitis, haemoperitoneum), but is also encountered in isolated air sacs and cysts, or as synovial fluid in the joints. Effusions can be classified as transudate, exudate, synovia or haemorrhage.

The normal cytology of abdominal fluid, which is usually not present, occasionally shows mesothelial cells and macrophages. Mesothelial cells are round or oval and variable in size, have a homogenous basophilic cytoplasm and have a centrally positioned round nucleus. Reactive mesothelial cells may show cytoplasmic vacuolisation and eventually may contain phagocytised material. It is difficult to differentiate transformed mesothelial cells, active histiocytes and monocyte-derived macrophages.

Transudate and Exudate

Transudate fluids are characterised by low cellularity; exudate is characterised by high cellularity. Purulent exudate may demonstrate bacteria or degenerated heterophils. Plasma cells frequently occur in chronic inflammatory lesions. They are lymphoid cells with an eccentric nucleus, dark blue cytoplasm and a prominent Golgi apparatus. An egg-related peritonitis (yolk peritonitis) can be recognised by the presence of yolk drops, which are homogeneous, round, highly variable in size and deeply basophilic in smears stained with quick stains. The same basophilic droplets can often be found in macrophages within the spleen, liver or lung.

Synovia

Most normal avian joints contain a fluid volume that is too small for aspiration. Normal synovial fluid has poor cellularity; the majority of the cells are mononuclear.

Septic joints usually have an increased synovial fluid volume. Cytology reveals large numbers of heterophils (see Figure 5.6) and bacteria. The eosinophilic granules have often disappeared. Chronic traumatic arthritis demonstrates many macrophages and erythrophago-cytosis. Articular gout is often diagnosed by the gross appearance of the affected joint. The fluid is dense, white or yellow in colour, and cloudy. Large numbers

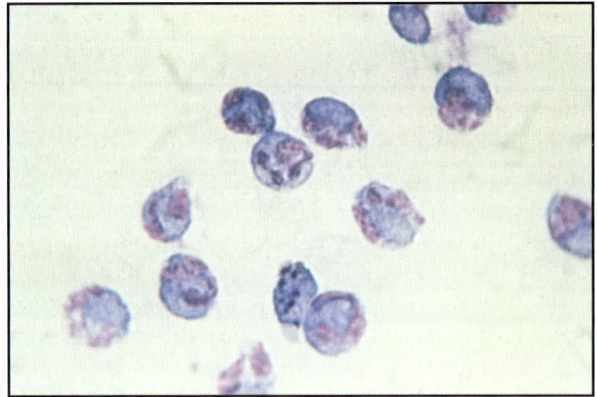

Figure 5.6: Septic joints with large numbers of heterophils; the eosinophilic granules have disappeared. (Hemacolor® - Oil Immersion x1000.)

of inflammatory cells are present. Urate crystals are birefringent needle-like crystals and are best seen under polarised light in a wet-mount.

Haemorrhage
Acute haemorrhagic effusions resemble peripheral blood smears.

DIGESTIVE TRACT

Oral Cavity, Oesophagus and Crop
Examination of the oral cavity is part of the routine physical examination of a bird. White or yellow plaques, nodules or ulcers may be found. Cytological examination of these lesions will aid in the diagnosis of candidiasis, trichomoniasis, poxvirus, bacterial infections, abscesses and squamous metaplasia due to hypovitaminosis A.

Wet-mount slides will aid the identification of live *Trichomonas* spp. or other protozoa. At necropsy these flagellate protozoa can be identified, after staining, by their undulating membrane, their axostyle and their anterior flagella (see Figure 5.7). Some other species of flagellates, without axostyle or membrane, may also be present.

The oesophageal and crop lumina are lined by stratified squamous epithelium. These cells are polygonal

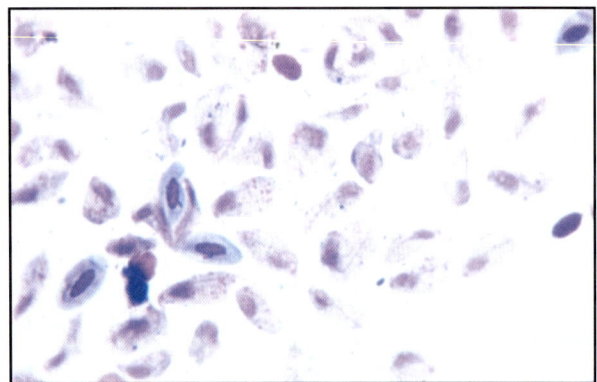

Figure 5.7: Crop: Trichomonas spp. (budgerigar). (Hemacolor® - Oil Immersion x1000.)

with varying degrees of keratinisation and possess a condense nucleus. Many extracellular bacteria (a variety of morphological types) are visible and are often found in association with squamous cells.

Bacterial infections are indicated by leucocytes. Smears with a large number of bacteria of one morphological type should be considered abnormal and an indication for bacterial culture. Candidiasis can be detected by demonstration of the oval, thin-walled yeasts (3-6μm). They stain dark blue with quick stain (see Figure 5.8) and Gram-positive (purple) with Gram stain.

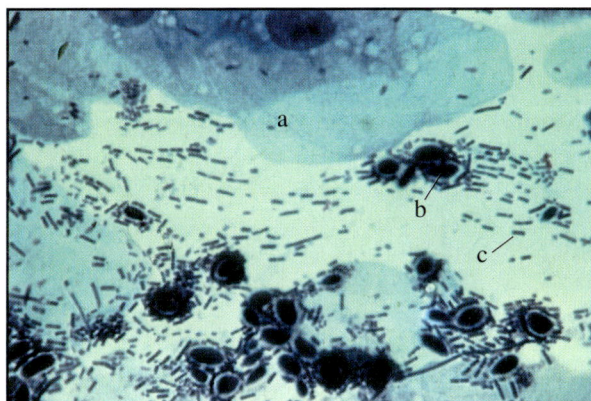

Figure 5.8: Crop: Candida spp. (African Grey). (Hemacolor® - Oil Immersion x1000.) a. epithelial cell; b. yeast; c. rod-shaped bacteria.

Cloaca

Cloacal cytology in a live bird is indicated when inflammation, prolapse or masses are detected. Wetmount preparations will aid in the detection of helminth eggs, coccidial oocysts or protozoa.

Normal cloacal cytology reveals a variable number of squamous cells that have varying degrees of keratinisation, but most cells appear non-keratinised and have a central vesicular nucleus. The normal mucosal cells of the intestinal lining are of the columnar type, often arranged in multicellular rows. In smears, the same changes may be found at necropsy (see later).

Stomach, Intestinal Tract and Cloaca at Necroscopy

In many species of birds a dilated ventriculus may be seen. In mucosal scrapings, so-called 'megabacteria' can often be demonstrated (see Figure 5.9). Candidiasis may be a cause of gastric ulceration.

In most psittacines no bacterial flora is present in the intestinal tract. At necropsy a mucosal scraping (mostly from the rectum) is prepared for cytological evaluation. A variable amount of bacteria (rods, cocci, *Campylobacter* spp. [see Figure 5.10], *vibrio*-forms, 'megabacteria', spores), fungi and yeasts, protozoa (coccidial schizonts, macro- and microgamonts [see Figure 5.11], intra- and extracellular trophozoites, *Microsporidia* spp., flagellates), inflammatory cells,

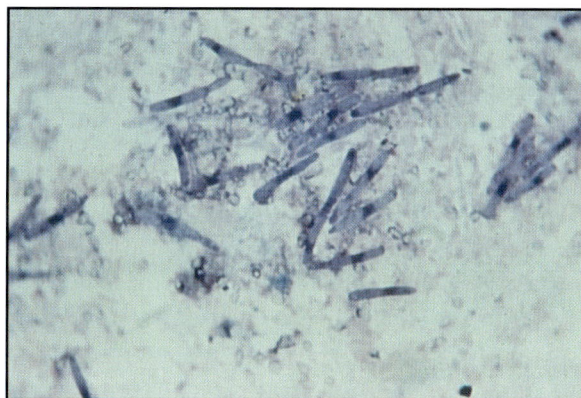

Figure 5.9: Proventriculus: 'megabacteria' (budgerigar). (Hemacolor® - Oil Immersion x1000.)

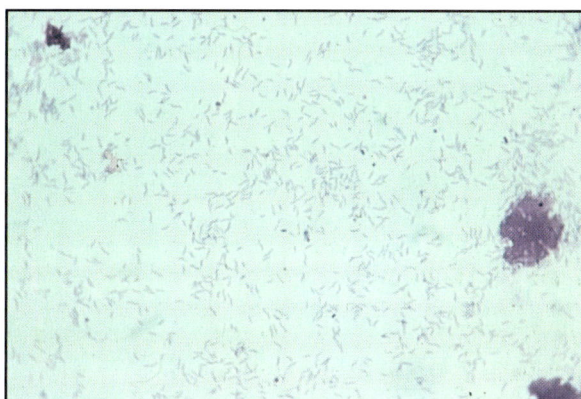

Figure 5.10: Intestinal tract: Camplyobacter spp. (Hemacolor® - Oil Immersion x1000.)

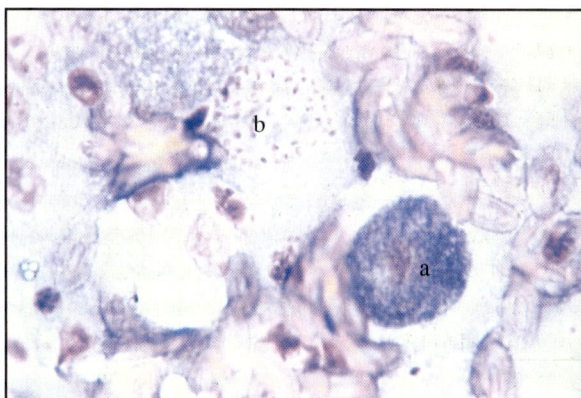

Figure 5.11: Intestinal tract: coccidiosis. (Hemacolor® - Oil Immersion x1000.) a. macrogamete; b. microgamete.

spermatozoa, starch or amylum particles, brown-black denatured haemoglobin and debris (plant material, chitin-skeletons of insects, urates) may be present. *Chlamydia* spp. may be demonstrated with a Stamp or Macchiavello's stain; *Mycobacterium* spp. with a Ziehl-Neelson stain.

RESPIRATORY TRACT

A sinus aspirate is indicated in avian patients with

sinusitis. The left and right sinuses communicate in psittacines. Therefore, a single aspirate from one side will represent the sinus material from both sides. Sinusitis cytology demonstrates a moderate amount of background debris and a variable number of inflammatory cells, depending on the severity of the inflammation. Sometimes, the aetiological agent can be detected phagocytised by leucocytes. An initial examination with a magnification of x100 is essential to detect fungal elements (see Figure 5.12).

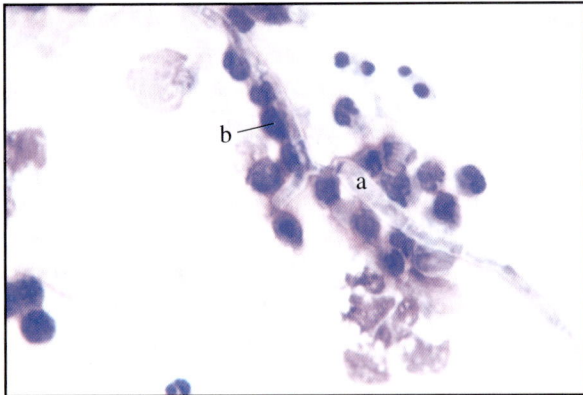

Figure 5.12: Sinus: Aspergillus spp. (Red-fronted Parakeet). (Hemacolor® - Oil Immersion x1000.) a. mycotic hypha; b. macrophage.

Transtracheal aspiration is one method for evaluating upper respiratory disease in birds. The procedure is simple, but requires general anaesthesia. A large-bore hypodermic needle can be inserted into an air sac to aid respiration during the procedure if the bird is severely dyspnoeic (see Chapter 6). Tracheal swab samples can be obtained by passing a small cotton swab directly into the trachea. The trachea and primary bronchi are lined by pseudostratified, ciliated columnar epithelium with goblet cells, whereas the syrinx (located at the junction of the trachea and bronchi) consists of either bistratified squamous cells or columnar epithelial cells.

Tracheal material exhibiting large numbers of heterophils and macrophages suggests tracheobronchitis even in asymptomatic birds. Mycotic tracheal or bronchial (or syringeal) lesions may be confirmed by the presence of fungal elements in a tracheal wash or *post-mortem* scrapings.

Air sac samples can be obtained in a live bird using an endoscopic laparotomy technique such as that used for surgical sexing of birds. At necropsy, scrapings can be made from the epithelial surface. The air sacs are lined by simple squamous epithelium. Air sacculitis is indicated by many inflammatory cells and a variable amount of background debris. Intracellular bacteria indicate a bacterial aetiology, and fungal hyphae or elements confirm mycotic involvement. Special stains are required to confirm chlamydial infections (see Figure 5.13).

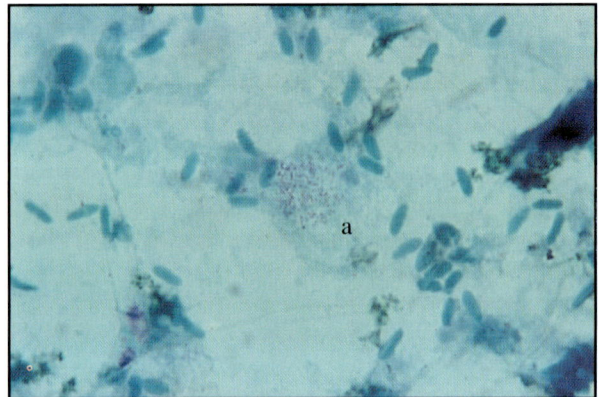

Figure 5.13: Lung: Chlamydia psittaci (Rosella spp.). (Stamp stain - Oil Immersion x1000.) a. macrophage with chlamydial inclusions.

LUNGS

At necropsy the lungs are removed from the thoracic cavity and a freshly cut surface is blotted dry on a clean paper towel. A microscope slide is touched gently several times onto this dry surface. The impression smear should be as thin as possible.

The impression smear of normal lung tissue consists mainly of blood cells mixed with columnar epithelial cells, ciliated cells, isolated cilia, pieces of striated muscle fibres and an occasional macrophage or lymphocyte.

Pneumonia is characterised by the presence of many heterophils and vacuolated macrophages, often in an eosinophilic background due to oedema and/or protein-containing fluids (exudate) within the respiratory tissue. The impression smear will give information on chlamydial, fungal, cryptococcal, bacterial respiratory or neoplastic disorders (see Figure 5.14). With severe anthracosis, macrophages containing black phagocytised particles may be found. Lung tissue smears will also show the composition of the blood cells. In anaemic conditions many young erythrocytes or their precursor cells may be recognised with a basophilic cytoplasm and a large round and vesiculated nucleus. Extracellular blood parasites (*Trypanosoma* spp., [see Figure 5.15] *Microfilaria* spp.) and intracellular schizonts (*Plasmodium* spp.) are easily seen under low power magnification. Under high power magnification intracellular blood parasites can be seen within erythrocytes - *Plasmodium* spp., *Haemoproteus* spp. (both with brown pigment), *Leucocytozoon* spp. (without pigment) - and within leucocytes - *Leucocytozoon* spp., *(A)toxoplasma* spp., *Toxoplasma*-pseudocysts.

SPLEEN

The avian spleen is a blood-forming and blood-destroying organ; it also contains lymphoid tissue. Impressions of the normal spleen show a significant amount of blood cells and heavy background cellular debris.

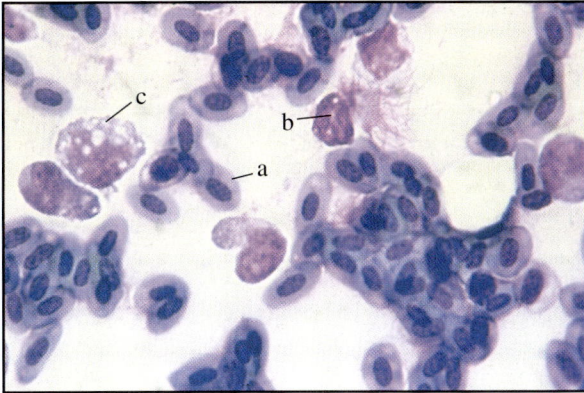

Figure 5.14: *Lung: myeloid leucosis (budgerigar). (Hemacolor® - Oil Immersion x 1000.) a. erythrocytes; b. ciliated cell; c. tumour cell.*

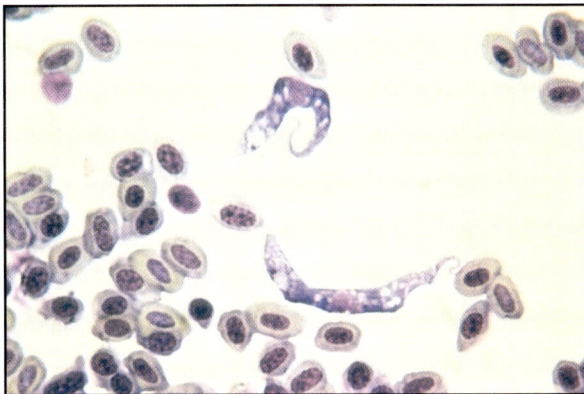

Figure 5.15: *Lung: Trypanosoma spp. (Sulphur-crested Cockatoo). (Hemacolor® - Oil Immersion x 1000.)*

Frequently, groups of lymphocytes in various stages of maturity can be seen. Macrophages showing varying degrees of erythrophagocytosis and iron accumulation are common. Cells with a variable amount of pale blue cytoplasm and indistinct cytoplasmic borders are present. These cells have an eccentric round or oval nucleus with coarse granular chromatin. They probably represent cells of the reticular stroma.

Splenic impressions are good samples for the detection of bacterial infections, intra- and extracellular blood parasites or chlamydial inclusions.

LIVER

Liver cytology can be examined from smears or imprints made from aspiration biopsy or excisional biopsy. At necropsy, the freshly cut surface should be blotted very thoroughly until almost no cells are exfoliated. Liver specimens tend to provide a smear which is too cellular with an abundance of circulating blood cells. Background material is thick and basophilic (hepatocyte cytoplasm with many mitochondria) with a marked amount of cell fragments and free hepatocyte nuclei. Normal hepatocytes occur singly, in sheets or in clusters. They are large and have abundant

basophilic cytoplasm with coarse granulation (mitochondria). Fine eosinophilic granulation and iron particles can be detected in most cells. The nuclei are round or oval, slightly eccentric in location, contain coarse chromatin and have a single prominent nucleolus (see Figure 5.16). The nuclei are uniform in appearance; an occasional binucleated cell can be seen. Occasionally, spindle-shaped stromal cells, lymphocytes, plasma cells and macrophages are present.

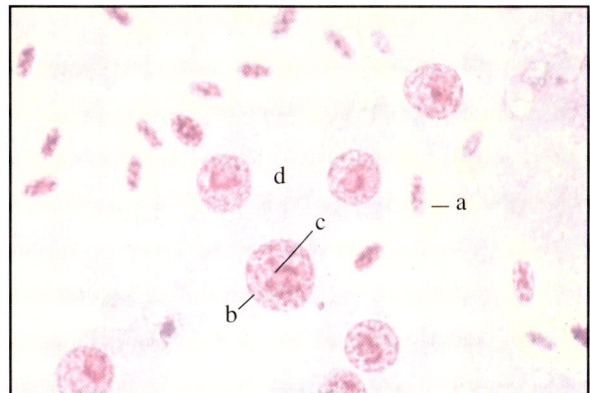

Figure 5.16: *Liver: normal (Torquoise Parrot). (Hemacolor® - Oil Immersion x 1000.) a. erythrocyte; b. hepatocyte nucleus; c. hepatocyte nucleolus; d. hepatocyte cytoplasm.*

Macrophages often contain iron pigment or phagocytised material. Lymphoid aggregates may be found in most normal avian livers. These consist primarily of small mature lymphocytes. Reactive lymphoid aggregates contain a large number of plasma cells and often also heterophils. Lymphoid neoplasia is indicated by large numbers of immature lymphocytes. Microfilarial larvae are sometimes found in liver cytology in birds without peripheral blood microfilarial infection. *Mycobacterium* spp. may be seen (sometimes even in birds without conspicuous macroscopic alterations) as empty, uncoloured, rod-shaped ghosts, often grouped together in the basophilic background. An acid fast staining technique will confirm the diagnosis (see Figures 5.17.1, 5.17.2).

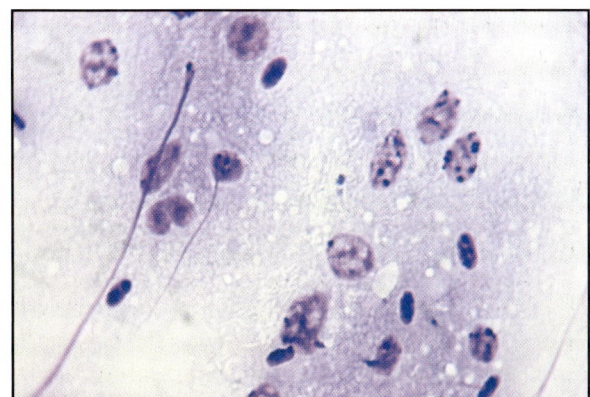

Figure 5.17.1: *Liver: Mycobacterium spp. (Blue-fronted Amazon). (Hemacolor® - Oil Immersion x 1000.)*

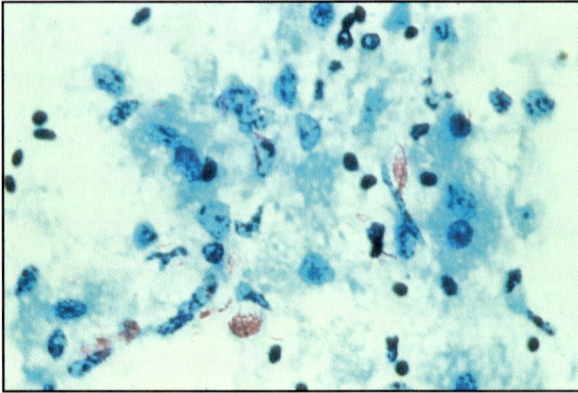

Figure 5.17.2: *Liver: Mycobacterium spp. (Blue-fronted Amazon). (Ziehl-Neelsen stain - Oil Immersion x 1000.)*

Degenerated hepatocytes are seen with *post-mortem* autolysis or hepatic disease. Fatty livers show swollen hepatocytes with intracellular and extracellular lipid droplets. Inflammatory hepatic lesions are characterised by degenerate hepatocytes and marked inflammatory cell infiltration. Bacterial infections are recognised by intra- and/or extracellular bacteria; some viral infections may show intracytoplasmic or intranuclear inclusion bodies (see Figure 5.18). Neoplastic lesions contain cells with cytological features of neoplasia.

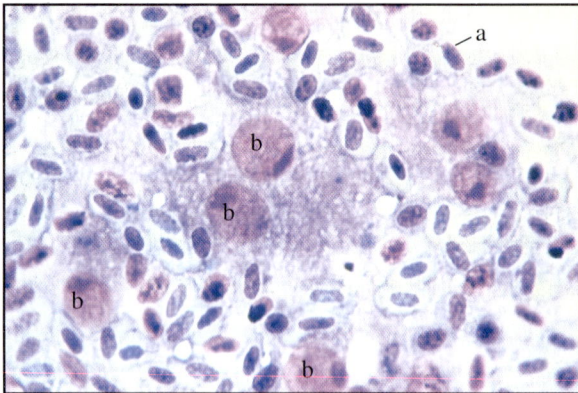

Figure 5.18: *Liver: herpesvirus inclusion bodies (Sulphur-crested Cockatoo). (Hemacolor® - Oil Immersion x 1000.) a. erythrocyte; b. intranuclear inclusion bodies.*

REFERENCES

Campbell TW (1984) Diagnostic cytology in avian medicine. *Veterinary Clinics of North America: Small Animal Practice* **14**, 317.

Campbell TW (1986) Cytology. In: *Clinical Avian Medicine and Surgery, including Aviculture.* Eds GJ Harrison and LR Harrison. WB Saunders, Philadelphia.

Campbell TW (1988) *Avian Hematology and Cytology.* Iowa State University Press, Ames.

Campbell TW (1994a) Cytology. In: *Avian Medicine: Principles and Application.* Eds BW Ritchie, GJ Harrison and LR Harrison. Wingers, Lake Worth.

Campbell TW (1994b) Hematology. In: *Avian Medicine: Principles and Application.* Eds. BW Ritchie, GJ Harrison and LR Harrison. Wingers, Lake Worth.

Fudge AM (1988) Avian clinical cytology. In: *Proceedings of the Association of Avian Veterinarians Annual Conference 1988.* AAV, Lake Worth.

Hawkey C and Gulland F (1989) Clinical haematology. In: *Manual of Parrots, Budgerigars and Other Psittacine Birds.* Ed CJ Price. BSAVA, Cheltenham.

Ingh TSGAM van den and Vos JH (1989) Technical aspects of fine-needle aspiration cytology. *Tijdschrift voor Diergeneeskunde* **114**, 713.

Lucas AJ and Jamroz C (1961) *Atlas of Avian Hematology.* United States Department of Agriculture, Monograph 25, Washington DC.

CHAPTER SIX

Anaesthesia

Martin P C Lawton

INTRODUCTION

Sedgwick (1980) considered that prior to the introduction of isoflurane, avian anaesthesia was difficult and had to be of short duration to improve the likelihood of a successful outcome. With the advances brought about by the newer, safer anaesthetic agents, there is now no reason why any psittacine may not be successfully anaesthetised, providing the basic principles of anaesthesiology are observed. The rapid metabolism, the peculiarity of the respiratory system and the physical size of the patient are all factors that must be assessed in the approach to avian anaesthesia. An approach to anaesthetising birds is given in Figure 6.1.

REQUIREMENTS OF SEDATION/ANAESTHESIA

The aims of anaesthesia should be to provide a smooth, safe, reliable induction with adequate restraint, muscle relaxation and analgesia, followed by a fast, but full, uneventful recovery.

Restraint
The degree of restraint required depends upon the purpose for which the bird is being sedated or anaesthetised. Sedatives or low anaesthetic doses may be sufficient to immobilise a bird for a brief but thorough clinical examination or for the obtaining of laboratory samples. Heavier sedation or a light plane of anaesthesia may, however, be required for radiography, laparoscopy, biopsy or minor surgery. Total restraint with moderate to deep anaesthesia is required for most surgery. The choice of anaesthetic agent depends upon the degree of restraint that is required.

Muscle Relaxation
The requirements for muscular relaxation depend on the procedure or investigation to be performed. Radiography requires only sufficient relaxation to allow correct positioning and non-manual restraint of the patient. More relaxation will be required when abdominal or orthopaedic surgery is contemplated and this will therefore affect the choice and depth of anaesthetic.

Analgesia
All birds undergoing surgery require analgesia both intra- and postoperatively. In many cases the correct choice of anaesthetic agent(s) will provide all the intraoperative analgesia that is required. The use of reversible anaesthetics should be considered carefully, especially if the analgesia may be affected by the antagonists. Anaesthetic agents which provide a good degree of analgesia will often allow better restraint and muscle relaxation, as well as proving safer by allowing the anaesthetist to maintain the bird on a lower plane of anaesthesia.

PRE-ANAESTHETIC CONSIDERATIONS

Handling
Handling should be as gentle and stress free as possible. Although the bird has to be handled for a full clinical examination, this should ideally be done some time before the anaesthetic, to allow time for recovery from any stress. Handling of birds directly before induction should be kept as short as possible. Equipment and agents required to anaesthetise the bird should be prepared well in advance.

Clinical Examination
The importance and techniques of a full clinical examination have been covered elsewhere (Chapter 4). Assessment of the health status of any bird prior to an anaesthetic is mandatory in order to establish possible complications or requirements for medication or treatment prior to anaesthetic induction. The bird should be in as fit a state of health as is possible. Dehydration should be corrected. Some thought should be given to performing routine biochemical examination for liver and kidney function in older birds. Birds with kidney disease should not be given ketamine, as elimination relies on renal excretion. Halothane is contraindicated in birds with hepatic dysfunction. It is also contraindicated in excited (increased catecholamine sensitisation) or debilitated birds due to the risk of cardiac arrest (Harrison, 1986). Altman (1991) advised that all surgical patients should at the very least have a HCT (PCV) and blood glucose estimation. Birds with a PCV greater than 55% require fluid therapy prior

Clinical examination ⟶ PCV (<25% - severe, significant anaemia;
        >55% - suggests dehydration).
      Urea (>2mmol/l - marked dehydration).
      Glucose (<3mmol/l - marked hypoglycaemia).

Weigh ⟶ Assess fluid requirements.
      Calculate drug dosages.

Premedication? ⟶ Pre-anaesthetic ⟶ Fluid therapy if necessary.
      Antibiotics (previous day or just prior to surgery).
      Starvation (if crop surgery).

Handling ⟶ Gentle.
      Subdued lighting.
      Use towels (new ones for each bird).
      Experienced staff.

Anaesthetic ⟶ Gaseous v. Injectable.
      Mask v. Intubation.
      (Air sac intubation.)

Monitoring ⟶ Cardiac function.
      Respiration.
      Reflexes ⟶ Corneal reflex.
        Palpebral reflex.
        Cere reflex.
        Wing reflex.
        Pedal reflex.

Post-anaesthetic ⟶ Fluids
      Respiration.
      Analgesia.
      Warmth.
      Reduce self-trauma (wrap up).

Recovery

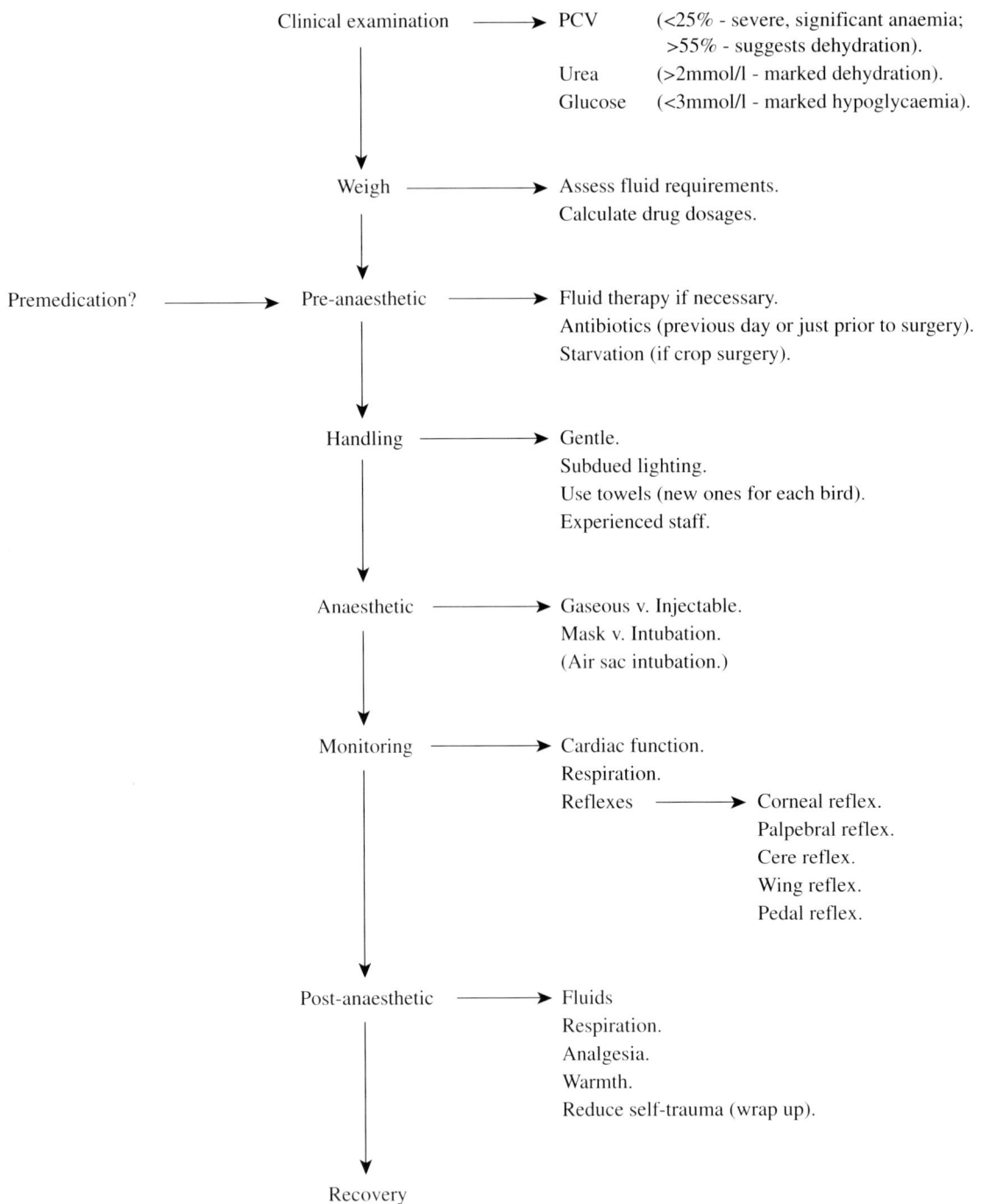

Figure 6.1: An approach to anaesthetising birds.

to anaesthesia; birds with hypoglycaemia should be given intravenous glucose 5% before, during and after surgery (Altman, 1991; Fitzgerald and Blais, 1993).

Weight

Birds should always be accurately weighed. It is impossible to calculate an accurate and safe dosage of an injectable agent (anaesthetic, analgesic or antibiotic), unless the exact weight of the bird is known. This is not so important if a gaseous anaesthetic agent is to be used, but is important for administration of medications or fluid therapy (in which case the bird can be weighed once anaesthetised).

Warmth

Warmth should be provided before induction, during anaesthesia and in the recovery period. The high metabolic rate of birds produces a high core body temperature (CBT), typically 40-44°C. Sick or anaesthetised birds may not be able to maintain their CBT adequately. Sick birds attempting to maintain their normal high temperature may become hypoglycaemic. Anaesthetising a bird, especially if placed on a cold operating table, may result in a rapid fall in body temperature. Excessive removal of feathers or pre-operative washing or application of surgical spirit at the surgical site will result in lost insulation and heat loss. Anaesthetised birds should be placed onto a towel or Vetbed (Animalcare); heating pads or lights or insulatory materials can also help reduce heat loss. The use of OpSite (Smith and Nephew) will reduce the need to pluck a bird bald, yet maintain an adequately clear surgical site. Cold anaesthetic gases will also have a chilling effect on the bird, but there is little that can be done to prevent this.

Fluid Therapy

Any dehydration should ideally be corrected before an anaesthetic is given, although it is considered less stressful to administer fluids immediately after induction with isoflurane. Most surgical cases will benefit from fluid therapy even if the patient is not dehydrated. Birds, like reptiles, are uricotelic. Uric acid is extremely insoluble and even a slight degree of dehydration may result in renal damage and/or gout. The blood concentration of uric acid will be highest in the kidneys and liver. Tophii (micocrystals of urates) formation will, therefore, affect the kidneys and liver the most. Fluids may be administered by the intravenous, intramuscular, intraosseus or subcutaneous routes (see Chapter 4). Fluids should be given at 37-40°C. If birds are showing signs of severe dehydration or gout, allopurinol should be administered.

Starvation

Pre-anaesthetic starvation is normal for dogs and cats, but should be considered more carefully for avian patients. Starvation is seldom harmful for larger psittacines (over 250g), but should be avoided for smaller birds (less than 120g). Cooper (1989) stated that small birds should never be deprived of food for longer than three hours. Starvation of budgerigars or cockatiels may result in hypoglycaemia and an increased anaesthetic risk. The period of food deprivation should be calculated from the start of starvation until the bird is recovered and is willing to eat again. The author does not routinely starve birds, but may delay anaesthesia if the crop is full, unless the bird has an impacted crop requiring surgery. Starvation may also reduce hepatic detoxification of certain anaesthetic agents (Carter-Strom, 1988). Larger psittacines, such as Amazons, African Greys, cockatoos and macaws, may be starved, but for not longer than 1-2 hours. Regurgitation is seldom a problem in granivorous psittacines, unlike waterfowl or frugivorous birds, where subsequent starvation for 4-10 hours is recommended (Mandelker, 1987).

PREMEDICATION

The decision whether or not to premedicate will depend upon which anaesthetic regime is to be used. Consideration must be given to the additional handling and stresses involved in administering the premedicant. If sedatives or tranquillisers are used, they should not delay the recovery from anaesthesia or cause more disorientation and increased flapping than is experienced with the anaesthetic itself. The use of atropine (0.04-0.1mg/kg) is debatable. Altman (1991) considered that there is an advantage in reducing respiratory secretion, although Sinn (1994) stated that the respiratory secretions become thickened and could cause complications. The author does not advise the use of atropine, unless there is excessive oral secretion in the larger species.

ANALGESIA

Whatever the anaesthetic regime there must be adequate analgesia throughout the period of anaesthesia, and postoperatively if surgery has been performed. The degree of analgesia will depend on the anaesthetic agent or agents used and the plane of anaesthesia at which the bird is maintained. An anaesthetic agent that provides good analgesia, eg. isoflurane or medetomidine, may allow the bird to be maintained under a lighter plane of anaesthesia than with agents where the analgesia is poor, eg. halothane or ketamine. True analgesics have received little attention, although the use of very high doses of butorphanol (3-4mg/kg) and flunixin meglumine (1-10mg/kg) have been reported as safe in parakeets (Bauck, 1990). Ketoprofen (5-10mg/kg) can also be used, although the author prefers to use buprenorphine (0.01-0.05mg/kg i/m) or carprofen (5-10mg/kg) in the postoperative period to provide analgesia.

ANATOMICAL CONSIDERATIONS

On inspiration, air enters through the nares into the nasal cavity, then out of the choana and into the pharynx via the glottis, and down the trachea (which contains full rings of cartilage) to the bifurcation of the two primary bronchi where the syrinx is situated. The primary bronchi extend to the medioventral aspect of the lungs. When intubating a bird, it is important that the cuff is not overinflated as this will damage the tracheal cartilage rings (Fitzgerald and Blais, 1993).

Within the lungs are the secondary bronchi and parabronchi. These contain the avian equivalent of the alveolar (McLelland, 1990). There is some debate as to whether inspired air passes over the lung tissue twice (James et al, 1976) or only once (Scheid and Piiper, 1971; Fitzgerald and Blais, 1993). Although inspired gases pass through the neopulmonic tissue of the lungs twice (this tissue has only a minimum gaseous exchange function), inspired air passes only once through the paleopulmonic tissue of the lungs (responsible for gaseous exchange) (Scheid and Piiper, 1971; Fitzgerald and Blais, 1993).

There are eight air sacs: the unpaired cervical, unpaired clavicle, paired cranial thoracic, paired caudal thoracic and the paired abdominal sacs (McLelland, 1990). Air sacs themselves have very poor vascularity so that gaseous exchange does not take place other than in the lungs.

Air sacs extend into some of the long bones (pneumatised bones) and into the skull sinuses. The sternum and humeri are always pneumatised, reducing their overall weight and thus aiding flight. Depending on the species, some or all of the following are also pneumatised: cervical vertebrae, thoracic vertebrae, synsacrum, ribs, sternum, scapula, coracoid, femur and pelvis (McLelland, 1990).

Birds have no diaphragm. Muscular contractions, mainly of the abdomen, cause the air sacs to act as a bellows, blowing the air back into and through the lungs. A deeply anaesthetised bird may not be generating sufficient muscular contractions to allow adequate 'pumping' of air back into the lungs. Sinn (1994) advised the routine use of positive pressure ventilation (20-40/minute at 15mmHg) to overcome any possibility of hypocapnoea and to maintain adequate oxygenation. The air sacs hold 80% of the volumetric capacity (Coles, 1985). There is some recirculating of the air between the anterior thoracic and clavicular air sacs (as well as the connections with the pneumatised bones) and then into the abdominal and posterior thoracic air sacs. This bellow system will act as a reservoir for anaesthetic gases within the bird. After induction, the concentration of anaesthetic within these air sacs could lead to a further deepening of the plane of anaesthesia, even though the vaporiser concentration has been reduced. Positioning birds on their backs may compromise the bellows action of the air sacs. Figures 15.6 and 15.7 (see Chapter 15) show in schematic form the air flow through the avian lower respiratory tract.

It is during the second passage through the lungs (the first is through the neopulmonic tissue) that the majority of gaseous exchange occurs. Avian lungs are fixed, and not divided into lobes as in mammals. The capillary blood supply to the lungs is, however, greater than that found in mammals. Air diffuses into the air capillaries in a cross-current direction to the arterial blood flow, resulting in an extremely effective gaseous exchange system (McLelland, 1990). Efficiency is also increased because of the thinner barrier between blood and air in the tertiary bronchi. This is possible because of the fixed lungs. Avian lungs are thought to be 10 times more effective than mammalian lungs (James *et al*, 1976; Coles, 1985), and are therefore more sensitive to smaller changes in the concentration of gaseous anaesthetics.

CHOICE OF ANAESTHETIC CIRCUITS

The relative ease of induction by face mask with isoflurane reduces many of the complications of handling and injecting and the stresses that are involved with these procedures (see Figure 6.2). The subsequent fast recovery eliminates the complications of trauma due to incoordination or wing flapping. Therefore, the most basic anaesthetic circuit consists of a vaporiser, a source of carrier gas (usually oxygen) and a face mask. A face mask does have disadvantages, especially if examining or operating around the head. Whatever the circuit, the flow rate of oxygen to the lungs must be kept high in order to prevent hypercapnoea. The gaseous flow rate should be a minimum of three times the normal minute volume, ie. approximately 3ml/g bodyweight (a 400g Amazon needs 1.2 litres/minute). The author uses 2-3 litres/minute irrespective of size. The flow rate should never be less than 0.75 litres/minute.

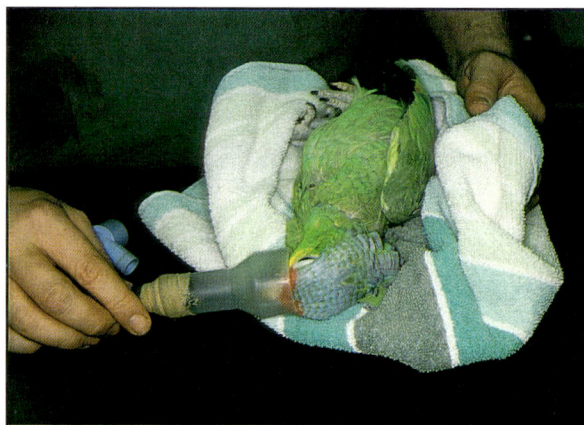

Figure 6.2: *Amazon masked down with isoflurane anaesthesia.*

Psittacines have a large fleshy tongue. When placed on their backs, the tongue may flop back into the mouth and obstruct the glottis. This risk can be eliminated by either intubation of the bird or the use of a paper clip bent around the mandible to prevent the tongue from falling back onto the glottis. Other than for the shortest procedure, the author advises intubating of birds and maintaining them via a Bethune or Ayre's T-piece system. This will allow ventilation of the bird should this prove necessary, and also allows scavenging of waste gases. Scavenging of waste gases is difficult with an open face mask unless a more expensive active scavenging system such as the Fluvac (International Marketing Supplies) (designed for a face mask) is used.

Intubation of birds is easy, due to the forward placed glottis on the base of the tongue. Even small budgerigars or cockatiels may be intubated using cut-down cannulae or catheters, although these small diameter tubes may become blocked with respiratory secretions (see Figure 6.3). An airway should be provided to allow maintenance of the bird under anaesthesia, but also for ventilation should apnoea occur. An intubated bird is less likely to have complications from regurgitation or glottis obstruction from the tongue when on their backs.

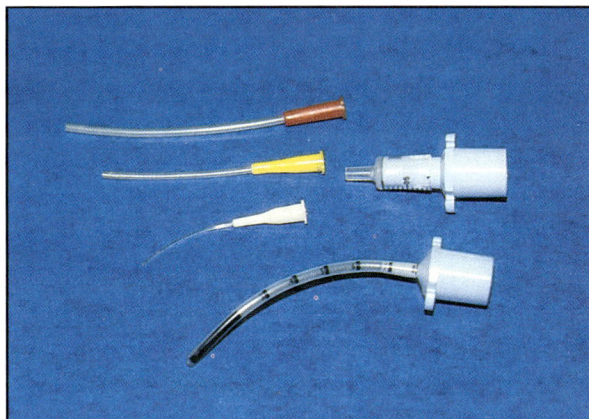

Figure 6.3: Various small endotracheal tubes made from urinary catheters. A cut-down 2ml syringe is put onto an 8mm endotracheal tube adapter to allow luer fitting of the catheters onto an anaesthetic circuit.

Air Sac Intubation

There are often occasions where the use of a face mask or endotracheal tube is not possible. Surgery around the head makes the use of a face mask difficult. Oral or beak surgery, or surgery in cases of airway obstruction require alternative techniques. The presence of air sacs and the unique air flow from the abdominal and caudal thoracic air sacs into the lungs means that when a tube is placed into one of these air sacs, anaesthetic gases (or just oxygen where there is an air way obstruction) can be introduced. Placement of an air sac tube is usually performed after induction by injection or face mask. However, in cases of airway obstruction it is possible to place the tube with the bird restrained. In emergency situations the author restrains the bird with its head in a mask into which 100% oxygen is being delivered; this should reduce the risks that are associated with handling a respiratory embarrassed bird. Placement of a tube in a conscious bird is quick and appears to cause no discomfort or distress.

The site for placement of an air sac tube is similar to the site for endoscopic examination. Traditionally, this is the left side just behind the ribs, although Sinn (1994) has suggested the use of short endotracheal tubes or rubber tubes into the clavicular or caudal thoracic air sacs. An additional site is behind the left leg below the lumbar muscle; this is easily accessed and less likely to block. However, any available approach to an appropriate air sac can be used (Dustin, 1993). After extending the leg, the skin over the sternal notch is incised using a stab incision and the underlying muscles spread with haemostats (or a trocar used) to gain entry into an air sac. As large a tube as possible (French Guage 14) should be placed into the air sac

and sutured in place with a purse-string suture. The end of the tube is attached to the anaesthetic circuit (see Figure 6.4). It is best to apply positive pressure ventilation via the placed tube whilst the bird is under anaesthesia. A higher rate of gas flow is required (unless 2-3 litres/minute is being used) to allow for loss of gas via the trachea and mouth. Korbel *et al* (1993) reported that following ventilation of birds with air sac intubation the birds stopped breathing spontaneously due to the expulsion of all carbon dioxide from the respiratory system. Ventilated birds will not breath again spontaneously until after perfusion via the air sac is terminated and the blood carbon dioxide levels rise. The tube can be removed postoperatively or left *in situ* in cases of dyspnoea, eg. after surgery to the neck or in cases of aspergillosis plugs of the syrinx.

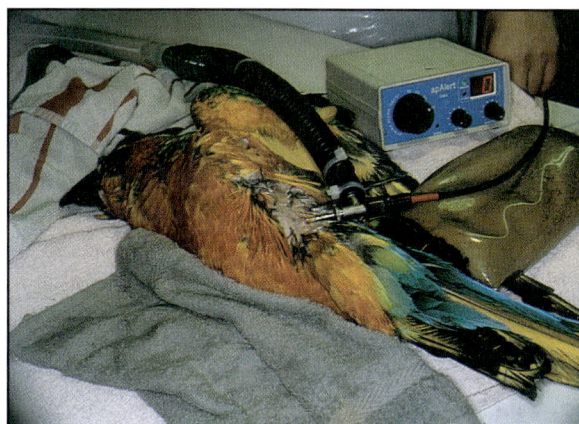

Figure 6.4: Macaw with air sac intubation connected via a Bethune circuit to an anaesthetic machine.

CHOICE OF ANAESTHETIC DRUGS

Injectable Anaesthetics

Although the author considers isoflurane is the anaesthetic agent of choice and would not advise or recommend the use of other agents, there may be circumstance when isoflurane is not available. Suggested dose rates for injectable anaesthetic agents are given in Table 6.1. Before the introduction of a reliable and safe gaseous anaesthetic (isoflurane), injectable agents were used routinely. These agents should only be used in psittacines if gaseous anaesthesia is not available.

Volatile Anaesthetics

The use of volatile anaesthesic agents in birds allows greater control of anaesthesia than the use of injectable agents (Flammer, 1989). There are four volatile anaesthetics that may be found in veterinary practice: ether, halothane, isoflurane and methoxyflurane. Of these, ether has no place in avian practice as an anaesthetic. Ether has a poor safety margin in birds, and is irritable to the mucous membranes. Under COSHH regulations, careful consideration has to be given to its use in any veterinary practice. Although halothane is the volatile anaesthetic most commonly used in small animal practice, it is not the most suitable in avian practice. The three volatile anaesthetic agents that can be used in birds are described and compared in Table 6.2.

The combination of isoflurane's safety, rapid induc-

tion and recovery makes it the gaseous anaesthetic of choice. Rapid induction with isoflurane, within 4-5 breaths, is substantially less stressful for the bird than continued restraint with a mask over its face, as occurs with methoxyflurane. Although halothane induction can be almost as fast as isoflurane, the decreased safety margin requires a lower concentration (3%) for

Table 6.1. Injectable anaesthetic agents.

Agent	Dose rate	Comments
Alphaxalone/ alphadalone	5-10mg/kg i/v; 36mg/kg i/m, i/p.	Alphaxalone/alphadalone is a relatively good anaesthetic agent (Harcourt-Brown, 1978), although there is often a transient apnoea following intravenous administration (Cooper and Frank, 1973, 1974). This can be alarming and, when compared to other anaesthetic agents, is a major disadvantage. Despite this, there is a wide safety margin but only a short length of action (Mandelker, 1987). The large volumes required make intravenous the preferred route. Intraperitoneal or intramuscular routes produce immobilisation but poor analgesia (Cooper and Frank, 1973, 1974). There are better alternatives to this agent.
Ketamine	20-50mg/kg s/c, i/m, i/v (smaller species require a higher dose rate than larger birds).	Use first reported in birds in 1972 (Mandelker, 1972). Ketamine was considered one of the drugs of choice; it is now used less often in avian practice. Ketamine by itself is a good sedative but a poor anaesthetic, with poor muscle relaxation and little analgesia, although there is little respiratory or cardiovascular depression (Flammer, 1989). The dose rate of ketamine is inversely proportional to the body size (Boever and Wright, 1975). Ketamine may provide up to 30 minutes anaesthesia with full recovery taking up to three hours (Ensley, 1979). There is often wing flapping during recovery, even when used in combination with tranquillisers, and this may continue for several minutes (Mandelker, 1987). With ketamine, hippus (rhythmic contraction and dilation of the pupil) is seen until the bird becomes deeply anaesthetised (Lawton, 1984). Ketamine is eliminated by the kidneys in birds, as it is in mammals. Toxicity may be noted in debilitated or dehydrated birds, or in birds with renal dysfunction (Mandelker, 1987). Intravenous fluids can hasten recovery from ketamine due to the diureses caused (Flammer, 1989).
Ketamine with diazepam or midazolam	25mg/kg ketamine + 1-2mg/kg diazepam or 0.2mg/kg midazolam s/c, i/m.	These are good combinations. The benefit of midazolam is that it can be mixed in the same syringe as ketamine, while diazepam has to be given as a separate injection. These were considered by Mandelker (1988) as the most effective combinations available, but with the introduction of medetomidine, which can be reversed, this is no longer true.
Ketamine/ medetomidine	1.5-2mg/kg ketamine + 60-85μg/kg medetomidine i/m. (Reversed by atipamezole - 250-380μg/kg i/m).	Medetomidine has sedative and analgesic properties, but it also has hypotensive, bradycardic and hypothermic effects. Medetomidine and ketamine combination provides deep sedation and good muscle relaxation with no arrhythmias or respiratory depression (Jalanka, 1989).

Table 6.1. Continued.

Agent	Dose rate	Comments
Ketamine/ xylazine	4.4mg/kg ketamine + 2.2mg/kg xylazine i/v (reversed by yohimbine hydrochloride - 0.1mg/kg i/m or s/c). (Atipamezole [250-380µg/kg i/m] can be used to reverse the effects of xylazine).	The synergistic action of xylazine and ketamine produces a smooth induction and improved muscle relaxation. There are no difficulties in recovery due to the residual ketamine effect. Unreversed, there is prolonged recovery and postoperative depression that may result in the bird being unable to perch properly or unable to feed, leading to hypoglycaemia and even death (Lawton, 1984). Lumeij (1993) reported two deaths postoperatively (24 hours and 50 hours) which were attributed to severe sinus bradycardia.
Propofol	1.33mg/kg i/v.	Propofol is metabolised far too quickly in birds to be of realistic use as an induction agent. This rapid elimination is especially disadvantageous if isoflurane is to be the maintenance gaseous anaesthetic. The combination of these two agents may lead to difficulty in keeping the bird anaesthetised long enough for intubation. Intravenous propofol is more stressful than mask induction with isoflurane.
Tiletamine/ zolazepam	5-10mg/kg i/m.	Tiletamine is a phencyclidine derivative which is more potent than ketamine, although it causes convulsions unless combined with a sedative. It provides good immobilisation and is considered to be safe (Kreeger *et al*, 1993).
Xylazine	1-20mg/kg i/m, i/v. (Reversed with yohimbine hydrochloride [0.1-0.2mg/kg i/v] or atipamezole [250-380µg/kg i/m]).	Xylazine by itself is unreliable, causes bradycardia and A/V block, and is extremely respiratory depressant (Mandelker, 1987).

Table 6.2. Volatile anaesthetic agents.

	Isoflurane	Halothane	Methoxyflurane
Safety margin This is the ratio of lethal dose to anaesthetising dose (Dohoo, 1990).	5.7 Rosskopf *et al* (1992) considered this safety margin alone makes other agents obsolete.	3.0 Reservoir effect of high concentrations of anaesthetic agent in the air sacs after inductions may lead to fatalities.	3.7 Reservoir effect of high concentrations of anaesthetic agent in the air sacs after inductions may lead to fatalities.
Blood gas partition coefficients This reflects the solubility in blood and the potential for tissue distribution and, more importantly, tissue retention.	1.4 at 37°C Very low solubility allows rapid induction and rapid recovery.	2.3 at 37°C Potential for more redistribution from the body compartments back into circulation after induction.	12.0 at 37°C High solubility means a slower induction and recovery. Induction is slow but easy to maintain (Dolphin and Olsen, 1977).

Table 6.2. Continued.

	Isoflurane	Halothane	Methoxyflurane
Metabolism	0.3% Virtually no metabolism means that excretion is solely on expiration, therefore liver and kidney pathology does not affect recovery. 2% isoflurane has been used for prolonged anaesthesia and recovery was still rapid, occurring within six minutes and considered fully recovered within 21 minutes (Clutton, 1986).	15-20% Due to distribution in body tissues and metabolism, there is a slower recovery than isoflurane. There is a delayed recovery if underlying liver damage is present.	50% High level of metabolites leads to 'hang-over' effect and depression.
Muscular relaxation	Very good.	Poor.	Moderate to good.
Analgesia	Good.	Poor.	Good.
Respiratory effects	Little respiratory depression.	Markedly respiratory depressive.	Markedly respiratory depressive.
Cardiac effects	Slight myocardial depression which often results in little or no change in the heart rate (Jenkins, 1993).	Moderate myocardial depression. Potential for catecholamine sensitisation.	Moderate myocardial depression.
Contraindications	None reported.	Hepatic dysfunction or cardiovascular disease.	Hepatic dysfunction or cardiovascular disease.
Overdose	Apnoea before cardiac arrest. Good chance of prompt artificial ventilation leading to full recovery.	Apnoea and cardiac arrest usually simultaneously.	Apnoea and cardiac arrest usually simultaneously.

induction (isoflurane 5%), thus making safe halothane induction much slower.

The cost of isoflurane and the need for a dedicated vaporiser may dissuade veterinary surgeons from its use. Isoflurane can be used in a halothane vaporiser (Harvey, 1990) and, although the concentration settings are not totally correct, the difference is probably of minimal significance (Werner, 1987). Isoflurane has a similar vapour pressure to that of halothane: 239.5mmHg and 244.1mmHg respectively (Dohoo, 1990; Harvey, 1990). Isoflurane cannot, however, be used in a vaporiser that has been used previously with halothane unless it has been serviced and cleaned. The preservatives that maintain the stability of halothane and methoxyflurane will make the vaporiser 'sticky' and affect the accuracy if isoflurane is used subsequently. Servicing or several flushes with ether are required before isoflurane is used in a halothane vaporiser (Harrison, 1986).

MONITORING OF ANAESTHESIA

Avian anaesthesia, especially with isoflurane, is now considered a very safe and routine procedure. However, there is no excuse for complacency over monitoring during anaesthesia (Lawton, 1993). Fatalities may and will occur without adequate monitoring of the anaesthetised bird. The depth of anaesthesia may only be controlled if the bird is carefully and continuously monitored. Monitoring of birds should be approached in exactly the same way as monitoring of any other mammalian species, although it is considered to be more challenging (Flammer, 1989).

Reflexes

Palpebral reflexes, corneal reflexes, cere reflexes, toe pinch reflexes and wing twitch are all good indications of the depth of anaesthesia. As the bird becomes more deeply anaesthetised, the standard reflexes usually slow and decrease in strength, or will eventually disappear. The toe, cere and wing reflexes disappear as the bird enters a medium plane. The corneal reflex is usually the last reflex to be abolished and shows that the bird is very deeply anaesthetised. The tone of the jaw should also be assessed; it becomes less tense as the bird enters a medium plane of anaesthesia.

Respiration

Respiration is the best indicator of the depth and stability of anaesthesia. Both the respiratory rate and depth should be monitored, electronically if possible (see Figure 6.5). The pattern of respiration is also important; it should be stable during anaesthesia (Lawton, 1993). Sudden change in pattern, especially in the depth of respiration (from shallow to deep), may indicate that the bird's plane of anaesthesia is lightening or the bird is feeling pain. As the bird enters a deeper plane of anaesthesia, the rate and depth usually decrease. Depending on the bird's body size, the respiration rate should not fall below 25-50bpm (Doolen and Jackson, 1991); below this there is a risk of hypercapnoea. The respiratory rate of any anaesthetised bird should never fall below half its normal resting rate (Coles, 1985).

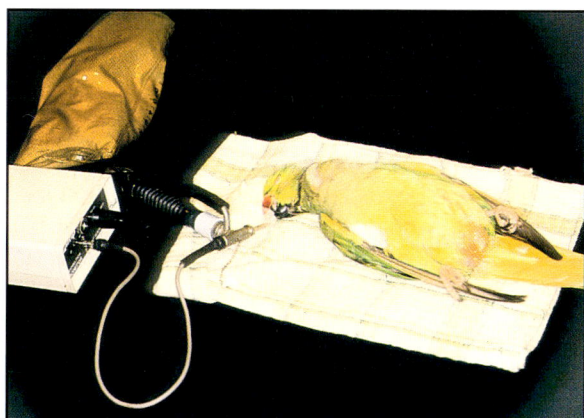

Figure 6.5: *Parakeet intubated and fixed to a respiratory monitor. The bird is on a tea towel to reduce heat loss.*

Heart Rate

Routine use of cardiac monitors is recommended, although an oesophageal stethoscope can be of use (Lawton, 1993). Heart rate is affected dramatically by pain and, therefore, is the best indicator of analgesia and the depth of anaesthesia provided. It is not uncommon for a cockatiel, on feeling pain, to increase its heart rate from 300bpm to over 700bpm. The heart rate should never fall below 120bpm (Doolen and Jackson, 1991).

Use of a cardiac monitor is reassuring to show that there are no abnormalities, such as A/V blocks that may occur with xylazine. The standard lead placements are over the distal lateral tarsometatarsus and the carpal joints of each wing (Burtnick and Degernes, 1993) using atraumatic clamps or silver needles (see Figure 6.6). Careful monitoring of respiration and heart rate will allow immediate resuscitation and administration of drugs, such as doxapram (5-10mg/kg i/m, i/v, s/c or p/o), should this be required.

Figure 6.6: *An anaesthetised cockatiel with ECG leads placed on the skin of the leading edge of the wings and on the right thigh.*

Temperature

The high metabolic rate of birds results in their temperature fluctuating while under anaesthesia, often with considerable heat loss (Mandelker, 1987; Altman, 1991). The CBT of birds is usually between 40-44°C (Carter-Storm, 1988), with that of smaller birds being 41°C (Cooper, 1989). The cloacal temperature should be monitored during anaesthesia (Doolen and Jackson, 1991). The temperature drop is particularly noted if the bird is kept on an operating table. It is advisable to keep an anaesthetised bird on a towel, Vetbed or other insulatory layer (Dolphin and Olsen, 1977). Heated water ripple blankets or heated lamps have been used to maintain CBT during prolonged anaesthesia (Clutton, 1986). Cold anaesthetic gases may also cool the bird, but preventing this effect is difficult. Although body temperature does return rapidly to normal postoperatively, usually within 10-20 minutes (Altman, 1991), the stress or shock involved in reduced body temperatures during surgery could cause fatalities.

Fluid Balance

The control of haemorrhage during surgery is important; however, some loss may be unavoidable. Whether or not haemorrhage is anticipated, fluid therapy should be given prior to surgery. Fluid therapy is dealt with in more depth elsewhere (see Chapter 4).

POSTOPERATIVE CARE OF BIRDS

Birds should be carefully monitored not only during anaesthesia, but in the recovery phase as well. Respiration, in particular its depth, should be constantly observed. If an anaesthetic regime other than isoflurane is used, the bird should be wrapped in a towel during the recovery phase (see Figure 6.7). This allows CBT to be maintained, as well as preventing damage from excessive wing flapping. Wrapping is required especially when ketamine has been used. When the bird is able to crawl out of its wrapping, it is usually recovered enough to perch. When isoflurane has been used, the bird should be held until a full recovery is made, and then placed straight back onto its perch (Lawton, 1993).

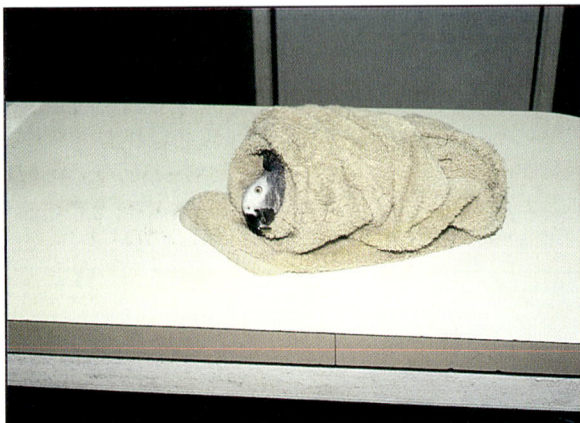

Figure 6.7: An African Grey recovering from ketamine sedation has been wrapped to prevent damage from wing fluttering.

If a bird is not eating within an appropriate length of time for its size (from 10 minutes for a budgerigar up to two hours for a large macaw), it should be crop tubed with fluids and nutrients. Small birds may become hypoglycaemic and die. Fluid intake is also important. Although many different figures for fluid requirements exist, Sinn (1994) suggested that the normal daily requirement is approximately 5% of bodyweight in millilitres while up to 10% of bodyweight in millilitres may be required for a dehydrated bird. If a daily intake of less than 5% is achieved, supplementation should be considered.

REFERENCES

Altman RB (1991) Avian anesthesia. In: *Exotic Animal Medicine in Practice. Vol. 1.* Ed DE Johnston. Veterinary Learning Systems, New Jersey.

Bauck L (1990) Analgesics in avian medicine. In: *Proceedings of the Association of Avian Veterinarians Annual Conference 1990.* AAV, Lake Worth.

Boever WJ and Wright W (1975) Use of ketamine for restraint and anesthesia of birds. *Veterinary Medicine/Small Animal Clinician* **70**, 86.

Burtnick NL and Degernes LA (1993) Electrocardiography on fifty-nine anesthetized convalescing raptors. In: *Raptor Biomedicine.* Eds PT Redig, JE Cooper, JD Remple and DB Hunter. University of Minnesota Press, Minneapolis.

Carter-Storm A (1988) Special considerations for general anaesthesia of birds. *Clinical Insight* **2(3)**, 61.

Clutton RE (1986) Prolonged isoflurane anesthesia in the Golden Eagle. *Zoo Animal Medicine* **17**, 103.

Coles BH (1985) *Avian Medicine and Surgery.* Blackwell Scientific Publications, Oxford.

Cooper JE (1989) Anaesthesia of exotic species. In: *Manual of Anaesthesia for Small Animal Practice.* 3rd Edn. Eds ADR Hilbery, AE Waterman and GJ Brouwer. BSAVA, Cheltenham.

Cooper JE and Frank LG (1973) The use of the steroid anaesthetic CT 1341 in birds. *Veterinary Record* **92**, 474.

Cooper JE and Frank LG (1974). The use of the steroid anaesthetic CT 1341 in birds. *Raptor Research* **8(1/2)**, 20.

Dohoo SE (1990) Isoflurane as an inhalational anesthetic agent in clinical practice. *Canadian Veterinary Journal* **31**, 847.

Dolphin RE and Olsen DE (1977) Anesthesia in the companion bird. *Veterinary Medicine/Small Animal Clinician* **72**, 1761.

Doolen MD and Jackson L (1991) Anesthesia in caged birds. *Iowa State University Veterinarian* **53(2)**, 76.

Dustin LR (1993) Surgery of the avian respiratory system. *Seminars in Avian and Exotic Pet Medicine* **2(2)**, 83.

Ensley P (1979) Cage bird medicine and husbandry. *Veterinary Clinics of North America: Small Animal Practice* **9(3)**, 391.

Fitzgerald G and Blais D (1993) Inhalation anesthesia in birds of prey. In: *Raptor Biomedicine.* Eds PT Redig, JE Cooper, JD Remple and DB Hunter. University of Minnesota Press, Minneapolis.

Flammer K (1989) Update on avian anesthesia. In: *Current Veterinary Therapy X.* Eds RW Kirk and JD Bonagura. WB Saunders, Philadelphia.

Harcourt-Brown NH (1978) Avian anaesthesia in general practice. *Journal of Small Animal Practice* **19**, 573.

Harrison GJ (1986) Anesthesiology. In: *Clinical Avian Medicine and Surgery, including Aviculture.* Eds GJ Harrison and LR Harrison. WB Saunders, Philadelphia.

Harvey RC (1990) Isoflurane anaesthesia in small animal practice. *Veterinary Technician* **11(2)**, 97.

Humphreys PN (1985) Water-birds. In: *Manual of Exotic Pets*. Eds JE Cooper, MF Hutchison, OF Jackson and RJ Maurice. BSAVA, Cheltenham.

Jalanka HH (1989) Chemical restraint and reversal in captive markhors (*Capra falconeri megaceros*): a comparison of two methods. *Journal of Zoo and Wildlife Medicine* **20(4)**, 413.

James AE, Hutchings G, Bush M, Natarajan TK and Burns B (1976) How birds breathe: correlation of radiographic with anatomical and pathological studies. *Journal of the American Radiological Society* **17**, 77.

Jenkins JR (1993) Postoperative care of the avian patient. *Seminars in Avian and Exotic Pet Medicine* **2(2)**, 97.

Korbel RR, Milovanovic A, Erhardt W, Burike J and Henke J (1993) Aerosaccular perfusion with isoflurane - an anaesthetic procedure for head surgery in birds. In: *Proceedings of the European Conference of the Association of Avian Veterinarians, Utrecht, 1993*. AAV, Lake Worth.

Kreeger TJ, Degernes LA, Kreeger JS and Redig PT (1993) Immobilization of raptors with tiletamine and zolazepam (Telazol). In: *Raptor Biomedicine*. Eds PT Redig, JE Cooper, JD Remple and DB Hunter. University of Minnesota Press, Minneapolis.

Lawton MPC (1984) Avian anaesthesia. *Veterinary Record* **115(3)**, 71.

Lawton MPC (1993) Monitoring the anaesthetised bird. In: *Proceedings of the Association of Avian Veterinarians European Conference, Utrecht, 1993*. AAV, Lake Worth.

Lumeij JT (1993) Effects of ketamine-xylazine anesthesia on adrenal function and cardiac conduction in goshawks and pigeons. In: *Raptor Biomedicine*. Eds PT Redig, JE Cooper, JD Remple and DB Hunter. University of Minnesota Press, Minneapolis.

Mandelker L (1972) Ketamine hydrochloride as an anesthetic for parakeets. *Veterinary Medicine/Small Animal Clinician* **67**, 55.

Mandelker L (1987) Anesthesia and surgery. In: *Companion Bird Medicine*. Ed EW Burr. Iowa State University Press, Ames.

Mandelker L (1988) Avian anesthesia - part II: injectable agents. *Companion Animal Practice* **2(10)**, 21.

McLelland J (1990) *A Colour Atlas of Avian Anatomy*. Wolfe Publishing, London.

Rosskpof WJ, Woerpel RW, Reed S, Snider K and Dispirito T (1992) Part 1. Anesthetic agents: anesthesia administration for pet birds. *Veterinary Practice Staff* **4(2)**, 34.

Scheid P and Piiper J (1971) Direct measurement of the pathway of respired gas in duck lungs. *Respiratory Physiology* **11**, 308.

Sedgwick CJ (1980) Anesthesia of caged birds. In: *Current Veterinary Therapy VII*. Ed RW Kirk. WB Saunders, Philadelphia.

Sinn LC (1994) Anesthesiology. In: *Avian Medicine: Principles and Application*. Eds BW Ritchie, GJ Harrison and LR Harrison. Wingers, Lake Worth.

Werner RE (1987) Isoflurane anesthesia: a guide for practitioners. *Compendium on Continuing Education for the Practicing Veterinarian* **9(6)**, 603.

CHAPTER SEVEN

Radiography

Maria-Elisabeth Krautwald-Junghanns and Susanne Hendrich-Schuster

INTRODUCTION

Radiography in avian clinical practice is a very important diagnostic technique as birds are often at an advanced stage of disease when presented to the veterinarian and, therefore, in need of a rapid, but accurate, diagnosis.

When assessing a radiograph, profound knowledge of the anatomy and the physiological variants between different avian species is necessary. Every opportunity should be taken to collect normal radiographs of different species. Whenever an extremity is being investigated, the normal limb should be radiographed as well as the abnormal limb, and a comparison made.

This chapter describes the principles of radiography in avian medicine, as well as the reading of radiographs with regard to physiological characteristics and pathological alterations.

TECHNICAL PRINCIPLES

Exposure Time and Screens

Since birds have a relatively high respiratory rate, a short exposure time is necessary (maximum 0.015-0.05 seconds) to prevent movement blur. This requires radiographic equipment with a minimum performance of 200-300mA, eg. a two- or multiphase generator. The kV setting should be kept as low as possible (45-55kV) in order to obtain pictures of high contrast with many different shades of grey. Good intensifying screens cut down the exposure time. Green light-emitting, rare-earth screens provide a better definition and, when used with an appropriate high-definition film, they are a good choice for radiography of birds. Grids should not be used except in radiography of very large birds, ie. birds > 1kg.

The recommended film/focus distance is one metre, but if using a high definition film/screen combination it can be reduced to 60-70cm.

Restraining and Positioning

Using a perspex plate (maximum 0.5cm thickness) the veterinarian can restrain the bird non-manually. Small birds can be restrained additionally with adhesive tape. Crepe tape is suitable for feathered parts of the body

as it causes less damage to skin and feathers (see Figure 7.1.1). Sedation or light anaesthesia (see Chapter 6) may be necessary. Generally, sedation or anaesthesia is useful to achieve readable radiographs of the head (Murphy *et al*, 1986; Kostka *et al*, 1989).

Radiographs of at least two planes should be taken. With small birds it is of advantage to have both views on one film, masking one half of the cassette with a lead plate while taking the first radiograph.

Ventrodorsal Projection (v/d)

The bird is placed in dorsal recumbency on the table with the head restrained with crepe tape or fixed onto the perspex plate. The legs are extended caudally and fixed by tape or with shoe laces onto the plate. The body should be in an exact symmetrical position to achieve a readable radiograph (see Figure 7.1.1).

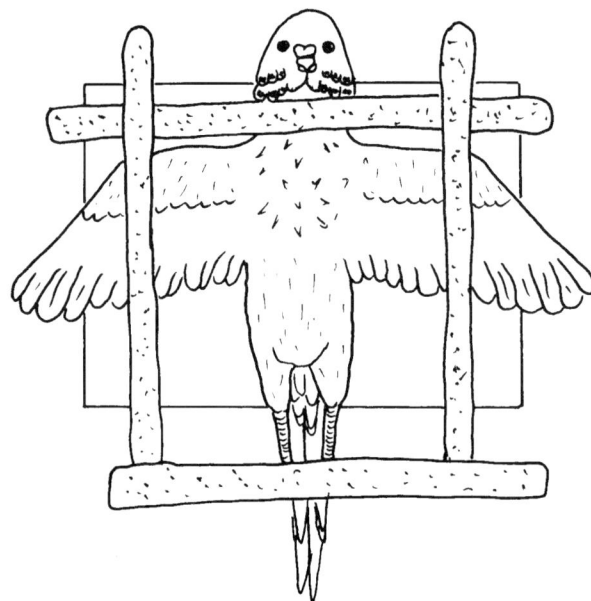

Figure 7.1.1: *Ventrodorsal projection, dorsal recumbency.*

Lateral Projection

The bird is positioned with its right side on the table the legs extended caudally as far as possible and the wings pulled dorsally (dorsocranially/caudally) to the bird's back. When using a perspex plate the wings can be fixed by laying lead gloves over them (see Figure 7.1.2).

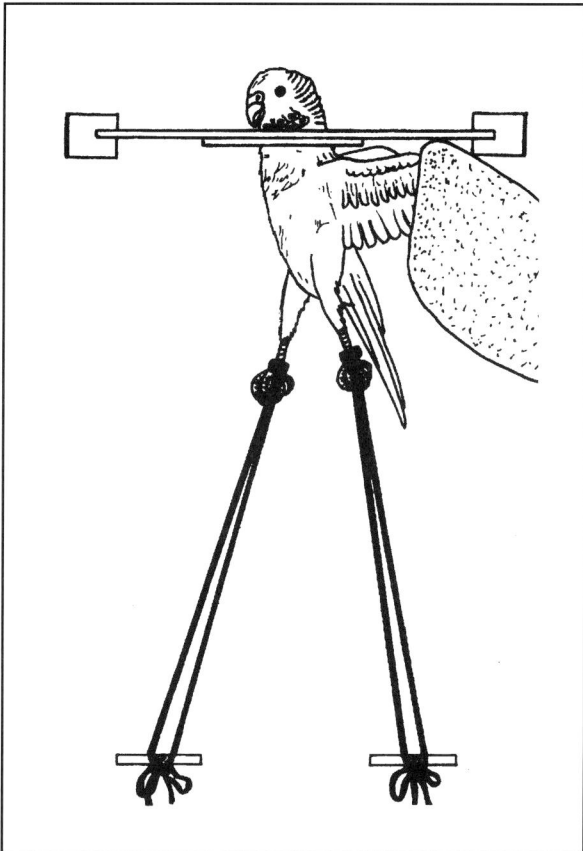

Figure 7.1.2: Lateral projection, right lateral recumbency. Restraint with a perspex plate (body) and using a lead glove (wings).

Other Projections

When taking radiographs of the head a third projection is necessary: the dorsoventral (d/v) view. In all three planes the neck is stretched to its limit by using adhesive tape or a sling on the beak (Murphy *et al*, 1986; Kostka *et al*, 1989).

If a wing fracture is suspected, dorsal and lateral recumbency offer the same perspective of the wing and its bones. Therefore, a caudocranial (c/c) view is necessary. The bird is positioned downwards perpendicular to the table with the wing extended laterally over the table so that the cranial border of the wing is on the plate. This is the only exposure where manual restraint may be required.

PHYSIOLOGY AND COMMON PATHOLOGIES

Skeletal System

General Characteristics

Avian bones are characterised by a thin cortex and a very delicate pattern of trabeculae. Most birds have pneumatisation of their long bones and, to a lesser extent, other parts of the skeleton, eg. skull, pelvis, vertebrae, coracoid. In young birds the skeleton is only poorly demonstrated by radiography. Persistent cartilaginous parts are typical in growing birds, eg. the distal sternum, the scapula and the diaphyses. The smaller the species, the earlier ossification occurs.

Avian bones have no ossification centres in the epiphyses. In young birds the tarsal bones can only be differentiated in the intertarsal joint. The air sac diverticula into the humeri are very small during the first weeks of life and they enlarge as pneumatisation of the bone marrow progresses.

Physiological variations/pathological findings

Homogenous polyostotic hyperostosis is a physiological characteristic seen in female birds prior to egg production. It is a physiological calcium-storage site, whereas irregular hyperostosis is a result of excessive hypercalcification, often caused by an extremely high oestrogen level and associated with pathological findings such as laminated eggs, gonadal tumours or cysts (see Figure 7.2).

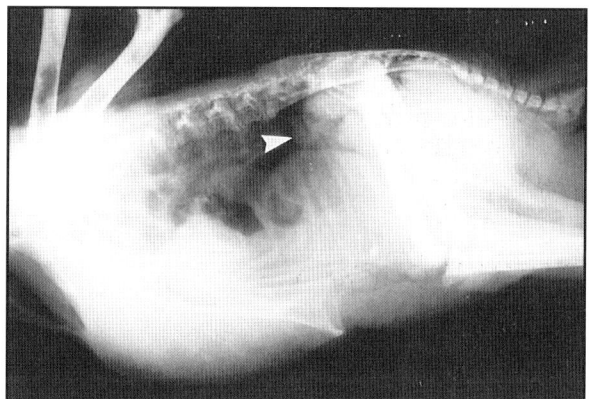

Figure 7.2: Body. Lateral projection. Eclectus Parrot. Non-homogenous hypercalification in both humeri, femurs and tibiotarsi. Enlarged proventriculus partially filled with gas, active ovary (arrow), radiodense abdominal mass. (Laminated egg: enlarged proventriculus was caused by partial obstruction of the gastrointestinal tract by the laminated egg.)

Periosteal reactions and osteolysis indicate an inflammatory process (see Figure 7.3). Periostitis frequently occurs with fracture healing (especially compound fractures). In pneumatised bones these alterations can spread via the air sacs. Mycobacterial infection may show multiple osteolytic and sclerotic lesions in the medullary cavity of long bones. Granulomata in the lungs, liver and/or spleen, as well as in the gastrointestinal tract, are frequently associated with *Mycobacterium avium* (Krautwald *et al*, 1991).

Rhinitis and sinusitis with oversecretion may be seen as increased radiodensity of the sinuses of the head. Surrounding bones may show osteolytic changes.

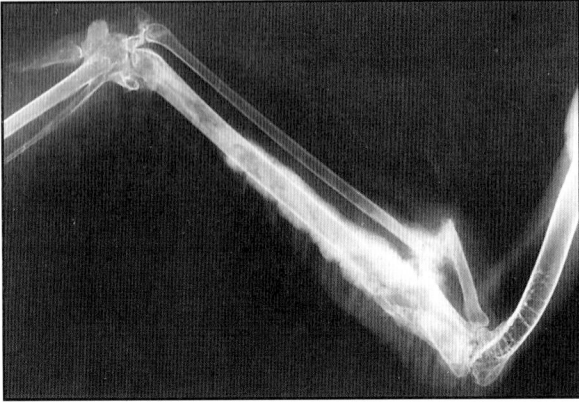

Figure 7.3: Wing. Mediolateral projection. Three weeks old radius/ulna fracture. Inflammatory periosteal reactions. Intramedullary pin (ulna) has just been removed. (Periostitis.)

Septic pododermatitis shows as various degrees of arthritic and osteolytic lesions of the toes and joints and the tarsometatarsae.

The more severe these changes, the less favourable the prognosis. Soft tissue swelling in this area is indicative of inflammation. Multiple deformities of the skeleton are often a consequence of Ca:P:vitamin D_3 imbalance at the nestling age. The typical appearance in the mature bird is that of a convex vertebral column (kyphosis) and bent bones with old pathological fractures. Older birds can also succumb to osteomalacia or secondary hyperparathyroidism; the latter can be recognised by increased radiodensity in different parts of the skeleton, mainly in the shoulder girdle and the skull (see Figure 7.4). This hypercalcification may lead to pain and restricted movement. Osteoporosis and osteomalacia show a decrease in skeletal radiodensity; the differentiation between these causes is not certain (Kostka *et al*, 1988).

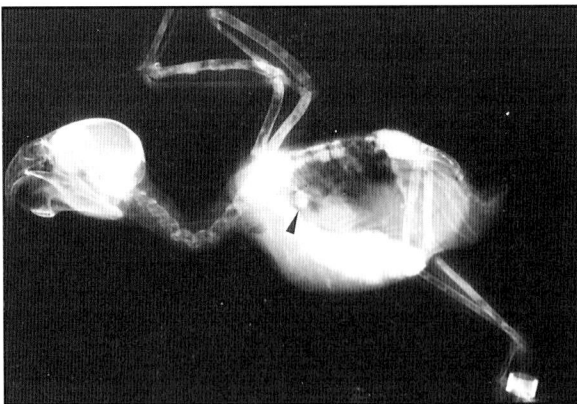

Figure 7.4: Body. Lateral projection. Plum-headed Parakeet. Massive non-homogenous calcium storage in skull, shoulder girdle, vertebral column, pelvis, sternum, long bones of wings and legs, and in the syrinx (arrow). (Polyostotic hyperostosis.)

Primary neoplasms of avian bones are rare; they are often characterised by extensive osteolysis. Secondary neoplasms are shown with various alterations, such as pathological fractures or osteolysis. The bones of the shoulder girdle - the scapula, coracoid and clavicle - are superimposed by overlaying muscles. Therefore, the diagnosis of fractures or alterations of these bones is more difficult than for long bones. In the lateral view it is impossible to distinguish the coracoids and the scapulae from each other. Asymmetrical positioning may help in these cases. Fractures of the vertebral column usually involve the last or second last thoracic vertebrae and the synsacrum. Posterior paralysis and non-defecation are suggestive of a fractured vertebral column (see Chapter 13). To achieve an exact diagnosis of fractures, an oblique positioning may sometimes be required. Periosteal reactions, such as formation of a callus, cannot be compared to those seen in mammals.

Fracture healing in birds should be assessed by the extent of the endosteal callus formation (Bush *et al*, 1976). A large formation of callus is not necessarily a sign of progressing stability; it is more an indication of movement at the fracture site. Increased radiodensity as a result of calcium deposition at the fracture site followed by formation of bone, in the absence of signs of inflammation, is the sign of primary healing.

Respiratory Tract

General Characteristics

The upper and lower respiratory tracts are of particular interest in avian internal medicine as they are involved in many serious diseases. Clinical examination of the upper respiratory tract might provide more information than a radiograph of the head; if this is not the case, a sinography should be undertaken in order to show the nasal sinus.

The cartilaginous rings of the trachea are well demonstrated on the radiograph. In older birds the rings may be partially calcified. Foreign bodies in the upper respiratory tract are better visualised using endoscopy.

The lungs show a typical honeycomb structure. Radiographically, the air sacs are almost the same shade of blackish grey as the surrounding air (see Figures 7.5.1, 7.5.2). Any radiodensity of the air sacs indicates an abnormality.

Physiological Variations/Pathological Findings

In fat birds the lungs, and especially the air sacs, appear much more dense because of the internal fat layers. During the inspiratory phase the air sac appears wider than during the exspiratory phase.

Enlarged inner organs, neoplasms, laminated eggs or ascites can narrow the air sacs and lead to dyspnoea (see Figures 7.9.1, 7.9.2). The membranes of normal air sacs cannot be demonstrated on the radiograph but they can be well defined at a later stage of chronic inflammatory disease, eg. air sacculitis. Air sac walls may be thickened by bacterial, chlamydial or fungal infection. The latter may lead to aspergillomata filling the air sac. These thickened structures, the so-called

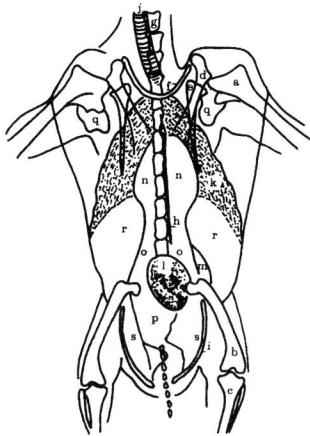

Figure 7.5.1: Body. Ventrodorsal projection. Blue-fronted Amazon.

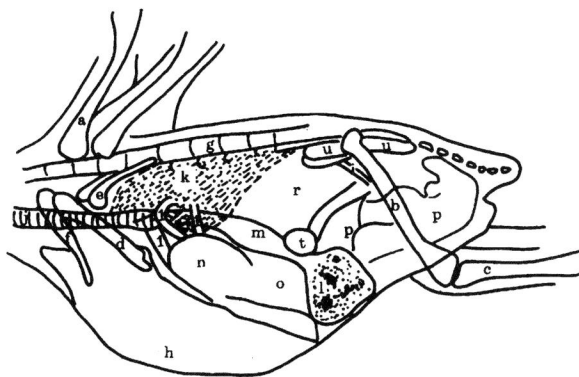

Figure 7.5.2: Body. Lateral projection. Blue-fronted Amazon.

7.5.1 and 7.5.2:

a - Humerus	l - Gizzard containing grit
b - Femur	m - Proventriculus
c - Tibiotarsus	n - Heart
d - Coracoideum	1 - Vessels
e - Scapula	o - Liver
f - Clavicula	p - Intestines
g - Vertebral column	q - Axillary diverticulum
h - Sternum	r - Thoracic air sac
i - Os pubis	s - Abdominial air sac
j - Trachea	t - Spleen
k - Lung	u - Kidney

'cavern formation', are due to chronic aspergillosis with mycotic coats on the air sac walls (see Figure 7.11).

An homogenous increased density of the lung field and the air sacs can be caused by fat deposits, which are of 'physiological' origin. It can also be a sign of pneumonia, but requires comparison with a radiograph of a normal bird of the same species for a definitive diagnosis.

Mycotic infections show as an irregular distribution of increased pulmonary density. This is also valid for the increased density of air sacs infected with

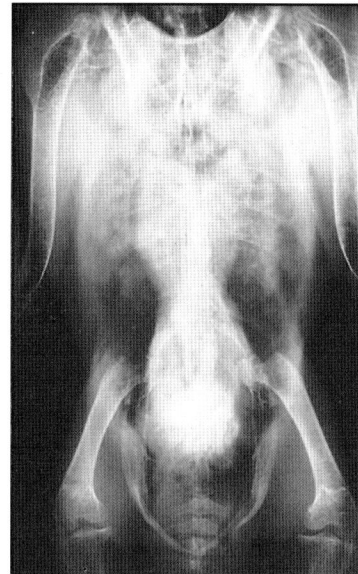

Figure 7.6.1: Body. Ventrodorsal projection. Green-winged Macaw. Slight overdistension of the axillary diverticulum. Massive, non-homogenous increased radiodensity of the lungs. (Severe mycosis.)

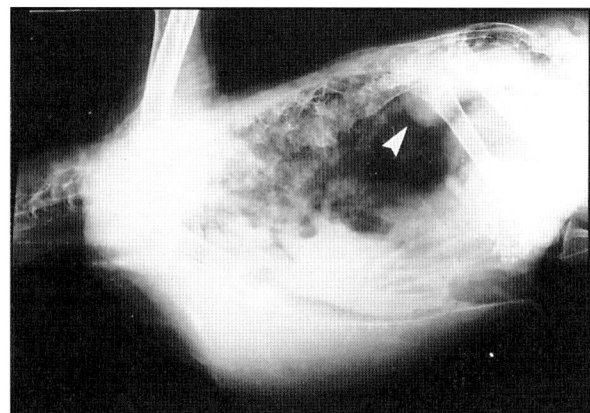

Figure 7.6.2: Body. Lateral projection. Green-winged Macaw. Massive, non-homogenous increased radiodensity of the lungs. Kidney swollen (arrow).

Aspergillus spp. (see Figures 7.6.1, 7.6.2).

Complete absence of movement blur is necessary to achieve a diagnostic radiograph.

Mycotic granulomata may be seen as irregular focal dense areas. As a differential diagnosis one should consider mycobacterial granulomata. Other signs, such as hepatic or renal enlargement, or nodular alterations in the gastrointestinal tract, increase the likelihood of mycobacteriosis. Nevertheless, granulomata of different origin cannot be distinguished from one another by radiography alone.

On the v/d view an overdistension of the axillary air sacs is sometimes seen in birds with severe respiratory distress - often clinically diagnosed as severe dyspnoea.

Overdistension of the abdominal air sacs is specific to a stenosis of the upper respiratory tract (Ruebel,

1985). The rounding of the caudal parts of the abdominal air sacs in the v/d view occurs in chronic air sacculitis. A massive overextension (air trapping) can be caused by a valve-like stenosed syrinx (commonly caused by syringeal aspergillomata) making expiration more difficult (Ruebel, 1985).

Gastrointestinal Tract

General Characteristics
The gastrointestinal tract of birds can best be identified on the lateral view, especially within seed-eaters in which the grit-filled (radiopaque stones) ventriculus can be clearly visualised. Its physiological localisation is between the two acetabuli, paramedian and to the left.

The proventriculus can be found dorsocranially above the ventriculus. In birds that prefer soft food it is not always possible to distinguish the proventriculus from the ventriculus.

Identifying the different loops of the intestines is almost impossible without the use of contrast medium. More importantly, contrast medium allows differentiation of gut from other internal organs, tumours and products of the reproductive tract.

The crop should be examined by palpation and endoscopy but, nevertheless, radiography can give some information about the thickness of the crop wall or the structure of the inner mucous membrane - the latter is best visualised by the double-contrast method (see later). A thickened wall may be a result of hypovitaminosis A or a sign of chronic inflammation, eg. candidiasis or trichomoniasis.

Metallic foreign bodies (see Figure 7.9.1) in the alimentary tract can easily be identified. Typically, they are in the gizzard. These foreign bodies must be distinguished from normal grit. In most cases they are more radiodense than grit and their identification is straightforward. Birds which show any central nervous signs, vomiting or bloody diarrhoea should be radiographed for the presence of metallic foreign objects.

Excessive grit in the gizzard may pass into the proventriculus and the intestines in an attempt to compensate for nutritional deficiency or malabsorption caused by intestinal parasites, eg. nematodes or cestodes. Where helminths are involved the walls of the intestines are often thickened and a gas filling can be seen occasionally. Gas filling may be indicative of parasitic ileus, but it can also be caused by bacterial gastroenteritis or an obstruction.

Displacement of the gizzard is always indicative of enlargement, swelling or neoplasia, or of a tumourous change in a neighbouring organ. Dorsocranial or caudal displacement suggests hepatic enlargement; ventrocranial or caudal displacement suggests renal or gonadal enlargement. Ventrocranial movement can also be caused by a laminated egg within the oviduct,

ovarian cysts or enlarged intestinal loops (Silverman, 1989).

Contrast Studies
In order to improve the interpretation of gastrointestinal radiographs, a contrast study is necessary. Contrast media should not be administered to a bird that is or has just been anaesthetised as peristalsis will be reduced, thus influencing the passage time. The patient should have been fasted for approximately two hours (see Figures 7.7, 7.8.1, 7.8.2, 7.9.1, 7.9.2, 7.11.1).

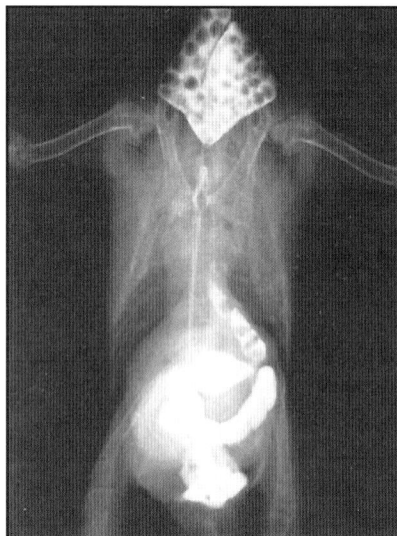

Figure 7.7: Body. Ventrodorsal projection. Budgerigar. Gastrointestinal contrast - 45 minutes after administration of 1ml of 25% barium sulphate suspension. Barium sulphate is surrounding grains in the crop and the proventriculus. The contrast study was necessary to define the gastrointestinal tract against a large soft tissue mass in the abdomen.

Barium sulphate suspension (25-45%) is administered into the crop with a tube-feeder at a dose of 20ml/kg bodyweight.

The passage time differs according to species, food type, age and presenting disease. Birds who live on a mushy diet have a fast passage time compared to whole-seed eaters.

In large psittacines that have been fasted prior to administration of contrast medium, the contrast suspension should have reached the cloaca after two hours; the crop should be empty after three hours. To ensure that the barium sulphate will not lead to constipation, liquids should be administered orally after completing the radiographic study.

Dilatation of the digestive tract is clearly demonstrated by contrast radiography. It may be caused by neurogenic infections, neurotoxic poisons, food stasis or ileus of the distal segments (probably caused by helminth infestation etc.).

Massive dilatation of the proventriculus can be a symptom of a very serious disease. Formerly only seen in New World parrots, but now increasingly observed in Old World parrots, neuropathic dilatation of the proventriculus, also known as 'macaw wasting disease', is an insidious incurable disease of suspected viral origin (see Figures 7.8.1, 7.8.2). Other characteristics include retarded passage time, thinning of the wall, atrophy and deformation of the gizzard. As a less serious disease, the differential diagnosis of candidiasis should be considered; the radiographic image would be similar.

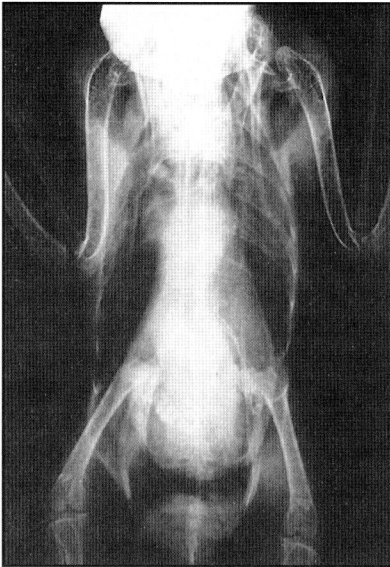

Figure 7.8.1: Body. Ventrodorsal projection. African Grey. Contrast study - six hours after administration of 10ml of 25% barium sulphate suspension. Massively retarded transit time due to extreme dilatation of the oesophagus and the proventriculus. Displacement of the ventriculus caudally and to the right side of the body. (Proventricular dilatation syndrome.)

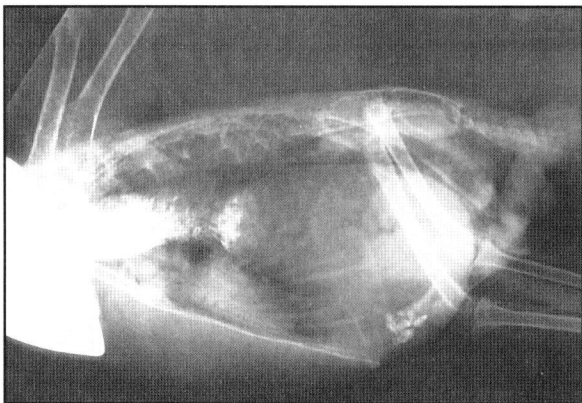

Figure 7.8.2: Body. Lateral projection. African Grey. Contrast study - six hours after administration of 10ml of 25% barium sulphate suspension. Massively retarded transit time due to extreme dilatation of the oesophagus and the proventriculus. Displacement of the ventriculus ventrally. (Proventricular dilatation syndrome.)

Double contrast study is used to show the surface of the mucous membrane of the crop or cloaca, eg. when lesions are suspected. Barium sulphate (10ml/

kg bodyweight) followed by air (20ml/kg) is administered either orally or *per cloacam* depending on the indication.

Liver

On a v/d view the combined shadow of the heart and liver form the shape of an hour glass. A well-filled or even massively enlarged proventriculus can be seen on the left side of the liver shadow on this view.

The size of the liver is dependent on the species and the nutritional status of the individual, but physiologically it does not differ too much from the general rule that in the v/d view the outer limit of the liver should not extend beyond an imaginary line drawn between the coracoid and the acetabulum (McMillan, 1986).

If the liver shadow is enlarged on the radiograph, there could be two different explanations:
● The liver is swollen due to an infectious or non-infectious cause (see Figures 7.9.1, 7.9.2).
● The liver is normal itself but organs below it are enlarged or, in case of the gut, massively filled. In these cases the liver has lost its shape and seems to be broader than it really is.

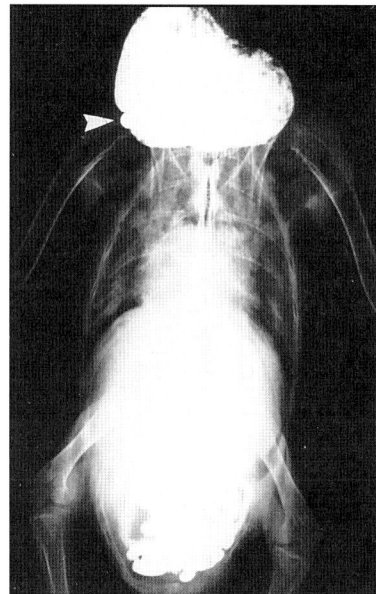

Figure 7.9.1: Body. Ventrodorsal projection. Blue and Gold Macaw - eight hours after administration of 20ml of 25% barium sulphate suspension. Massively retarded transit time. Large soft tissue shadow with lateral displacement of the proventriculus and caudal displacement of the intestinal tract. Massive compression of the air sacs, overdistension of the axillary air sacs. Metallic foreign body in the crop, nearly overlaid by barium sulphate (arrow). (Adenocarcinoma of the liver.)

One of the most common diseases in budgerigars is hepatic neoplasia. Biopsy or diagnostic laparotomy is required to differentiate a tumour from an enlarged liver due to a different cause.

Infections which can lead to an enlarged liver include chlamydiosis, tuberculosis and Pacheco's

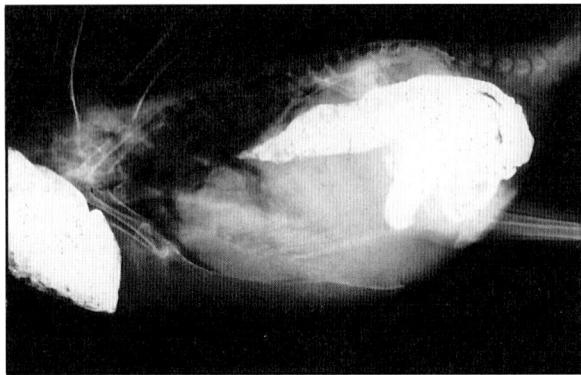

Figure 7.9.2: *Body. Lateral projection. The same Blue and Gold Macaw as in Figure 7.9.1. Eight hours after administration of 20ml of 25% barium sulphate suspension. Massively retarded transit time. Extreme liver enlargement with dorsal displacement of the proventriculus and caudal displacement of the gastrointestinal tract. Massive compression of the air sacs. (Adenocarcinoma of the liver.)*

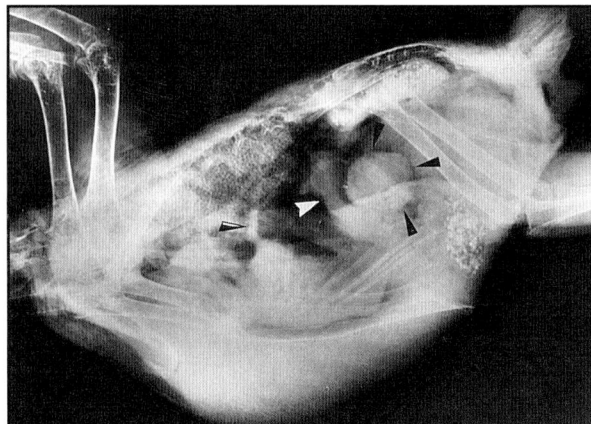

Figure 7.10: *Body. Lateral projection. African Grey. Increased non-homogenous radiodensity in the ventral part of the lung. Increased radiodensity of the vena cava caudalis (black/white arrow). Massively enlarged spleen (black arrows). Dilated proventriculus. Uric acid crystals within the kidneys. Curved soft tissue shadow cranial to the enlarged spleen revealed to be a massively thickened thoracic air sac wall (white arrow). (Chlamydiosis, aspergillosis and uric acid crystals within the kidneys.)*

disease, as well as other bacterial and viral infections. The gizzard is often displaced dorsocaudally. As in many other cases a contrast study will be helpful in establishing a diagnosis.

Diseases such as haemochromatosis are commonly diagnosed clinically because of the extensive ascites. Radiographically, the whole abdomen, except for the air-filled lungs, is the same shade of grey without any differentiation. Nevertheless, in most cases the liver is enlarged. Ultrasonography will confirm the diagnosis (Krautwald-Junghanns *et al*, 1991a). The prognosis in these cases is poor and treatment is supportive only.

Spleen

Except in cases of a massive enlargement, the spleen can only be identified in the lateral view with the bird lying on either side. The spleen can be seen dorsal to the lower part of the proventriculus. The normal diameter in Amazons or African Greys, for example, is about 5mm.

Neoplasia of the spleen is occassionally seen in budgerigars, but rarely in larger psittacines.

Heart and Vascular System

The apex of the heart is directed ventrocaudally and lies between the fifth and sixth ribs, with some interspecies variability. The heart has contact with the sternum and is partially overlaid by the liver. As already mentioned in connection with the liver, these two organs form the shape of an hour glass in the v/d view.

In cockatoos the contours of the heart can be seen distinctly on the radiograph (Ruebel, 1985).

In macaws, on the lateral view, the ventrally directed kink between heart and liver shadow is normal. In the v/d view the aorta and other large vessels are projected in an oblique direction and seen as round radiodense structures. These structures must not be confused with pulmonary granulomata. In the lateral view the

brachiocephalic trunk, the arteria pulmonalis and the caudal vena cava may be seen. In older birds these vessels tend to be calcified and appear radiodense (see Figure 7.10).

Indications for radiography of the heart are limited. An enlargement and/or an increased radiodensity of the heart shadow may occur in pericarditis or epicarditis.

Ultrasonography and electrocardiography are better methods for diagnosing heart and circulatory disturbances. Ultrasonography permits study of the heart's movement, the chambers and the vessels, and may indicate, for instance, the presence of a hydropericardium (Krautwald-Junghanns *et al*, 1991b). Nevertheless, in avain patients these techniques require practise and experience.

Urinary Organs

The kidneys can only be seen on the lateral view, lying caudodorsally along the vertebral column with their physiological length from about the level of the last rib to the end of the synsacrum. Depending on their functional state, the gonads might be visible cranial to the anterior pole of the kidneys (McNeel, 1981).

The kidneys, ureters and cloaca are easily demonstrated when impacted with radiodense crystalline deposits such as uric acid (see Figure 7.10). This is not necessarily a sign of renal insuffiency, but may be a result of temporary dehydration or chronic bacterial infection. The presence of these radiodense deposits can be suggestive of gout, but it is not diagnostic. In these cases uric acid blood levels should be assayed.

Enlargement of the kidney shadow (see Figure 7.6.2) is frequently seen in combination with an enlargement of other organs as a sign of generalised infection, eg.

chlamydiosis, or in connection with vitamin A deficiency or renal neoplasia (common in budgerigars).

Kidney cysts may cause changes to the kidney shadow. However, they can be diagnosed more accurately using ultrasonography (Krautwald-Junghanns and Enders, 1994). Contrast study (urography) using organic iodine compounds is indicated if functional disturbances of the urinary organs are suspected, or simply to highlight expected defects (McNeel, 1981; Krautwald, 1987). The patient should be fasted for approximately two hours. Warm contrast medium is administered intravenously as a 70-80% solution (or a compound containing 200-400mg iodine/ml) at a dose of 2ml/kg bodyweight. The first radiograph should be taken immediately after the injection of the contrast medium; the kidneys are highlighted 30-60 seconds after injection. The cloaca is visualised after 2-5 minutes.

Reproductive Tract

The gonads are demonstrated particularly well during their active state. On a lateral view they are seen cranial to the anterior pole of the kidneys.

An active ovary appears as a non-homogenous lumpy shadow (see Figure 7.3). Active testes have a large round or oval soft tissue shadow, but they must not be confused with a traumatically enlarged kidney pole, cysts or even a tumour. Ovarian cysts or tumours often lead to a massive increase in oestrogen levels. High levels of oestrogen lead to enhanced storage of calcium; non-homogenous polyostotic hyperostosis of the long tubular bones is the corresponding radiographic sign (see Figure 7.3). Homogenous storage of calcium signifies a preparation for laying eggs.

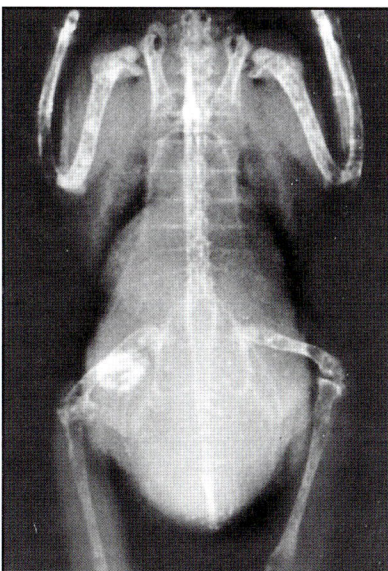

Figure 7.11.1: Body. Ventrodorsal projection. Budgerigar. Loss of hour glass shape, massive compression of the air sacs. Displacement of the ventriculus caudally and to the left. Non-homogenous hypercalcification of all long bones. Soft tissue mass in the abdominal cavity. (Laminated egg.)

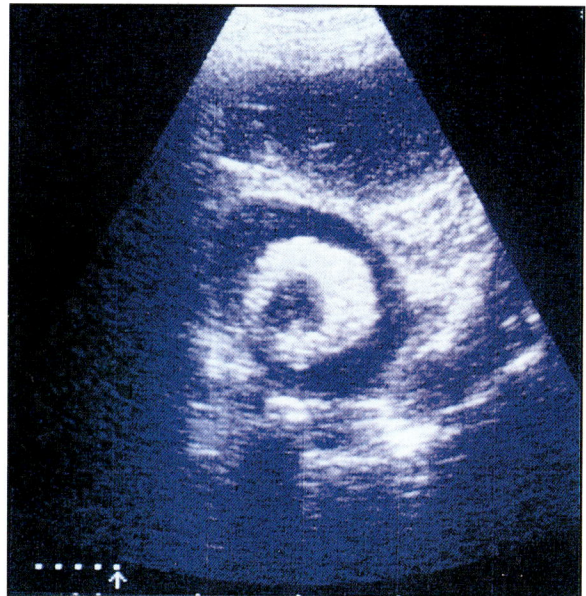

Figure 7.11.2: Ultrasonography. Ventromedial approach. Budgerigar. Abdomen. Round structure in the abdomen with different echogenicity. (Laminated egg.)

Conversely, persistent (excessive) egg laying hens may show depletion of calcium stores and, eventually, thinning of the long bone cortices.

Despite the descriptions above, sexual differentiation by radiography is not a reliable method.

When enlarged, the oviduct can be demonstrated in the abdominal region as a distinct soft-tissue shadow. Eggs can be seen clearly by the radiodensity of the calcified shell. Laminated non-shelled eggs (see Figures 7.3, 7.11.1) can only be presumed (most often accompanied by non-homogenous hyperostosis of the long bones). However, they are readily visualised by ultrasonography (see Figure 7.11.2).

REFERENCES

Bush M, Montali RI, Novak RG and James FA (1976) The healing of avian fractures - a histological xeroradiographic study. *Journal of the American Animal Hospital Association* **12(6)**, 768.

Kosta AV, Krautwald M-E, Tellhelm B and Schildger B (1988) A contribution to radiologic examination of bone alterations in psittacines. In: *Proceedings of the Association of Avian Veterinarians Annual Conference 1988.* AAV, Lake Worth.

Kostka V, Krautwald M-E and Tellhelm B (1989) Radiology of the avian skull. In: *Proceedings of the Association of Avian Veterinarians Annual Conference 1989.* AAV, Lake Worth.

Krautwald M-E (1987) Radiographic examination of the urinary system of birds with organo iodinated contrast media. In: *Proceedings of the Association of Avian Veterinarians Annual Conference 1987.* AAV, Lake Worth.

Krautwald M-E, Riedel U and Neumann W (1991)

Diagnostic use of ultrasonography in birds. In: *Proceedings of the Association of Avian Veterinarians Annual Conference 1991*. AAV, Lake Worth.

Krautwald-Junghanns M-E, Kostka V and Pieper K (1991) Pathologische Röntgenzeichen bei der Tuberkulose von Zier- und Greifvögeln. *Tierärztliche Praxis* **19**, 156.

Krautwald-Junghanns M-E and Enders F (1994) Ultrasonography in birds. *Seminars in Avian and Exotic Pet Medicine* **3(3)**, 140

McMillan M (1986) Radiographic diagnosis of avian abdominal disorders. *Compendium on Continuing Education for the Practicing Veterinarian* **8(9)**, 616.

McNeel SV (1981) Avian urography. *Journal of the American Veterinary Medical Association* **178**, 366.

Murphy JP, Koblik P, Stein G and Penninck D (1986) Psittacine skull radiography. In: *Proceedings of the Association of Avian Veterinarians Annual Conference 1986*. AAV, Lake Worth.

Ruebel A (1985) *Röntgendiagnostik bei inneren Erkrankungen der Psittaciden*. Veterinarmedizinische Dissertation, Zürich.

Silverman S (1989) Basic and advanced avian radiology. In: *Proceedings of the Association of Avian Veterinarians Annual Conference 1989*. AAV, Lake Worth.

FURTHER READING

Krautwald M-E, Tellhelm B, Hummel GH, Kostka V and Kaleta EF (1992) *Atlas of Radiographic Anatomy and Diagnosis of Cage Birds*. Paul Parey Company, Berlin.

McMillan M (1983) Avian gastrointestinal radiography. *Compendium on Continuing Education for the Practicing Veterinarian* **4(5)**, 273.

McMillan M (1986) Radiology of the avian respiratory tract. *Compendium on Continuing Education for the Practicing Veterinarian* **8(8)**, 551.

Ruebel A, Isenbügel E and Wolvekamp P (1991) *Atlas der Röntgendiagnostik bei Heimtieren*. Schlütersche Buchhandlung, Hannover.

Silverman S (1980) Avian radiographic technique and interpretation. In: *Current Veterinary Therapy VII*. Ed RW Kirk. WB Saunders, Philadelphia.

Smith BJ (1990) The normal xeroradiographic and radiographic anatomy of the Orange-winged Amazon Parrot (*Amazona amazonica amazonica*). *Veterinary Radiology* **3(7)**, 660.

Walsh MT (1986) Radiology. In: *Clinical Avian Medicine and Surgery, including Aviculture*. Eds GJ Harrison and LR Harrison. WB Saunders, Philadelphia.

CHAPTER EIGHT

Post-Mortem Examination

Victor R Simpson

INTRODUCTION

This chapter is intended as a guide for those in general practice and describes the author's recommended *post-mortem* procedure. However, the chapter should be regarded as a framework for developing a personal protocol. As with a clinical examination, it is important to work systematically, but unlike a clinical examination a *post-mortem* examination cannot be repeated. It is therefore doubly important that samples are taken in a logical sequence and that no systems are omitted from examination. Samples can always be stored and disposed of later if not required.

Before starting on the *post-mortem* examination it is sensible to satisfy the following questions:
● Is time available to do the job properly ?
● Are there adequate facilities to carry out the procedure correctly and safely ?

If adequate time is not available it is likely that mistakes will be made or systems missed. Facilities must include protective clothing and gloves and, in particular, a Class I safety cabinet (see Chapter 23), as well as instruments, a microscope, various sample pots, staining facilities, etc. If the answer to both questions is not a confident 'yes', it may be preferable to submit the carcase to a specialist pathology laboratory.

RECORDING

At the time that the bird is presented for *post-mortem* examination it is important to take a full history from the owner. Clinical signs and details of any treatment given should be recorded and a note made of when and from where the bird was obtained. If the bird has a history of illness and laboratory tests have been performed, a copy of the reports should be requested. Enquiries should be made as to whether or not any other birds are kept and, if so, whether they have shown signs of disease. Details of husbandry and feeding should be recorded.

The bird should be given a unique laboratory reference number and this number should be written on all specimen pots and samples subsequently collected. All these data, together with the date of submission, the owner's name and address, etc., should be recorded on a standard submission form.

The *post-mortem* findings should be written up immediately after completing the examination. It is helpful to use a standard 'prompt' sheet, with headings for each organ system (see Appendix 8.1). The reverse side of this sheet can be used to record details of any samples taken, test results and/or where samples have been sent for further examination. The 'prompt' sheet should be permanently attached to the submission form.

EQUIPMENT AND STAINS

The equipment required will depend largely on how much laboratory work it is intended to carry out in the practice. A list of basic equipment and stains is given in Appendix 8.2.

COLLECTION AND HANDLING OF SAMPLES

In addition to the information provided in the text, further notes on the collection, handling and despatch of samples is provided in Appendix 8.3.

PROCEDURE

1.   Before examining the body, check the bag or wrappings in which the specimen was carried; ectoparasites may be more evident here than on the carcase itself. If it is necessary to euthanase a sick bird, do not inject barbiturate into the body cavity or the liver. The author prefers to give a small dose of intravenous barbiturate, but an anaesthetic gas, such as halothane, can also be used. If the brachial vessels are too small, use the right jugular vein.

2.   Record the species and any identifying leg ring details. In cases where litigation is possible it is wise to retain any ring(s) and take photographic evidence. A label showing the bird's laboratory reference number and the date should appear in the photographs.

In certain cases, particularly when dealing with valuable birds, it is advisable to check for the presence of a microchip. If using a scanner, bear in mind that the different systems currently available in the United Kingdom (UK) are not necessarily compatible, and therefore a negative reading does not automatically mean the absence of a microchip. A radiograph provides a more certain way of locating a microchip and is also an advisable procedure when investigating cases of suspected malicious shooting or vandalism. Any shot or foreign bodies subsequently recovered during the *post-mortem* examination should be labelled, carefully wrapped and retained as possible exhibits.

3.   Record the weight of the bird. (When doing this note whether the plumage is wet or dry.)

4.   Examine the external features, specifically the eyes, ears, nares, beak, feet, skin and vent. Check the plumage for abnormalities, including evidence of fret marks, ectoparasites and moult (see Chapter 10).

If there are ocular or nasal discharges, take a sample with a sterile swab. Inoculate blood agar, MacConkey agar and Sabouraud's medium for bacterial and fungal cultures, and make a smear on a microscope slide for staining by Gram. Submit a second swab for examination by polymerase chain reaction (PCR) for *Chlamydia psittaci*. **Do not use transport medium when submitting samples for the PCR test as this may lead to false positive results**. (See Section 11 and Chapters 17 and 23 for further details on *C. psittaci*).

Any scaly or proliferative skin lesions should be excised and samples taken for histological examination. Although poxvirus infection is not common in psittacine species in the UK, any raised, plaque-like lesions, particularly around the mouth and eyes, should be taken for examination by electron microscopy. Submit these samples **without transport medium**. If the legs or the skin around the face appears thick and scaly, take scrapings for evidence of *Cnemidocoptes* spp. mites. In small birds it is often very difficult to get an adequate sample. Therefore, add a spot of microscope immersion oil to the skin, scrape backwards and forwards with a scalpel blade, and transfer the resulting oily paste onto a microscope slide for direct examination.

5.   Wash the carcase in warm water and liquid detergent. This reduces significantly the risk of inhaling dust particles containing microorganisms, in particular *C. psittaci*. It also facilitates detailed examination of the body surface and, when the carcase is opened, prevents dry feathers contaminating the viscera. Water will not be taken into the respiratory system providing care is taken not to squeeze the carcase whilst it is immersed. Pluck the feathers from the ventral body surface. 70% alcohol, instead of water and detergent, may be used to wet the plumage. However, this is unnecessarily expensive and it also carries a fire risk.

6.   Palpate the carcase, especially the limbs. Check for swellings or fractures, and confirm that all joints are fully mobile. Check for proper bone mineralisation by attempting to bend a long bone.

7.   Pin the carcase out - tightly stretched - on a *post-mortem* (PM) board. The author prefers a cork board (30 x 30 x 1.5cm) for small birds and a soft wood board (50 x 50 x 2cm) for the larger parrots. Dissection pins are useful, but round headed nails (5-6.5cm) work well in wood and are cheaper. A useful tip is to pin the legs over the wing tips; this keeps the feathers out of the way. In larger birds, eg. macaws, the long tail feathers can be amputated.

8.   Transfer the bird to the safety cabinet.

9.   Make a midline incision along the sternum. This is extended up the neck to the mandible, taking care to avoid the oesophagus and crop. Hold the skin with rat-tooth forceps and, using a scalpel, reflect the skin away from the pectoral muscles, the neck, the abdominal wall and the medial aspect of the legs (see Figure 8.1). Note the extent of any subcutaneous fat deposits and check for the presence of lipomata, particularly in cockatiels and budgerigars.

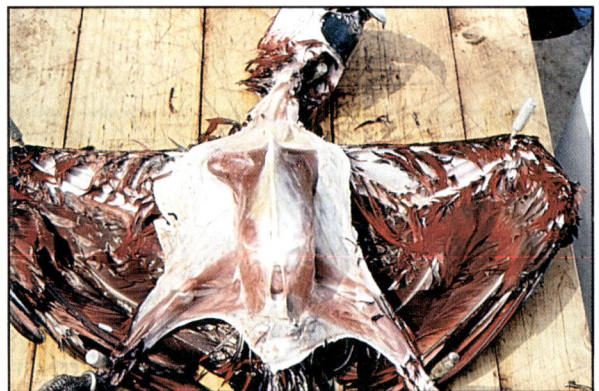

Figure 8.1: Green-winged Macaw pinned out for post-mortem examination. Note the wasted pectoral muscles.

Examine the muscles for lesions, eg. abscesses, bruising or evidence of injections. Pale parallel streaks following the alignment of the muscle fibres may be seen in cases of infection with so-called *Leucocytozoon* sp. infection (Simpson, 1991) (see Figure 8.2). Such cases are only likely to occur between June and September. Similar lesions may also be seen in cases of *Sarcocystis* sp. infection, although this condition is much less common and there is no obvious seasonal incidence (Borst and Zwart, 1973). If lesions are present, place a sample of muscle approximately 3-4mm thick into 10% buffered formal saline for histological examination (see also Sections 14 and 20).

Starting at the level of the coracoid bone, make a longitudinal incision through the pectoral muscles

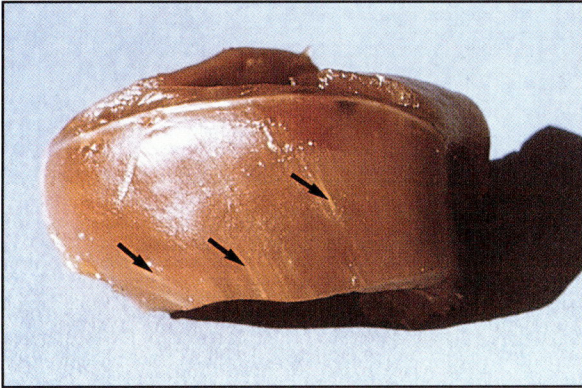

Figure 8.2: Pectoral muscles of a Turquoisine Parakeet showing pale parallel streaks (arrows) caused by infection with so-called *Leucocytozoon sp.*

down either side of the thorax. Hold the caudal edge of the sternum with forceps and make a transverse incision through the abdominal wall just caudal to the ribs. Take care not to incise the liver which lies immediately beneath. Lift the sternum and use the scalpel to free it from the pericardium. Cut through the rib joints down either side using large scissors. Elevate the sternum further still and, using bone shears, cut through the coracoid and clavicle bones on both sides. Using scissors or scalpel cut through any remaining tissue and lift the sternum away. During this whole process take care not to cut the brachiocephalic arteries, particularly in freshly dead birds, or blood will enter the lungs via the thoracic air sacs. Should this happen, subsequent examination of the lungs becomes more difficult. Reflect the remainder of the abdominal wall back to the cloaca.

10. The exposed organs should now be examined visually before they are further disturbed (see Figure 8.3). Note the general appearance and whether any organs appear congested, discoloured, swollen, etc. Beware of artefactual lesions caused by injection of barbiturate into the body cavity if the bird had been euthanased by this method. This typically results in brownish discolouration, often with crystalline deposits. In cases of visceral gout, many organs, especially the liver and heart, may appear white or frosted due to the superficial deposition of urates. Pay particular attention to the appearance of the liver and also observe the pancreas. Examine the pericardium for adhesions (often seen in cases of *C. psittaci* infection) and the pericardial cavity for excess fluid, blood or fibrin deposits. Also observe the thyroid and parathyroid glands, which lie just cranial to the thoracic inlet (see Figure 8.4). If the thyroids are abnormal, eg. hyperplasia in budgerigars, place a representative sample in fixative for histological examination. Hypertrophy of the parathyroid glands is seen occasionally in parrots and may be associated with an all seed diet, which is high in phosphates and low in calcium (Wallach and Flieg, 1969).

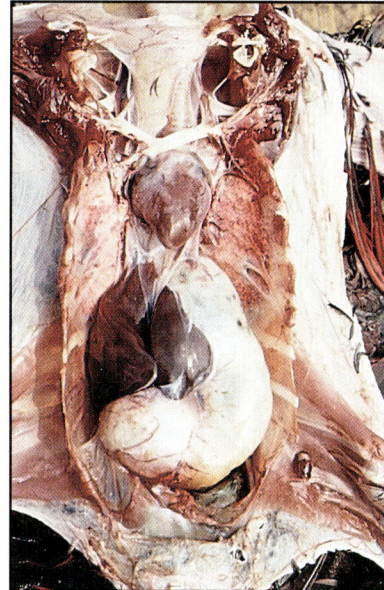

Figure 8.3: Green-winged Macaw with sternum removed and major organs exposed. Note the markedly dilated proventriculus in this case of psittacine proventricular dilatation syndrome.

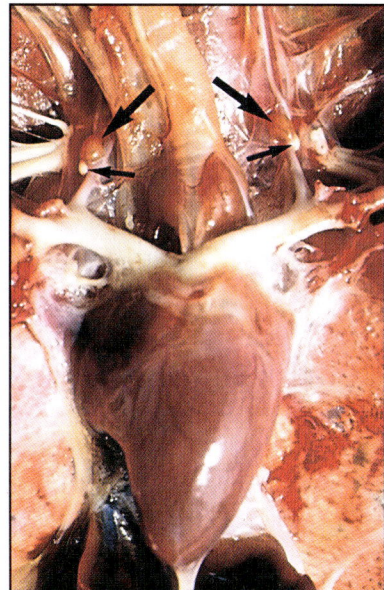

Figure 8.4: The thyroid glands (large arrows) and parathyroid glands, which are much smaller and whitish (small arrows), lie either side of the thoracic inlet.

The air sacs should be transparent and any opacity, thickening or discreet lesion is evidence of disease. Fungal infections of the respiratory system, principally due to *Aspergillus fumigatus*, are common in parrots, especially in recently imported birds. Lesions can occur almost anywhere, but the larger ones occur most commonly in the caudal thoracic or the abdominal air sacs (see Figure 8.5). The lesions vary greatly, ranging from discreet, cream coloured, roundish plaques, often with a bluish-grey mass of sporing bodies over the exposed surface, to yellow exudative masses or chronic granulomatous lesions. In advanced cases these lesions may cover most of the surface of one or more air sacs. If lesions are present, tear a hole in the affected air sac using forceps, insert a sterile swab and take a sample from the surface of the lesion. Inoculate onto Sabouraud's medium, blood agar and MacConkey agar plates. After doing this cut out a small fragment of the lesion, place it on a microscope slide, add lactophenol cotton blue and examine microscopically for fungal hyphae. (Cultural examination of granulomatous lesions should be carried out as described later for bacterial infections, but with the additional inoculation of Sabouraud's plates - see Section 12). Mixed infections with *Aspergillus* spp. and *Mycobacterium avium* or *C. psittaci* are not uncommon, and gross lesions should therefore be interpreted with care.

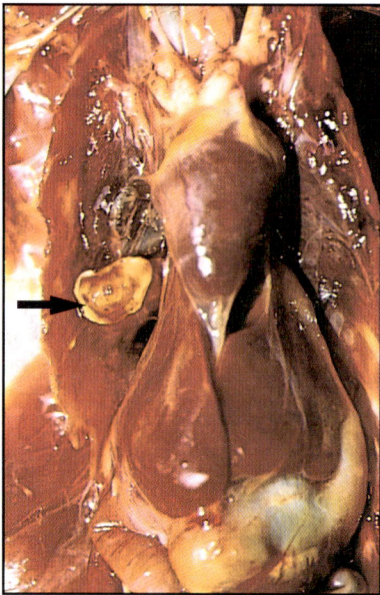

Figure 8.5: Caseous air sac lesion (arrow) caused by aspergillosis infection in a cockatoo. Death was from pulmonary haemorrhage, an occasional sequel to chronic infection.

11.   Because chlamydiosis represents a significant zoonotic risk (see Chapter 23) it is recommended that examination is made for the presence of this infection before proceeding further.

In many cases of chlamydial infection there are visible lesions, such as pericarditis, air sacculitis, hepatomegaly (see Figure 8.6) (often with serofibrinous deposits over the surface) and/or a swollen and inflamed spleen (see Figure 8.7). In some cases, however, no such lesions are apparent. The spleen is the organ of choice when testing for chlamydiosis. To locate the organ, take hold of the body of the gizzard, preferably with large rat-tooth forceps, and reflect and rotate it towards the bird's right hand side. The spleen will be seen lying immediately behind the gizzard, close to its junction with the proventriculus (see Figure 8.8). Irrespective of its appearance the spleen should **always** be tested for *C. psittaci*, at least by microscopic examination.

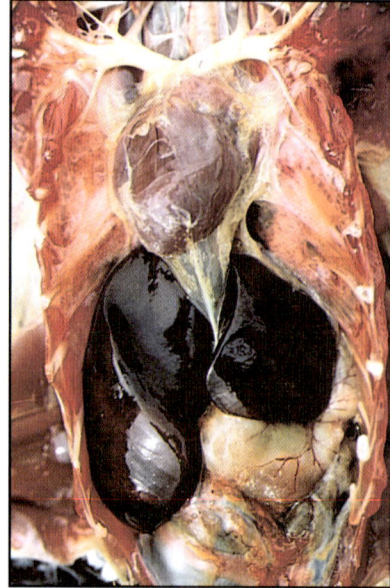

Figure 8.6: C. psittaci infection in a Blue and Gold Macaw. Note the yellow pericardial adhesions and the rounded edges to the grossly swollen and inflamed liver. The spleen was similarly affected.

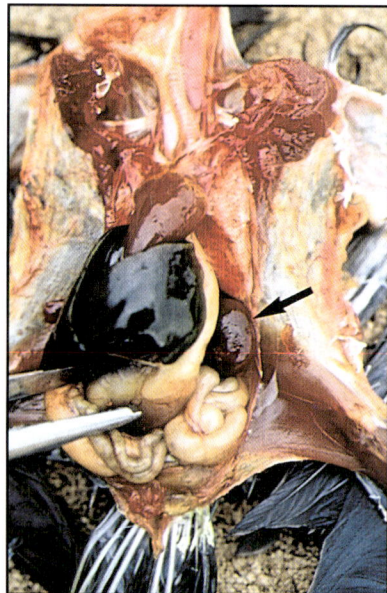

Figure 8.7: Classical enlarged spleen (arrow) in a lovebird infected with C. psittaci. The greenish discolouration of the liver is atypical.

Take hold of the spleen in forceps, cut it free and then cut it in half. Retaining one half in the forceps, touch the cut surface at two or three points along a microscope slide. Prepare a second slide as a spare. The slide should be air dried, stained by modified Ziehl-Neelsen (MZN) and examined under a high power (x100) objective. Chlamydial organisms appear as clusters of tiny magenta-pink bodies within the blue staining cytoplasm of the host cell (see Figure 8.9). Some bacteria, eg. *Yersinia pseudotuberculosis, M. avium* and *Salmonella typhimurium,* will stain pinkish,

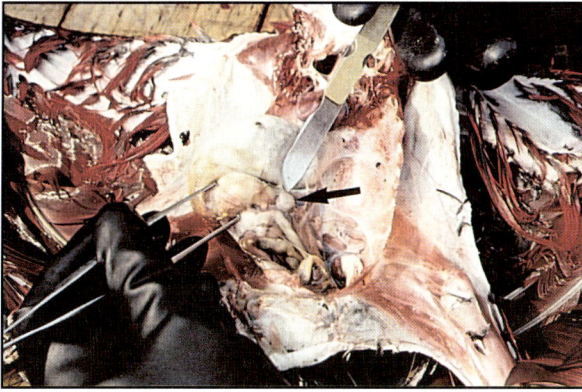

Figure 8.8: With the gizzard reflected to the bird's right side, the spleen of this Green-winged Macaw is visible. In this case the spleen is of normal appearance (arrow).

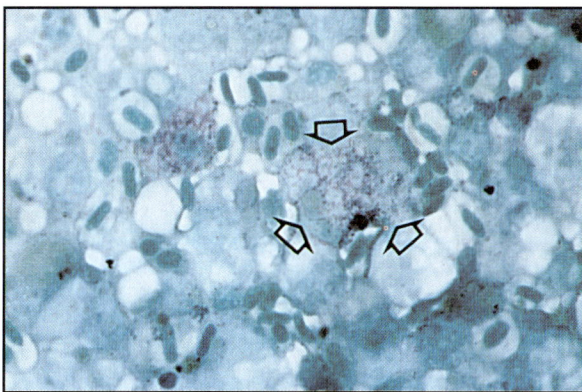

Figure 8.9: MZN stained spleen impression smear showing numerous magenta staining chlamydial inclusions (arrows).

but they are much larger and are morphologically distinct from *C. psittaci*.

If the bird has a history and/or lesions suggestive of *C. psittaci* infection, microscopic examination should be performed before proceeding further with the *post-mortem* examination. If the spleen smear proves positive for chlamydiosis it is questionable whether one can justify completing the *post mortem*. Although other intercurrent diseases may be missed, they are unlikely to be of the same significance. Continuing with the examination increases the zoonotic risk to the veterinarian and his/her staff. There are implications for veterinarians under the Health and Safety at Work Act 1974 if they or their staff are exposed to material which is known to be infected with an organism such as *C. psittaci* (Gresham, in press). The carcase should be wrapped up in paper towels which have been soaked in disinfectant and transferred to a polythene bag for safe disposal. This latter procedure must be carried out within the safety cabinet.

If total reliance is not to be placed on microscopic examination for diagnosing chlamydiosis, there are several additional tests available, but all involve a significant delay in obtaining a result. The traditional confirmatory test has been cultural examination; for

this test spleen must be submitted in special chlamydia transport medium (CTM) to a reference laboratory. However, this test has now been largely replaced by the enzyme-linked immunosorbent assay (ELISA) test for chlamydial antigen and, even more recently, by the PCR test which detects chlamydial DNA. The PCR test is extremely sensitive and works equally well on live or dead chlamydial organisms. The very sensitivity of the test means that particular care has to be taken to avoid contamination during collection of samples. A new scalpel blade must be used for every case, along with scrupulously clean instruments and new sample pots. For the same reason, the spleen should not be cut on the PM board; instead the author cuts it on the medial aspect of the bird's own thigh. It is also vital **not to use any form of transport medium** as this can give false positive results. The PCR test is carried out by the Chlamydia Unit at the Central Veterinary Laboratory, Weybridge (samples should be submitted through the local Veterinary Investigation Centre) and by Vetgen Europe.

Several ELISA test kits are commercially available, eg. Clearview (Unipath) and Ideia (Dako). The latter kit is used by the Veterinary Investigation Service and gives good results when applied to tissue samples. Results take approximately five hours to complete. The ELISA test is less satisfactory for the examination of faecal specimens, as false positive results may occasionally occur. Samples submitted for the ELISA test should be in CTM. If swabs are used to collect the samples they should have wire or plastic stems - swabs with wooden stems produce erroneous results.

12.   If on-site facilities for bacteriology are available it is highly desirable to culture direct from the organs which are, as yet, relatively undisturbed. This will yield superior results to those obtained by removing tissue samples and culturing them later. Tissues which have to be posted for bacteriological examination tend to give poor results, as they often suffer from overgrowth of contaminant organisms.

As a routine, culture heart blood, liver and intestines. If there are visible lesions in other organs, especially the lungs, these should also be cultured. The assistance of a technician greatly facilitates the taking of good quality samples with minimum risk of contamination.

Heat the blade of a spatula (or scalpel blade) in a Bunsen flame and apply this briefly to a cardiac atrium. Immediately insert the point of a finely drawn, sterile Pasteur pipette (or hypodermic needle) through the seared area and collect a small sample of blood. Inoculate this onto blood agar and MacConkey culture plates - if the bird is freshly dead this sample can also be used to make a blood smear for haematological examination (see Chapter 5).

Sear a small area of one lobe of the liver and, again, take a sample using a Pasteur pipette. If there are discreet lesions, try and take a sample through the edge of a lesion. If there are no on-site cultural facilities, remove one lobe of the liver, using a sterile scalpel blade and forceps, and transfer it directly into a sample pot. Hold the sample in a refrigerator at 4°C until it can be posted, preferably with an ice pack in an insulated container. Most organisms will survive at 4°C for about 48-72 hours, but wherever possible prolonged storage should be avoided.

Multiple, discreet white or cream nodular lesions in the liver are typically due to *Y. pseudotuberculosis* (see Figure 8.10), although *M. avium* can cause very similar lesions. As a rapid check, excise a lesion and make touch preparations from the cut surface on at least two microscope slides. Air dry them and stain one by Ziehl-Neelsen (ZN) and the other by Gram. *M. avium* will appear as slender acid-fast bacilli (see Figure 8.11) and *Y. pseudotuberculosis* are short Gram-negative bacilli. (Mycobacteria stain Gram-positive, but this stain should not be used to try and identify them). It should also be borne in mind that psittacines may be infected with *M. bovis* or even *M. tuberculosis*. Where mycobacteria are demonstrated they should, ideally, be cultured and identified. In practice, this is seldom done. Cultural examination of intestines is dealt with later (see Section 20).

13.   Some viral conditions, such as Pacheco's parrot disease and reovirus hepatitis, may cause severe liver damage. In both these diseases the lesions may appear similar, with the liver swollen, yellowish or bronzed, and showing an extensive pattern of necrosis (Pacheco and Bier, 1930; Martin *et al*, 1979; Ashton *et al*, 1984) (see Figure 8.12). Swelling of the liver is also seen with other infections, such as *S. typhimurium* and

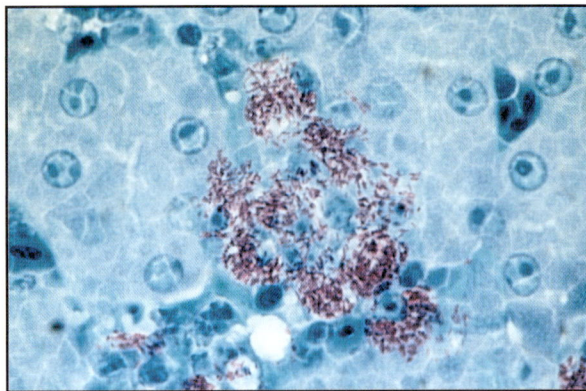

Figure 8.11: M. avium in a liver section stained by ZN.

Figure 8.12: The liver of this African Grey is enlarged, bronze coloured and showing multiple necrotic foci. This is a case of reovirus hepatitis.

C. psittaci. If samples are to be taken for virological examination, transfer tissue directly to a sterile container, as described earlier for posting bacteriological samples. However, before posting contact should be made with the reference laboratory to enquire whether or not they wish to receive samples in virus transport medium (VTM). The samples should be kept cool and packaged as described earlier in Section 12 for bacteriology samples.

Avian polyomavirus infection (budgerigar fledgling disease) was first diagnosed in the UK in 1994 (Scott, 1994). Although the virus classically causes acute mortality in budgerigar chicks aged 1-3 weeks, in other psittacine fledglings, notably Eclectus Parrots, conures and macaws, it results in marked hepatomegaly, splenomegaly and subepicardial and subserosal haemorrhages. In these species the condition appears to be restricted to fledglings aged 2-14 weeks of age and in most cases they are hand reared birds (Phalen *et al*, 1993). The PCR test for polyomavirus is carried out

Figure 8.10: Multiple cream, focal lesions in the liver of a King Parrot caused by Y. pseudotuberculosis. Very similar lesions may be caused by M. avium.

by Vetgen Europe (see Appendix 8.3 for address).

When removing tissues for bacteriology, virology or toxicology (see later) take care not to contaminate the samples. If gloves, instruments and PM boards are wet with disinfectant or formalin, disappointing results can be expected.

14.   Returning to the heart, open the pericardial sac and check for adhesions to the myocardium, as well as for urates, blood or pus. Examine the surface of the ventricles for lesions, eg. areas of necrosis, nodules, etc. So-called *Leucocytozoon* sp. infection, most commonly seen in Antipodean parakeets, may result in subepicardial nodules and/or haemorrhages (Simpson, 1991).

Using forceps, take hold of the base of the large arteries emerging from the heart, sever these vessels distally and free the heart from the surrounding tissue. Take care not to cut through the wall of the proventriculus, which lies immediately dorsal to the heart. It is often easier to remove the liver along with the heart, maintaining a grip on the heart and freeing the liver with a scalpel.

Separate the heart from the liver and lay it on the PM board. Hold the heart on its side and cut transversely across the ventricles, starting near the apex. Repeat this two or three times, progressing towards the atria and cutting slices approximately 3-4mm thick. Check the cut surfaces for lesions, particularly for areas of necrosis. Place any slices showing lesions in fixative. Using a small pair of sharp scissors cut through from the lumen of each of the ventricles into the atria and up into the arteries. Check for endocardial or valvular lesions. If the walls of the arteries appear thick, rubbery or calcified, place samples in fixative. Arteriosclerosis is not uncommon, particularly in old psittacines, and may be confirmed by histological examination.

15.   Examine the liver for evidence of swelling, discolouration, inflammation, congestion and diffuse or focal lesions. If the liver appears abnormal, cytological or histological examination may be carried out in addition to the previously described examination for microorganisms. Lay the organ on the PM board and, avoiding the seared area, cut one lobe longitudinally. Place a 3-4mm slice (or, in small birds, half the liver) in fixative. To make cytological preparations hold the other half of the lobe in forceps, blot off any excess blood using filter paper and make touch preparations from the cut surface onto at least two microscope slides. Stain by Hemacolor (or Diff Quik) and Gram or ZN as appropriate (see Chapter 5).

Hypovitaminosis A is a common condition in captive psittacines (Zwart *et al*, 1979). To check on the bird's vitamin A status place approximately 5g of liver sample in a sterile universal container. An absolute minimum of 1g is required by the laboratory

(Shrewsbury VI Centre) and, therefore, analysis may not be possible for the smaller species. The liver sample should be held in a deep freeze at -20°C until it can be posted, together with a freezer pack, to the laboratory. Autolysed samples give invalid results.

16.   With the heart and liver removed the alimentary tract is more accessible. The size and appearance of the crop, proventriculus, gizzard, duodenum and pancreas should be noted, but it is best to leave detailed examination of these organs until later. Therefore, sever both the bronchi, reflect the trachea and reflect the alimentary tract to one side. Do not cut the rectum. If the intestines cannot be reflected because of peritoneal adhesions, check for a possible point of entry of infection, such as perforation of the gizzard or accidental damage to the intestine following laparoscopy. In a case of egg peritonitis there will be masses of yellow, inspissated yolk interspersed between adhering loops of intestine.

17.   Open the bird's beak, insert a pair of large scissors into the oropharynx (bone shears will be needed for larger parrots) and cut through one side of the mouth. Reflect the mandible and examine the oropharynx, including the choanae, the tongue and the glottis. Conditions which may be seen in this area include oral papillomata, lesions of vitamin A deficiency and avian pox. Excise any lesions and examine by histology or electron microscopy as appropriate. Insert a small pair of sharp scissors into the glottis and cut down the trachea both dorsally and ventrally, dividing it into two longitudinal halves (see Figure 8.13). It is important to do this carefully and cleanly, checking in particular for items of inhaled food and also for caseous

Figure 8.13: Division of the trachea into two halves in a Moluccan Coakatoo in order to check for possible lesions, eg. aspergillosis.

lesions adherent to the mucosa. Occasionally, these are localised within the syrinx or the bronchi where they may easily be missed. Such lesions are usually mycotic and, if present, should be examined microscopically (stain crushed preparations with lactophenol cotton blue) and/or cultured onto suitable media.

If the lungs appear congested or show discreet lesions they should be cultured for bacteria and fungi. Samples are best taken with the lung *in situ*. Trim away any protruding rib ends with scissors, sear the lung surface and collect a sample with a Pasteur pipette. If a viral condition is suspected, eg. paramyxovirus (PMV), place lung tissue plus a portion of trachea in a sterile bijou. Hold this at 4°C and post promptly to a reference laboratory (in the case of PMV it is a good idea to send - in separate pots - additional samples of brain and duodenum plus pancreas).

Removal of lungs is not particularly easy and requires practice. Hold the apex of a lung with large forceps and, whilst pulling gently away from the ribs, use the flat face of the scalpel to free the organ. Try not to cut into the lung substance or it will readily tear. Place each lung on the PM board and cut transversely. If any lesions are seen, or if the bird had shown signs of respiratory disease, place a section about 3-4mm thick in fixative. In the case of small species, place both cut halves into fixative.

18.   Examine the adrenal glands, which are normally orange or yellow, and the gonads which lie immediately caudal and ventral to them. In most species the paired testes are cream coloured, elongated bodies, but in some species they may be black, eg. cockatoos. Normally, only the left ovary is present and is a roughly triangular whitish body with an irregular surface. If the ovary is active, check for any ova which appear discoloured, inflamed or shrunken. In this case take samples for bacteriological examination, including inoculation of selenite F for *Salmonella* spp. Check the oviduct for abnormalities. In cases where a valuable bird has died due to 'eggbinding' it may be worth collecting the egg for attempted artificial incubation.

19.   Check the appearance of the kidneys and the ureters. A small quantity of urates in the ureters is normal, but they should not be distended. In cases of acute nephritis the kidneys appear pale and swollen with the individual lobules forming a fine reticular pattern over the surface. Additionally, there may be fine, whitish, focal deposits of urates, particularly in cases of visceral gout. In cases of chronic nephritis, one or both kidneys may appear shrunken. Where the bird has a history of leg paralysis check carefully for space occupying lesions in the kidneys, eg. tumours or granulomata caused by *Aspergillus* spp., as these can cause pressure on the sciatic nerves. If the kidneys appear abnormal, histological examination is

recommended, but as a general rule bacteriological examination is unrewarding.

To remove the kidneys use rat-tooth forceps to take hold of the connective tissue just cranial to the adrenal glands. Lift gently and use the scalpel to free the kidneys from the pelvis along with the adrenal glands and gonads. As with the removal of the lungs, this procedure requires practice. Place the kidneys on a board and cut transversely at several points. If any discolouration or other abnormality is seen, place material in fixative (see Appendix 8.3). In the smaller species it is possible to include gonads and adrenal glands along with the kidneys in a single histological section.

20.   To commence examination of the alimentary tract, open the oesophagus and crop using a pair of scissors. Check the mucosa for necrotic or proliferative lesions. Conditions such as avian pox, hypovitaminosis A and trichomoniasis (see Figure 8.14) may all appear very similar or, indeed, may be present simultaneously. In cases of candidiasis, lesions are usually more obvious in the crop, rather than the oesophagus, with the mucosa having a greyish, floccular appearance. Take swabs from any abnormal mucosa and examine for *Candida* spp. by Gram-stained smear and by culture onto blood agar and Sabouraud's medium. If the bird is freshly dead take a mucosal scraping, mix with a few drops of normal saline and examine microscopically by the 'hanging drop' technique for *Trichomonas* spp. Under a medium power lens (x20) and with the condenser racked down, the organisms will be seen swimming around rapidly. The parasites die soon after the death of the host, whereupon they become very difficult to see; therefore, care should be taken in reporting negative results. When examining budgerigars it is also necessary to consider idiopathic

Figure 8.14: The mucosal surface of the oesophagus of this budgerigar is showing advanced lesions of trichomoniasis.

oesophageal necrosis (Keymer, 1961). Although the gross lesions resemble those of chronic trichomoniasis, the aetiology is obscure and there is no confirmatory test.

Cut through the oesophagus just distal to the crop. Holding on to the gizzard, gently pull on the intestines and, as far as possible, cut the intestinal loops free but leave the duodenal loop and pancreas intact. Cut the duodenum immediately where it emerges from the gizzard and remove the proventriculus and gizzard for examination. Place the greater curvature of the proventriculus and gizzard on the PM board and, with a sharp knife or scalpel, make a longitudinal incision starting with the gizzard and extending forward to the proventriculus. Note the size of each organ, the contents and the condition of the mucosa. Although most psittacine species have a well developed muscular gizzard, in lories and lorikeets, which feed on soft fruit and nectar, the gizzard is a simple thin-walled structure and this should not, therefore, be regarded as an abnormality. However, if such birds are incorrectly fed, impaction of the gizzard with fibrous debris readily occurs.

In cases of psittacine proventricular dilatation syndrome (PPDS) (also known as macaw wasting syndrome or psittacine neuropathic gastric dilatation) the proventriculus may be distended with large quantities of undigested seed (see Figure 8.3). In some cases, undigested food is present within the crop, gizzard or intestines (Woerpel et al, 1984; Mannl et al, 1986). The aetiology of this condition is currently obscure, but a diagnosis can be confirmed on histological examination of a range of tissues, which must include the proventriculus, gizzard and brain.

In small psittacine species, particularly budgerigars, check the proventriculus for signs of megabacteriosis (Baker, 1992). In these cases there is usually excess mucus, often blood stained. The condition is readily diagnosed by taking a mucosal scraping with a scalpel blade and making a smear for Gram stain. Examine microscopically using a high power lens (x40 or x100). The organisms appear as very large Gram-positive

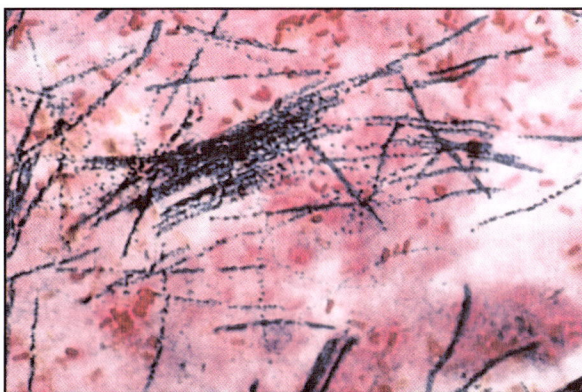

Figure 8.15: Photomicrograph showing clumps of megabacteria in a mucosal scraping from a budgerigar's proventriculus Gram stain.

filamentous bacilli, often in parallel clumps (see Figure 8.15).

Check the gizzard contents for foreign bodies. Larger psittacine species sometimes ingest items such as splinters of wood or pieces of wire. These may lead to ulceration or perforation of the gizzard and subsequent peritonitis. Ingestion of galvanised wire may also cause a syndrome known as 'new wire disease' (see Chapter 2). This is believed to be principally due to zinc toxicity. Confirmation is by analysis of liver, or preferably pancreas, for zinc concentration (Howard, 1992) (see Toxicological Examination).

Examine the gizzard muscle for lesions. In budgerigars suffering from so-called *Leucocytozoon* sp. infection the muscle may appear extremely pale, almost like ground glass. Histological examination will reveal megaloschizonts in the muscle (Simpson, 1991). Before placing proventriculus or gizzard into fixative for histological examination, briefly rinse the mucosa under a cold tap to remove as much grit as possible.

Examine the duodenum and pancreas. If the duodenum is dilated or inflamed, sear a small area in the upper part of the loop. Take a sample with a Pasteur pipette for bacterial culture and make a smear for Gram stain. If large numbers of *Clostridia* spp. are present, culture the contents anaerobically on blood agar. Examine duodenal contents by the 'hanging drop' method for *Giardia* spp. Although rarely diagnosed, this protozoal infection is capable of causing heavy losses in budgerigars (Panigrahy et al, 1978).

Avoiding the seared area, cut transversely across the loop and place the lower part, together with the pancreas, into fixative for histological examination.

The pancreas is composed of two main lobes, one either side of the duodenum, and if either appears abnormal, eg. shrunken, distorted or with haemorrhages, it should be examined histologically. Pancreatic lesions may be seen in conditions such as zinc toxicity (Reece et al, 1986) and PMV infection in parakeets (Uyttebroek et al, 1991; Simpson, 1993). Although diabetes mellitus has been described in psittacines, the role of the pancreas in these cases is uncertain. Affected birds show hepatic fibrosis and lipidosis but no pancreas pathology. Therefore, there would appear to be no case for examining pancreas histologically when trying to confirm a diagnosis of diabetes in a psittacine (Altman and Kirmayer, 1976).

Examine the remainder of the intestines, checking for helminth and protozoan infections. Although both coccidiosis and cryptosporidiosis are apparently uncommon in psittacines, cryptosporidiosis, at least, is probably underdiagnosed. Cryptosporidia have been shown to cause severe enteritis in species such as lovebirds (Belton and Powell, 1987). Mucosal scrapings may be stained by Giemsa and examined under a high power (x100) objective, where they appear as tiny, spherical bodies, little larger than bacteria. Alternatively, a section of intestine may be placed in fixative for histological examination. To check for coccidiosis make a wet preparation of a mucosal scraping on a microscope slide and examine using a x20 or x40 objective.

Although cestodes are uncommon parasites of psittacines, the nematode *Ascaridia platyceri* is commonly seen in first year birds, especially Rosella Parakeets. Heavy infection will often lead to death due to impaction of the intestine (see Figure 8.16). Capillaria or hairworm infections may be overlooked because of the small size of the worms, but they, or their characteristic eggs, will be revealed by routine examination of wet preparations of intestinal contents (see Chapter17).

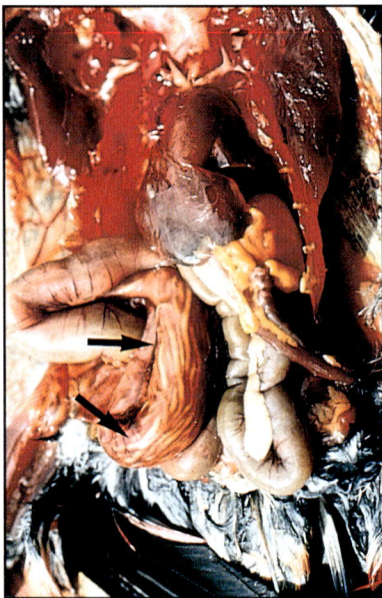

Figure 8.16: Severe infections with Ascaridia platyceri can cause impaction of the intestine, particularly in young birds. The case illustrated is a Rosella Parakeet.

The rectum should be checked for evidence of impaction. The author has seen cases in cockatiels where the rectum was impacted with sand caused by the bird eating sandpaper from the cage floor. Examine the cloaca and check for polyps or papillomata. These are most commonly seen in New World species, such as Amazons. In most cases they can be diagnosed on gross appearance, but if in doubt, excise the lesion and examine it histologically. The bursa of Fabricius, which lies dorsal to the cloaca, should be well developed in young birds, but in some conditions, eg. psittacine beak and feather disease (PBFD), it may be vestigial. In cases of PBFD it is sometimes possible to demonstrate the causal virus by electron microscopic examination of the bursa and, if still present, thymic tissue.

Irrespective of the appearance of the intestines it is wise routinely to culture intestinal contents for the presence of *Salmonella* spp. Either take a cloacal swab and inoculate into selenite F medium or, preferably, sear the rectum wall and sample using a Pasteur pipette.

21.   Check the brachial and sciatic plexi and the sciatic nerves. If the bird has been exhibiting abnormal locomotor signs, particularly of one limb, consider histological examination of the appropriate nerves. Place a straight section of nerve on a piece of Whatman filter paper, leave it for a few minutes and then carefully slip the filter paper plus nerve into fixative. The nerve will remain adherent to the paper and will be fixed in a straight length. This permits the cutting of good longitudinal sections, which is almost impossible if the nerve is simply dropped into fixative, as it then tends to curl or twist.

Remove the skin over the skull and examine for evidence of traumatic injuries. Beware of attributing too much significance to areas of haemorrhage into the cancellous bone of the cranium, as in most cases this is an agonal artefact. As a routine the skull should be opened and the brain examined for obvious lesions, such as intracranial or submeningeal haemorrhages. The simplest way of doing this is to place the skull normal way up on a PM board and hold it with the beak towards the hand with the finger and thumb in the orbits. Insert the point of a knife vertically into the midline just caudal to the eyes. Keep the point of the blade pressed into the PM board and then bring the blade down caudally in a 90° arc. The brain will be split cleanly into left and right halves. This technique is also suitable for obtaining brain for virological examination, eg. PMV. In this case put brain plus small portions of lung and trachea into a sterile bijou and submit for virological examination. If intestine is also submitted this should be put into a separate pot to minimise bacterial contamination of the other tissues.

Where birds have been showing neurological signs, and particularly in cases of suspected PPDS, it is important to examine the brain histologically. Whilst it is possible to use halves of brain obtained as described earlier, it is generally preferable to fix the whole brain. This is best done with the brain *in situ*, as it is difficult to remove fresh brain without damaging it. Trim away all excess tissue from the cranium and cut the skull transversely just caudal to the orbits (if brain is also required for virus culture it is possible to use the anterior portion of the optic lobes for this purpose, plus a small portion of spinal cord). Place the cranium in fixative and, after several days, carefully cut away the bone using bone shears and remove the brain.

22.   Check the nasal and infraorbital sinuses. Fungal infection of the nasal sinuses by organisms such as *Rhizopus* spp. or *Aspergillus* spp. is occasionally seen, particularly in hand-reared young birds, and may lead to distortion of the beak. Because it is impossible to collect uncontaminated samples from the sinuses, any cultural examinations are of doubtful value. However, histological examination is useful. Tissues need to be decalcified after fixation and should be stained by

periodic acid Schiff or Grocott in order to demonstrate any fungal hyphae.

23.   Finally, check all the major limb joints. Long slender nematodes are occasionally found in psittacines' leg joints. In most cases these are *Pelecitus* sp., and although the worms produce microfilariae, they are normally of little significance. If a joint appears swollen it is worth attempting bacteriological culture. Sear the joint capsule and aspirate a sample using a Pasteur pipette. In cases of articular gout, large deposits of urate crystals are often found in the knee, hock and foot joints. The identity of the urates may be confirmed by the murexide test (see Table 8.1).

TOXICOLOGICAL EXAMINATION

Occasionally, it is necessary to consider carrying out toxicological examination, eg. where birds have been exposed to herbicides, insecticides, etc. In such cases there are seldom specific lesions. As a general rule collect as much liver, kidney and stomach contents as possible and wrap these separately in aluminium foil before placing them in sample pots or polythene bags. If organophosphate or carbamate insecticide poisoning is suspected then, in addition to the above samples, remove the brain for analysis for cholinesterase activity. Store the samples in a deep freeze until they can be sent for analysis. Analysis for organic compounds can be very expensive.

If there is a possibility that agricultural pesticides are involved, the case should be discussed with the nearest VI Centre and with the Wildlife Officer of the Agriculture Development Advisory Service (ADAS). Such cases may be eligible for examination under the Wildlife Incident Investigation Scheme run by the Ministry of Agriculture, Fisheries and Food (MAFF). However, this is not a diagnostic service and although analysis is carried out free of charge, the results may not be available for several months.

In cases of suspected heavy metal poisoning, eg. lead, take samples of liver and kidney. If zinc poisoning is suspected, collect pancreas and liver. The samples should be placed in disposable plastic universal pots and held at -20°C until they can be sent for analysis. Take particular care not to contaminate your samples by using instruments which have been in contact with objects such as lead pipes or galvanised surfaces.

Birds which have died due to exposure to polytetrafluoroethylene fumes (PTFE, 'Teflon') as a result of overheated 'non-stick' pans, show intense bright red discolouration of the tissues, especially the lungs (Blandford *et al*, 1985). Unfortunately, no analytical confirmation for this as a cause of death is currently available.

Confirmed cases of death due to the ingestion of poisonous plants are extremely uncommon, but where such a case is suspected, stomach contents as well as liver and kidney should be collected. Hold the samples at -20°C and check with your laboratory to see if analysis is possible.

Table 8.1. Some diseases of psittacine birds: a *post-mortem* guide to diagnosis.

Causal agent or disease	Major sampling sites	Tests required
Fungal infections		
Aspergillus spp., *Rhizopus* spp.	Trachea, air sacs, lungs.	Wet prep: lactophenol cotton blue. Culture on Sabouraud's medium. Histology.
Candida spp.	Oesophagus, crop, proventriculus.	Mucosal scrape: Gram stain or 'Diff Quik'. Culture on blood agar and Sabouraud's medium.
Trichophyton spp.	Skin.	Histology. Microscopy on KOH preparation.
Bacterial diseases		
Megabacteria sp.	Proventriculus.	Mucosal scraping: Gram stain. Histology.
Mycobacterium avium	Spleen, liver, intestines (lesions occur in any organ).	Lesion smear: ZN stain. Histology. Culture (specialist laboratory).

Table 8.1. Continued.

Causal agent or disease	Major sampling sites	Tests required
Salmonella spp.	Liver, intestines, peritoneal granulomata.	Culture: MacConkey agar, selenite F and subculture onto brilliant green agar.
Yersinia pseudotuberculosis	Liver, spleen, lungs.	Culture onto blood agar.
Escherichia coli	Heart blood, liver.	Culture on blood agar and MacConkey agar.
Chlamydial infections		
Chlamydia psittaci	Spleen (liver).	Spleen smear: MZN stain. Spleen: ELISA test. Spleen: PCR test (**no transport medium**).
	Eyes, nares.	Swab: PCR test (**no transport medium**).
Viral diseases		
Pacheco's parrot disease	Liver.	Histology. Virus isolation: tissue culture.
Paramyxovirus (serotypes 1, 2, 3 and 5)	Brain, lungs, trachea, pancreas, intestines.	Virus isolation: egg inoculation. Histology on pancreas. Serology on recovered and/or in-contact birds.
Poxvirus	Skin lesions: eyelid, face, feet; mucosal lesions in pharynx.	Lesion (**without transport medium**): electron microscopy. Histology
Reovirus	Liver.	Tissue culture. Histology.
Psittacine beak and feather disease	Plucked developing feathers; thymus, bursa of Fabricius, blood.	Histology: feather follicles. Lymphoid tissue: electron microscopy. Feather follicles (pulp) and/or blood: PCR test.
Budgerigar fledgling disease (polyomavirus)	Liver, spleen, kidney.	Histology. Electron microscopy. PCR test.
Inclusion body hepatitis (adenovirus)	Liver.	Histology. Electron microscopy.
Parasitic diseases		
Ascaridia platyceri	Intestines.	Gross visual examination, low power microscopy.
Capillaria spp.	Intestines.	Microscopy on contents.
Cnemidocoptes spp.	Skin (of face or legs).	Skin scrape: microscopy on KOH or oil cleared sample. Histology.

Table 8.1. Continued.

Causal agent or disease	Major sampling sites	Tests required
Coccidiosis	Intestines.	Mucosal scrape: direct microscopy. Histology.
Cryptosporidium spp.	Intestines.	Mucosal scrape: Giemsa stain. Histology.
Giardia spp.	Duodenum.	Intestinal contents: 'hanging drop', low power microscopy.
Leucocytozoon sp. (so-called)	Skeletal muscles, heart; (gizzard in budgerigars).	Histology.
Microsporidium spp.	Kidney, liver, duodenum.	Histology.
Pelecitus sp.	Leg joints, body cavities.	Direct visual examination, low power microscopy.
Sarcocystis spp.	Skeletal muscles, heart.	Histology.
Sternostoma spp.	Air sacs, trachea.	Direct microscopy.
Metabolic diseases		
Hypovitaminosis A	Salivary glands, tongue, liver.	Histology: salivary glands, tongue. Vitamin A analysis on liver.
Visceral gout	Kidney, liver, heart.	Kidney: histology.
Articular gout	Joint cavities, tendon sheaths.	Urates: Murexide test*.
Fatty liver syndrome	Liver.	Histology.
Toxic disorders		
Lead	Kidney, liver.	Analysis.
Cadmium	Kidney, liver.	Analysis.
Zinc	Liver, pancreas.	Liver, pancreas: analysis. Histology on pancreas.
Organophosphorus pesticides (OPs)	Liver, ingested food, brain.	Liver, food: analysis. Brain: acetylcholinesterase estimation.
Most pesticides (except OPs)	Liver, ingested food (body fat for organochlorines).	Analysis.
Aflatoxin	Liver, kidney, pancreas.	Histology. (Analysis of feed if available.)
Neoplastic diseases	All systems.	Histology.

Table 8.1. Continued.

Causal agent or disease	Major sampling sites	Tests required
Conditions of unknown aetiology Psittacine proventricular dilatation syndrome (macaw wasting syndrome)	Proventriculus, gizzard, brain, coeliac plexus, adrenal glands.	Histology.

* Mix a spot of suspect material with a drop of nitric acid on a white porcelain dish. Evaporate carefully over a flame. Cool and then add a drop of ammonia. A reddish purple colour indicates the presence of uric acid. (Minsky and Petrak, 1982)

REFERENCES

Altman R and Kirmayer A (1976) Diabetes mellitus in the avian species. *Journal of the American Animal Hospital Association* **12**, 531.

Ashton WLG, Randall CJ, Dagless MD and Eaton TM (1984) Suspected reovirus-associated hepatitis in parrots. *Veterinary Record* **114**, 476.

Baker JR (1992) Megabacteriosis in exhibition budgerigars. *Veterinary Record* **131**, 12.

Belton DJ and Powell IB (1987) Cryptosporidiosis in lovebirds (*Agapornis* sp.). *New Zealand Veterinary Journal* **35**, 15.

Blandford TB, Seaman PJ, Hughes R, Pattison MJ and Wilderspin MP (1975) A case of polytetrafluoroethylene poisoning in cockatiels accompanied by polymer fume fever in the owner. *Veterinary Record* **96**, 175.

Borst JHA and Zwart P (1973) Sarcosporidiosis in Psittaciformes. *Zeitschrift fur Parasitenkunde* **42**, 293.

Howard BR (1992) Health risks of housing small psittacines in galvanised wire mesh cages. *Journal of the American Veterinary Medical Association* **200**, 1667.

Keymer IF (1961) Post-mortem examinations of pet birds. *Modern Veterinary Practice* **42**, 35.

Mann LA, Gerlach H and Leipold R (1986) Neuropathic gastric dilatation in Psittaciformes. *Avian Diseases* **31**, 214.

Martin HT, Early JL and Bridger JC (1979) The isolation of a herpesvirus from psittacine birds. *Veterinary Record* **105**, 256.

Minsky L and Petrak ML (1982) Metabolic and miscellaneous conditions. In: *Diseases of Cage and Aviary Birds*. 2nd Edn. Ed ML Petrak. Lea and Febiger, Philadelphia.

Pacheco G and Bier O (1930) Epizootic chez les perroquets du Bresil. Relations avec le psittacose. *Comptes Rendus de la Societe de Biologie* **105**, 109.

Panigrahy B, Elissalde G, Grumbles L and Hall C (1978) Giardia infection in parakeets. *Avian Diseases* **22**, 815.

Phalen DN, Wilson VG and Graham DL (1993) Avian polyomavirus biology and its clinical applications. *Proceedings of the Association of Avian Veterinarians European Conference, Utrecht, 1993*. AAV, Lake Worth.

Reece RL, Dickson DB and Burrows PJ (1986) Zinc toxicity (new wire disease) in aviary birds. *Australian Veterinary Journal* **63**, 199.

Scott PW (1994) Psittacine polyomavirus in Britain. *Veterinary Record* **135**, 168.

Simpson VR (1991) Leucocytozoon-like infection in parakeets, budgerigars and a common buzzard. *Veterinary Record* **129**, 30.

Simpson VR (1993) Suspected paramyxovirus 3 infection associated with pancreatitis and nervous signs in *Neophema* parakeets. *Veterinary Record* **132**, 554.

Uyttebroek E, Ducatelle R and Alexander DJ (1991) Steatorrhoea and pancreatic lesions in Neophema parrots with paramyxovirus serotype 3 infection. *Vlaams Diergeneeskunde Tijdschrifd* **60**, 55.

Wallach JD and Flieg BS (1969) Nutritional secondary hyperparathyroidism in captive birds. *Journal of the American Veterinary Medical Association* **155**, 1046.

Woerpel RW, Rosskopf WT and Hughes E (1984) Proventricular dilatation and wasting syndrome: myenteric ganglioneuritis and encephalomyelitis of psittacines: an update. *Proceedings of the International Conference on Avian Medicine 1984*. ICAV, Toronto.

Zwart P, Schreurs WHP and Dorrestein GM (1979) Vitamin A deficiency in parrots. *Sonderdruck aus Verhandlungsbericht des XXI Internationalen Symposiums über die Erkrankungen der Zootiere, Mulhouse*. Akademic-Verlag, Berlin.

Appendix 8.1. Standard *Post-Mortem* 'Prompt' Sheet.

Date of Post Mortem:	**Case Ref. Number:** ....
Ring/Microchip Number:	**Bodyweight:** ....

Plumage and external features
    Eyes
    Nares
    Feet
    Skin
    Cloaca (external)	

Subcutaneous tissues	

Musculo-skeletal system
    Long bones
    Joints	

Thyroid and parathyroid
Thymus
 	
Alimentary tract
    Oesophagus
    Crop
    Proventriculus and gizzard
    Small intestine
    Pancreas
    Large intestine
    Bursa of Fabricius and cloaca	

Liver Spleen	

Kidneys
    Gonads
    Adrenals	

Sinuses Trachea **Lungs** Air sacs	
Nervous system	

CONCLUSION:

Appendix 8.2. Basic Equipment, Stains and Media.

Equipment

Rubber gloves, PM gown, safety cabinet (Class 1), 'sharps' pot, detergent, sink with hot and cold water supply.

10% buffered formal saline, 70% alcohol, normal saline, 10% KOH.

Supply of disposable plastic pots, including 5ml (bijou), 30ml (universal) and 300ml (honeypot), cotton wool swabs (preferably 'Ear, Nose and Throat', wire stemmed), Pasteur pipettes (sterile), rubber teat, microscope slides and cover slips, small quantity of plasticine (for 'hanging drop' technique), freezer packs, absorbent packing materials, polythene bags (various sizes), felt tip pen, diamond marker pen, Bunsen burner (or spirit burner), searing spatula, filter paper.

Post-mortem board, dissection pins or nails, claw hammer. Scalpel with disposable blades, PM knife, scissors (large and small, pointed, straight), tissue forceps (large - rat-tooth; small - fine point), bone shears.

Scales (accurate to 1g), compound microscope with x10, x20, x40 and x100 objectives.

Stains	**Reagents required**
Gram	Crystal violet (0.5%), Lugol's iodine, acetone (pure), carbol fuchsin (dilute).
Ziehl-Neelsen	Carbol fuchsin (concentrated), acid alcohol (3%), methylene blue or malachite green (1%).
Modified Ziehl-Neelsen	Carbol fuchsin (dilute), acetic acid (0.5%), methylene blue or malachite green (1%).
Giemsa	As supplied. Phosphate buffer pH7.2.
Lactophenol cotton blue	As supplied.
'Diff Quick' or 'Hemacolor'	As supplied.
Culture Media (to include)	Sheep blood agar (5%), MacConkey agar, Brilliant green agar, Selenite F liquid medium, Sabouraud's medium (or malt extract agar).

Appendix 8.3. Notes on Collection, Handling, Packaging and Posting of Samples.

General

- Work cleanly: sample major organs before opening alimentary tract.
- Avoid unnecessary handling of tissues.
- Use forceps, not fingers, to transfer tissues to containers.

Bacteriological Examination

- Collection of samples for inoculation of culture media requires the use of either a platinum wire (straight or loop), a disposable plastic loop, a cotton wool swab or a disposable glass Pasteur pipette plus a rubber bulb. The Pasteur pipette has the following advantages:
  - It can be inserted accurately into a lesion or organ, and provides a visible sample.
  - The sharp, snapped off tip will easily penetrate all tissues, including fibrous lesions, joint capsules, etc.
  - The end can be heated and then drawn thinner, enabling even the smallest site to be accurately sampled.
- Where on-site cultural facilities do not exist, tissue samples should be posted promptly to a diagnostic laboratory. An alternative is to take samples from tissues using swabs. The sampling site is lightly seared with a hot spatula and a small swab is inserted into the tissue. If the tissue has a tough capsule, first cut this with a hot scalpel blade. Ear, nose and throat (ENT) swabs with wire stems are useful, especially for sampling smaller organs.
- When an organism is isolated but cannot be identified, consider posting the isolate to a diagnostic laboratory for further identification (see notes on postage and packing of pathological specimens).

Virological Examination

- Virology laboratories differ in their requirements regarding the use of VTM (some laboratories prefer to receive samples without transport medium). Contact your laboratory before submitting samples.
- Try to collect fresh, uncontaminated samples and hold them at 4°C until they can be posted. Do not deep freeze.
- Samples to be examined by transmission electron microscopy, eg. suspected poxvirus lesions, should be sent in dry containers, without transport medium.

Examination for *Chlamydia psittaci*

- For PCR test send tissue, including spleen, in new, sterile containers. Do not use transport medium. Avoid faecal contamination.
- For ELISA or cultural examination use CTM. The indicator must be red - if it has turned yellow the medium should be discarded.

Histological Examination

- Handle tissues with care; do not crush.
- Cut cleanly using a sharp knife or scalpel. Do not use scissors.
- Many samples submitted for histological examination are too thick and are in insufficient fixative. This results in autolysis. Therefore:
  - Cut tissue samples no more than 4mm thick.
  - Place samples in **at least** 10 times their volume of fixative.
- Use 10% buffered formal saline (BFS) as fixative for all routine samples.
- Use 70% alcohol rather than 10% BFS if you wish to preserve urate deposits. In this case clearly state your requirements on the submission form. (In practice the presence of urate deposits and tophi are normally recognisable in formalin fixed sections, eg. in nephrotic kidneys.)
- For electron microscopy on ultra thin sections, fix very small samples, about 2mm^3, in 3% glutaraldehyde.

Examination for Parasites

- Ectoparasites and helminths may be preserved in 70% ethyl alcohol or 10% BFS.
- Blood films should be rapidly air dried and briefly fixed in pure methanol.

Packaging and Posting

- All sample containers must be properly sealed and identified.
- Sufficient absorbent material must be present to soak up any fluid which might leak from the specimen.
- Where samples are submitted in fluid, eg. histology specimens, the risk of physical damage to the specimen is reduced if the pots are almost full of fluid.
- Specimens, surrounded in absorbent material, must be sealed in a leak proof container, eg. a polythene bag, and then packed in a box.
- The letter/form submitted with the samples should be included in a separate, sealed, polythene bag.
- When submitting fresh tissues for bacteriology or virology, pack the samples in an insulated container together with an ice pack.
- Parcels should be sent by first class post and must be clearly marked 'Pathological Specimens - Handle with Care'.
- The name and address of the sender should be clearly written on the outside of the package.

Useful Addresses

Central Veterinary Laboratory, Woodham Lane, New Haw, Addlestone, Surrey KT15 3NB.

Lasswade Veterinary Laboratory, Bush Estate, Penicuik, Midlothian EH26 OSA.

Vetgen Europe, PO Box 60, Winchester, Hampshire SO23 7LS.

Parasitic Worms Division, Department of Zoology and/or Department of Entomology, Natural History Museum, Cromwell Road, London SW7 5BD.

CHAPTER NINE

Nursing the Sick Bird

Brian H Coles

INTRODUCTION

Admitting a sick bird to the veterinary surgery for intensive care has many advantages and few disadvantages.

Advantages of Hospitalisation

● The bird is under the direct observation of the veterinary surgeon and his/her experienced staff and its condition can be monitored daily, if not hourly. The bird's bodyweight, and food and water intake can be recorded accurately.

● The bird receives regular therapy if necessary.

● Immediate action can be taken if the bird's condition deteriorates.

● The veterinary surgeon has time to think about the case, to carry out any necessary laboratory tests etc. and to reconsider the original diagnosis.

● The bird can be kept in a controlled microclimate under optimum conditions for its recovery.

● Birds are by nature usually members of a flock; the sight of other hospitalised birds often has a beneficial psychological effect.

● Many owners are totally unable to medicate their birds or give them supplementary feeding.

Disadvantages of Hospitalisation

● The bird is in unfamiliar surroundings with an unfamiliar routine. This may increase stress and the bird may be less willing to eat.

● There may be a strong bond between the owner and the bird: this is broken and may increase stress.

● The owner is often prepared to give the bird 24 hours a day tender loving care, but against this an overanxious owner may cause more stress to an already sick bird.

● There is a risk of infection to other in-patients and to members of staff.

Factors to be considered when hospitalising birds are listed under the various headings in order of their importance.

HANDLING AND RESTRAINT

Proper examination or treatment cannot be carried out without first handling the sick bird. First class, gentle, but firm handling keeps stress to a minimum, whereas prolonged struggling may lead to heat stroke and/or a fractured bone. It is always wise to warn an anxious owner of a very sick bird that it may collapse in the process of handling and restraint. Doors and windows must always be kept shut and extractor fans turned off. Staff should always knock before entering the examination room in case a bird is loose.

Psittacines vary considerably in size from budgerigars to very large macaws. They all bite and the severity of the bite depends on their size, but it is the timorous operator who is bitten. The veterinary surgeon should know exactly what he/she wishes to do, and then confidently and quickly carry this out. Often, large macaws and some umbrella cockatoos can be the gentlest of birds, whilst many budgerigars resent handling. Skill in handling is only acquired by practice and an understanding of the bird's likely reaction. African Greys often growl if threatened and many parrots screech. Amazons will sometimes roll on their back defending themselves with their beak and claws. Cockatoos, if frightened, may erect their feathers. However, many very sick birds or juvenile birds can be handled with minimum restraint.

Whichever method of capture is employed, rather than trying to catch a bird through the door of the cage, it is always better, if possible, to remove the bottom of the cage. The cage is then tipped onto its side, the perches, and feeding and drinking bowls, etc. having been first removed. The operator then approaches the bird through the larger opening of the cage bottom.

Use of a Torch

For the uninitiated, one of the easiest methods of capturing birds is to work in a completely dark room with the only light source being a small hand torch which has been covered with either a red or, preferably, a blue filter. A piece of sweet wrapping can be used in an emergency. Birds do not see well in red or blue light. The light level should be kept low and just sufficient for the operator to see the bird. Sometimes, the bird can literally be picked off its perch. The initial approach with the hand should be slow so as not to create any air movement and then, at the last moment, the bird should be grabbed quickly round its neck (or head) and, almost instantaneously, the hands closed around the wings and body. This method works particularly well with smaller species of psittacines.

Use of Gloves

The time honoured method favoured by many inexperienced people when capturing psittacines is to protect their hands with a pair of strong gloves. It is probably the only safe method when handling a known bad tempered large macaw or cockatoo. Custom-made armoured gloves can be acquired, but a strong pair of welders' gloves purchased from the local industrial clothing store is much less expensive and quite adequate. However, gloves are cumbersome, particularly when handling smaller birds, as the operator loses his/her sense of touch. Also, they are difficult to keep clean and to sterilise, and they may act as fomites for the transmission of disease. Many intelligent psittacines soon learn to know what the sight of a pair of gloves means, and they become alarmed. Some people favour the use of a surgical glove to handle cockatiels; the bird will bite the glove rather than the operator's skin.

Use of a Towel

When used skilfully this is a much less stressful method of capturing a bird. The author favours a small sized hand towel (approximately 600mm x 470mm) or dish cloth. Many hand towels are too large and should be cut down to a suitable size. A towel draped over the hand with the fingers spread out acts as a visual barrier. The hand is slowly advanced towards the bird in order to trap it in one area of the cage and, at the last moment, a grab is made for the bird's neck so as to control the head and neck. Because the psittacine neck contains 12 cervical vertebrae (compared with seven in mammals) and is comparatively long and mobile, there is little chance of throttling the bird during the capture procedure. Most importantly, the powerful beak can be quickly controlled by keeping the thumb and forefinger over the temporomandibular joints of the bird's head (see Figure 9.1).

If the veterinary practice is treating birds regularly, a supply of suitable sized towels should be kept for catching purposes. They should be washed after each use, preferably in a washing machine rather than hand washed. Alternatively, owners should be encouraged to bring their own small hand towel.

Some veterinary surgeons use disposable paper towels. The same towel should not be used more than once, even for the same patient, because of the possibility of transferring infection.

Use of a Net

If a bird escapes into the room the use of a padded net is often helpful. However, all the lights should be

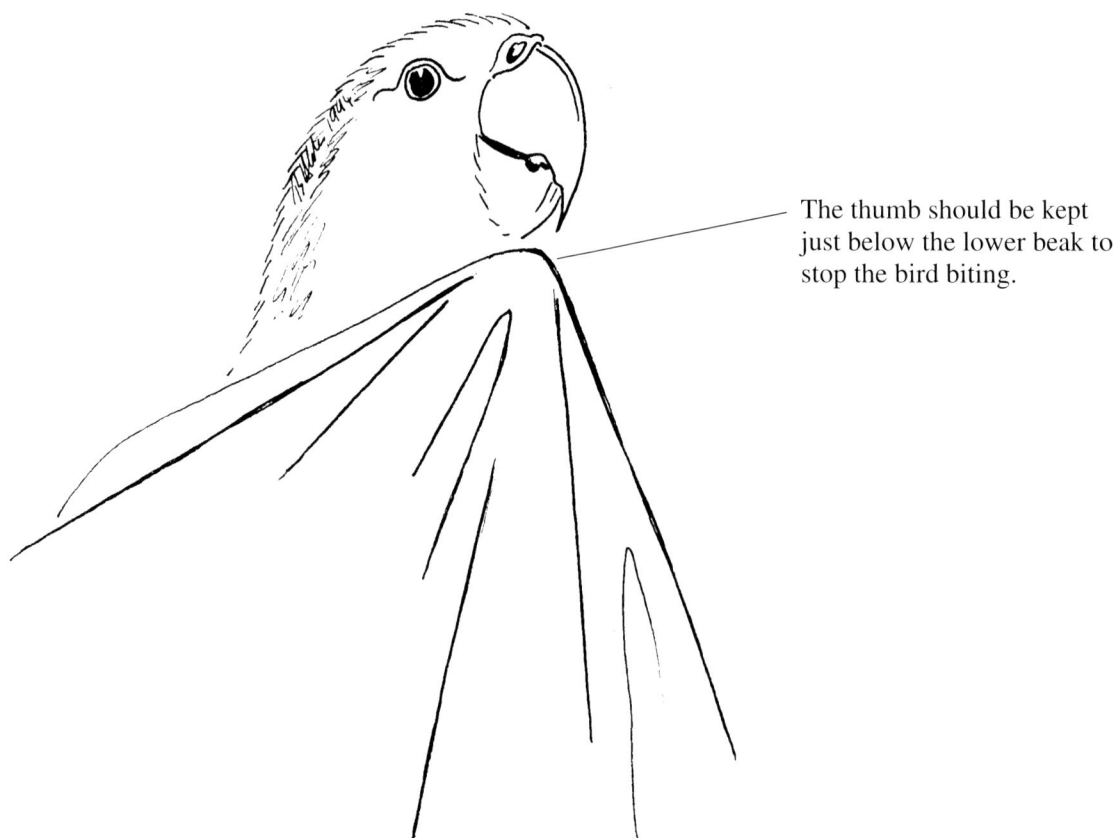

The thumb should be kept just below the lower beak to stop the bird biting.

Figure 9.1: Method of holding a psittacine by using a towel.

turned off first, and a red or blue torch only used as the light source.

Calming a Frightened Bird

Once the bird has been captured it should be talked to in a calm voice. Scratching or tickling the feathers on the back and sides of the head (but not the top of the head), which simulates the natural allopreening of another bird, will also help. Using this technique a confident and experienced handler can pick up and calm a strange bird with the minimum of restraint. Nurses should practise these methods for calming a bird and leave the painful procedures to the veterinary surgeon so that the bird does not resent handling by the nurses.

Note: If an owner offers to help and the bird or owner is injured in the process, the veterinary surgeon is ultimately responsible. It is better not to remove a bird directly from an owner as this may upset the owner-bird bond.

What to Do if Bitten and the Bird Hangs On

- Keep calm.
- Try blowing into the bird's face.
- Try gently squeezing the top of the bird's head as a predator would do.
- Use whelping forceps to open the beak very gently and release the finger or hand. Careless use of these forceps may damage the bird's beak.

FIRST AID

Only the most urgent problems which require immediate attention are dealt with in this section. Other less urgent problems, such as crop impaction in neonates and eggbinding, are dealt with elsewhere in this manual.

Haemorrhage

Common causes of haemorrhage include:
- Damaged claws due to being caught in the cage or frost bite.
- Bleeding from the wing tip due to self-trauma or from a damaged growing pin feather.
- Haemorrhage from a lacerated tongue or from a beak crushed by another psittacine.
- Lacerated skin wounds.
- Bleeding from an ulcerated neoplasm which may be situated in the vent.
- Conures may be presented with epistaxis or gastrointestinal haemorrhage. This is a well recognised syndrome and these birds require injections of calcium, vitamin K_1 and antibiotics.

Many of the above causes of haemorrhage can be dealt with using simple remedies, but occasionally general anaesthesia and suturing may be required. Some simple procedures to control haemorrhage

include:
- Use a silver nitrate pencil.
- Apply ferric chloride.
- Apply one or two crystals of potassium permanganate with a swab. This stains feathering and operator, but is effective.
- Apply talc, wound powder or even flour.
- Apply sustained pressure with cotton wool or a sterile swab.
- Apply Superglue. This only works if the site is relatively dry.

Bleeding pin feathers which are 'in the blood' and growing are a common problem. The damaged feather should be isolated from the surrounding matted feathers by cleaning, and the remainder of the damaged feather shaft gently pulled out, taking care to hold the surrounding skin and not to damage the papilla of the growing feather. A silver nitrate pencil or one of the methods mentioned earlier should be used. Suturing may be required, especially if primary wing feathers are involved.

Fractures

Sometimes, these need splinting temporarily to prevent a simple fracture becoming compound and until radiography and a proper evaluation can be carried out. However, unless a wing is trailing badly, when a temporary figure of eight bandage using Vetrap (see Figure 14.3) or similar material can be used, it is often wiser to do nothing at this stage. Many psittacines are notorious for trying to remove their dressings (see Figure 14.4), although, as with other animals, this is usually because the bandage is uncomfortable. Birds will often support themselves quite well on one leg, thus taking the weight off the injured side.

Applying Splints

In nearly all cases this is best carried out under general anaesthesia or deep narcosis since struggling can easily make the situation worse. Various materials can be used, but there is a danger that large birds may injure themselves by chewing aluminium or hard plastic splints. Probably, the best combination is well padded casting tape, eg. Hexcelite, protected by a Vetrap bandage. Sticky tapes can be used, but the adhesive tends to damage feathering. Splints are best padded using sheet (5-15mm thick) expanded polyurethane foam rather than cotton wool. This material can be bought cheaply from market stalls selling upholsterers' materials.

For small birds, such as budgerigars up to cockatiel size, a tape splint reinforced with cocktail sticks, paper clips, microbiological swab sticks or feather quills from larger birds can be used (see Figure 9.2). A precariously hanging fractured beak can be temporarily stabilised with Superglue, Araldite or Technovit.

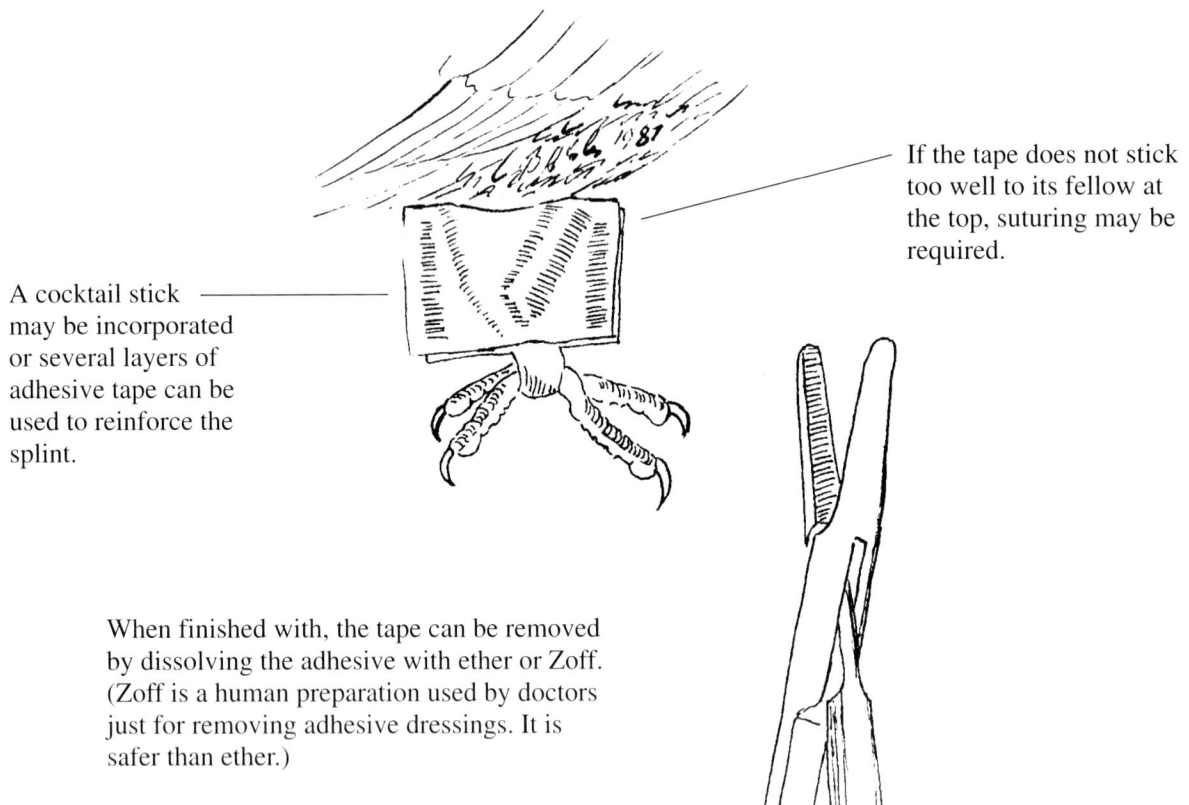

A cocktail stick may be incorporated or several layers of adhesive tape can be used to reinforce the splint.

If the tape does not stick too well to its fellow at the top, suturing may be required.

When finished with, the tape can be removed by dissolving the adhesive with ether or Zoff. (Zoff is a human preparation used by doctors just for removing adhesive dressings. It is safer than ether.)

Figure 9.2: The Altman type of tape splint for quickly stabilising fractures of small birds up to cockatiel in size.

Seizures

These are dealt with in more detail elsewhere (see Chapter 19). However, a bird may be presented actually in a fit (status epilepticus) or in a concussed state having flown into a window.

In African Greys, fits are commonly, but not always, due to hypocalcaemia. Consequently, it is always advisable to give an injection of calcium. Taking a blood sample first should be considered. This will enable the diagnosis to be confirmed retrospectively and will facilitate subsequent monitoring and any dietary changes or supplementation. Calcium gluconate 10% (0.5-2ml/kg) or calcium borogluconate 20% (0.25-1ml/kg) can be given by **slow** intravenous injection - preferably using the right jugular vein (see Figure 9.3) - or intramuscularly. Epilepsy is occasionally seen in all psittacine species. Diazepam (1-1.5mg/kg) can be given intramuscularly.

Birds Presented in a Collapsed or Semi-Comatose State

It is often wiser to try and improve a bird's clinical condition before undertaking a thorough clinical examination, blood sampling, radiography, etc. The following first aid measures should be considered:

● Most severely ill birds are dehydrated. This is considered in more detail later (see Fluid Replacement Therapy). Lactated Ringer's (Hartmann's) solution or normal saline solution (10ml/kg), warmed to 38°C, should be given by **slow** intravenous injection (over a period of 3-5minutes). If a vein cannot be found, the injection can be given subcutaneously over the dorsum between the scapulae. The intraosseus route via the distal end of the ulna or the proximal end of the tibiotarsus and injecting into the medullary cavity can be used.

● The use of non-steroidal anti-inflammatory drugs may help. Ketoprofen, flunixin and carprofen can all be used at a dose rate of 2mg/kg. However, they are contraindicated where nephropathy, hypotension or dehydration is suspected, and they may occasionally cause vomiting. Carprofen probably has the least side effects. Corticosteroids do not function so well as in mammals.

● An injection of either trimethoprim/sulphadoxine (0.2ml/kg i/m) or clavulanic acid/amoxycillin (0.2ml/kg i/m) can be given. Both these drugs are effective against many of the bacterial infections found in birds.

● The bird should be placed in an incubator or hospital cage at 26-30°C with the relative humidity raised to 50%.

● If the bird is severely dyspnoeic it should be placed in an oxygen-enriched atmosphere.

Birds Which Stop Breathing Whilst the Initial Consultation and Examination is Taking Place

These birds should be quickly intubated and ventilated. If no suitably sized endotracheal tube is available, a

The forefinger is placed under the neck in order to stabilise the mobile jugular vein.

The head is in an anaesthetic mask or controlled by an assistant.

The needle is bent to make access to the vein easier.

Wetting of the feathers is usually sufficient.

The jugular vein is very mobile and may be found anywhere over the right side of the neck.

The thumb raises the vein as near to the thoracic inlet as possible.

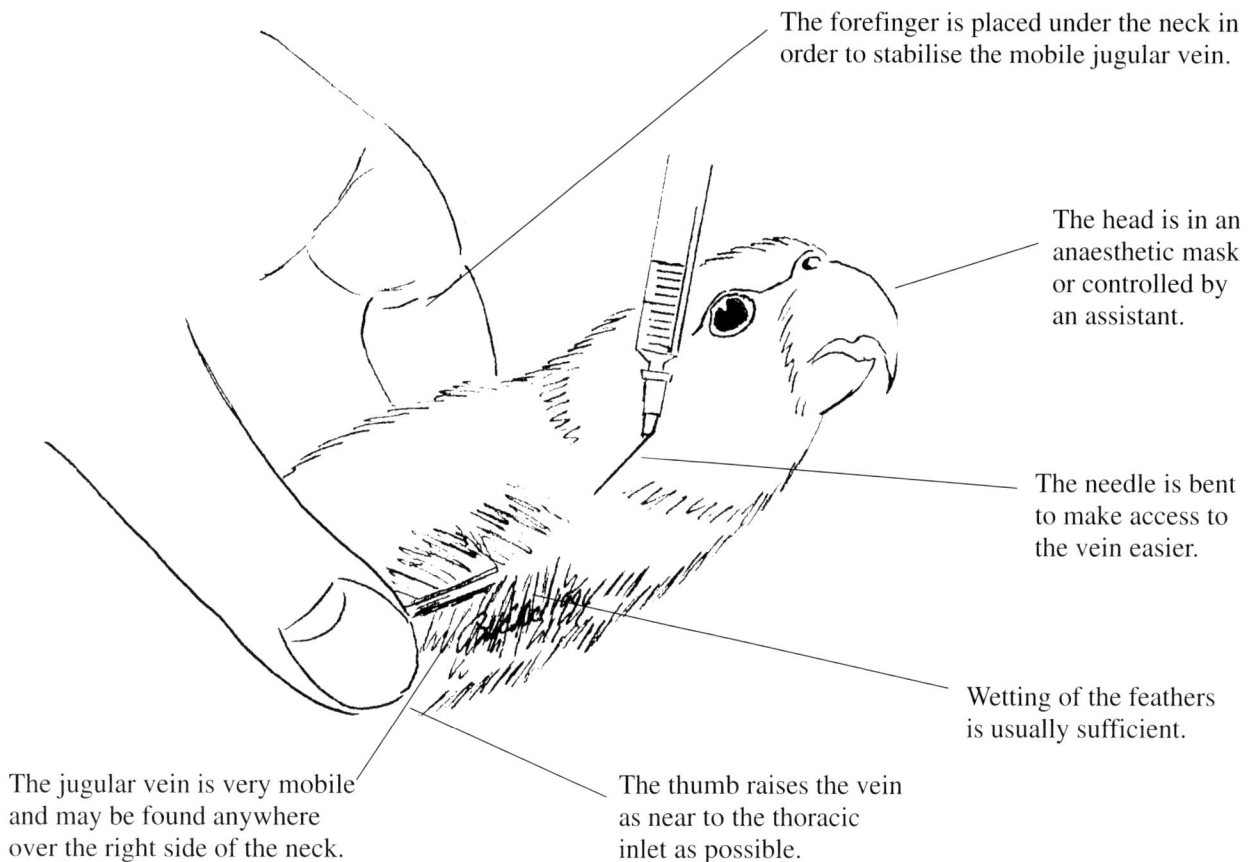

Figure 9.3: Method of using the right jugular vein to give an intravenous injection.

cut-off canine urinary catheter can be used. This is connected with sticky tape to an oxygen supply, preferably a 'T' piece anaesthetic or equivalent system. Intermittent (every five seconds) positive pressure ventilation of the respiratory system can be tried, but care must be taken not to overinflate. Doxapram can be dropped onto the tongue or given by slow intravenous injection (0.05ml for a budgerigar or lovebird - dilute the primary solution; 0.5ml for an Amazon or African Grey; 1-1.5ml for a macaw or large cockatoo).

Foreign Bodies in the Upper Alimentary Canal

Owners are notoriously careless with regard to what objects they let their birds play with. Larger psittacines can chew up and splinter wood, metal (aluminium) and bone (particularly poultry bones). They may also play with cotton or wool attached to needles and, sometimes, with large cactus house plants. Foreign bodies can become lodged in the tongue, oesophagus or crop. Metal or plastic crop feeding tubes can be lost down the upper alimentary canal unless care is taken.

In many cases it will be known what type of foreign body has been swallowed. The bird may be presented trying to regurgitate the offending object. This can sometimes be palpated in the oesophagus or crop, or demonstrated on radiography.

In some cases, eg. a swallowed metal or plastic catheter, the foreign body can be gently 'milked' out of the oesophagus with the bird conscious. However, general anaesthesia or deep narcosis and forceps removal is easier. Ingluviotomy (crop surgery) may be required in some cases. If the foreign body has been present for some time, ulceration and fistula of the crop may occur.

SPECIAL NUTRITIONAL REQUIREMENTS OF SICK BIRDS

After attending to the most obvious emergencies, the next most important factor to consider is the bird's nutritional state. This should be assessed in conjunction with the bird's state of hydration.

Many ill psittacines are presented to the veterinary surgeon having been anorexic for several days and many are on the verge of collapse due to hypoglycaemia and/or dehydration. The majority of these birds need force feeding with a crop tube (see later). Many sick birds may continue to eat whilst they are ill, but their nutritional intake may be insufficient. These birds also need crop tube feeding. One cannot rely on an owner's observations of food intake. A seed container may be filled with dehusked seed or a bird may pick up seed and drop the vast majority onto the floor without dehusking. Some psittacines are fed almost entirely on inappropriate food, such as potato chips.

Sick birds which are hospitalised need supplementing with an easily digestible diet which is low in protein, but high in vitamins, energy and minerals. The Milupa range of baby foods with added supplements will meet these requirements. They contain approximately 422Kcal/100g, added vitamins and some minerals, and are relatively low in protein (12.9%). Milupa Fruit Salad and Milupa with Tropical Fruit are the most suitable. To this mixture can be added Avipro (Vetark) or Enterodex (Vetex). These are probiotics which may help stabilise the gastrointestinal flora. Other medications can be added to the mix and, later, nutritional supplements, such as ACE-High (Vetark), MVS-30 or Nutrobal (Vetark), which will provide vitamins and minerals, can replace the probiotics. Bottled pureed baby foods can be used, but keeping these products fresh may be a problem. The veterinary practice could produce its own pureed and strained vegetables or cooked pulses, to which vitamin and mineral supplements, as already mentioned, are added.

Once the bird regains its strength, it may start feeding by itself. Enquiries should be made as to what the bird is usually fed, and this should always be tried first. Sometimes, clients will bring a supply of the bird's regular food. This should be accepted and used. Even sunflower seeds may vary and this may affect the bird. The diet should not be changed radically during the convalescence period and any changes should be made slowly. Birds are very much creatures of habit and slow to adapt to change. This needs careful manipulation and patience.

The following therapeutic agents can be added to the semi-liquid diet used for crop tube feeding:
● Methylycellulose or ispaghula husk may help to slow down the gastrointestinal transit time so allowing more efficient absorption of nutrients (Dimski, 1991). Also, this product may absorb enterotoxins and therefore help to restore normal functioning of the alimentary canal.
● Lactulose is another product which may help to absorb enterotoxins, but it has a mild laxative action (Harrison, 1986).
● Harrison (1992) considered that extract of Echinacea (extracted from all parts of the plant *Echinacea augusticolia*), which can be purchased in health food shops, helps to stimulate the immune system and is useful in many chronic conditions.

The bird must be weighed daily to make sure that it is at least maintaining and preferably gaining in weight. Fresh water (without additives) must always be available and be contained in a receptacle that is not so large that the bird is tempted to bathe in it. This receptacle must be cleaned regularly and not placed below the perches where it might become contaminated with faeces or urates.

THE TECHNIQUE OF CROP TUBING OR GAVAGING PSITTACINES

The best method of force feeding psittacines is to use a suitable metal catheter which can be fitted onto the end of a hypodermic syringe. Special curved catheters with a bulbous distal end long enough to reach into the crop are marketed for the purpose. However, any suitable diameter metal tube which is long enough, such as a Spreull's needle or a metal bitch catheter, will suffice, even though these may not be curved. Laboratory suppliers produce stainless steel tubes (straight and curved) for dosing laboratory animals and these are quite suitable. A plastic or rubber tube can be used, but there is a danger of these being bitten through and a length of tube becoming lodged in the oesophagus or crop. This problem can to some extent be overcome by using a suitable gag (see Figure 9.4).

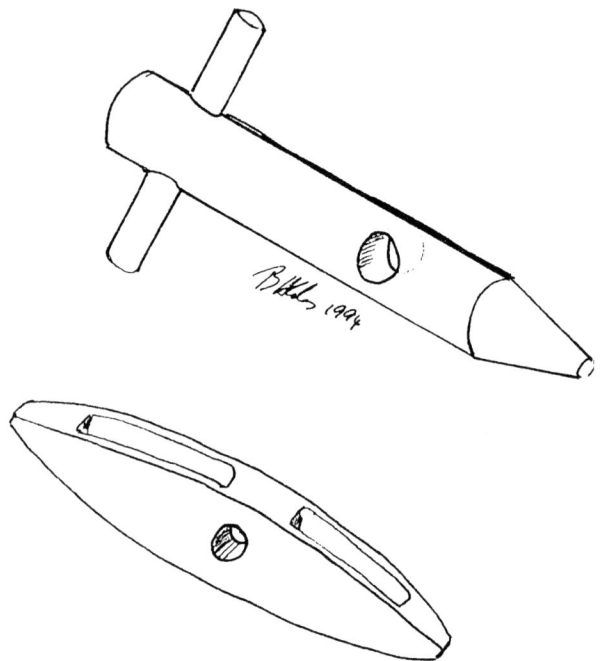

Figure 9.4: Two types of gag - the top one of perspex rod, the bottom one of moulded plastic - suitable for crop tubing psittacines when using a soft tube.

Before passing the tube it is necessary to estimate the length required to reach the crop. The neck should be extended by gripping the bird's head with forefinger and thumb and the tube, having been first lightly lubricated with liquid paraffin or K.Y. lubricating jelly, is then gently inserted into the side of the mouth between the commisure of the upper and lower beaks. The tube is directed towards the roof of the oropharynx and then down the posterior mucous membrane of the oesophagus. By inserting the tube in this

Figure 9.5: Schematic diagram to illustrate the method of crop tubing a psittacine using a rigid metal tube.

manner there is little likelihood of it entering the glottis, especially if the largest diameter tube consistent with the size of the bird is used (see Figure 9.5).

Even if only a small quantity of food enters the airway, at best an aspiration pneumonia will occur or, at worst, the bird will immediately succumb to asphyxia. Cough reflexes are poorly developed in birds. Care should be taken that the fingers are not clasped too tightly around the bird's neck, otherwise liquid food may reflux up the oesophagus. If this happens, feeding should be stopped immediately and the bird allowed to swallow. For this reason it is safer to give small quantities rather than try to fill the crop.

However, the entrance to the oesophagus in birds is relatively large because of the underdevelopment of the avian larynx. In nestlings the tube can be seen descending the oesophagus, and in feathered adult birds it can be felt as it transcends the oesophagus. A skilled operator can tube quite a large bird single handed, but the less experienced operator will require additional help.

In the author's opinion, safe amounts that can be given by crop tubing are as follows:

Budgerigars and lovebirds	1ml
Cockatiels	2ml
African Greys and Amazons	7ml
Cockatoos	10ml
Large macaws	15ml

Although an experienced person may be able to give two or even three times these quantities, it is wiser to stick to smaller amounts. Birds can be refed every two hours if necessary. Meticulous cleanliness and faultless hygiene must be maintained when crop tubing. The tubes, catheters and utensils must be washed and sterilised between each feed. Milton (Proctor and

Gamble), as used for human baby feeding bottles, teats, etc., is suitable and safe for this purpose.

FLUID REPLACEMENT THERAPY

Birds are inherently prone to becoming dehydrated very quickly. Many seed eaters obtain much of their water requirements from metabolised fat from the seed. The large internal surface area of the air sacs, combined with normal high body temperatures which may be even higher in sick birds, lead to high insensible water loss. However, most birds overcome these problems by needing very little water to excrete the waste products of the gastrointestinal and urinary tracts. Providing they remain healthy, many semi-desert species, eg. budgerigars, can go for relatively long periods without water. However, birds originating from tropical rain forest, eg. Amazons, need a constant fluid intake. Taking into account all the above factors, an anorexic or sick bird with a reduced appetite will very soon become dehydrated. Dehydration is more difficult to recognise in birds than in mammals so it is safer to assume that all sick birds are dehydrated and will benefit from fluid replacement therapy.

Choice of Fluid
Normal saline can be used but it is probably better to use Lactated Ringer's (Hartmann's) solution. The lactate acts as a precursor to bicarbonate formation, which helps to counteract the metabolic acidosis present in many dehydrated and anorexic birds.

How Much Fluid to Give
Fluid deficit, which may range from 4-10%, ie. 40-100ml/kg bodyweight, should be replaced over a 48 hour period, half in the first 24 hours and half in the

second 24 hours. In addition, the bird should be given its normal daily maintenance fluid requirement - 50ml/kg bodyweight (Bond, 1993; Huff, 1993) and 50-300ml/kg (Quesenberry and Hillyer, 1994) have been suggested as being the normal daily fluid requirement for birds. The author favours a figure of 75ml/kg bodyweight daily. Up to 50% more fluid per day may be given to very young birds.

On this basis 105ml/kg bodyweight daily for the first two days would be appropriate assuming 6% fluid deficit (60ml/kg), ie. 30ml/kg, on each of the first two days plus 75ml/kg maintenance requirement. The fluid deficit should be reassessed after two days by carrying out a packed cell volume (PCV) estimation.

The maximum amounts which should be given by i/v bolus (usually the basilic or jugular vein) or by the intraosseus route are:

Budgerigar	1ml
Cockatiel	2ml
African Grey or Amazon	8ml
Large macaw or cockatoo	12 - 14ml

This can be repeated 3-4 hours later and the same quantities can be given subcutaneously. Adding hyaluronidase to subcutaneous fluid helps dispersal and absorption. The remainder of the fluid can be given orally. All fluids should be given near body temperature (39°C).

Continuous drip fluids can be given to medium and larger birds using a 20G, 2.5cm catheter with a tape butterfly fed into the jugular vein and sutured or glued to the skin, and protected with a loose collar of Vetrap self-adhesive orthopaedic bandage. Bond (1993) used a capped-off, heparinised indwelling jugular catheter for all psittacines more than 60g bodyweight. Forbes (personal communication) uses a 21G, 2.5cm Jelco needle which is capped-off and sutured into the basilic vein. Both these routes allow repeated instant access and are accompanied by low stress levels.

A preferred method to continuous intravenous administration is to use a 20-22G needle inserted into the intraosseus medullary cavity of the distal ulna or the proximal tibiotarsus. The end of the needle and the drip line can be protected with Vetrap. Bond (1993) only used the intraosseus route in birds weighing less than 60g and in which the veins were generally too small to catheterise. If used as a continuous drip, a pump is often required to facilitate administration.

CHOICE OF CAGES FOR HOSPITALISATION

A number of specialised custom-made hospital cages for birds are available. The companies selling these products are listed at the end of this section. All these cages are designed to produce the optimum microenvironment for the sick bird. They are all fitted with electronically regulated humidity and heating systems. There is usually a supplemental oxygen inlet and many of these cages have a nebuliser fitted for administering drugs via aerosol. All these cages are easily cleaned with smooth interior surfaces and a clear glass or plexiglass door.

If a custom-made avian hospital cage is not available, many stainless steel or plastic hospital cages as used for dogs and cats can be adapted. A sheet of clear perspex or thick (5mm) rigid polythene sheet, which is cheaper and tougher, can be bolted to the cage door to produce an enclosed environment. Two or three holes of approximately 1cm diameter should be drilled at the top and bottom of this transparent sheet to allow for air circulation. Heating can be provided by a heat pad on the floor or an electric light bulb. In both cases the heater and its electrical lead need to be protected by a metal 'cage' and, if an electric light bulb is used, this needs to be supported free of adjacent surfaces and with its light shielded. Food and water containers can be attached to the door, or small, heavy ceramic bowls can be free standing on the floor. An oxygen pipeline can be fed in through the transparent sheet. A thermometer should be attached inside the door near the roof of the cage and a rheostat electrical switch should be incorporated in the electrical lead, or, ideally, the heating element can be wired to a Honeywell thermostat. A perch will make the bird more at ease and, particularly for long tailed species, it is important to keep the tail and wing tips from trailing on the floor so that the plumage does not become damaged or contaminated with droppings. Free standing perches can be made with a wide base which has been suitably weighted or stuck to the floor with a suction pad.

Alternatively, premature baby incubators surplus to hospital requirements are sometimes available and can be adapted. Their main disadvantage is that they have insufficient height for larger birds. For smaller birds, plastic plant propagators sold in many garden centres can be utilised. Another alternative is to use a glass aquarium with a wire mesh top, or to turn the aquarium on its side. However, although these are easy to keep clean, maintaining a suitable microenvironment within them is difficult. In all cases meticulous hygiene is of paramount importance.

Sick birds respond best to treatment if kept in a temperature of 26-30°C, which is uncomfortable for humans and other mammals. Ideally, the bird cages should be kept in a separate room where this required temperature can be maintained. In this situation birds can often be hospitalised in the cages in which they have been brought to the surgery However, a heated separate room may not be very practical, especially for only one or two birds. If this is the case, supplemental heating via a heat pad below the cage might help, particularly if the cage is almost entirely covered with a blanket, which, if wet, will increase the humidity. Care should be taken when using an infra-red lamp with a reflector to ensure that the whole cage is not subjected to the beam and that the bird does not become 'cooked'. Some heat lamps have been coated with Teflon to prevent them shattering. **NB.** The Teflon fumes produced can be toxic for birds.

Hospitalising birds in their own cage has the advantage that the familiar surroundings cause less stress. The cages are best kept on a shelf at or above human eye level where the bird will feel less threatened than if on the floor of the animal room. The sound of other animals, eg. barking or meowing, appears to worry psittacines much less than seeing the animals. Many psittacines will soon learn to mimic barking and miaowing. Many psittacines under natural conditions live in flocks, so the sight of other hospitalised birds, not necessarily of the same species (other than raptors), seems to have a beneficial psychological effect. **Care must be taken to avoid cross infection between hospitalised patients.**

The floors of the cages are probably best left clean of all bedding materials, eg. sawdust, wood shavings or sand, so that the character of the bird's droppings can be observed and clean specimens collected for laboratory examination. If any covering is used, commercial brown wrapping paper or biodegradable kitchen towelling is probably better than newspaper, although the bird may decide to rip up any paper.

The lights of the bird room are often best left on all night to encourage 24 hour period feeding.

Many parrots, eg. African Greys, Amazons and macaws, come from habitats of tropical rain forest where they are subjected to a tropical rainstorm most afternoons. In consequence, providing they are not too ill, their plumage often benefits from spraying with warm water once daily. This can be done with the fine spray from a household plant spray. The spray should not be held too close to the cage otherwise the bird becomes alarmed. The aim is to have a fine mist descending gently onto the bird so that the plumage becomes wet.

Suppliers of Hospital Cages

The AICV	Snyder M.F.G. Co.
RW and RM Gill	5500 East Pacific Place
Delaport Long Road	DENVER
Brampton en-le Morthen	Colorado 80222
ROTHERHAM	USA
South Yorkshire S66 9BJ	
Tel: 01709-548125	

Avtech Systems	Aquabrood
7955 Silverton Avenue	D & M Bird Farm
Suite 1217	P.O. BOX 191204
SAN DIEGO	SAN DIEGO
CA 92126	CA 92159
USA	USA

SURGICAL NURSING

The nurses should make sure that all hospitalised birds have a clean cloaca if they are passing abnormal fluid droppings or have cloacitis. Some birds will not leave wounds or sutures alone and the nurse should be aware of this possibility. A restraining collar may need to be fitted (see Figure 14.4). A bird with an oesophagotomy tube or an auxiliary airway tube inserted should have the tubes kept clean and unblocked. If splints have been applied to a leg or wing a careful watch should be made that the foot or wing tip does not become swollen. Birds should be kept on clean perches to prevent foot problems. Nurses should make a habit of examining the birds' droppings rather than just clearing them away. They should look for signs of blood, undigested seed or the occasional tapeworm segment (usually in imported birds), and note any changes in the normal colour or character of the droppings.

REFERENCES AND FURTHER READING

Bond MW (1993) Intravenous catheter therapy. In: *Proceedings of the Association of Avian Veterinarians Annual Conference 1993*. AAV, Lake Worth.

Coles BH (1984) Some considerations when nursing birds in veterinary premises. *Journal of Small Animal Practice* **25**, 275.

Coles BH (1985) *Avian Medicine and Surgery*. Blackwell Scientific Publications, Oxford.

Dimski DS (1991) Dietary fibre in small animal therapeutics. *Journal of the American Veterinary Medical Association* **199(9)**, 1142.

Harrison GJ (1986) Toxicology. In: *Clinical Avian Medicine and Surgery, including Aviculture*. Eds GJ Harrison and LR Harrison. WB Saunders, Philadelphia.

Harrison GJ (1992) Herbal immune stimulation. *Journal of the Association of Avian Veterinarians* **6(3)**, 144.

Huff DG (1993) Avian fluid therapy and nutritional therapeutics. *Seminars in Avian and Exotic Pet Medicine* **2(1)**, 13.

Quesenberry KE and Hillyer EV (1994) Supportive care and emergency therapy. In: *Avian Medicine: Principles and Application*. Eds BW Ritchie, GJ Harrison and LR Harrision. Wingers, Lake Worth.

CHAPTER TEN

Feather and Skin Problems

A Dermod Malley

BASIC EXAMINATION OF THE INTEGUMENTARY SYSTEM

Prior to clinical examination, the clinician should acquire a detailed history of the bird, following the procedure laid out in Chapter 4. Particular attention should be paid to the environment, nutrition, concurrent disease and sexual status of the bird, as well as its moulting and preening behaviour.

The clinical examination should follow the same protocol as if the bird was presented for any other reason. The quality of individual feathers should be assessed. Feather colour is best verified by reference to an authoritative, well-illustrated text, eg. Cooper and Forshaw (1977) or Alderton (1991). The barbules should interlock properly: separations and fret marks (see Figure 10.1) indicate possible nutritional problems. The retention of feather sheaths (see Figure 10.2) may not be a primary dermatological problem, as it may reflect other illnesses, eg. spinal disorders interfering with normal preening activities.

DIAGNOSTIC AIDS

Radiographs, laparoscopy, haematology and biochemical analysis may elucidate the causes of feather plucking or self-mutilation (see Chapter 22).

Sampling

Mature feathers can be transported without preservative and their examination may show parasites, structural deformities and colour changes. Immature feathers (in 'blood scape') should be transported in ethanol for DNA probe analysis or in neutral buffered formalin for histopathology. Glutaraldehyde is used as a preservative for thin section electron microscopy when cultures are not required. Samples for direct electron microscopy should not be preserved but should be submitted to the laboratory in a deep-frozen state; this method keeps open the option for the subsequent cultivation of microorganisms. The author uses biopsy skin punches of 4mm diameter, repairing the deficit by passing suture material (Supramid, Braun) through a hypodermic needle (without local anaesthesia) as described by Pavletic (1982). Proliferating lesions of

Figure 10.1: Feathers of an African Grey showing fret marks.

Figure 10.2: Rectrices of a macaw showing retained feather sheaths.

the cere and feet should be scraped gently with a scalpel blade to obtain samples for examination for ectoparasites, eg. *Cnemidocoptes* spp.

MOULTING

Moulting consists of the shedding and replacement of

plumage and the stratum corneum; at any one time a bird may have feathers derived from more than one moult (Cooper and Harrison, 1994). The development of a new feather is the natural instigation for the shedding of the older feather and is dependent on neurohumoral factors, regulated by the thyroid and gonads and triggered by an alteration in photoperiod, stresses and cessation of breeding activity. Humidity and heat promote moulting - psittacines require a relative humidity of 60% for an adequate moulting cycle (Krautwald, 1990).

Moulting generally occurs once a year, usually after breeding, but can occur twice and, in some species, eg. budgerigars, up to three times a year. Large psittacines may take up to two years to complete a full moult cycle, although powder down is shed continuously, especially from African Greys, cockatiels and cockatoos (Cooper and Harrison, 1994).

Moulted feathers should be replaced with normal feathers. However, a lack of normal plumage can be the cause as well as the result of disease. Regrowth is quick if the whole feather is pulled out, but is non-existent if the calamus has been broken and retained within the follicle.

Apterylae are normal featherless areas. They are found over the jugular furrows and on the brood patch which occurs on the belly and legs of some species of psittacines in the breeding season. In the latter the dermis becomes thickened and highly vascular, and feathers are lost in order to facilitate the transfer of body heat to the eggs.

Hypothyroidism can lead to symmetrical loss of feathers without pruritus. There is often delayed feather growth, feather anomalies and black tinting of the feather tip leading to a fringed, dull plumage (Krautwald, 1990). Diagnosis is made on a resting thyroxine blood level followed by stimulation with thyroid stimulating hormone (TSH) (0.25iu for small birds; 1iu for a macaw), retesting after six hours and comparing the blood levels (Hillyer, 1994). The clinician must ensure that the laboratory is equipped to do these tests on avian blood and can supply normal values for the species under consideration. Hypothyroidism can be treated with L-thyroxine (20mcg/kg p/o bid) (Cooper and Harrison, 1994).

Effect of Disease on Feather Replacement

Hepatopathies are often accompanied by plumage colour changes - grey to red (see Figure 10.3), dark brown to black, or green to black - feather loss on the abdomen, pruritus and dermatitis.

Renal disease can cause loss of feathers without pruritus, as well as retardation of the feather growth rate and dermatitis (Krautwald, 1990).

The presence of excessive numbers of 'pin feathers' may indicate normal 'recovery' from a recent moult. Affected areas of skin should be examined thoroughly and abnormal feathers subjected to further analysis. If

Figure 10.3: Hepatopathies are often accompanied by changes in the colour of feathers. In this case the feathers of a juvenile African Grey are pink instead of grey. Fret marks are also seen on some of the feathers. The colour and structure of the subsequent plumage was normal after appropriate changes were made to the diet.

feather plucking is suspected the clinician should follow the approach detailed in Chapter 11.

ECTOPARASITES

The clinician should be aware of the role that ectoparasites play in the transmission of disease (viral, bacterial or protozoal) in psittacines and search for these vectors at every opportunity. Clinical signs suggestive of ectoparasitism include restlessness, excessive and frantic preening, poor condition of the feathers (broken, rough or soiled), feather plucking, pruritus, marked irritation, bald patches and erythema (Greve, 1986; Krautwald, 1990). The occurrence of ectoparasites in caged psittacines is usually related to debilitation due to other causes, which must always be addressed. However, aviary birds may contract ectoparasites from wild birds and may be said to be exhibiting primary parasitic disease.

Ectoparasites that commonly infest psittacines include:

Flies
Louse flies (Hippoboscidae) do not cause disease, but irritate and can transmit pathogenic organisms, eg. *Haemoproteus* spp. (Keymer, 1982a), mites and lice (Philips, 1990).

Lice
Lice (see Figures 10.4, 10.5) feed on down feathers and lay their eggs on flight feathers. They are usually controlled by the host's own preening activity.

Ticks
Ixodidae (hard ticks) are ubiquitous and are known to secrete a toxin (Philips, 1990). There have been reports of aviary birds being found dead, with a tick bite, usually on the head, as the only clinical finding (see

Figure 10.4: *A louse (Order Mallophaga) on the vane of the flight feather of a Luteino Cockatiel.*

Figure 10.5: *The same parasite as in Figure 10.4 under greater magnification.*

Figures 10.6, 10.7) (Forbes and Simpson, 1993; Knott, 1993).

Feather Mites

Feather mites found on psittacines belong to many taxa, including *Protolichus* spp., *Dubinina* spp. and *Chiasmalges* spp. (Philips, 1993). Keymer (1982a) stated that feather mites are predominantly non-pathogenic, scavenging on feathers, skin scurf and lipids. They are known to have microhabitat preferences (Perez and Atyeo, 1984, cited by Philips, 1990).

Nest or Aviary Mites

Birds' nests contain many mites and insects which feed on nest litter and food remains. Other nidiculous invertebrates may climb onto birds accidentally. Some are genuinely parasitic.

The red or roost mite, *Dermanyssus gallinae*, is found most commonly. These parasites can cause anaemia in aviary birds. They are visible usually only at night. Investigation involves laying a white sheet cover on the floor of the aviary or cage (or wrapping one around the cage) overnight and examining for moving 'sand-like grains' the following morning. Treatment is by careful application of permethrin (Harker's

Figure 10.6: *Infestation of the head by a tick, Ixodes ricinus, lead to the death of this Golden-mantled Rosella. (Photo courtesy of Mrs CIF Knott)*

Figure 10.7: *The skin of the head of the bird in Figure 10.6 incised to show the haematoma caused by the tick bite. (Photo courtesy of Mrs CIF Knott)*

Louse Powder) or carbaryl and prevention of contact with sparrows or other wild birds. Mites can remain viable in nests in the absence of the hosts for up to 30 weeks (Philips, 1990).

Mites of the Family Macronyssidae, Sub-family Ornithonyssinae, can cause anaemia. *Ornithonyssus sylviarum*, the Northern fowl mite, lays eggs on host feathers and in the nest material.

Diptera

Mosquitoes can transmit poxvirus and cause painful bites and localised dermatitis on the featherless areas of the face of macaws or African Greys, whereas Simulidiae are thought to transmit leucocytozoon parasites. Treatment of both these groups involves the prevention of further attacks by the elimination of the flies' breeding sites.

Quill Mites
Krautwald (1990) considered quill mites to be rare in ornamental birds.

Skin Mites
The commonest skin mite found in psittacines is the genus *Cnemidocoptes*, which has its complete life cycle on the host. They form proliferative, honeycombed lesions (see Figure 10.8) on the feet and cere and around the base of the beak. The mites (see Figure 10.9) are demonstrated by means of skin scrapings cleared in 10% potassium hydroxide.

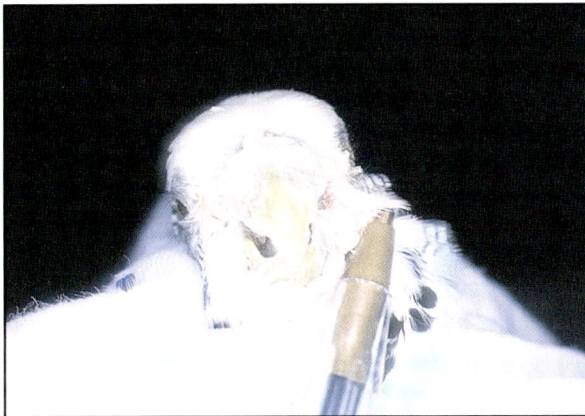

Figure 10.8: The honey-combed lesions of the rictus due to infestation with Cnemidocoptes pilae.

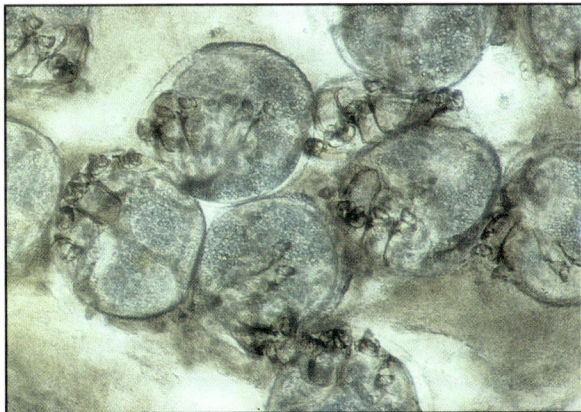

Figure 10.9: Photomicrograph of Cnemidocoptes pilae.

Treatment of Ectoparasites
Treatment requires great care because of the potential danger of pesticide toxicity to the bird. Topical applications should be used on the feathers to eliminate adult parasites; nests should be cleaned and treated every 2-3 weeks to eliminate free-living forms. In the case of lice, treatment must be repeated to eradicate nits (Cooper, 1985). Lice may act as shelter for moulting feather mites (Perez and Atyeo, 1984, cited by Philips, 1990). Products available include pyrethrin blended with piperonyl butoxide (Ridmite Powder, Johnson), high cis permethrin (Harker's Louse Powder) and cypermethrin (Dy-Sect, Deosan). Cypermethrin is diluted 1:200 and used as a spray, but care must be taken not to allow contact with the skin as some discomfort may occur. Ivermectin as a spray (0.5ml of 1% Ivomec Injection for Cattle in 1.1 litres of water) may be useful. Care should be taken not to exceed a total dose of ivermectin per bird of 200mcg/kg, although budgerigars have been shown to have a fair tolerance to external application of this product (Bishop, 1988).

The treatment of burrowing mites usually involves the use of ivermectin (200mcg/kg i/m, p/o or s/c, or by the spot-on technique, diluted 1:10 with propylene glycol and applied to the apteryla over the jugular furrow). There has been a report of a sarcoptid mite unresponsive to ivermectin in a macaw (Reavill *et al*, 1990).

ENDOPARASITES

Giardiasis has been confirmed as a cause of skin disease in cockatiels, especially if feather plucking (see Chapters 11 and 22). Affected birds appear to pluck the feathers over the abdomen, probably because of abdominal discomfort caused by *Giardia* spp. Chronic ingluvial trichomoniasis can cause feather loss over the crop in some affected birds.

BACTERIAL INFECTIONS

The psittacine skin is very resistant to infections due to the presence of bacteriostatic and mycostatic agents in the epidermal lipids and to the feather follicles being kept closed by the feathers lying flat against them. However, true folliculitis has been recorded in psittacines (Rosskopf *et al*, 1983) and may arise because of damage to a 'blood' or 'pin' feather after the previous feather has been moulted out. A feather base culture with antibiotic sensitivity is recommended - the affected feather is gently plucked out and a swab obtained from the follicle. Treatment should be maintained for at least three weeks.

Pododermatitis
Pododermatitis (bumblefoot) (see Figure 10.10) is fairly common in caged birds. The predisposing causes include arthritis, unsuitable perches, excessive trauma to the feet caused by obesity, puncture of the sole by foreign bodies, eg. sandpaper and dirt, and hypovitaminosis A. Microbial investigation is indicated, followed by surgical debridement and long-term use of antimicrobials. The clinician must also address the environmental, nutritional and behavioural factors involved.

'Septicaemic Alopecia'
Affected birds (see Figure 10.11) (usually solitary,

cage-bound African Greys) are presented as 'feather-pluckers', with dull plumage, feather loss and brittle feathers (Krautwald, 1990). Full clinical investigation frequently discloses involvement of bacteria such as *Chlamydia psittaci*. The excessive downy appearance of the breast of these birds may be attributed to the existence of chronic intracoelomic pain or malaise which the bird attempts to relieve by rubbing its beak over the affected area. Aviary birds may also be affected.

Figure 10.10: Bumblefoot in a budgerigar.

Figure 10.11: 'Septicaemic alopecia' in an African Grey.

Staphylococcal Infections

Staphylococcal infections are reported to be common in ornamental birds and are manifested by yellow vesicles and crusts which first develop under the wings and then spread to the plumage of the breast and abdomen (Krautwald, 1990). Clavanulate-potentiated amoxycillin (up to 100mg/kg p/o bid) is the author's preferred treatment.

Infected Skin Wounds

These are frequently encountered, especially on the sternal area of pet birds which crash land on their sternum because of improperly trimmed flight feathers and split the overlying skin (see Figure 10.12). Bacterial culture and sensitivity should be ascertained before

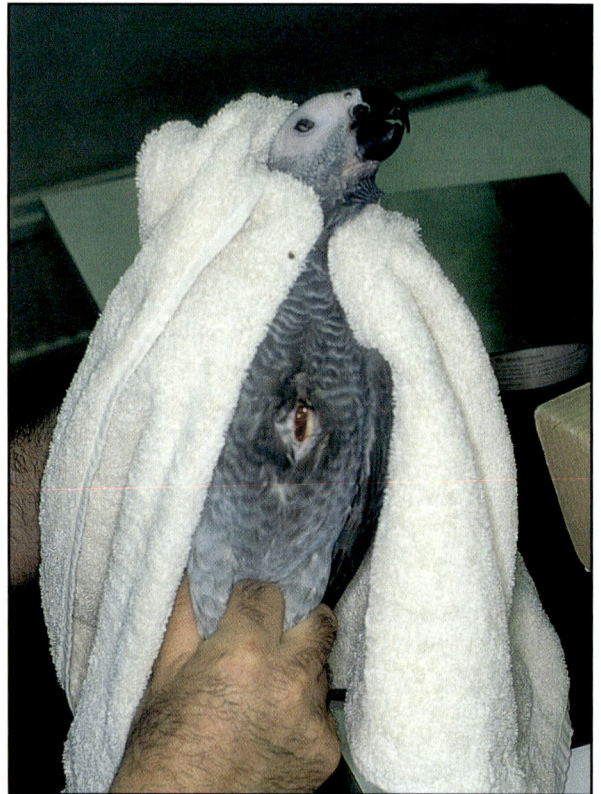

Figure 10.12: Sternal abrasion in an African Grey associated with improperly clipped wings.

antibiotic treatment and surgical repair are attempted.

Granulomatous lesions of the head, due to infection with *Mycobacterium tuberculosis*, have been reported in cockatoos (Eamens, 1981). The zoonotic potential of this infection must be considered by the clinician.

FUNGAL INFECTIONS

Where recalcitrant skin infections are encountered, especially in cases in which respiratory tract infection is also present, exfoliative cytology may show the presence of dermatophytes. Culture on Sabouraud's medium will confirm the diagnosis and treatment with an appropriate antimycotic agent should be initiated. Organisms encountered include: *Candida* spp., *Chrysosporium* spp., *Aspergillus* spp., *Malassezia* spp., *Microsporum* spp., *Helminthosporium* spp., *Malbranchea* spp, *Mucor* spp., *Rhizopus* spp., *Penicillium* spp. and *Trichophyton* spp. (Keymer, 1982b; Pass,1989; Krautwald, 1990; Dixit and Kushwaha, 1992; Andre, 1993; Tudor, 1983, cited by Cooper and Harrison, 1994).

The treatment of fungal dermatoses suggested by Cooper and Harrison (1994) included the use of STA (3g salicylic acid, 3g tannic acid and 100ml ethyl alcohol) applied twice weekly. Krautwald (1990) stated that enilconazole should be used at a dilution of 1:50 (1:100 for smaller species), but Forbes (personal communication) advises much stronger concentrations (1:10). The clinician must always investigate any predisposing disease, eg. hypovitaminosis A, when assessing dermatomycoses.

VIRAL INFECTIONS

There are several epitheliotrophic viruses that affect the psittacine integumentary system.

Avipox

Three species-specific antigenic strains of avipox occur in Psittaciformes - agapornis poxvirus, amazona poxvirus and budgerigar poxvirus (Gerlach, 1984). Clinical signs of cutaneous poxvirus infection are discrete nodular proliferations of the skin of the cere, eyelids (see Figure 10.13), tarsometatarsi and feet. These progress through papules, vesicles and pustules to scab formation. They are pruritic and prone to secondary infection. The clinician should consider the possibility of poxvirus infection when presented with slowly healing wounds (Cooper and Harrison, 1994).

Vectors may be involved, but transmission can also occur between individuals; from contaminated cages, food or water; via ingestion of contaminated food or drinking water; through inhalation of dust containing the virus; or by pecking (Clubb, 1986). Establishment of infection requires loss of integrity of the skin.

Diagnosis

Histological diagnosis involves the demonstration of ballooned epithelial cells with margination of nuclear chromatin and eosinophilic granular intracytoplasmic inclusions (Bollinger bodies). Cultural diagnosis requires isolation of the virus on chorioallantoic membranes of embryonated chicken eggs or fibroblast cell cultures of chicken embryos. The best source for recovery of avipoxvirus in psittacines appears to be from the feather quills (Gerlach, 1984).

Treatment

Effective treatment requires the removal of the virus lipid envelope using lipid solvents or dilute quaternary ammonium compounds. The author's preferred

Figure 10.13: Avipoxvirus infection in a Blue-fronted Amazon.

treatment is the topical application (by spraying) of a solution of 300mg tylosin and 150mg povidone-iodine in 100ml of sterile water. This is used as an ocular spray on affected birds. High doses of vitamin A (up to 125,000IU/kg i/m once a week), antibiotics and physical and nutritional supportive treatment are also recommended. Control of secondary bacterial and fungal infection is important.

Prevention

Commercial vaccines are available for use in other avian Orders, but are of little use in psittacines (Clubb, 1986). The use of quaternary ammonium compounds, eg. benzylkonium chloride, is recommended to disinfect affected premises.

Psittacine Beak and Feather Disease (PBFD) (see also Chapter 21)

PBFD (see Figure 10.14) is a fatal disease of major economic importance which has been reported in more than 35 species of psittacines: the causative agent is a circovirus (Latimer *et al*, 1991). However, the viruses involved in PBFD in different species of parrots are not necessarily identical (Graham, 1990) - this may be why lovebirds have been recorded as recovering from the disease (see Figures 10.15, 10.16, 10.17). The incubation period, although dose related, seems to be inversely proportional to the size of the bursa of

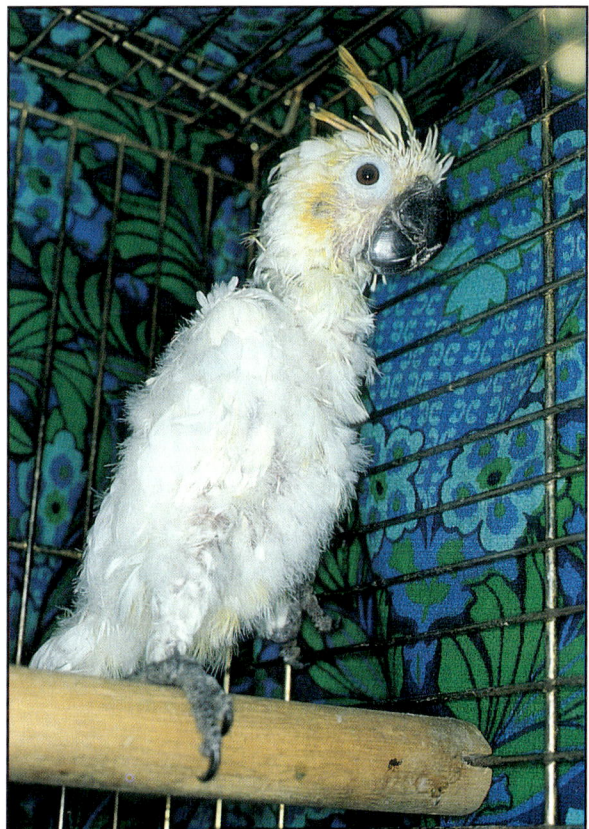

Figure 10.14: PBFD in a Sulphur-crested Cockatoo. Note the shiny beak (due to lack of powder down) and the badly formed contour feathers, particularly those of the crest.

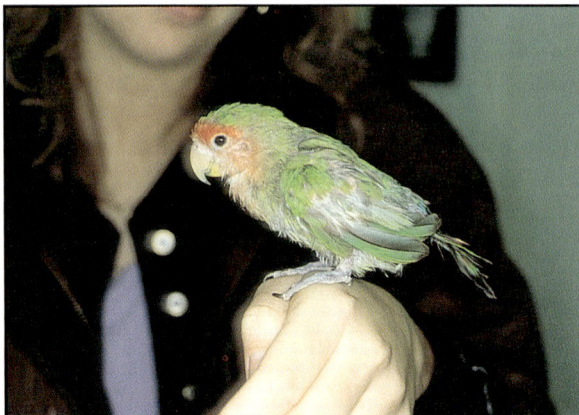

Figure 10.15: PBFD in a Masked Lovebird. The presence of the virus was confirmed by direct electron microscopy. The contour feathers, especially those of the tail and wing, are particularly badly affected.

Figure 10.16: PBFD in a Masked Lovebird. The bird in Figure 10.15 six months later. All contour feathers are now affected.

Figure 10.17: PBFD in a Masked Lovebird. The bird in Figures 10.15 and 10.16 after a further six months.

Fabricius at the time of infection. The virus may be carried by many birds without clinical signs for a long period after infection. Stress may induce an outbreak.

Clinical Signs

In general, the virus localises within feather follicles leading to feather dyscrasias (see Figure 10.14). However, in some young, intensively hand-reared chicks the immunosuppressive form is encountered without dermatological signs; the presenting signs depend on the nature and location of the secondary bacterial or mycotic infection. Viral infection causes premature atrophy of the thymus and bursa of Fabricius and suppression of the bone marrow, leading to an absolute neutropenia. Diagnosis of the immunosuppressive form of the disease is usually made on *post-mortem* examination, but the demonstration of panleucopenia in an unwell, hand-reared psittacine chick should suggest the existence of the disease.

Clinical signs and distribution of dermatological lesions depend on the stage of feather development at the time of infection and include haemorrhage, necrosis, fractures and bending or premature shedding of feathers (Latimer *et al*, 1991). Loss of feather pigment is sometimes observed, Vasa Parrots showing pathognomonic white feathers (Cooper *et al*, 1987; Andre, 1993). Persistence of a clot in the feather may also be seen but is not necessarily pathognomonic for this condition.

Beak and claw dyscrasias are discussed in Chapters 11 and 12 respectively. The beak pathology, together with the effects of immunosuppression, are the reasons for the fatal nature of this disease.

Diagnosis

Definitive diagnosis of the dermatological form is by histological examination of feather buds or follicles to demonstrate basophilic, intracytoplasmic or intranuclear inclusion bodies. Since PBFD can be diagnosed in plucked feathers preserved in neutral buffered 10% formalin, provided the feather epithelium (including the epidermal collar) and pulp are intact (Latimer *et al*, 1991), the requirement of a feather follicle biopsy for the detection of PBFD particles is debatable (although it is recommended to rule out polyomavirus, bacterial folliculitis or dermatophytosis).

Direct electron microscopical examination of a follicle biopsy of a deformed feather may provide a reliable diagnosis. A sharp biopsy punch may be used without general or local anaesthesia to obtain a suitable sample. This should be sent (without being fixed or preserved) to a laboratory experienced in the recognition of PBFD virus particles, eg. Central Veterinary Laboratory, Weybridge.

DNA probe diagnosis is available from Vetgen Europe on whole blood (collected initially in a capillary tube coated in EDTA) or on fresh feather pulp squeezed from abnormal feathers - both the whole blood and the fresh feather pulp should be preserved in ethanol (Vetgen Europe Information). The blood sample should be taken by venepuncture as the nail clip technique runs the risk of contaminating the sample with infected feather dust. All positive birds with normal plumage should be retested after 90 days to eliminate false positives (Dalhausen and Radabaugh, 1993). False-negative blood results (which arise due to the panleucopenia which accompanies the later stages of the disease) may be avoided by submitting feather pulp from obvious clinical cases in the same ethanol phial.

Transmission

Virus is shed in faeces and from infected epidermal tissue, including powder down, and in material from beak and claws. Nail clippers, burrs and files used for pedicures and beak trims must be disinfected with glutaraldehyde. Vertical transmission may be possible as can infection shortly after hatching by ingestion of regurgitated crop fluids from parent birds (Latimer *et al*, 1991). Many breeders practise hand rearing of chicks from hatching in an attempt to avoid horizontal transmission of the virus in crop fluids, but the benefits of this must be weighed against the dangers of rearing chicks devoid of 'maternal antibodies' which many workers consider are available in crop milk to parent-reared chicks.

Prevention

There is no vaccine currently available in the UK. Quaternary ammonium compounds and iodophors are the recommended disinfectants. Management procedures include culling infected birds, isolation of nestlings until over two years old and the use of segregation units (Graham, 1990). Prospective purchases should be blood tested and maintained in isolation until the results are known.

Treatment

The juvenile form (baby birds that show heteropenia) is usually very unrewarding to treat, but attempts to treat adults, especially lovebirds, may be successful. Treatment is supportive and includes probiotics and immunostimulants (vitamin A, levamisole and ivermectin). The use of autogenous vaccination gives variable results.

Papovaviruses

Papovaviruses cause persistent, latent infections that become acute or active following stresses (Ritchie *et al*, 1991a). Two types of papovaviruses affect psittacines: polyomavirus and papillomavirus.

● Polyomavirus (see also Chapter 21)

Many authors quote this virus as the cause of budgerigar fledgling disease and French moult. How-

Figure 10.18: *French moult in a nine-month-old budgerigar. (Photo courtesy of Mr TW Pennycott)*

ever, French moult (see Figure 10.18) is probably a multifactorial condition (Arnall, 1975; Taylor, 1982). Polyomavirus is an acute disease of chicks, with adult birds acting as chronically infected virus reservoirs (Ritchie *et al*, 1991b).

Clinical signs. Clinical signs depend on when the birds were infected. If birds are infected before two weeks of age they almost invariably die. *Post-mortem* findings include ascites, hepatomegaly and hydropericardium. Birds other than budgerigars seldom show clinical signs involving the integumentary system. Budgerigars infected after 15 days of age develop feather signs, including lack of production (retarded growth) of new flight and tail feathers (remiges and rectrices) in the juvenile plumage, lack of dorsal and ventral down feathers, and lack of filoplumes on the head and neck. Contour feathers grow more slowly than normal and lack barbs. The virus may be shed from gastrointestinal, renal and possibly reproductive tissues, as well as being present in feather dander (Ritchie *et al*, 1991b).

Histological diagnosis. Basophilic or amphophilic intranuclear inclusion bodies are seen in many tissues, including liver, spleen and renal glomeruli (Ritchie *et al*, 1991b).

DNA probe diagnosis (see earlier under PBFD). This may be performed on cloacal swabs or excrement and also on *post-mortem* tissues to demonstrate the presence of polyomavirus nucleic acid. A negative result on a cloacal swab or faecal sample shows only that the bird was not shedding at the time of testing. There is more chance of detecting the virus when the bird has been stressed (Dalhausen and Radabaugh, 1993).

Prevention. Birds found to be shedding the virus should be culled and the contaminated quarters (bird rooms, incubators, brooders) fumigated with formaldehyde gas.

Treatment. Currently, there is no treatment for this disease. Budgerigar breeding programmes should be interrupted for three months to allow adult birds to encounter the infectious agent and develop antibodies. Affected fledglings should be culled for fear of reintroducing the virus to the breeding flock (Scott, 1994).

● **Papillomavirus**
Papillomaviruses are associated with benign skin tumours (warts) (Ritchie *et al*, 1991a). They are non-enveloped, small, stable viruses containing double-stranded DNA.

Clinical signs. The disease is contracted through minor skin lesions. In African Greys the proliferative lesions are confined to the skin of the head (see Figure 10.19), including the palpebrae, the ricti and the skin contiguous with the lower beak. In Amazons the cloacal mucosa seems to the site of predilection. In macaws the lesions are commonly found in the buccal cavity. Epidermal biopsy for histological examination confirms the diagnosis of papillomavirus.

Figure 10.19: Papillomatosis in an African Grey.

Prevention. Clinical examination, confirmation of disease and culling of affected birds.

Treatment. Excision of the lesion and the production of an autogenous vaccine has been used with reasonable results, but the present treatment of choice, particularly in the treatment of cloacal papillomatosis, involves the use of lasers (Greenwood and Wild, 1993).

REFERENCES

Alderton D (1991) *The Atlas of Parrots*. TFH Publications, Neptune City.

Andre J-P (1993) La 'maladie du bec et des plumes' (PBFD). Son observation chez des perroquets malgaches (*Coracopsis vasa et Coracopsis nigra*). (PBFD - its observation in two Malagasy Parrots.) *Le Point Veterinaire* **25**, 779.

Arnall L (1975) The skin and its appendages. In: *Bird Diseases*. Eds L Arnall and IF Keymer. TFH Publications, Neptune City.

Bishop CR (1988) A study of the tolerance of ivermectin in budgerigars: In: *Proceedings of the Association of Avian Veterinarians Annual Conference 1988*. AAV, Lake Worth.

Clubb SL (1986) Avian pox in cage and aviary birds. In: *Zoo and Wild Animal Medicine*. Ed ME Fowler. WB Saunders, Philadelphia.

Cooper JE (1985) Parasites. In: *Veterinary Aspects of Birds of Prey*. 2nd Edn. Ed JE Cooper. Standfast Press, Saul.

Cooper JE, Gschmeissner S, Parsons AJ and Coles BH (1987) Psittacine beak and feather disease. *Veterinary Record* **120**, 287.

Cooper JE and Harrison GJ (1994) Dermatology. In: *Avian Medicine: Principles and Application*. Eds BW Ritchie, GJ Harrison and LR Harrison. Wingers, Lake Worth.

Cooper WT and Forshaw JM (1977) *Parrots of the World*. TFH Publications, Neptune City.

Dalhausen B and Radabaugh S (1993) Update on psittacine beak and feather disease and avian polyomavirus testing. In: *Proceedings of the Association of Avian Veterinarians Annual Conference 1993*. AAV, Lake Worth.

Dixit AK and Kushwaha RKS (1992) Occurrence of keratiniphilic fungi in Indian birds. *Folia Micobiologica* **36(4)**, 383.

Eamens GJ (1981) Zoonoses and other human diseases associated with cage and aviary birds. In: *Aviary and Caged Birds - Refresher Course for Veterinarians: Proceedings No 55*. University of Sydney Post-Graduate Committee in Veterinary Science, New South Wales.

Forbes NA and Simpson GN (1993) Pathogenicity of ticks on aviary birds. *Veterinary Record* **133**, 532.

Gerlach H (1984) Virus diseases in pet birds. *Veterinary Clinics of North America: Small Animal Practice* **14(2)**, 299.

Graham DL (1990) Feather and beak disease: its biology, management and an experiment in its eradication from a breeding aviary. In: *Proceedings of the Association of Avian Veterinarians Annual Conference 1990*. AAV, Lake Worth.

Greenwood AG and Wild DJ (1993) Laser surgery of psittacine internal papilloma. In: *Proceedings of the Association of Avian Veterinarians European Conference, Utrecht, 1993*. AAV, Lake Worth.

Greve JH (1986) Parasitic diseases (of birds). In: *Zoo and Wildlife Medicine*. 2nd Edn. Ed ME Fowler. WB Saunders, Philadelphia.

Hillyer EV (1994) Avian dermatology. In: *Saunders Manual of Small Animal Practice*. Eds SJ Birchard and RG Sherding. WB Saunders, Philadelphia.

Keymer IF (1982a) Parasitic diseases. In: *Diseases of Cage and Aviary Birds*. 2nd Edn. Ed M Petrak. Lea and Febiger, Philadelphia.

Keymer IF (1982b) Mycoses. In: *Diseases of Cage and Aviary Birds*. 2nd Edn. Ed M Petrak. Lea and Febiger, Philadelphia.

Knott CIF (1993) Ticks on aviary birds. *Veterinary Record* **133**, 376.

Krautwald M-E (1990) Befiederungsstoerungen bei Ziervoegeln. (Plumage disorders in ornamental birds.) *Der Praktische Tierarzt* **71(10)**, 5.

Latimer KS, Rakich PM, Niagro FD, Ritchie BW, Steffens WL, Campagnoli RP, Pesti DA and Lukert PD (1991) An updated review of psittacine beak and feather disease. *Journal of the Association of Avian Veterinarians* **5(4)**, 211.

Pass DA (1989) The pathology of the avian integument: a review. *Avian Pathology* **18**, 1.

Pavletic MM (1982) Suturing with a syringe needle. *Veterinary Medicine/Small Animal Clinician* **77(3)**, 378.

Philips JR (1990) What's bugging your birds? Avian parasitic arthropods. *Wildlife Rehabilitation* **8**, 155.

Philips JR (1993) Avian mites. *Compendium on Continuing Education for the Practicing Veterinarian* **15(5)**, 671.

Reaville DR, Schmidt RE and Fudge AM (1990) Avian skin and feather disorders: a retrospective study. In: *Proceedings of the Association of Avian Veterinarians Annual Conference 1990*. AAV. Lake Worth.

Ritchie BW, Niagro FD, Latimer KS, Davis RB, Pesti D and Lukert PD (1991a) Avian polyomavirus: an overview. *Journal of the Association of Avian Veterinarians* **5**, 147.

Ritchie BW, Niagro FD, Latimer KS, Vernot J, Pesti D, Campagnoli RP and Lukert PD (1991b) Polyomavirus infections in adult psittacine birds. *Journal of the Association of Avian Veterinarians* **5**, 202.

Rosskopf WJ, Woerpel RW, Sievers MJ and Pater C (1983) Treatment of feather folliculitis in a lovebird. *Modern Veterinary Practice* **64(11)**, 923.

Scott PW (1994) Psittacine polyomavirus in Britain. *Veterinary Record* **135**, 168.

Taylor TG (1982) French molt. In: *Diseases of Cage and Aviary Birds*. 2nd Edn. Ed M Petrak. Lea and Febiger, Philadelphia.

CHAPTER ELEVEN

Behavioural Problems

Martin P C Lawton

INTRODUCTION

Due to their intelligence, playfulness and ability of mimicry, psittacines are the most widely kept companion birds. In the wild these birds are normally social, living in groups. In captivity most are kept singly in a cage. Keeping captive birds away from others has advantages and disadvantages. The main advantage is that they are more likely to become tame and develop their powers of mimicry of sounds, some becoming very good 'talkers'. The disadvantages will be covered in this chapter. They are as varied as they are numerous and make up a large part of companion psittacine practice.

Psittacine species differ not only in their size, dietary requirements and environmental needs, but also in their behavioural attributes. Before purchasing a pet bird, some thought should be given to the needs of the bird as well as what is required from it as a companion. Hand-reared baby birds are in demand as pets because of the imprinting that has developed during their rearing. Although this is advisable as it can reduce the number of bites an owner may receive during training, aggression as they reach sexual maturity or vices, such as masturbation on the owners arm, will be more common.

If the bird is required to be a 'talker' it should be obtained as young as possible. The younger the bird, the easier it is to tame and the more agreeable it will usually become.

CAUSES OF BEHAVIOURAL PROBLEMS

The causes of behavioural problems are numerous and may be as odd as the problems they cause, but usually they relate to either boredom or neurosis (Lawton, 1988). Kennedy and Drapper (1991) claimed that most behavioural complaints arise during the breeding season associated with 'sweeping hormonal changes', although this author considers that the incidence is all year round and not just due to hormonal influences.

Boredom
Being intelligent, psittacines need to have variety and to be occupied, otherwise they become bored. The following aspects of their lifestyle may lead to boredom: small cages, insufficient toys, same view, never being let out of the cage, incorrect perches, being alone for long periods and insufficient attention from owners. Boredom may be a major contributory factor in any behavioural problem, but especially screeching and self-mutilation.

Neurosis
Neurosis is diagnosed in people who exhibit non-adaptive behaviour and attitudes or anxiety states in an attempt to come to terms with reality rather than to escape (Collocott, 1971). The term 'neurosis' can also be applied to the behavioural traits seen in psittacines which are failing to adapt to their surroundings and way of life (Lawton, 1988).

Psittacines are very sensitive and they can react to changes in the environment (Harrison, 1984). Therefore, the causes of neurosis may be other birds, lack of other birds, the size or type of cage they are housed in, the quantity and type of toys and furniture, or even the owner. Disturbances or changes at home may all play an important part; a recent move, additions to the family, frequent visitors or constant arguments may induce neurosis. Some birds are left unattended for long periods; others are frequently left with friends while the owner goes away. Some birds become very neurotic about a pet of another species kept in the same house. Psittacines require entertainment and attention and a regular, non-stressful routine. Changes to their regular routine may result in instability, neurosis or other behavioural problems.

Keeping a bird in a cage is probably the greatest cause of neurosis, due usually to frustration associated with the size of the cage or to attempts to escape from the cage. Dilger and Bell (1982) considered these unresolved frustrations responsible for many of the difficulties encountered in birds.

Some species, such as budgerigars and cockatiels, are highly social species and should not, therefore, be isolated from their own kind; they may gradually decline in general health and may eventually die (Dilger and Bell, 1982). Such birds may be isolated as individual pets, but they must not be in range of sight or hearing of other birds. If isolated birds can see each other, neurosis may develop due to the frustration of trying to achieve physical contact. Larger psittacines, such as Amazons and African Greys, may call out to each other continuously. A neurotic and aggressive bird in a normal group of budgerigars can upset the whole of the flock (Coles, 1985). In such a situation the identification and removal of that bird will often restore harmony in the flock.

Periods of privacy are necessary for psittacines. A dark box should be provided as a 'hide' into which the bird can enter and feel secure.

Wild psittacines spend a large part of their waking time foraging for food in addition to other activities. The provision of readily available food, usually *ad libitum*, allows more time for behavioural problems such as neurosis or psychogenic overeating and obesity (see Chapter 3) to develop. In order to relieve boredom and prevent this psychogenic overindulgence, it is a good idea to schedule specific feeding times and, if possible, to stimulate foraging activity.

Punishment by the owner may induce neurosis through fear, anger and/or resentment. The punishment is often carried out some time after the 'crime' has been committed and thus the bird may only be confused by the punishment and unable to relate it to a previous behaviour.

Neurosis in its early stages, whatever the original cause, may not be very noticeable; it may be shown as agitation, such as hopping from perch to perch or the continual shaking of the head in a figure of eight on its side (Dilger and Bell, 1982), or just a continuing dipping of the head from side to side. Subsequently, the neurosis develops into flighty and scatty birds and eventually, in extreme cases, may present as self-mutilation (see Figure 11.1).

Normal preening may develop into an exaggerated and aggressive chewing or pulling of the feathers in cases of neurosis (Galvin, 1983; Harrison, 1984). It has been suggested (Harrison, 1984) that the bird may

Figure 11.1: Peach-face Parakeet showing feather plucking and evidence of self-mutilation to the right wing.

be chewing the feathers because it develops 'a taste for them'. Self-mutilation is the most commonly presented behavioural problem. Self-mutilation includes nail biting, toe biting, feather chewing and feather plucking. In severe cases, birds may also go off their food and lose weight (Perry, 1987).

FEATHER PLUCKING

Birds with feather loss should be subjected to a thorough step by step investigation as discussed in Chapter 22. It is important to eliminate infectious, parasitic and nutritional causes of feather loss by taking a complete clinical history; by examination of the feathers both on and off the bird; by noting the environment and the diet; and by a full clinical examination and performing all necessary laboratory investigations (Lawton, 1993; Harrison, 1994) (see Chapters 4 and 10). Giardiasis, in particular, has to be ruled out in budgerigars and cockatiels as it is a common cause of feather picking (Levine, 1984). Only after a thorough clinical examination has been carried out and all other possible causes of feather loss have been ruled out by extensive investigations, can a diagnosis of 'behav-

Table 11.1. Some causes of feather plucking (in decreasing order of frequency).

Cause	Comments
Neurosis	Similar to fingernail biting in humans (Ensley, 1979; Harrison, 1984; Davis, 1987).
Boredom	Intelligent birds need to be exploring and investigating new surroundings or objects.
Poor quality feathers	Due to malnutrition; a smoky, dry or poorly lit environment; poor husbandry; badly clipped primaries; or hormonal imbalance. Poor quality feathers are often plucked by birds and they may be the stimulus for further self-mutilation.
Folliculitis	Due to bacterial, viral or mycotic agents. May result in feather plucking. A stained smear of feather pulp from the follicles may yield useful information.
Feather mites	Often thought to be the cause by the owner, but rarely found (Galvin, 1983).

ioural' feather plucking be made (see Figures 11.2, 11.3). Some causes of feather plucking are listed in Table 11.1.

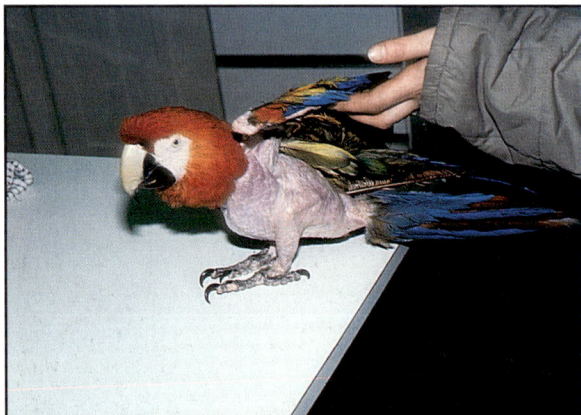

Figure 11.2: Macaw showing the classic distribution associated with behavioural feather plucking. Note the normal feathering on the head where the bird cannot pluck feathers.

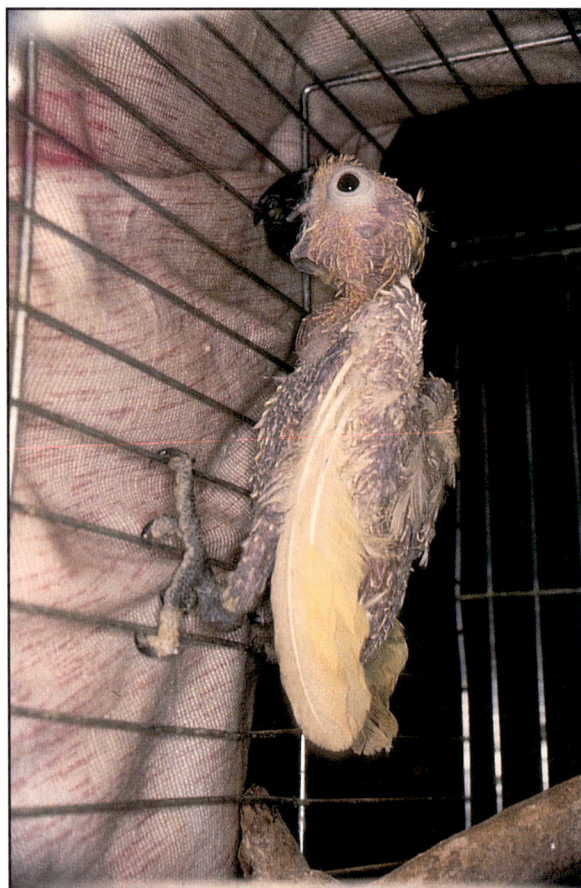

Figure 11.3: Cockatoo with feather loss associated with psittacine beak and feather disease (see Chapter 10). Note the loss of the feathers on the head (cf. Figure 11.2). Such a bird should never be considered a behavioural feather plucker.

Self-mutilated feathers, especially at the bottom of the cage, must be distinguished from normal growing and feather sheath removal. If the feather plucking is psychological the feathers are not deformed or discoloured and they are lost from the areas that the bird is able to chew. Initially, flight and contour feathers are plucked (Perry, 1987), but eventually the bird may be bald except for the head (see Figure 11.2). The use of an Elizabethan collar is often helpful, not only for treatment (see later), but also to assess feather follicle activity in cases of doubt.

Treatment

The suspected underlying causes of the neurosis should be corrected. The aim should be not just to gain feather regrowth, but to prevent feather plucking from recurring or being replaced by another vice.

Treatment should include the following:

● An **Elizabethan collar or neck brace** should be fitted. This is often useful as a first approach: it prevents further mutilation while the original cause of the neurosis can be dealt with as outlined below. Ideally, the collar should be clear so that the bird can see almost normally; it must also be large enough to prevent the bird from reaching the feathers. Psittacines do not like Elizabethan collars, but they work well. Birds should be hospitalised initially for a few days to allow them to adapt to the collars and ensure that they are able to feed normally. If this is not done, owners may remove the collar as soon as they get their bird home if it appears to upset the bird. However, if birds have been given sufficient time to accept the collars and learn to feed while wearing them, owners are much more likely to leave them on. Collars should be left *in situ* until feathers have regrown, which is usually after about two months.

There are a number of variations on the fitting of Elizabethan collars (see Figures 11.4, 11.5, 11.6); these are described by Galvin (1983). Lennox and Van der Heyden (1993) have even used a hexcelite 'T-shirt' to prevent tissue damage in birds that react badly to collars.

● The plane of **nutrition** should be improved. Particular attention should be paid to protein, calcium, vitamin and energy levels, to allow replacement of the feathers (see Chapter 3).

● In some cases the owner should provide more **attention** to the bird, either directly or indirectly, in an attempt to reduce the boredom factor, although care should be taken to ignore attention seeking (see Chapter 22).

● The **environment** should be changed frequently by moving the cage around the house or placing it in an area where there are distractions. Toys should be given to occupy the bird, but changed regularly and not allowed to overclutter the cage. A more suitable cage should be provided where necessary. The cage should be sufficiently large to allow exercise. Use of natural branches for perches provides something at which the bird can peck. If the bird is tame it should be allowed out of the cage.

Figure 11.4: Peach-face Parakeet with a 'classic' Elizabethan collar fitted; staples are sufficient in smaller psittacines.

Figure 11.5: African Grey with a partially inverted Elizabethan collar; this design allows slightly better access to food bowls; notice that pop-rivets have been used to secure the collar.

Figure 11.6: African Grey with a neck brace fitted to prevent further mutilation of skin over the keel; this type of device can also have a circular plate fitted to further limit mutilation.

● In order to give some **privacy and security** to the bird, a 'hide' should be provided. A dark box is suitable.

● The **photoperiod** should be altered to a more normal level of 8-12 hours per day. Often birds are kept in the lounge and subjected to as much as 18 hours of light per day. Ensley (1979) recommended covering the cage at dusk and uncovering it at sunrise.

● Birds should be allowed to **bathe** or should be sprayed daily. This is especially important in African Greys which tend to get very dusty and, therefore, often become overzealous groomers.

● **Medication** should only be considered as a 'last resort' (Johnson-Delaney, 1992). The above suggestions should be followed through and attempted first, and only if they do not eliminate the problem should the bird be put onto medication. Once on medication, the bird may have to remain on that treatment permanently. The large number of drugs that have been reported as useful in birds (Lawton, 1988; Lennox and Van der Heyden, 1993; Turner, 1993) suggest that there is no one 'cure all' available. Davis (1987) postulated that some feather pluckers may respond to sex

hormones if the neurosis is sexual frustration. In an attempt to treat feather picking, even acupuncture has been advised (Worell and Farber, 1993). The more useful drugs are listed in Table 11.2.

In general, all drugs used are behavioural modifiers, although their mode of action may differ quite markedly. Tranquillisers can be used to calm the state of neurosis, although they usually also cause sedation and ataxia at effective doses. The modern psychotropic drugs, which have been developed and are used for obsessive compulsive behaviour (OCB) in man, are the drugs which currently seem to be giving the best results when used in birds. Often these OCB-aimed drugs have to be used for up to six weeks before it is possible to say that they are not helping. In most cases an improvement is expected within two weeks of starting the therapy. Dopamine antagonists, eg. haloperidol, are thought to be useful because neuropeptides, eg. dopamine, are believed to play a part in self-mutilation (Iglauer and Rasim, 1993). Haloperidol is able to allow sedation and inhibition of psychomotor agitation as well as having antipsychotic effects (Lennox and Van der Heyden, 1993). The principal use of haloperidol in man is to treat psychomotor agitation. The tricyclic antidepressants, such as doxepin and amitryptyline, do have some antihistaminic, anticholinergic and local anaesthetic properties (Johnson-Delaney, 1992); this makes them even more useful for the treatment of self-mutilators.

● Culture and sensitivity and appropriate **antibiotic** therapy should be administered if bacterial folliculitis has been diagnosed.

● Ensley (1979) stated that the **introduction of a cage mate** sometimes helps, but the author has found that this often leads to the new bird being shown how to feather pluck and two bald birds result. An alternative is to introduce a 'stuffed' bird which may be groomed by the affected bird and cause the bird to stop feather plucking itself.

● **Training** of both the owner and the bird is useful. If the owner sees the bird plucking its feathers, he/she should not run in and yell at the bird as this is often seen as a 'reward' by the bird and simply reinforces

Table 11.2. Drugs that may prove useful in treating behavioural problems.

Drug	Dosage	Uses	Comments
Amitryptyline	1-5mg/kg p/o bid.	Behavioural modifier.	A tricyclic antidepressant which can be mixed in fruit drink or Millupa.
Delmadinone	1mg/kg (0.02ml/ 30g) i/m.	Sexual behavioural problems.	May be useful in regurgitation.
Diazepam	0.6mg/kg i/m or i/v sid. Two drops (5mg/ml) per 30ml of drinking water.	Feather plucking.	Ataxia and sleepiness are common side-effects. Should only be considered as a short-term treatment to allow healing and give time until the underlying cause or problem is treated.
Doxepin	0.5-1mg/kg p/o bid.	Behavioural modifier.	A tricyclic antidepressant which can be mixed in fruit drink or Millupa.
Fluoxetine	0.4mg/kg p/o sid.	Feather plucking.	An antidepressant which is not meant to cause sedation.
Haloperidol	0.4mg/kg p/o sid.	Self-mutilation, feather plucking and other vices.	An antipsychotic which is a neuroleptic and a dopamine antagonist. Side-effects on the extrapyramidal centre result in Parkinson-like symptoms which disappear on withdrawing the drug. This drug works best in feather plucking where there is also self-mutilation.
Medroxyprogesterone	25-50mg/kg i/m.	Feather plucking and sexual behavioural problems.	Has a calming effect in most birds, but may cause obesity, polydipsia, polyuria or fatty liver syndrome.
Megestrol acetate	2.5mg/kg p/o sid for seven days then once or twice weekly.	Feather plucking and sexual behavioural problems.	Recommended by Galvin (1983).
Naltrexone	1.5mg/kg p/o bid.	Self-mutilation.	An opioid antagonist. Water soluble.

Table 11.2. Continued.

Drug	Dosage	Uses	Comments
Phenobarbitone	0.003mg/gm, ie. 3mg/kg, p/o bid (Galvin, 1983).	Feather plucking.	May cause deep sedation and inability to perch.
Thyroxine	Dissolve a 1mg tablet in 28.4ml of drinking water; 0.4-0.5ml/kg sid or, 100mcg/kg every other day for two weeks, will induce a moult.	Hypothyroidism.	Helpful if primary hypothyroidism or to induce a moult.

the negative behaviour. Often the bird is feather pluck-ing because insufficient attention is being provided (see Attention); by yelling at the bird, the owner is giving the attention the bird craves.

● If a bird is seen feather plucking, **punishment** by placing it into a dark cupboard or covering the cage can be attempted. Initially, this should be for three minutes, but subsequently the length of time can be increased up to 15 minutes (Harrison, 1984). The use of a water pistol is also helpful. Use of high pitched alarms is not advised as this just scares the bird and worsens the neurosis (Lawton, 1988).

SEXUAL PROBLEMS

There are several problems that can be considered to be sexual in origin. These include:

Regurgitation

The desire to pair bond is a strongly physiological fac-tor in a bird's life. In the absence of another bird (of the opposite sex) there is often a pairing or imprinting on the owner, toys, mirrors, other objects or a bird of the same sex. If the imprinting is abnormal there may be sexual advances towards the owner or object upon which it has imprinted.

A common clinical presentation of abnormal pair bonding is regurgitation. It is seen especially in male budgerigars, but it can also occur in Amazons and macaws which have pair bonded with the owner (Harrison and Davis, 1986). Generally, the regurgita-tion is over the objects with which the bird has pair bonded, usually toys and mirrors (Harrison, 1984). The owner often presents the bird as 'vomiting'. Diagno-sis should be on the type of regurgitation and the site, ie. the toys or mirror.

This problem can usually be prevented by the re-moval of the objects of the bird's affection. Initially, this requires removal of all toys and mirrors from the cage. Later, a rotation of toys will allow the limited

returning of some of the objects. If the owner is the object of the bird's affection, limiting the time the bird is 'petted' should be implemented. If regurgitation con-tinues despite the removal of the toys and mirrors, or reduced owner contact, medication may be tried (see Table 11.2).

Persistent Egg Laying

Persistent egg laying is a problem of sole hen birds which continuously produce large numbers of eggs. It is often due to pair bonding with the owner. This con-dition is seen especially in cockatiels and budgerigars, and may result in other problems due to the depletion of the body calcium stores (see Chapter 20).

The owner often removes each egg as it is produced; this stimulates the production of more eggs (Harrison and Davis, 1986). It is often advisable to leave one egg, as the bird is then able to go through the com-plete brooding cycle, at the end of which the egg can be removed. A period of time will then elapse before the bird lays again.

Egg laying in cockatiels can be controlled to some degree by lowering their calorific intake, by avoiding the owner stroking and handling the bird, or by the use of hormones, similar to those for regurgitation (see Table 11.2). Ovariohysterectomy or salpingohysterec-tomy are the treatments of choice (Harrison and Davis, 1986).

Brooding Problems

Neurosis in birds can lead to desertion of eggs and abandoning of chicks, or ceasing to feed at any stage of the brooding (Coles, 1985).

Coles (1985) also described egg eating as a vice which, in the aviary situation, can be copied by others.

DOMINANCE

The establishment of a pecking order is a normal behavioural feature of birds; it is essential for the establishment of a hierarchy. Usually, once the pecking order has been established it is unnecessary for the dominant bird to assert its dominance unless its place in the hierarchy is threatened. Dominance becomes a behavioural problem once it is exhibited beyond the realms of the normal hierarchy. Two specific forms of dominance are recognised - dominance towards other birds and dominance towards people. Both forms of dominance may also be associated with sexual maturity and be classed as 'sexual aggression', especially where imprinting is involved.

Dominance Towards Other Birds

In the case of two birds, even if they are of opposite sexes, incompatibility may lead to one becoming dominant over the other and actively bullying the submissive bird. This can lead to feather picking, usually off the head of the submissive bird. The aggression may be so severe as to result in the death of the submissive partner or, at best, infertility due to stress. Treatment for such a situation is by separation of the two birds.

Parental dominance may be shown as aggression, especially prior to and after fledging, and thus it is best to separate the young once they are feeding independently. This is seen especially in rosellas, parakeets and lovebirds. The cock bird, in particular, appears to be aggressive and should be removed about one week before the expected fledgling time, or else the chicks should be hand reared (Alderton, 1987).

Dominance Towards People

In a single pet bird a hierarchy must still be established, but between the bird and the owner or others in the household. Problems arise when the bird becomes dominant over its owner and may even become aggressive towards him or her. This is particularly a problem in young Amazons which have a reputation for being tyrants.

A bird can show it is dominant by being possessive over one person (to whom it is imprinted) and aggressive towards other people or other birds. This is particularly noted in macaws. This behaviour is only really a problem in a family situation, where the bird is possessive over one member of the family and aggressive towards the other members. Treatment is difficult and relies upon other members of the family becoming more involved with the bird and the imprinted person less so, until the bird becomes a family pet once more.

A bird that is trying to become dominant over its owner is often skittish and untameable. Dominance is often shown by nipping at the owner's fingers (see Biting), refusing to perform tricks and being difficult to handle. In extreme cases the bird may even attack its owner.

A bird whose head is much higher than the mid-chest of its owner may think it is the dominant household member (Davis, 1987). When dealing with a

dominant bird it is a good idea to lower the perches to below chest level. Harrison and Davis (1986) recommended waist level, to convey the dominance of the owner. If the bird is placed constantly below waist level it becomes panicky and neurotic (Davis, 1987). A bird that is allowed to roam the house may see itself as the owner of that house and, in some cases, will develop an 'attack' behaviour where it will try to bite anyone it chooses in order to reaffirm its status (Davis, 1991).

The owner must also be assertive but not aggressive, or the bird may revert to being neurotic. If a parrot attacks, the use of a water pistol helps fend off the bird. Food can also be used to reduce the dominance of the bird, especially if *ad libitum* feeding is stopped. Food can then be given by the owner after the bird has allowed the owner to stroke it, or it has performed a trick.

BITING

Biting comes naturally to psittacines. They can inflict substantial damage with their large, powerful jaws so this habit has to be curtailed at an early stage. Young birds need to be trained early on not to use their beaks in playing or affection.

Most birds bite due to fear, especially on sudden or quick movements, or as a warning behaviour (Harrison and Davis, 1986). Biting due to dominance occurs in Amazons and especially in macaws, which Davis (1987) classed as nippers by nature.

In order to train a bird not to be a biter, the opportunities for it to do so must first be avoided. If it is a dominance response, as in the tyrant Amazon, the dominance must be squashed (see earlier). Harrison and Davis (1986) recommended a verbal 'No' or punishment by isolation. This is achieved by placing the bird in a dark cupboard and removing the bird from the owner for a set period, starting with three minutes and working up to a maximum of fifteen minutes for repeated offences. Blowing in the face of the bird may also be useful, but is not considered as effective as the 'earthquake' effect of administering a jolt to the cage, perch, shoulder or whatever the bird is on, resulting in a startling effect to the bird without appearing confrontational (Davis, 1991).

Food may also be used as a training aid, similar to that described for dominance. Hand feeding in itself is a good way of getting a nippy bird used to the hand that feeds it, and may go a long way to calming the bird.

SCREECHING

Of all the behavioural problems this is the most annoying, hardest to live with and most difficult to modify. Some psittacines learn that their 'favourite person' will give them attention when they screech (Davis, 1991). It is mainly heard in cockatoos but also displayed by Amazons, African Greys and macaws (Harrison, 1994).

Screechers can be classified according to the reason for screeching. This will also affect the prognosis for treatment of the problem.

Dawn and Dusk Screechers

Some psittacines screech in the morning and/or at night. This is a common problem which is considered similar to the crowing of the rooster and, therefore, natural (Harrison and Davis 1986; Harrison, 1994).

This type of screeching often wakes the owner as the psittacine welcomes the dawn each morning. Being a natural behaviour it is very difficult to modify. Attempts can be made to feed the psittacine or occupy it prior to the expected screeching time. If this is attempted, it is very important that no reward is given once the screeching has begun or this will only serve to reinforce the negative behaviour. The bird should be kept covered until the owner wishes it to wake up, ie. when the owner wishes to start the day.

Attention Screechers

This type of screeching is mainly seen in cockatoos (Davis, 1987; Harrison, 1994) as they are so demanding of attention. It is essential that the owner does not give the bird the attention it is requesting during a screeching episode as this further reinforces the negative behaviour (Davis, 1991).

An attention screecher must be ignored and attention only given once silence is obtained. Even shouting at the bird to be quiet just serves to reward the screeching, and should be avoided. The use of a thick cover to put the cage into darkness until the screeching stops is helpful. Once the screeching has stopped the bird should receive attention as a reward for not screeching.

If ignoring or covering does not work, squirting the bird with a water pistol or placing it in a different room or cupboard for a variable length of isolation (as previously described) may be useful.

Happy Screechers

Some psittacines start screeching as a welcome to the owner, especially on their return home. This type of behaviour is to be encouraged as it helps build the bond between bird and owner. Any attempt at modification only results in other neuroses developing. In order to keep the screeching to a minimum, the owner should go straight to the bird and return the welcome.

Harrison and Davis (1986) stated that good talkers are often noisier than non-vocal birds, especially if there are other birds in the house and they can produce deafening noises calling out to each other. This type of screeching may be reduced by having the birds within sight of each other. If this is not desired for any reason, ie. isolation of a sick or new bird, then a water pistol or thick dark cloth should be utilised.

Unhappy Screechers

Some birds screech because they are discontented. This may be noticed after they have been placed in a new cage or moved from their original site. If the reason is obvious it should be corrected, eg. returning the bird to its original site or cage.

Adult African Greys which have recently been purchased as pets may develop their screeching powers as a protective and warning weapon. The owner must try to ignore this screeching when approaching the bird. If the owner retreats from the bird when it starts screeching, this further convinces the bird that screeching works. Trying to hand feed the bird may help to calm it and with time the screeching should stop as people approach. Squirting such a bird with a water pistol simply increases its neurosis. Patience and kindness are the only answers.

ANY TREATMENT BY THE OWNER

This is included here as many owners are reluctant to comply with veterinary advice on treatment, especially medication, as they feel the bird will remember and hate them forever. Neurosis can be induced during treatment and certainly some birds will act differently to owners after restraint for nail clipping or examination, or after administration of medicine. So, to some extent, the owner's fear is justified.

Birds, however, are not able to recognise a 'changed' person (Harrison, 1984) and this can be used to the owner's advantage during treatment. If a mask, hood or hat is used as a disguise during the capture and medication, the bird will not associate the owner with these 'dreadful' deeds.

Fear on behalf of the bird can sometimes be carried too far by owners. The author has been presented with sick psittacines which he was not allowed even to take out of the cage for fear that they might be 'upset'. Similarly, some owners insist on leaving the room before the handling of a parrot for fear it will associate them with the action of capture and handling. This option should be routinely offered to all owners of single psittacine birds, as often the bird is easier to handle with an anxious owner out of sight.

REFERENCES

Alderton D (1987) Captive breeding. In: *Companion Bird Medicine*. Ed EW Burr. Iowa State University Press, Ames.

Colocott TC (1971) Ed *Dictionary of Science and Technology*. W & R Chambers, Oxford.

Coles BH (1985) *Avian Medicine and Surgery*. Blackwell Scientific Publications, Oxford.

Davis C (1987) Avian behaviour. In: *Companion Bird Medicine*. Ed EW Burr. Iowa State University Press, Ames.

Davis CS (1991) Parrot psychology and behaviour

problems. *Veterinary Clinics of North America: Small Animal Practice* **21(6)**, 1281.

Dilger WC and Bell J (1982) Behavioural aspects. In: *Diseases of Cage and Aviary Birds.* 2nd Edn. Ed ML Petrak. Lea and Febiger, Philadelphia.

Ensley P (1979) Caged bird medicine and husbandry. *Veterinary Clinics of North America: Non-Domestic Pet Medicine* **9(3)**, 499.

Galvin C (1983) The feather picking bird. In: *Current Veterinary Therapy VIII.* Ed RW Kirk. WB Saunders, Philadelphia.

Harrison GJ (1984) Feather disorders. *Veterinary Clinics of North America: Caged Bird Medicine* **14(2)**, 179.

Harrison GJ (1994) Perspective on parrot behaviour. In: *Avian Medicine: Principles and Application.* Eds BW Ritchie, GJ Harrison and LR Harrison. Wingers, Lake Worth.

Harrison GJ and Davis C (1986) Captive behaviour and its modification. In: *Clinical Avian Medicine and Surgery, including Aviculture.* Eds GJ Harrison and LR Harrison. WB Saunders, Philadelphia.

Iglauer F and Rasim R (1993) Treatment of psychogenic feather picking in psittacine birds with a dopamine antagonist. *Journal of Small Animal Practice* **34**, 564.

Johnson-Delaney C (1992) Feather picking: diagnosis and treatment. *Journal of the Association of Avian Veterinarians* **6(2)**, 82.

Kennedy KA and Drapper DD (1991) Common psittacine behavioural problems. *Iowa State University Veterinarian* **53(1)**, 21.

Lawton MPC (1988) Behavioural problems. In: *Manual of Parrots, Budgerigars and Other Psittacine Birds.* Ed CJ Price. BSAVA, Cheltenham.

Lawton MPC (1993). Feather loss in birds. In: *Manual of Small Animal Dermatology.* Eds PH Locke, RG Harvey and IS Mason. BSAVA, Cheltenham.

Lennox AM and Van der Heyden N (1993) Haloperidol for use in treatment of psittacine self-mutilation and feather plucking. In: *Proceedings of the Association of Avian Veterinarians Annual Conference 1993.* AAV, Lake Worth.

Levine BS (1984) Psychogenic feather picking. *Avian/ Exotic Practice* **1(1)**, 23.

Perry RA (1987) Avian dermatology. In: *Companion Bird Medicine.* Ed EW Burr. Iowa State University Press, Ames.

Turner R (1993) Trexan (naltrexone hydrochloride) use in feather picking in avian species. In: *Proceedings of the Association of Avian Veterinarians Annual Conference 1993.* AAV, Lake Worth.

Worell AB and Farber WL (1993) The use of acupuncture in the treatment of feather picking in psittacines. In: *Proceedings of the Association of Avian Veterinarians Annual Conference 1993.* AAV, Lake Worth.

Martin P C Lawton

CHAPTER TWELVE

Head Problems

INTRODUCTION

Sufficient time should be spent on a thorough examination of the head so that none of the systems or possible problems are overlooked. Many systemic infections may result in clinical signs affecting the head. These should be noted during examination. Respiratory disease should be suspected when there are ocular or nasal discharges. Evidence of these discharges may only be found on the feathers around the cere or lateral canthus. Vitamin A deficiencies are more easily diagnosed or suspected based on changes to the lacrimal or salivary glands, often resulting in caseous swellings or plaques, especially under the tongue or around the choana. Changes to the ocular structures should be particularly noted. Not only can these allow an assessment of age in some species (the iris of African Greys changes from blue to yellow after about six months of age), but various changes in the conjunctiva, cornea or anterior chamber may provide evidence of systemic infection or metabolic disease (such as xerophthalmia associated with hypovitaminosis A or uveitis associated with chlamydial infection). Excessive flaking of the beak may signify vitamin/mineral deficiencies, whilst an excessively shiny surface may indicate feather abnormalities or lack of grooming.

HEAD FEATHERS

Careful attention must be paid to the plumage on the head and neck. The finding of feather loss on the body, but the head plumage being normal, suggests self-mutilation rather than parasitic or viral causes. Feather loss of the head and neck as well as the body is rarely seen in the behavioural feather plucker or chewer. Feather loss and trauma to the skin on the head and neck alone may be associated with overgrooming by a mate or with parasitic infection. Cockatoos with psittacine beak and feather disease (PBFD) often have a poor crest with missing or damaged feathers. In all cases of abnormality of feathers of the head and body it is advised that a blood sample is taken for PBFD testing. Birds with only head and neck feather loss should be examined under magnification for evidence of parasitic infections (see Chapter 10). Skin scrapings

and biopsies may also be required to establish a diagnosis.

Birds that are generally ill may not preen as frequently or as thoroughly as normal, and this may result in excessive sheathed pin feathers on the head. The presence of these, especially in budgerigars, is usually a worrying sign.

SKIN OF THE HEAD

Although the skin of the head should not be considered in isolation to the rest of the integument (see Chapter 10), there are a number of conditions which primarily affect this area.

Congenital Abnormalities
Ankyloblepharon has been reported in cockatiels (Buyukmihci *et al*, 1990). Surgical attempts to reconstruct the palpebral fissures were unsuccessful. The skin overlying the globe frequently returned to the preoperative state within one month of surgery.

Hyperkeratosis
The skin around the eyelids and cere should be examined for signs of hyperkeratosis which may be associated with 'scaly face' caused by *Cnemidocoptes pilae* (see Figure 12.1). This parasite may cause eyelid or cere deformities which can result in predisposition to other eye infections or obstruction of the nostrils. Treatment is with ivermectin (200mcg/kg s/c repeated once after 14 days).

Swellings
Any swelling of the skin should be investigated further. Although neoplasia may be found (squamous cell carcinoma in African Greys), the most usual cause is squamous cell metaplasia associated with hypovitaminosis A. The resultant swellings are commonly found either dorsal and/or lateral to the orbit due to changes to the lacrimal gland tissue in these areas (see Figure 12.2) (Lawton, 1988), or located between the mandibles associated with salivary gland changes (see Figure 12.3). These areas may be affected individually or simultaneously. Concurrent swellings may also be found within the oral cavity (see later). These

caseous swelling should be removed surgically under general anaesthetic. The diet should be changed to provide adequate levels of vitamin A and to prevent further occurrences (see Chapter 3).

Poxvirus may result in excessive crusting and thickening of the eyelid margins which are seldom responsive to treatment (Lawton, 1993a). Diagnosis is made on biopsy. Pox lesions are generally seen 10-14 days after infection, initially starting as a mild blepharitis. Later, a serous ocular discharge appears, the lids swell and they then stick together. Caseous masses of white fluid collect under the lid, resulting in the cornea becoming oedematous and ulcerated; corneal perforation is a possible complication. Dry crusty scabs form around the margins of the lids 12-18 days after infection, and these may seal the lids completely shut. The clinical illness lasts between 2-6 weeks in parrots (Karpinski and Clubb, 1986). Treatment is usually palliative, with corticosteroid and antibiotic topical drops to reduce the inflammation and secondary bacterial infections (see Chapter 10).

Fluid swellings in front of and below the orbits are often associated with sinusitis. Nasal discharges may be present, manifested especially when gentle pressure is applied to the swellings. Treatment is by flushing of the sinuses, via the nostrils, with a suitable antibiotic solution (see Chapter 15).

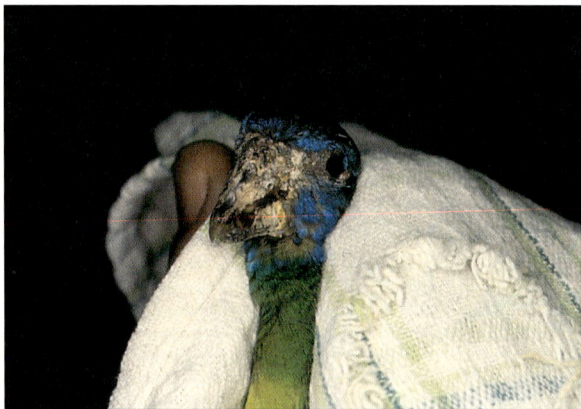

Figure 12.1: Rosella with severe deformation of the eyelids and beak associated with chronic scaly face (Cnemidocoptes pilae).

Figure 12.2: African Grey with a dorsal periorbital swelling caused by squamous cell metaplasia of the lacrimal glands.

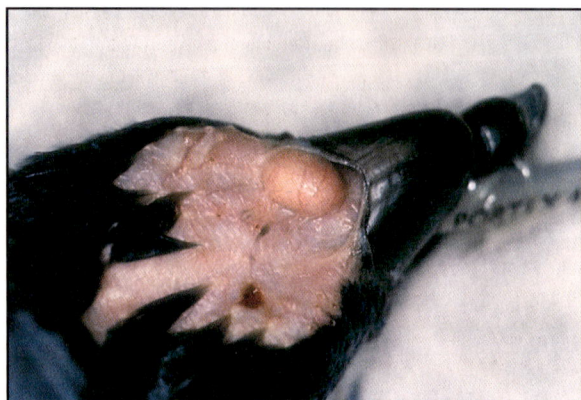

Figure 12.3: African Grey with a intramandibular swelling associated with hypovitaminosis A.

Trauma

Trauma to the eyelids is frequently encountered, especially in cockatiels. If the damage is to the leading edge of the eyelid margin, repair should be attempted under general anaesthetic using a fine suture material such as 6/0 Vicryl (Ethicon), as described for mammals.

Wounds on the back of the head are usually not self-induced, although it is more difficult to assess wounds on the neck. A trial separation from any mate may be required to rule out overgrooming. Treatment of traumatic wounds to the head caused by other birds requires separation to prevent repeated trauma and to allow healing. Wounds should be cleaned with an antiseptic, such as povidone-iodine, and antibiotics used if indicated. Trauma to the skin from other causes, including flying into windows or lacerations against a sharp edge of the cage, will require cleaning and, where possible, suturing with fine suture material, eg. 6/0 Vicryl. Antibiotic cover is advised for all traumatic wounds. Concussion or neurological signs may also be noted following 'crash' trauma (see Chapter 19).

EARS

The ear canals open bilaterally, caudoventral to the lateral canthus of each eye, and they are well hidden by feathers. Parting the feathers will expose the auditory opening which should be obvious and show no swelling or discharges (see Figure 12.4). If there is a bacterial infection the tissues become hyperaemic and swollen, and the opening is no longer clear. Treatment is by cleaning and application of topical antibiotics. Corticosteroids may also be helpful in reducing inflammation. It has been reported (Harrison and Ritchie, 1994) that the ear openings may also appear hyperaemic in birds with sinusitis.

Figure 12.4: Amazon with otitis media and accumulation of material in auditory canal.

Granulomata and neoplasia may be found affecting the ear canal or surrounding tissues. Treatment, if they are detected early enough, is by surgical removal and submitting samples for histopathology for confirmation of the diagnosis and prognosis.

NOSTRILS AND CERE

The nostrils should be clear and with no discharge or blockage. Any discharge may indicate a respiratory infection and should be investigated further (see Chapter 15). It is possible for the nostrils to become blocked. This may be due to changes (thickening) of the cere or material accumulating within the nostrils themselves.

Hyperkeratosis and Brown Hypertrophy

Cnemidocoptes spp. infection can result in hyperkeratosis to such an extent that there is physical blockage of the nostrils. Even when a *Cnemidocoptes* spp. infection has been treated successfully, there may be chronic changes to the cere; this may also be associated with 'brown hypertrophy', where there is an overgrowth of the cere. Brown hypertrophy can also occur with some endocrine disorders. However, some browning of the cere is normal in budgerigar hens which are reproductively active (Harrison and Ritchie, 1994). Brown hypertrophy is most commonly seen in budgerigars. Excessive overgrowth of the cere can lead to blockage of the nares. This overgrown keratin can usually be removed in the conscious bird by being cracked off the cere. Treatment with ivermectin is routinely advised in case there is still an active but low grade *Cnemidocoptes* spp. infection (Lawton, unpublished data).

Rhinoliths

Chronic low grade infection (such as associated with sinusitis) or vitamin A deficiency can result in an accumulation of mucus and keratin debris within the nostrils and the formation of a rhinolith (see Figure 12.5). These are keratin whorls which can eventually become very large and cause distension and disruption of the nostrils. They may be found unilaterally, although they are more usually bilateral but of varying sizes. Treatment is by removal of the plug of keratin whorls using a small dental scraper or bent hypodermic needle. The nostrils can then be medicated with topical antibiotic with or without steroids. The bird's diet should also be changed or supplemented to correct the vitamin A deficiency. Blockage of the nostrils may also occur from chronic aspergillosis or candidiasis which can result in granulomata affecting one or both nostrils.

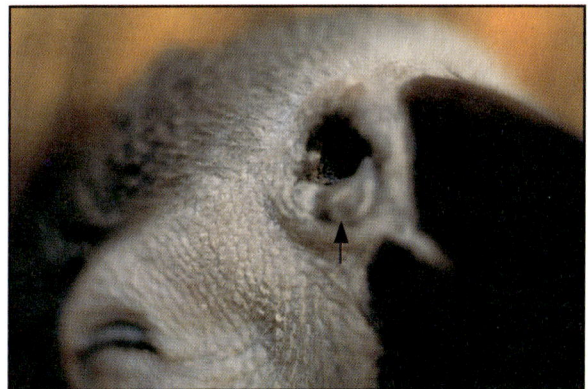

Figure 12.5: Large rhinolith (arrow) in the right nare of an African Grey.

BEAK

The beak is important for prehension, therefore any abnormality, trauma or disease will interfere with the bird's ability to feed and groom, and its mobility about the cage (Lawton, 1993b). Beak abnormalities will also affect the look of the bird. Many owners will request treatment of beak abnormalities for cosmetic reasons. The healthy beak should be smooth and even, and with good apposition between the mandibular and maxillary parts.

The psittacine beak consists of an upper sharp section and a lower blunt mandible. The beak has a keratin covering over bone. The keratin is cornified and known as rhamphotheca (Coles, 1985). The cornified layers grow continuously from the cere region towards the edges and the tip of the beak, where they are worn during eating and other activities.

The beak is subject to a variety of conditions, including infections, neoplasia and trauma. Damage, distortion or even loss of the beak is not unusual and is often the reason for a bird being presented to the clinician (Lawton, 1993b). Where the damage is due to parasitic, bacterial, fungal or viral disease, it is important that this is diagnosed and treated where possible. If distortion of the beak is identified, it is important to establish if dietary deficiencies are a cause of any bony abnormalities of the mandible or maxilla. Grooves in the beak which have originated from the nostril region may be indicative of previous episodes of sinusitis or pox (Harrison and Ritchie, 1994). A dry and flaky beak may be indicative of malnutrition or systemic infections. Where there is severe damage, usually due to trauma or neoplasia, surgical repair is required. A good knowledge of the anatomy of the beak is required before surgery is undertaken. This is covered in more depth in Clipsham (1994).

Some common presenting problems associated with the beak are described below.

Congenital Abnormalities

Attempts can be made to correct congenital dysplasia or aplasia surgically. In some cases a prosthesis may be required to fill any deficit that is present (Lawton, 1993b). Prostheses may be made from a variety of materials, including wire, pins and plates, the dental acrylics, hoof repair material (Technovite), or anything that is considered suitable and is likely to adhere to the beak (Sleamaker, 1983; Coles, 1985). Experience and practice are required in the choice and use of the prosthetic materials. Malaligment can be treated with prosthetic posts (see Figure 12.6) or tension bands (see Chapter 21).

Figure 12.6: Technovite prosthesis for attempted correction of 'scissors' beak in an Amazon.

Fractures

Simple fractures may be treated by stabilisation with pins or wires. The pins and wires may be placed in a cruciate pattern or be transfixing. External support is often advised until full healing has occurred. Some fractures may be repaired by splints alone (Amand, 1977). More serious fractures may lead to interference of the circulation to the beak and result in necrosis. In these cases a prosthesis may be required. This may be temporary or permanent, although the latter may

develop problems associated with infection, pressure necrosis or loosening, and need further attention. The use of cyanoacrylates should only ever be considered as temporary, as they will be lost after about three weeks due to desquamation of the keratin (Clipsham, 1994). If there is loss of keratin following injury, it may be years before the keratin is replaced.

Neoplasia

Neoplasia is typically highly destructive. If neoplasia is suspected, histopathology will confirm a diagnosis and ultimately provide a prognosis. As the tumours encountered are most commonly squamous cell carcinomata or other malignancies, the prognosis is always guarded. However, if neoplasia is diagnosed, surgical treatment is more likely to be effective at an early stage. In some cases of neoplasia, radiotherapy or cryotherapy may be more appropriate than conventional surgery. The use of a prosthesis may be required to repair any permanent defect.

Overgrowth

In small psittacines such as cockatiels and budgerigars, the commonest presenting beak problem is overgrowth. In some birds the growth of keratin is faster than the wearing activity and this results in overgrowth. More often the overgrowth is due to an underlying malocclusion which prevents normal beak wear and thus leads to overgrowth (Lawton, 1993b). The continued discrepancy will result in further abnormality. These cases require continual regular attention and trimming or burring.

If normal beaks show overgrowth, all that is required is simple trimming and remodelling. For deformed beaks it is often possible partially to correct the beak with repeated trimmings on a regular basis. Beaks may be trimmed with bone forceps, a jewellery file or a burr. After trimming they should always be smoothed with sandpaper. Care must be taken not to cut the sensitive structures under the keratin as this could result in infection or further growth abnormality. Some deformation of the beak may be caused by *Cnemidocoptes* spp., especially in chronic cases; treatment with ivermectin and cosmetic remodelling may be all that is required. Beak abnormalities may also result from infections associated with *Aspergillus* spp. or *Candida* spp.

Trauma

If a bird is presented with a traumatic beak injury, therapy should include analgesics and fluid therapy to control pain and shock. Once the bird is in a fit state to be anaesthetised, the damage may be assessed, the beak cleaned and the method of repair chosen. A review of the techniques used in the repair of beaks is given in Lawton (1993b) and Clipsham (1994). Radiography may be useful in assessing the extent of the damage and the planning of surgery or the fitting of a prosthesis.

If there is contamination, the use of systemic antibiotics is recommended. If the beak is lost and there are feather abnormalities, a blood test for PBFD should be performed. If positive, consideration should be given as to whether further treatment of the bird is in its best interest. If there are abnormal swellings or unexplained loss of beak structure, swabs or biopsies may be considered for further evaluation and diagnosis.

Punctures, lacerations, fractures and tears are considered to be most often caused by bites from cage mates (Clipsham, 1994). Compressed fragments of beak may need to be elevated with blunt instruments. After cleaning, the fragments are secured in place using cyanoacrylates.

MOUTH AND TONGUE

The mouth and tongue warrant special attention during examination. Any abnormalities or evidence of infection could result in anorexia. Small wart-like lesions may be associated with viral infection (see Figure 12.7). These can result in papillomata, which may even extend to the oesophagus and crop (Cooper *et al*, 1986) (see Chapter 10). White or yellow plaques within the oral cavity, especially around the choana (see Figure 12.8) and the tongue (sublingual glands) (see Figure 12.9), are often found in cases of hypovitaminosis A. These should be differentiated from fungal, yeast or protozoal (*Trichomonas* spp.) infections by taking a smear for examination under a microscope. Treatment is by surgical removal of the lesions. In some cases it is not possible to close the defect (especially if it involves the tongue). In these cases, antibiotic cover is advised. Recurrence can be prevented by improving the diet and by the use of suitable supplementation (see Chapter 3).

Chewing of wooden perches or unsuitable toys may lead to foreign bodies, such as splinters, or lacerations to the tongue. Anaesthesia is usually required for a thorough examination and the removal of any foreign body or suturing of the lacerations. In both cases it would be advisable to provide antibiotic cover.

EYES

The eyes should be examined carefully as they may often show clinical signs associated with systemic illness or nutritional deficiency. An opthalmoscope must always be used as a routine part of the examination. The ophthalmoscope is not only useful for examining the fundus, but in birds the +15 lens is also useful for providing some degree of magnification when examining the cornea, anterior chamber and lens (see Figure 12.10). The use of ancillary aids, such as fluorescein stains and Schirmer tear test strips, will also assist in diagnosis (Lawton, 1993c). Where there are any ocular discharges, routine testing for chlamydiosis is advised (see Chapter 22).

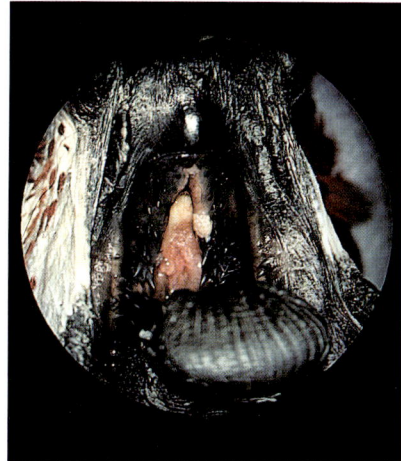

Figure 12.7: Oral papillomatosis around the choana in a Scarlet Macaw.

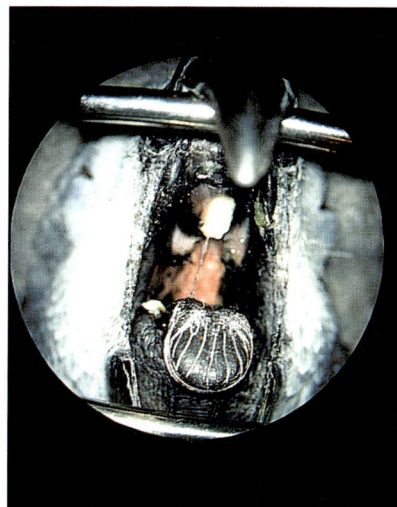

Figure 12.8: Hypovitaminosis A associated plaque around the choana in an African Grey.

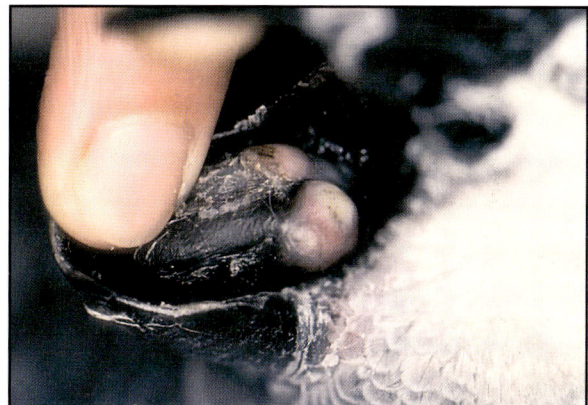

Figure 12.9: Bilateral sublingual swellings due to squamous cell metaplasia in an African Grey with hypovitaminosis A.

Mydriatics such as atropine or tropicamide are often ineffective in birds due to striated muscle in the iris allowing voluntary control of pupil size (Walls,

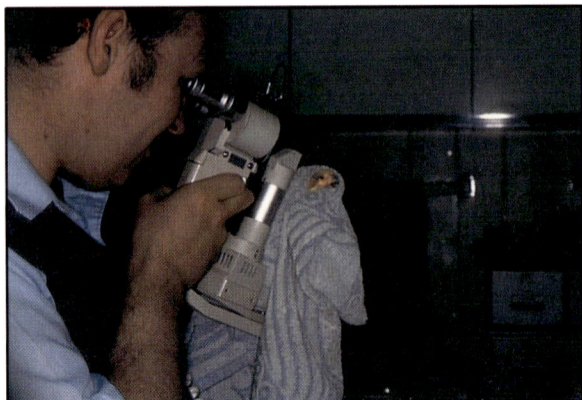

Figure 12.10: Examination of the ocular structures of a cockatiel with a biomicroscope.

1942). Mydriasis is best achieved in these cases by general anaesthesia or by the use of tubocurare either installed topically or injected into the anterior chamber. Several applications over a 15 minute period of D-tuborcurare (3mg/ml solution) has been reported as useful (Karpinski, 1986).

Cataracts

Birds with cataracts may be identified because they fail to feed properly. Lendectomy is possible, but due to the size and accommodation power of the lens, the bird's sight may be impaired afterwards. Surgery should therefore only be contemplated in cases of bilateral cataracts. Although true phacoemulsification in birds has been described (Murphy and Riis, 1984), because the avian lens is mainly fluid, simple aspiration without ultrasonic fragmentation may be used through a small corneal incision (Lawton, 1993c) in the majority of cases, although mature cataracts may be more dense and benefit from phacoemulsification. Hereditary cataracts have not so far been reported in psittacines, but the possibility should be considered when performing lendectomies.

Conjunctivitis

Upper respiratory tract infections are frequently associated with conjunctivitis and must therefore be considered as a possible cause. Conjunctivitis is usually due to bacterial infection, eg. chlamydiosis or sinusitis, or an irritant. If there is bacterial conjunctivitis, this seldom causes a purulent discharge due to the lack of lysozymes in the tears. However, inspissated pus can usually be seen as a swelling either under the third eyelid or under the lower or upper eyelids. Treatment involves initial removal of the pus by flushing the conjunctival fornix with Hartmann's solution via a fine flexible cannula (Lawton, 1993c). Cytology and bacteriology may be performed, although a suitable antibiotic, such as tobramycin, is often successful in curing the condition. Lesions of the eyelids can also result in signs of conjunctivitis, such as may occur with poxvirus infections.

Corneal Ulceration

Corneal ulceration may be associated with trauma, infection or foreign bodies, or with dry eye (see later). Budgerigars kept on loose sand may experience problems if sand gets into the eye. Other foreign bodies encountered include grass awns, seed husks or gravel. Rubbing the face at the bottom of the cage tends to exacerbate the problem as more irritant material may enter the eye. Treatment is by flushing out the foreign material with Hartmann's solution. Topical antibiotics are also recommended.

If corneal damage is suspected the use of fluorescein or rose bengal will allow the extent of the injury to be established. If swabs or scrapings are taken these should be done first and from the edge of any lesion. Leakage of fluorescein into the aqueous of the anterior chamber may be observed following foreign body penetration of the cornea.

Severe corneal ulceration should be treated with a third eyelid flap. Under general anaesthesia the third eyelid is brought down from its position in the superior medial fornix of the conjunctiva and sutured onto the inferolateral bulbar conjunctiva with two small 6/0 Vicryl mattress sutures (Lawton, 1993c). Magnification is essential. Often, the flap needs to stay in place only for two weeks.

Dry Eye

Keratoconjunctivitis sicca (dry eye) occurs in birds and is often associated with hypovitaminosis A. Xerophthalmia results because of damage to the lacrimal glands (Lawton, 1991). This condition should be suspected when there is a mucoid discharge on the eyelid margins. The condition is diagnosed on a Schirmer tear test using cut down strips (normal values are >10mm per minute) (see Figure 12.11). This test should be performed before local anaesthetic or any dyes have been used. If local anaesthetic has already been used it is important to remember that only the basal resting tear production will be measured. Corneal damage may not be irreversible; improving the diet and providing vitamin A supplementation may

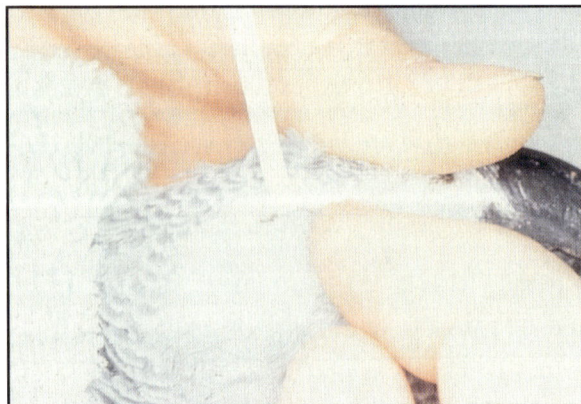

Figure 12.11: Performing a Schirmer tear test on an African Grey.

be beneficial. Treatment using an artificial tear preparation, eg. acetylcystine/hypromellose combination (Ilube, Glaxo-Wellcome) is useful, especially if there is damage to the cornea.

Although not a true dry eye, keratitis or corneal ulceration may result if the tear film is interfered with in any way. The eyelids should be functioning properly in order to spread the tear film over the cornea. At the time of examination it must be established that there are no underlying abnormalities of the eyelids.

Enophthalmos

Sunken eye disease in macaws is often associated with sinusitis which results in the eyes sinking into the orbit (enophthalmos). This should not be confused with an anterior uveitis and a reduction of intraocular pressure. There is often a copious mucopurulent nasal discharge. This condition responds to antibiotics, often combined with flushing out the sinuses (see Chapter 15).

Glaucoma

This is a rare condition in birds. Where glaucoma is encountered it is usually as a result of trauma and resulting hyphaema, or iatrogenic associated with cataract surgery. Glaucoma can be diagnosed (in larger birds) on the increase in intraocular pressure as measured with a tonometer. Treatment may be attempted with a carbonic anhydrase inhibitor (Korbel and Braun, 1995).

Iridal Colour

Iridal colour in some species may be an indication of age or sex (Karpinksi and Clubb, 1986). Fledgling macaws have brown irises which fade to grey within the first year of age; young Amazons have brown irises which become red/orange as they age; African Greys have irises which change from a dark blue through to a grey, brown or yellow colour (see Figure 12.12). Many species of cockatoos show sexual dimorphism. Adult males have a dark brown to black iris; adult females have red irises; and the young of both sexes have brown irises.

Rupture of the Globe

Because of the presence of scleral ossicles, traumatic rupture of the eye does not result in collapse of the globe. If the cornea can be repaired, this should be done, otherwise a third eyelid (see earlier) or conjunctival flap (similar to that performed for mammals) should be considered. If the cornea cannot be repaired, enucleation could be carried out. This should only be performed as a last option. The technique of enucleation is similar to that described for mammals, except that the globe is often proportionately larger for the size of the head. A lateral canthotomy together with gentle manipulation of the globe is essential in order to achieve good exposure (Murphy, 1987). Scissors should be introduced between the globe and the orbit, and the extraocular muscles, connective tissue and eventually the optic nerve severed. Care must be taken on handling the globe to prevent traction to the optic chiasma which will result in bilateral blindness (Lawton, 1993c).

Uveitis

Trauma or penetrating injury may result in hyphaema which often regresses within a few weeks (Lawton, 1993a). Conservative treatment with topical antibiotics, with or without non-steroidal anti-inflammatories, eg. Ocufen (Allergan), or, providing there is no corneal ulceration, corticosteroids, eg. prednisolone acetate, is usually all that is required. Macaws appear to be particularly prone to recurrent idiopathic uveitis (see Figure 12.13) (Lawton, 1991). Response to topical steroids and atropine (to control the ciliary body spasm) brings temporary relief. Often the uveitis may not recur for several months. Ultimately, recurrent bouts result in secondary cataracts and posterior synechiae. Other causes of uveitis include systemic disease, autoimmune conditions and parasitic, mycotic, bacterial or viral disease. Many cases of uveitis remain undiagnosed or idiopathic (Lawton, 1993a).

Hypopyon is always associated with a systemic infection. This should be treated with systemic antibiotics. It is possible to remove a small sample of aqueous

Figure 12.12: Juvenile African Grey with blue iris.

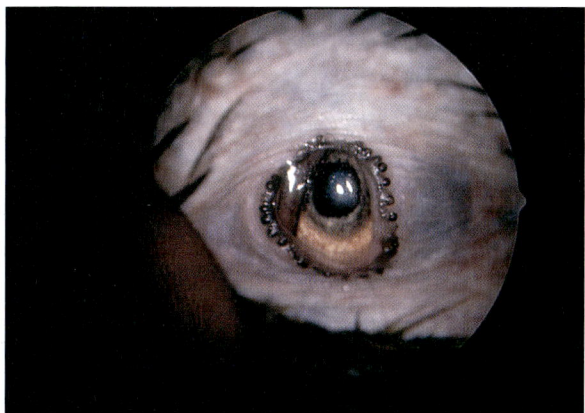

Figure 12.13: Uveitis and early cataract development in a macaw.

for culture and cytology via a 27G needle, although this risks causing further uveitis.

Vitreal Haemorrhage

Because birds have an anangiotic retina, they have modified vessels protruding into the vitreous which are responsible for supplying nutrients and removing metabolic wastes produced by the retina; this is the pecten (see Figure 12.14). Rupture of the pecten will result in massive haemorrhage into the vitreous. This may be encountered following severe trauma to the head, such as flying into a window. It is possible for this haemorrhage to regress, but it may take many months and may also result in traction and detachment of the retina as the haemorrhage contracts into a clot, followed by scar and adhesion formation (Lawton, 1991).

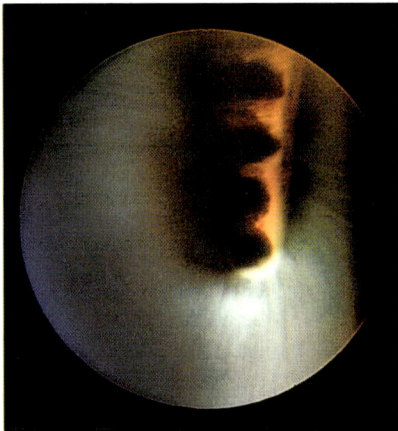

Figure 12.14: Retina and pecten of a macaw.

REFERENCES

Amand WB (1977) General techniques for avian surgery. In: *Current Veterinary Therapy VI*. Ed RW Kirk. WB Saunders, Philadelphia.

Buyukmihci NC, Murphy CJ, Paul-Murphy J, Hacker DB, Laratta LJ and Brooks DE (1990) Eyelid malformation in four cockatiels. *Journal of the American Veterinary Medical Association* **196 (9)**, 1490.

Clipsham R (1994) Rhamphorthotics and surgical correction of maxillofacial defects. *Seminars in Avian and Exotic Pet Medicine* **3 (2)**, 92.

Coles BH (1985) *Avian Medicine and Surgery*. Blackwell Scientific Publications, Oxford.

Cooper JE, Lawton MPC and Greenwood AG (1986) Papillomas in psittacine birds. *Veterinary Record* **119**, 535.

Harrison GJ and Ritchie BW (1994) Making distinction in the physical examination. In: *Avian Medicine: Principles and Application*. Eds BW Ritchie, GJ Harrison and LR Harrison. Wingers, Lake Worth.

Karpinski LG (1986) Ophthalmology. In: *Clinical Avian Medicine and Surgery, including Aviculture*. Eds GJ Harrison and LR Harrison. WB Saunders, Philadelphia.

Karpinksi LG and Clubb SL (1986) Clinical aspects of ophthalmology in caged birds. In: *Current Veterinary Therapy IX*. Ed RW Kirk. WB Saunders, Philadelphia.

Korbel R and Braun J (1995) Further investigations on tonometry in avian ophthalmology using an electronic tonometer. In: *Proceedings of the Association of Avian Veterinarians European Conference, Jerusalem, 1995*. AAV, Lake Worth.

Lawton MPC (1988) Nutritional diseases. In: *Manual of Parrots, Budgerigars and Other Psittacine Birds*. Ed CJ Price. BSAVA, Cheltenham.

Lawton MPC (1991) Avian ophthalmology. In: *Proceedings of the Association of Avian Veterinarians European Conference, Vienna, 1991*. AAV, Lake Worth.

Lawton MPC (1993a) Avian anterior segment disease. In: *Proceedings of the Association of Avian Veterinarians Annual Conference 1993*. AAV, Lake Worth.

Lawton MPC (1993b) An approach to surgical repair of beaks. In: *Proceedings of the Association of Avian Veterinarians European Conference, Utrecht, 1993*. AAV, Lake Worth.

Lawton MPC (1993c) Ophthalmology of exotic species. In: *Manual of Small Animal Ophthalmology*. Eds SM Petersen-Jones and SM Crispin. BSAVA, Cheltenham.

Murphy CJ (1987) Raptor ophthalmology. *Compendium on Continuing Education for the Practicing Veterinarian* **9 (3)**, 241.

Murphy CJ and Riis RC (1984) Lens extraction by phacoemulsification in two raptors. *Journal of the American Veterinary Medical Association* **185 (11)**, 1403.

Sleamaker TF (1983) Prosthetic beak for a Salmon-crested Cockatoo. *Journal of the American Veterinary Medical Association* **183(11)**, 1300.

Walls GL (1942) The vertebrate eye and its adaptive radiation. *Cranbrook Institute of Science Bulletin* **19**, 607.

CHAPTER THIRTEEN

Pelvic Limb Problems

Nigel H Harcourt-Brown

ANATOMY

The pelvic limb (see Figures 13.1, 13.2) can be considered to start caudal to the last movable thoracic vertebra. Articulating with this vertebra is the synsacrum, which is formed from the fusion of a series of vertebrae homologous to the thoracic, lumbar, sacral and caudal vertebrae of mammals. The pelvis is attached to the synsacrum and together they form a single unit. The acetabulum is not a solid cup, the acetabular foramen being closed by the acetabular membrane. The head of the femur articulates with the acetabulum. The trochanter of the femur articulates with the antitrochanter of the pelvis, and when the leg is in its normal position the femur is prevented from abduction.

The tibiotarsus is formed from a fusion between the tibia and the proximal row of tarsal bones. The tendon of the long digital extensor muscle runs through a fibrous canal on the cranial aspect of the distal end of the tibiotarsus (see Figure 13.5). The fibula is short and is attached by fibrous tissue to the tibiotarsus at the fibular crest. The femoral condyles are attached by ligaments to, and articulate with, the tibiotarsus and head of the fibula. Various ligaments permit movement between the tibiotarsus and the fibula and allow some rotation of the femorotibial joint around its long axis. The femorotibial joint (knee) is otherwise similar to that of mammals as it contains two menisci, cranial and caudal cruciate ligaments, and collateral ligaments.

The second, third and fourth metatarsal bones fuse at an early age and combine with the distal row of tarsal bones to form the tarsometatarsus. The first metatarsal bone is separate, but joined by ligaments to the tarsometatarsus. The joint between the tarsometatarsus and the tibiotarsus is known as the intertarsal joint.

The intertarsal joint has a meniscus and a single ligament homologous to the cranial cruciate ligament. There is little longitudinal rotation in this joint. The main flexor tendons of the digits arise from the tibiotarsal region and run over the caudal aspect of the intertarsal joint through the tibial cartilage and also in hypotarsal grooves or canals. The tendon of the long digital extensor muscle runs around the craniomedial aspect of the proximal tarsometatarsus

All psittacines have their digits arranged with the first and fourth toes facing caudally and the second and third facing cranially (zygodactyl). It should be noted that the hallux (first digit) is extended by a well developed branch of the long digital extensor, which is rare among birds; it is usually extended by a separate muscle, the musculus (m.) extensor hallucis longus.

The pelvic limb is covered with feathered skin to the intertarsal joint. From the intertarsal joint the skin is thickened and is covered by scales (scutes). Each digit ends in a claw, consisting of a phalangeal bone covered with a layer of germinal epithelium which gives rise to a keratinised and calcified dorsal plate and a softer plantar plate.

The musculature of the pelvic limb of the White-fronted Amazon has been fully described by Berman (1984).

FRACTURES

Methods of fracture repair are discussed in Chapter 14. Redig (1986) suggested the use of a modified Schroeder-Thomas splint (which can be made from coat-hanger wire padded with bandage) to support the pelvic limb from the hip to the digits. More sophisticated methods of repair are made difficult by the small size of the bones in most psittacines. Full pin fixation and shuttle-pin techniques are possible in macaws but are difficult in birds as large as Blue-fronted Amazons and virtually impossible in small parakeets.

It is vital that all fractures are examined radiographically for signs of osteodystrophy, osteomyelitis and tumours (see Chapter 7).

Synsacrum
Rarely fractured. Nerve damage frequently occurs and can be severe and irreversible. In some species, eg macaws, the pelvis is incompletely fused to the synsacrum; this incomplete fusion can become completely separated by trauma.

Pelvis
Rarely fractured. The fractures frequently trap nerves

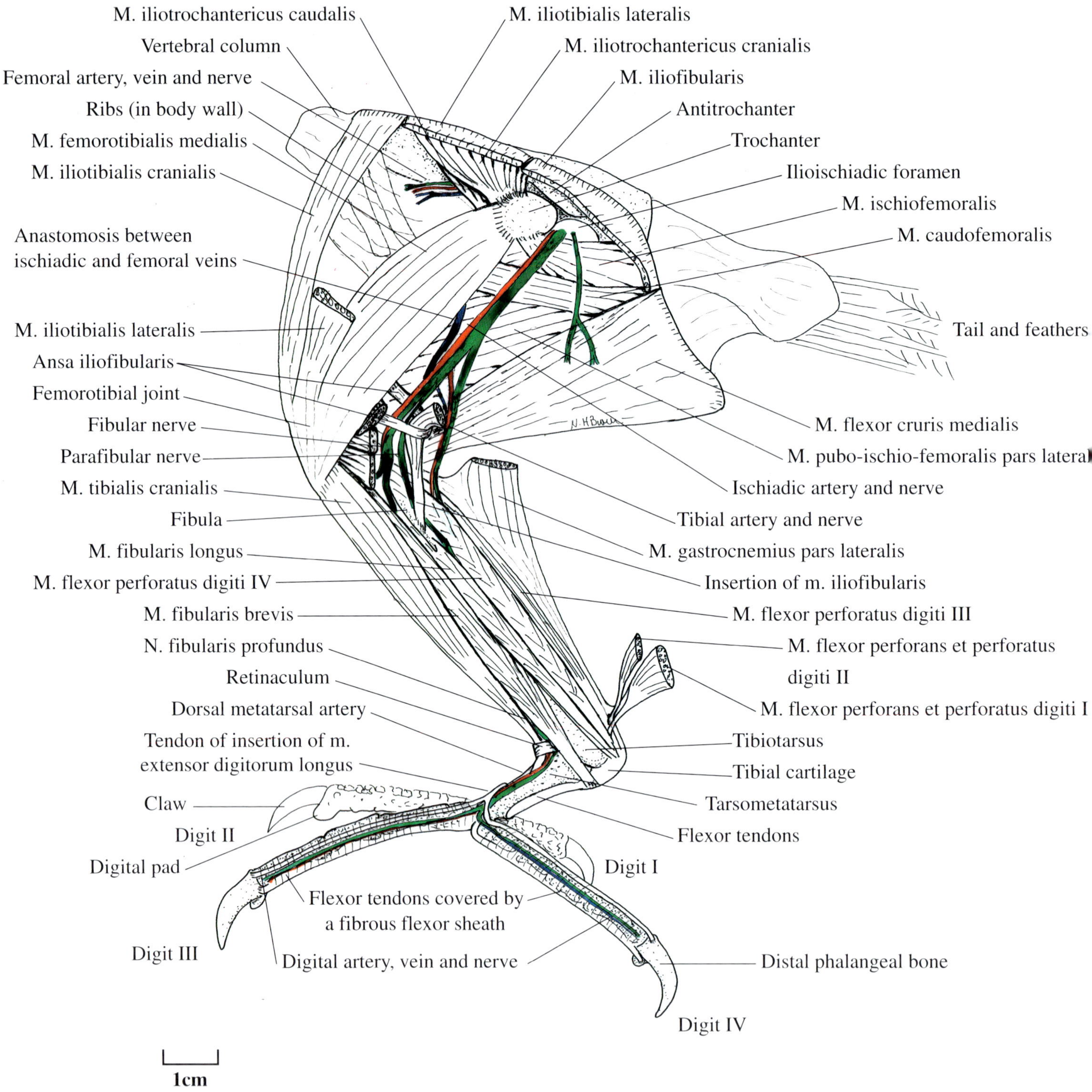

M. iliotrochantericus caudalis
Vertebral column
Femoral artery, vein and nerve
Ribs (in body wall)
M. femorotibialis medialis
M. iliotibialis cranialis

Anastomosis between
ischiadic and femoral veins

M. iliotibialis lateralis
Ansa iliofibularis
Femorotibial joint
Fibular nerve
Parafibular nerve
M. tibialis cranialis
Fibula
M. fibularis longus
M. flexor perforatus digiti IV
M. fibularis brevis
N. fibularis profundus
Retinaculum
Dorsal metatarsal artery
Tendon of insertion of m.
extensor digitorum longus
Claw
Digit II
Digital pad

Digit III

Flexor tendons covered by
a fibrous flexor sheath
Digital artery, vein and nerve

Digit IV

M. iliotibialis lateralis
M. iliotrochantericus cranialis
M. iliofibularis
Antitrochanter
Trochanter
Ilioischiadic foramen
M. ischiofemoralis
M. caudofemoralis

Tail and feathers

M. flexor cruris medialis
M. pubo-ischio-femoralis pars lateral
Ischiadic artery and nerve
Tibial artery and nerve
M. gastrocnemius pars lateralis
Insertion of m. iliofibularis
M. flexor perforatus digiti III
M. flexor perforans et perforatus
digiti II
M. flexor perforans et perforatus digiti I
Tibiotarsus
Tibial cartilage
Tarsometatarsus
Flexor tendons

Digit I

Distal phalangeal bone

1cm

Figure 13.1: *Lateral view of the left pelvic limb of an African Grey.*
The limb, including the pelvis and synsacrum, has been removed from the vertebral column, and the integument removed,
except for digits I and II. To illustrate the course of the main nerves, arteries and veins, mm. iliofibularis and iliotibialis
lateralis have been removed, and mm. gastrocnemius pars lateralis and flexors perforatus digiti II and III
have been sectioned at their origins and reflected.

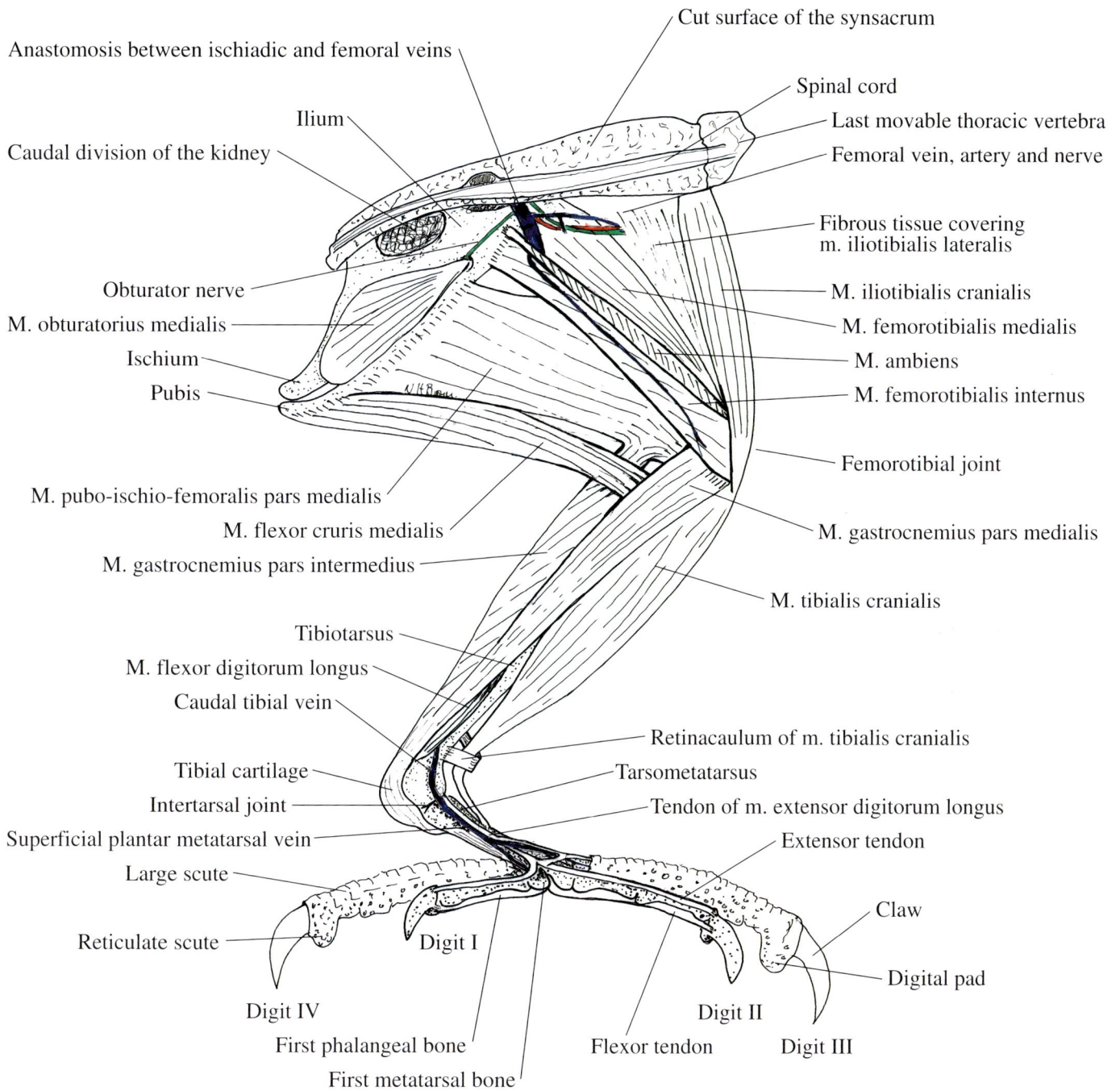

Cut surface of the synsacrum

Anastomosis between ischiadic and femoral veins

Spinal cord

Ilium

Last movable thoracic vertebra

Caudal division of the kidney

Femoral vein, artery and nerve

Fibrous tissue covering
m. iliotibialis lateralis

M. iliotibialis cranialis

Obturator nerve

M. femorotibialis medialis

M. obturatorius medialis

M. ambiens

Ischium

M. femorotibialis internus

Pubis

Femorotibial joint

M. pubo-ischio-femoralis pars medialis

M. gastrocnemius pars medialis

M. flexor cruris medialis

M. gastrocnemius pars intermedius

M. tibialis cranialis

Tibiotarsus

M. flexor digitorum longus

Caudal tibial vein

Retinacaulum of m. tibialis cranialis

Tibial cartilage

Tarsometatarsus

Intertarsal joint

Tendon of m. extensor digitorum longus

Superficial plantar metatarsal vein

Extensor tendon

Large scute

Claw

Reticulate scute

Digital pad

Digit I

Digit IV

Digit II

First phalangeal bone

Flexor tendon

Digit III

First metatarsal bone

1cm

Figure 13.2: *Medial view of the left pelvic limb of an African Grey.*
The limb, including the pelvis and synsacrum, has been removed from the vertebral column. The synsacrum and vertebral column
have been divided longitudinally to isolate one limb. The limb has had the integument removed, except for digits III and IV.
This illustration shows only the superficial musculature and no muscles have been removed.

as they leave the lumbosacral plexus and run through foramina in the pelvis (see Figures 13.1, 13.10.1). The pelvic muscle mass usually holds the fractured bones in place, but if there are signs of nerve damage then surgical intervention is necessary.

Femur

The femoral head is always fractured when the hip is dislocated (see later). The surgical approach to the femur should be from the lateral aspect (see Figure 13.1), dissecting between the iliofibularis muscle and the femorotibialis muscle (which is attached to the body of the femur). Care should be taken to avoid the major arteries, nerves and veins. Proximal femoral fractures can be repaired with a tension band technique using one or several pins (see Figure 13.3). Mid-shaft femoral fractures can be repaired using one of several techniques: pinning with a single pin if the bird is small, eg. a lovebird, or stack pinning with occasionally a cerclage wire in larger parrots, eg. an African Grey; shuttle pinning, full or half pin fixation are possible techniques for femoral fractures in macaws. The shaft of the femur has a slight craniocaudal curve, which is often lost when pinned; this is of no consequence. Fractures of the condylar region require cross pinning, the pins running from the epicondyles and bending up the inner edge of the cortex, or half pin fixation (see Figure 13.4).

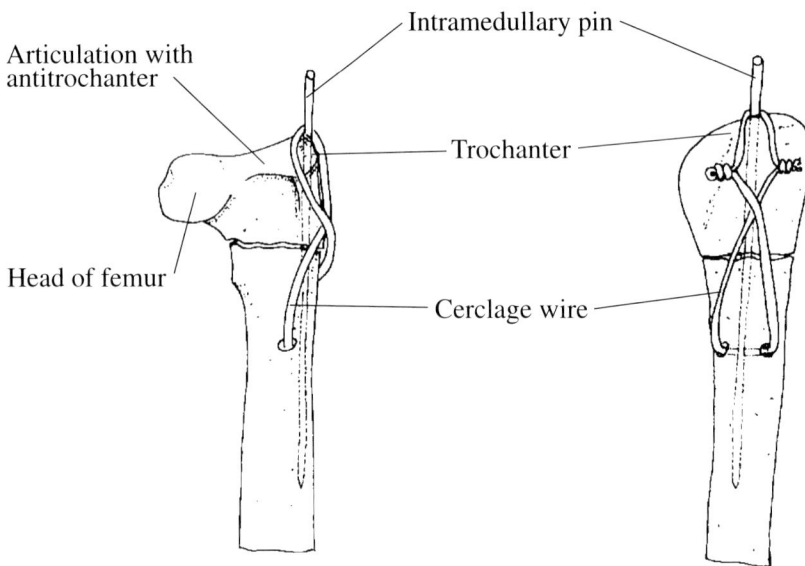

Figure 13.3.1: Cranial view of the proximal femur of a parrot to show tension band wiring.

Figure 13.3.2: Lateral view, of the proximal femur of a parrot to show tension band wiring.

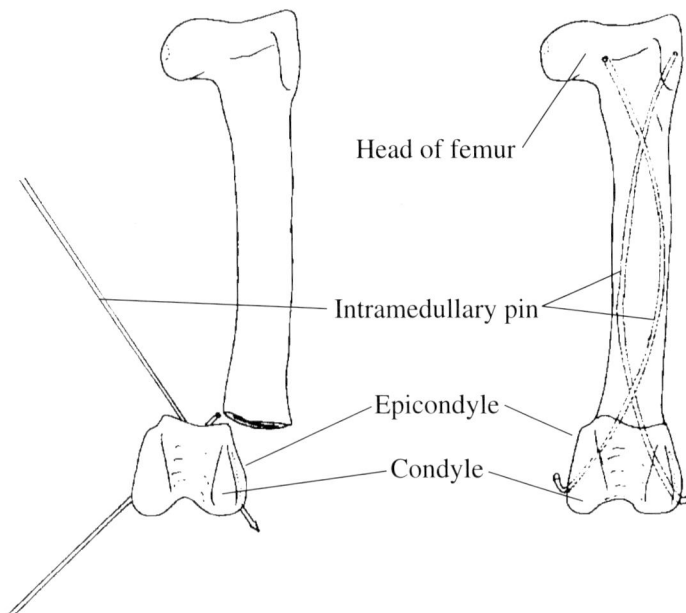

Figure 13.4: Cross pinning to repair a fracture of the distal femur.

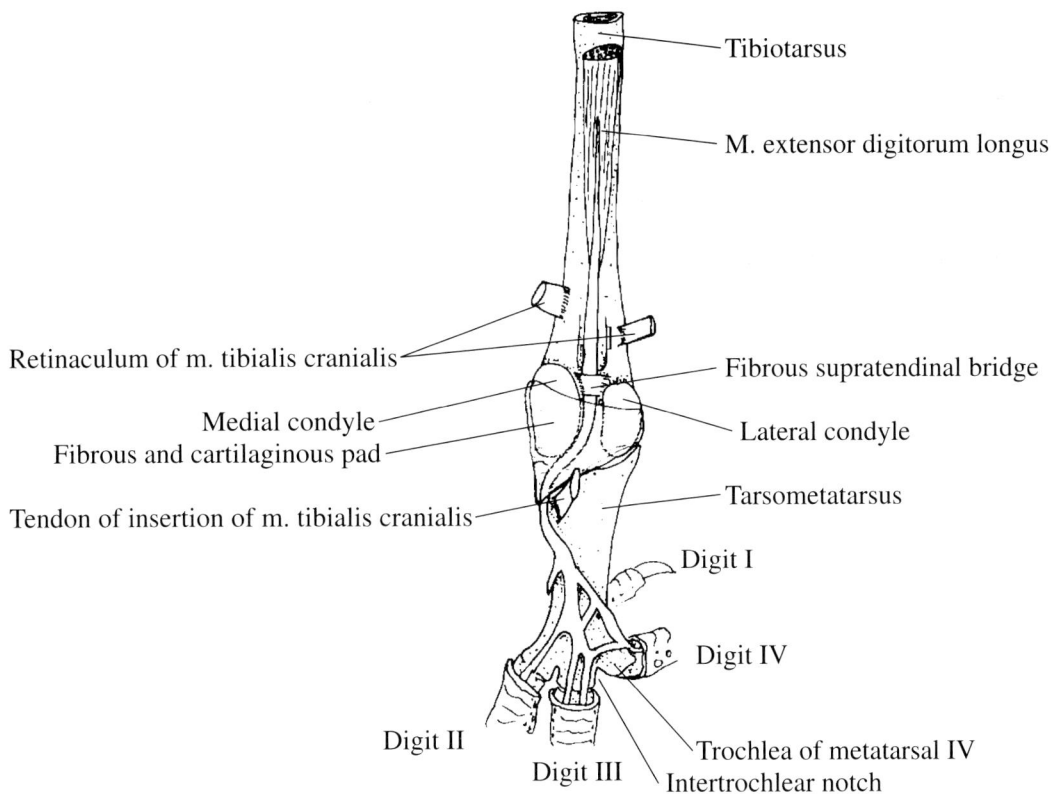

Figure 13.5: *A cranial view of the left intertarsal joint of an African Grey showing the path of the tendon of insertion of m. extensor digitorum longus. M. tibialis cranialis has been removed leaving the tendon of insertion; its retaining retinaculum has been sectioned.*

Tibiotarsus

This bone is the most frequently fractured. The surgical approach should be through a craniomedial incision, between the cranial tibial muscle and the medial gastrocnemius muscle (see Figure 13.2). This approach avoids any nerves, arteries and veins. The lateral approach should not be used (see Figure 13.1). Mid-shaft fractures occur just distal to the fibular crest. Intramedullary pins emerging through the cranial aspect of the femorotibial joint give good results when combined with a splint for 10 days. Shuttle pinning and full pin fixation can also be used to repair this fracture, but these are difficult techniques and only suitable for larger psittacines. If attempting these techniques it should be remembered that the arteries in this region are very close to the lateral tibiotarsus. The repair of fractures of the distal tibiotarsus are complicated by two tendons. The tendon of insertion of the cranial tibial muscle runs over the cranial surface of the intertarsal joint through a fibrous retinaculum. The tendon of insertion of the long digital extensor muscle runs under the fibrous supratendinal bridge, on the cranial aspect of the bone deep to the cranial tibial muscle (see Figure 13.5). Great care should be taken to avoid compromising the free running of these ten-

dons. Any involvement of these tendons in bony callus or fibrous scar will stop the intertarsal joint extending and flexing fully. Care must be taken during surgery, or when casting or applying tight bandages in this region, not to allow scar tissue to compromise the function of this joint. Cross pinning will usually allow adequate fixation of distal tibiotarsal fractures without the need for external support. The tibiotarsus in most psittacines is usually too small to allow full pin fixation.

Tarsometatarsus

This short bone is often fractured. Many fractures are the result of the leg band, used for identification purposes, becoming caught in the wires of the cage or aviary; the bird panics, tries to pull its leg away, and a fracture is the result. Because of the lack of soft tissue in this region the fracture is invariably compound. Bruising may lead to necrosis and loss of skin and tendons. Tendons of the extensor and flexor muscles run on the cranial and caudal aspect of the bone, as do the small intrinsic muscles. The veins are lateral and medial, but the arteries and nerves are mainly cranial. Cross pins can be inserted through the lateral aspect of the epicondyles to digit IV and the medial aspect of the epicondyles to digit II, and pushed cranially up the intramedullary cavity, which is well developed in this bone in psittacines. Full pin fixation is also satisfactory, especially if the fracture is compound and therefore infected. Small birds can be supported with an Altman tape splint (Altman, 1977).

Digits

In most cases the phalangeal bones are damaged beyond repair and amputation is required. Injured toes are usually removed by the bird itself, but may require professional amputation: sufficient skin should be saved to cover the bone end; the toe should be cut through the phalangeal bone and not the joint; the skin should be sutured with 3/0 or 4/0 cat gut and no dressing should be applied.

DISLOCATIONS

Vertebral-Synsacral Joint

The synsacrum can be dislocated partially or completely from the thoracic vertebrae (see later - Paralysis).

Hip Joint

This joint can be dislocated. The femoral head is always fractured as the bone is weaker than the ligament. The fracture will eventually lead to arthritis and loss of function. When the bird extends its leg the trochanter moves dorsal to the antitrochanter and 'locks', leaving the limb in extension. The diagnosis is confirmed on radiographic comparison of both hips (under general anaesthesia). Removal of the femoral head through a cranial approach to the hip joint and the placement of a strip of the iliofibularis muscle through the joint is an excellent salvage procedure (MacCoy, 1989). Most birds make a good recovery.

Femorotibial Joint

This joint is only dislocated as a result of severe trauma (see Figure 13.6). It is possible to make a satisfactory repair by replacing damaged ligaments with Teflon suture material (WL Gore and Associates). Complete disruption of the joint has been salvaged by using half-pin fixation on the cranial aspect above and below the joint, holding the joint in reasonable apposition whilst a fibrous union takes place (Rosenthal et al, 1994). Meniscal damage is rarely diagnosed.

Intertarsal Joint

In adult birds this joint is usually injured by severe trauma, and dislocation is generally accompanied by damage to tendons, ligaments, integument, etc. It is not usually possible to repair the joint. The tibial cartilage can be damaged: growing birds can easily dislocate many of the structures within or attached to the tibial cartilage. This dislocation can occasionally be secondary to a growth defect involving the bones; any

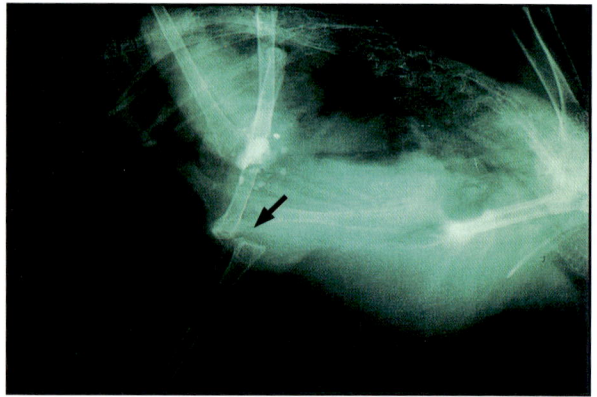

Figure 13.6: This Lord Derby Parakeet has a dislocated femorotibial joint (arrow). The two cruciate and the medial collateral ligaments have been ruptured. The menisci and lateral collateral ligament have escaped damage. Ligament replacement with Teflon suture material was successful and resulted in the bird being sound.

growth defect should be corrected. The most frequent dislocation in the intertarsal joint involves the tendon of m. flexor hallucis longus. The tendon bursts out of position and lies to the lateral aspect of the tibial cartilage, usually as a sequel to trauma. The displacement of the tendon causes the bird to be unable to use the affected leg; there is an obvious thickening of the joint and, if recently displaced, the tendon can be palpated; the foot is abducted from the body. If seen within a day or two of the event, the tendon is easily repositioned surgically. The tunnel that the tendon occupied is identifiable and the tendon can be repositioned. The tear is repaired with 4/0 polydioxanone (PDS II, Ethicon). No external support is needed for the limb, but the bird should be kept in a narrow, deep container for seven days to prevent any tendency for the leg to splay and therefore repeat the damage. Unfortunately, it may be weeks before these cases are presented, by which time it may be impossible to reposition the tendon. In cases of chronic displacement it is better to leave the tendon rather than attempt to reposition it surgically. The lateral and medial hypotarsal crests are well formed once growth has stopped. In the adult bird the deep flexor tendons, those of mm. flexor hallucis longus and flexor digitorum longus, are completely contained in hypotarsal grooves. In many psittacine species the bone that forms the grooves fuses over the tendon to form bony tunnels which contain these deep flexors, thereby preventing displacement. In growing birds the hypotarsal crests are less developed and are fibrous and cartilaginous: this predisposes the displacement and relocation of the tendon(s).

Less frequently, the insertion of the medial gastrocnemius muscle will pull away from the tibial cartilage and allow the tibial cartilage, flexor tendons and the tarsometatarsus to rotate laterally. Immediate surgical correction is required, but is difficult to achieve as the sutures tend to pull through the tissue used to anchor the muscle insertion.

Phalangeal Joints

These joints can be dislocated without any permanent ligamentous damage. They are easily replaced under general anaesthesia and require no external support. External support usually causes loss of function. If a collateral ligament is broken and there is no additional trauma; the ligament should be sutured.

NUTRITIONAL OSTEODYSTROPHY

This is a very common problem seen in two separate groups of psittacines.

Growing Birds

Many psittacine species are hand reared. The more easily bred and popular species, eg. African Grey, are frequently presented with osteodystrophy. These birds are easy to breed and rear; therefore they are often reared on a deficient diet by ill-informed owners. The most easily recognised deficiency is of calcium, though calcium deficiency is only one of many dietary deficiencies in these individuals. The signs of osteodystrophy are usually not evident to the inexperienced breeder; often the parent bird is wrongly accused of sitting on the chick. The pelvic limb is often the most affected (see Figure 13.7). Mild cases usually have lordosis of the synsacrum, variable diameter of the shafts of the femur and tibiotarsus, folding fractures of the distal femur just proximal to the condyles, and bowing of the tibiotarsus in either craniocaudal or lateromedial planes. More serious cases have dramatic bone deformities and often partially healed fractures of the long bones. Mild cases that are seen during active bone growth can be helped by placing the young bird into a narrow, deep plastic cup so that the limbs and body are supported. The cup must be cleaned frequently and lined with paper towels. This support is vital whilst the new vitamin and mineral enriched diet is used. In more serious cases, growing limbs can be encouraged to straighten by the use of external leg

braces (Clipsham, 1991). Cases with multiple fractures, especially those that have stopped growing, are destined to be crippled for life. Because of their poor quality of life, euthanasia should be considered for many of these birds.

Adult Birds

Dietary deficiency of calcium, due to inadequate supplementation or selective feeding by the bird, will lead to osteoporosis (see Figures 13.8.1, 13.8.2). Osteoporosis is made more dramatic if the bird is continually laying eggs, a frequent event in pet cockatiels.

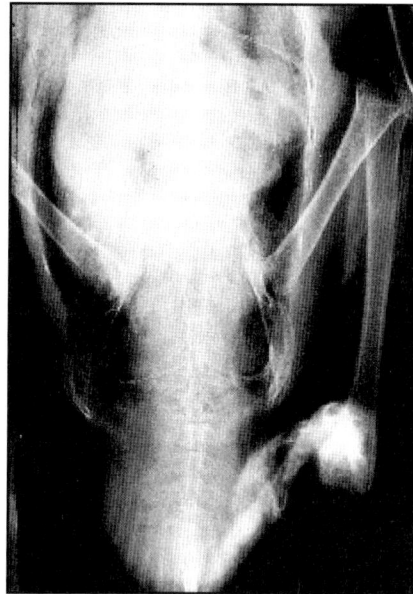

Figure 13.8.1: *Normal radiographic appearance of the pelvic region of a Blue and Yellow Macaw.*

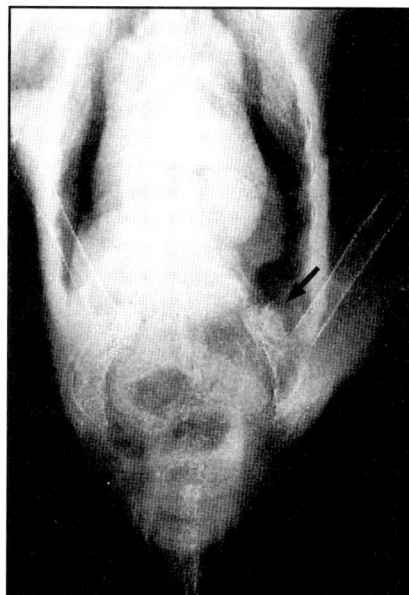

Figure 13.8.2: *A female Blue and Yellow Macaw that had laid 19 eggs: the diet was sunflower seed and very little vitamin supplementation. Note the very reduced bone density, thin irregular cortices of the long bones and a fracture of the proximal right femur (arrow).*

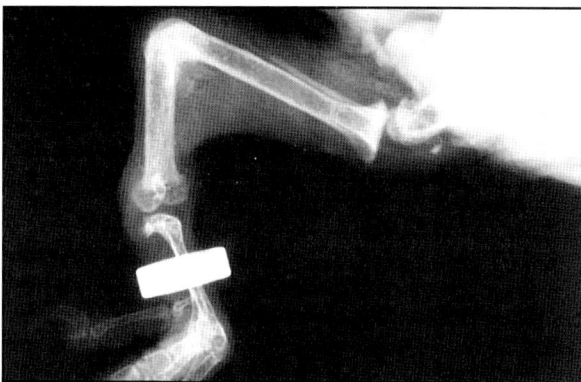

Figure 13.7: *The pelvic limb of a young African Grey. The bird had initially been fed a diet deficient in calcium which resulted in bowing of the tibiotarsus. The diet was then correctly supplemented. The radiograph shows normally mineralised bones.*

Spontaneous fractures are accompanied by loss of density and irregular thinning of the cortices of the long bones. A bird with a single fracture is often treated by surgical repair, only to have a second or third fracture appear a few weeks later on the opposite limb. These cases carry a poor prognosis. A suitable vitamin and mineral supplement must be added to the diet (see Chapter 3). Calcium deficiency in adult birds will be accompanied by many other nutritional problems.

PARALYSIS

Psittacines are frequently presented with paresis of one or both pelvic limbs. There are a number of distinct causes.

Luxation or Subluxation of the Vertebrae

Free-flying household pets may fly into a window with disastrous results. Fractures and dislocations of the vertebrae are usually easily diagnosed. The prognosis is often hopeless. Radiography under general anaesthesia with the vertebral column being 'stretched' may show a dislocation that has returned to its 'normal' position; there will be an increase in the intervertebral space that is greater than expected between the last, free thoracic vertebra and the synsacrum. The bruising and swelling of tissues in the vertebral canal will cause paresis or paralysis. Careful nursing, corticosteroids and antibiotics will sometimes help a patient presented with paresis and little bony damage. Osteoporosis often underlies this condition.

Abscessation of the Intervertebral Space

Some birds that fly into a window appear to recover or are apparently uninjured. However, haematogenously spread bacteria may invade the bruised intervertebral space and produce a slow-developing abscess (see Figures 13.9.1, 13.9.2). The abscess will cause increasing pressure on the spinal cord, producing paresis and finally paralysis of both pelvic limbs. The abscess is easily visible on radiographs. Haematology reveals an elevated leucocyte count with a heterophilia. Treatment is usually unsuccessful; the caseous nature of avian pus makes drainage impossible and antibiotics will not kill bacteria in the presence of pus. It is important that birds that have suffered a traumatic incident should be given a prophylactic course of antibiotic, even if they appear to be uninjured. *Staphylococcus* spp. or coliforms are commonly encountered in these abscesses.

Lead Poisoning

In the early stages of this disease affected birds may show marked paresis of the limbs (see Chapter 19).

Renal Infection

The pelvic limb is innervated by the femoral, obturator and ischiadic nerves (see Figures 13.1, 13.2). These

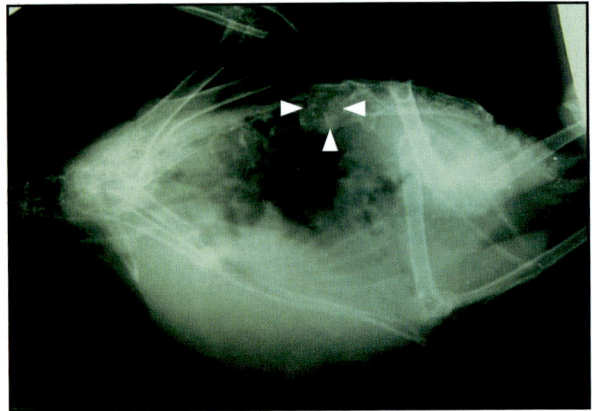

Figure 13.9.1: Lateral view of a vertebral synsacral abscess in a pet Blue-fronted Amazon. Note the area of increased bone density around a lytic area (arrows) at the vertebral synsacral junction. (A barium meal showed a massive soft tissue enlargement that pushed the intestines ventrally.)

Figure 13.9.2: The same case post mortem. Note the large abscess (arrows) displacing the kidneys. When opened the abscess was found to have eroded into the vertebral canal.

nerves all arise in the synsacral area and run across the ventral synsacrum and through the pelvis to the limb (see Figures 13.10.1, 13.10.2). The ischiadic nerve innervates the majority of the limb and runs from the synsacrum to the ilioischiadic foramen in close proximity to the middle and caudal divisions of the kidneys. This relationship is sufficient for a nephritis to cause a neuritis to develop. Many birds are presented with paresis and no history of previous trauma. Plain radiographs and intravenous pyelography using an intravenous bolus of 175-700mg iodine in the form of iohexol (Omnipaque, Nycomed) may show increased renal density and, occasionally, a difference in functional ability between the divisions of the kidney (see Chapter 7). Gentle palpation *per cloacam* will sometimes confirm enlargement of the kidneys if radiographs are not available. The birds may have an increased blood uric acid level (uricaemia) and often a leucocytosis. Antibiotic therapy is usually sufficient to effect a rapid improvement and cure. Co-trimazine (100mg/kg p/o or i/m bid) is usually the drug of choice,

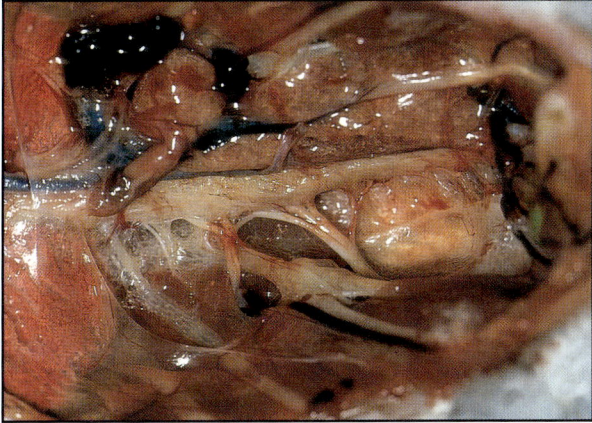

Figure 13.10.1: *The normal left lumbrosacral plexus of an African Grey after the removal of the left kidney. This bird died due to renal tubule damage and the resulting visceral gout. The right kidney is very pale and contains excessive urates.*

Figure 13.10.2: *The dorsal aspect of the kidneys of a Blue-headed Parrot. Note the close proximity of the nerves to the kidney tissues.*

in spite of the compromised renal function, as this condition is usually coliform related.

Tumours

Tumours of the gonad or the kidney may cause a unilateral paresis or paralysis. Plain and contrast radiography is usually sufficient to confirm the diagnosis.

Cage or Perch Paralysis

This condition is seen in many pet budgerigars and, occasionally, in other parrots and parakeets (see Figure 13.11). The birds are usually over-fed, overweight, reluctant to fly, never allowed out of their small cage, and have hard doweling perches. Often, they have pressure necrosis on the soles of their feet. Affected birds are incapable of flying or running, even if encouraged to do so. Most of these birds are deficient in calcium, iodine - and therefore thyroid hormone - and vitamin E. Treatment requires vitamin and mineral supplementation, followed by a weight reducing diet.

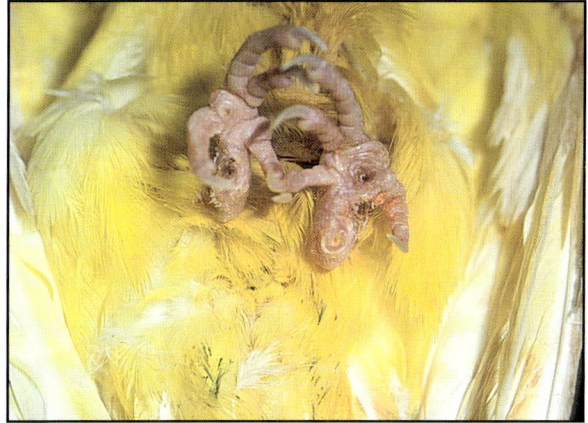

Figure 13.11: *The plantar aspect of the feet of a white cockatiel which had been fed on a diet of "cockatiel mix" with no additional supplements. This bird was treated with vitamin and mineral supplementation, antibiotic (lincomycin), application of Dermisol Cream (Pfizer) to the feet ulcers. Padding the cage floor with cushioned rubber carpet-underlay allowed the feet to heal and the bird to be able to fly. After six months the bird was approaching normality.*

Figure 13.12: *A healthy Scarlet Macaw with a deep groove under its stainless steel closed ring. The ring was placed around the tarsometatarsus when the bird was a few weeks old.*

Increased exercise will return some of these birds to normal, and most of them will be considerably improved.

INTEGUMENTARY DISEASES OF THE PELVIC LIMB

Ring Damage

A large proportion of psittacines have rings (leg bands) around their tarsometatarsal region. These rings may provide proof of identity, sex and captive status. There are, however, a number of ways in which rings can cause problems.

Most species of macaw walk on the plantar aspect of the foot and the entire caudal tarsometatarsus to the intertarsal joint. A ring in this position causes the formation of a deep groove and can lead to skin and tendon pressure necrosis (see Figure 13.12).

Some makes of ring are too wide for the tarsometatarsus and may cause pressure necrosis on the dorsal aspect of digits I and IV. This is especially common in some *Amazona* spp. and *Pionus* spp.

Closed rings on budgerigars may allow a build-up of scale between the ring and the skin. In time this can cause a complete stricture, resulting in oedema and even necrosis of the limb distal to the ring.

The best treatment is removal of the ring. In larger birds, where the rings are usually stainless steel, this requires general anaesthesia, narrow-jawed mole grips and a hacksaw or bolt-cutter. If the ring was present for identification purposes it must be replaced, eg. with a microchip (see Chapter 22). Some small rings can be removed with nail clippers or a special ring remover.

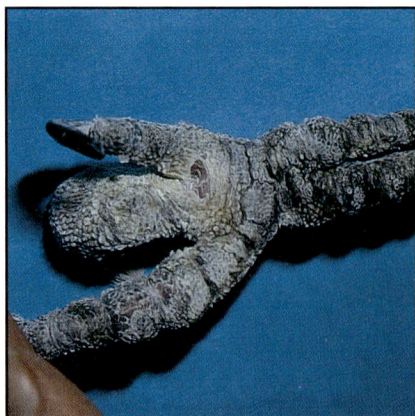

Figure 13.13: The plantar aspect of the right foot of a Salmon-crested Cockatoo. The foot shows two areas of early pressure necrosis; there is also epidermal proliferation in areas that are not under pressure.

Pressure Necrosis of the Foot

Many captive birds have too little exercise, are too fat and suffer from malnutrition; this leads to pressure necrosis, followed by infection, of the plantar aspect of the foot. The condition is made worse if the bird is chronically lame on one leg (see Figure 13.13). Plastic or doweling perches should be replaced with natural branches of different sizes and textures. Any edible fruit wood would be suitable, or ash or sycamore. In aviaries the perches should be mobile but stable. This can be achieved either by suspending one or both ends of the perch from a wire, or by using longer and thinner perches anchored at one end, so that they 'give' when the bird lands on them. Dietary supplementation, more flying exercise and treatment, if possible, of the lameness will allow the feet to return to normal.

Loss of Claws

Many birds lose a claw either in a fight with another bird or, if the claw is too long, by it becoming caught in the cage wire. It is quite possible for a bird to bleed to death from a broken claw, especially if it is malnourished, with associated low levels of vitamin K$_1$ or liver disease.

Crystals of potassium permanganate or ferric chloride on a swab should be applied firmly to the end of the damaged claw to stop any bleeding. Placing the bird in a cage with no perches for a few hours will help prevent the clot being rubbed off when the bird moves; the bird clings to the bars and the claw is therefore not in contact with a surface which will rub off the clot. Occasionally, general anaesthesia and thermocautery is needed. Vitamin K$_1$ (2-5mg i/m) should be given if a deficiency is suspected.

If the claw and its germinal layer are stripped to the bone, it is usually necessary to amputate the protruding bone. If this is done carefully, so as to conserve the germinal bed of the nail, a stub of nail will grow and the digit will remain functional.

Cnemidocoptes spp. Infection

This parasitic infection occurs occasionally in budgerigars and is known as 'scaly-face' or 'scaly-leg'. Ivermectin is completely curative (see Chapter 10). This condition should not be confused with the epidermal proliferation seen so commonly in old and malnourished birds.

Gout

Gout is commonly seen in budgerigars and occasionally in other psittacines. Accumulations of uric acid crystals (tophi) are deposited under the skin, especially on the feet and around the phalangeal joints. The skin can be lanced and the uric acid crystals squeezed out like paste (see Figure 13.14). Many of these birds can be shown at *post-mortem* examination or on kidney biopsy to be suffering from advanced renal disease. The uric acid level in the blood may be elevated but it seems that the body maintains its uric acid levels at close to normal by depositing these precipitates. Biopsy can give misleading results as the uric acid is dissolved while the tissues are processed.

Allopurinol has been used to treat avian gout. A

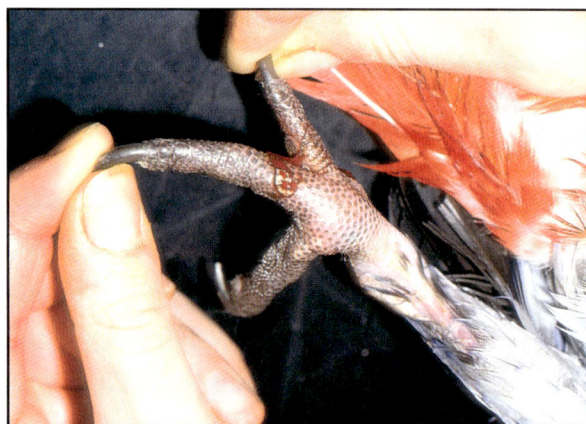

Figure 13.14: The dorsal aspect of the right foot of a four-year-old African Grey with gout. Note the creamy-pink discoloration in swollen areas of the foot.

100mg tablet crushed and dissolved into 10ml of water allows budgerigars to be dosed with one drop four times daily.

It is sometimes possible to reverse or even cure this condition by feeding a low protein diet and using antibiotic therapy, especially if there is an elevated leucocyte count indicative of a bacterial nephritis.

Fibrous Bands Around the Digits

Some birds are presented with swollen toes. Adult pet cockatiels and, occasionally, budgerigars get hair or thread wrapped around their toes as a constrictive band. The digit distal to the thread swells and can become gangrenous. The thread should be removed, which usually requires magnification and a needle. Young birds which are being hand reared can also be presented with swollen toes. This is usually caused by a complete fibrous epithelial band constricting the blood supply; occasionally, it is caused by a hair from the feeder. Again, the band should be cut. It has been suggested that the fibrous band results from the brooder being too dry, similar to the pathogenesis of ring-tail in laboratory rats.

REFERENCES

Altman RB (1977) Fractures of the extremities of birds. In: *Current Veterinary Therapy VI.* Ed RW Kirk. WB Saunders, Philadelphia.

Berman SL (1984) The hindlimb musculature of the White-fronted Amazon (*Amazona albifrons, Psittaciformes*). *The Auk* **101**, 74.

Clipsham RC (1991) Correction of pediatric limb disorders. In: *Proceedings of the Association of Avian Veterinarians Annual Conference 1991.* AAV, Lake Worth.

MacCoy DM (1989) Excision arthroplasty for management of coxofemoral luxation in pet birds. *Journal of the American Veterinary Medical Association* **94(1)**, 95.

Redig PT (1986) Evaluation and non-surgical management of fractures. In: *Clinical Avian Medicine and Surgery, including Aviculture.* Eds GJ Harrison and LR Harrison. WB Saunders, Philadelphia.

Rosenthal K, Hillyer E and Mathiessen D (1994) Stifle luxation repair in a Moluccan Cockatoo and a Barn Owl. *Journal of the Association of Avian Veterinarians* **8(4)**, 173.

CHAPTER FOURTEEN

Wing Problems

Brian H Coles

PREVENTION OR REDUCTION OF FLIGHT

Techniques for prevention or reduction of flight have been reviewed by Seidal (1991).

Clipping the Primary and Secondary Flight Feathers

This is the common method of flight prevention since most psittacines brought to the surgery are household pets. Breeders do not usually ask for their birds to be deflighted since this could interfere with breeding. It is important to explain to owners that clipping flight feathers does not completely eliminate flight, and that it is unwise to let these birds loose in the garden, particularly in windy weather.

The technique for clipping primary and secondary flight feathers is illustrated in Figure 14.1. The feathers of one wing only should be cut. This will reduce the aerodynamic lift so that the bird will not be able to maintain sustained flight. However, many birds are able to get airborne for short distances even when the flight feathers have been cut properly. Each primary feather should be cut individually just below the level of the covert feathers so that the trimmed end is not visible. If the last two or three distal primaries are left uncut the appearance of the resting and folded wing is more aesthetically pleasing as well as providing some stability. When cutting the feathers care should be taken to avoid any which are in the growing stage and said to be 'in the blood' or 'pin' feathers, since these will bleed quite profusely. If this occurs the feather shaft should be plucked and the bleeding follicle cauterised. All cut feather stumps are eventually moulted and replaced with new feathers at the next moult. Since moulting in psittacines, like most tropical birds, does not take place at specific times of the year, the cut feathers will be replaced irregularly. Recutting of the flight feathers will usually need to be repeated at least annually, and sometimes more frequently. Various modifications to this basic trim are suggested by Harrison and Harrison (1986a).

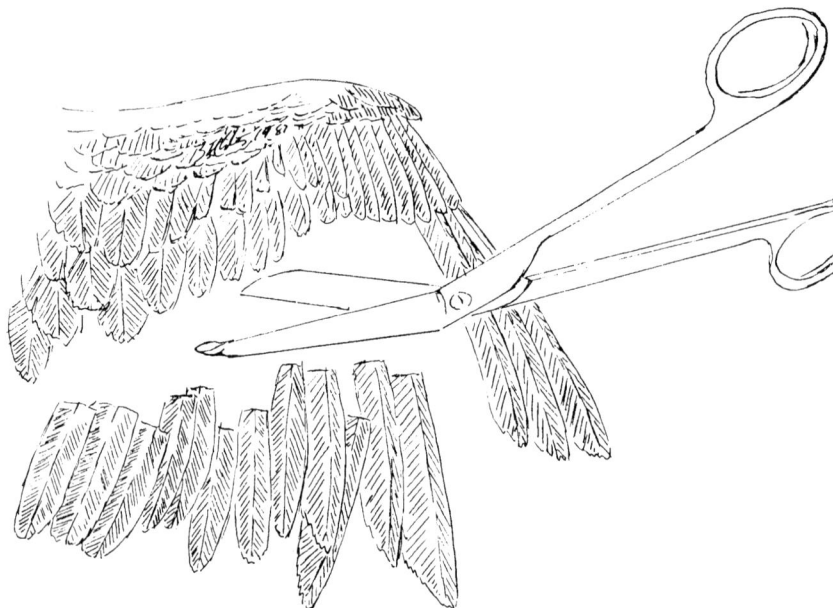

Figure 14.1: Cutting the flight feathers of one wing to restrict flight: the last two or three feathers are left so that when the wing is folded the effect is cosmetically more acceptable. **Owners must be warned that even after cutting the feathers some birds can still get airborne and it is not safe to take the uncaged bird outside.**

Other methods of flight prevention are surgical and permanent. However, some authorities, including the Royal College of Veterinary Surgeons (RCVS), consider these methods to be an unnecessary mutilation and, as such, unethical (RCVS, 1993). They are mentioned here only for reference purposes. Whichever method is used, only one wing is operated on.

Pinioning
This is usually carried out in fledglings before the bones are fully calcified, although there is a danger that the parent birds may kill their offspring. The second digit carrying the alula is preserved, but the tip of the wing is amputated by cutting through the two metacarpal bones with scissors, a heated scalpel blade or electrocautery. The operation can be carried out in mature birds, but a double figure of eight ligature just proximal to the carpus will be needed to control bleeding. The skin should be left long enough to suture over the stump. However, the cosmetic results in parrots are not acceptable.

Patagiectomy
The protopagium ligament is a complex sheet of tissue filling the space in the angle formed by the humerus and the radius when the wing is extended. This ligament forms the leading edge of the wing and if it is surgically removed the bird cannot fly. Providing the wound heals properly the end result is effective and aesthetically acceptable, but the procedure is time consuming and healing may be a problem, particularly in some species (Mangili, 1971; Coles, 1985; Seidal, 1991; Robinson, 1995).

Radial and Ulna Neurectomy
This method is effective and easy to carry out as both nerves are located subcutaneously. The ulnar nerve is located running obliquely and parallel to the brachial vein over the ventral and distal half of the humerus. The radial nerve lies more dorsally but also crosses the distal half of the humerus diagonally from the medial to the lateral aspect (see Figure 14.5.1). However, after the operation the wing may be permanently dropped and the result is not always aesthetically pleasing (see Figure 14.2.2).

Tendonectomy of the Muscle Extensor Pollicis Longus et Brevis
The tendon is exposed by a short incision along the leading edge of the wing over the flexed radial carpal joint starting just proximal to the alula. About 10mm of this tendon is removed. This method is effective, easy to perform and aesthetically acceptable.

Wiring of the Metacarpus and Ulna
This technique is not difficult and is effective. A series of simple interrupted stainless steel wire sutures are passed around the metacarpus and ulna so that the

carpometacarpal joint is permanently flexed. The anterior aspect of the radial carpal joint is opened just sufficient to scarify the articular cartilage and allow subsequent arthrodesis. Birds tend to leave the operation site alone. The wing may be dropped for several days postoperatively, but it soon regains its normal position. The end result is aesthetically acceptable.

FRACTURE DIAGNOSIS

A definitive diagnosis must be made before any method of treatment is contemplated and an accurate prognosis given to the owner. The veterinarian should be aware that even if a wing is in an apparently normal position it may still be fractured. Nevertheless, some fracture sites can be deduced from the position in which the wing is held by the bird when perched (see Figures 14.2.1, 2.2, 2.3).

Careful palpation of the bones of the wing can sometimes locate a fracture in the conscious bird, but if the bird struggles under examination a simple fracture may be converted into a compound fracture. An accurate diagnosis requires radiography. Without radiographs the surgeon cannot tell if a fracture is transverse or oblique or if it is comminuted. In cases of suspected fracture the whole body should be radiographed since there may be less obvious fractures or pathologies in other parts of the skeleton. Failure to carry out whole body radiography in a traumatised bird might be considered to be negligent. Radiography should be carried out under general anaesthesia so as to avoid any further injury due to struggling or unnecessary radiation exposure to the handlers.

Figure 14.2.1: The wing hangs down if the fracture is distal to the middle of the radius and ulna and if both these bones are fractured.

Figure 14.2.2: Injury to the humerus or elbow does not usually result in a markedly dropped wing, although it may be noticed to be swollen and held out from the body if viewed from the front of the bird and if compared with the normal side.

Figure 14.2.3: Injury to the coracoid or shoulder usually results in the anterior edge of the wing being dropped and the primary feathers canted above those on the other wing.

The following factors affect the decision as to the most appropriate method of treatment:

● All owners want their bird returned to complete normality, but this may not be possible and the likelihood of achieving this should be discussed with the client.

● Account should be taken of the bird's future life style. Many captive psittacines spend most, if not all, of their life in a cage or at best on a perch in the living room where their flying potential is negligible. They may already have had their feathers clipped to prevent flight. Alternatively, if the bird is to be kept in a breeding aviary or as a zoological specimen, some flight capacity is desirable. Consideration should be given as to whether or not the bird can live comfortably if it is permanently disabled.

● The final cosmetic appearance will be important to the owner, so the wing should appear normal when the bird is resting and perching .

● If the fracture is severely comminuted it may be wiser to decide on a conservative method of treatment. A widely distracted and distally fractured humerus will usually result in large callus formation which may, in time, trap nerves, muscle tendons or blood supply. The position in which the wing is initially held may worsen.

● If the fracture is compound it will usually be contaminated with blood clot, debris and matted feathering, and will almost certainly be infected. A swab should be taken for microbiological culture and sensitivity.

● A fracture which is close to or actually involves a joint will reduce considerably the chances of the bird flying normally again. This is because of the marked tendency of traumatised avian joints to stiffen or become ankylosed however much movement is allowed during the healing period.

● The time interval between the initial injury and the clinical examination should be considered. If the interval is more than a few days the natural healing processes will have progressed to the stage where granulation tissue will have formed at the fracture site. Some muscle contraction will have occurred in the adjacent muscles, possibly causing overriding of the fracture. How far this has progressed can sometimes be judged by the clarity of the cortices of the ends of the fractured bone as seen on the radiograph. If the fracture is in an advanced state of healing, any surgical interference can often prove to be much more difficult than originally anticipated.

● The cost to the client is an important consideration, particularly in the case of the smaller psittacines.

● There is little doubt that in the majority of cases wing fractures will heal satisfactorily with cage rest and appropriate bandaging. However, many of these birds will not be able to fly again.

FRACTURE MANAGEMENT

Clavicle

The clavicle is not present in all psittacine species and when present it is vestigial. However, where present it may be fractured as a result of collision injury. The clavicle is well supported by the pectoralis muscle and fractures of this bone are not usually compound or grossly displaced. Unless grossly displaced, when the clavicle is best removed, it is wiser to leave the fracture alone. If the fracture is compound the protruding bone should be removed, the fracture site debrided and cleaned, and any infection treated.

Coracoid

The coracoid is a substantial bone which helps to support the wing and counteracts the compression of the thorax by the main flight muscles. Fracture of this bone results in a very disabling and disfiguring injury. A large callus may impinge on the crop or oesophagus, causing dysphagia.

In small birds, eg. budgerigars, the fracture is probably best left to heal with cage rest. In larger birds, particularly if the bone fragments are not aligned, an attempt should be made to reduce the fracture by intramedullary pinning techniques. The coracoid lies deep below the cranial edge of the pectoralis muscle and just lateral to the right and left brachiocephalic trunks and their subclavian and common carotid arteries as well as the two jugular veins. Care should be taken to prevent these being snagged by the jagged edge of a fractured bone.

Shoulder Joint

Impact injury can sometimes result in the severing of the tendon of the supracoroideus muscle just after its emergence from the foramen triosseum and near to its insertion on the dorsum of the humerus (see Figure 14.5.3). The bird is then unable to elevate the injured wing. The shoulder joint can easily be palpated. It lies just beneath the skin and the overlying propatagius muscle, and is therefore not difficult to approach surgically. However, finding the severed end of the supracoroideum tendon is not as easy. Often, the distal part of the tendon still attached to the body of the muscle has disappeared out of sight down through the triosseal canal. If this injury is diagnosed it is probably best left alone.

Humerus

There are a variety of methods for dealing with fractures of the humerus, all of which have advantages and disadvantages. The method of choice will to some extent depend on the type and position of the fracture. Proximal fractures of the humerus are well supported by muscle and will often resolve satisfactorily with cage rest and bandaging. The medullary cavity of the humerus is connected to the lateral diverticulum of the clavicular air sac at its proximal end. Compound fractures of this region or surgery of this area carry a risk of air sac infection or emphysema. On the other hand, distal fractures of this bone are usually distracted and may require internal fixation.

Bandaging

The method of bandaging a wing is illustrated in Figure 14.3. Psittacines often interfere with their bandages so that a collar or neck brace may need to be used.

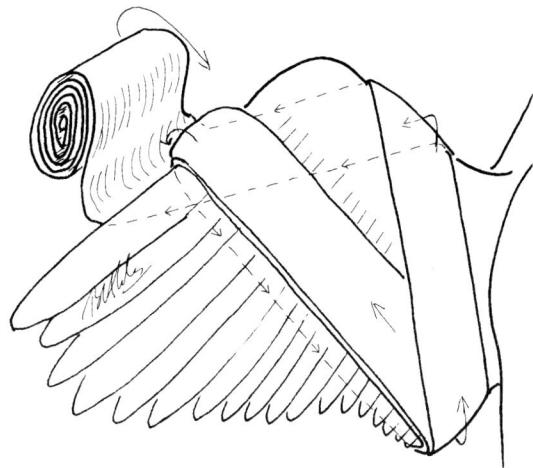

Figure 14.3: *The principles of bandaging the wing with Vetrap to give external support for fractures of the humerus, radius or ulna. For the purpose of clarification the wing is shown partly extended, but when this method is used the primary feathers would be bunched together so that their quills would act as a lightweight splint. The arrows indicate the direction in which the bandage is applied.*

The method of fashioning one of these is illustrated in Figure 14.4.

Intramedullary Pinning

The surgical approach and the important features of this method are illustrated in Figures 14.5.1 and 14.5.2.

Shuttle Pinning

This technique has been described by Coles (1985), Redig (1986) and Tom and Norbet (1991). All used the same principle technique but with slight variations. Coles and Tom and Norbet used the polypropylene cruciate section stem of a 1ml or 2ml syringe to make the shuttle.

Polypropylene is well tolerated by the body's tissues. It has been used as a surgical implant material by this author in many cases (and has also been used by human surgeons). The method of anchoring the shuttle in the medullary cavity of the humerus varies. Tom and Norbet used bone cement, but Coles favoured using a figure of eight tension band wire which, although a more difficult technique, puts more compression on the point of union of the fracture site and so promotes healing as well as stopping rotation of the bone.

The recommended surgical approach to the bone is from the dorsal aspect, ie. the same as for intramedullary pinning as illustrated in Figure 14.5.1. Either a dorsal or ventral approach to the humerus can be used but the dorsal one makes correct alignment of the fractured segments of bone easier. The technique of shuttle pinning as used by Coles is illustrated in Figures 14.6.1, 14.6.2, 14.6.3, 14.6.4, 14.6.5.

Shuttle pinning has all the advantages of intramedullary pinning but keeps away from the joints and does not require postoperative bandaging. Although cage

The lower (caudal) end can
be tapered to enlarge the
diameter slightly; this will
make it more comfortable
and able to accommodate a
distended crop.

Hospital sticky tape wound round the 'Pipe
Wrapp' to keep the cut side together and
keep it in place.

5cm external diameter 'Pipe Wrapp'
with an internal diameter of 2.5cm cut
to a suitable length to stop the bird
getting to a bandaged wing. Such a
collar can also be made from a roll of
Vetrap tape cut to a suitable length.

The length of 'Pipe
Wrapp' is cut so as to
allow it to open and to
fit over the neck, when
it closes back in
position.

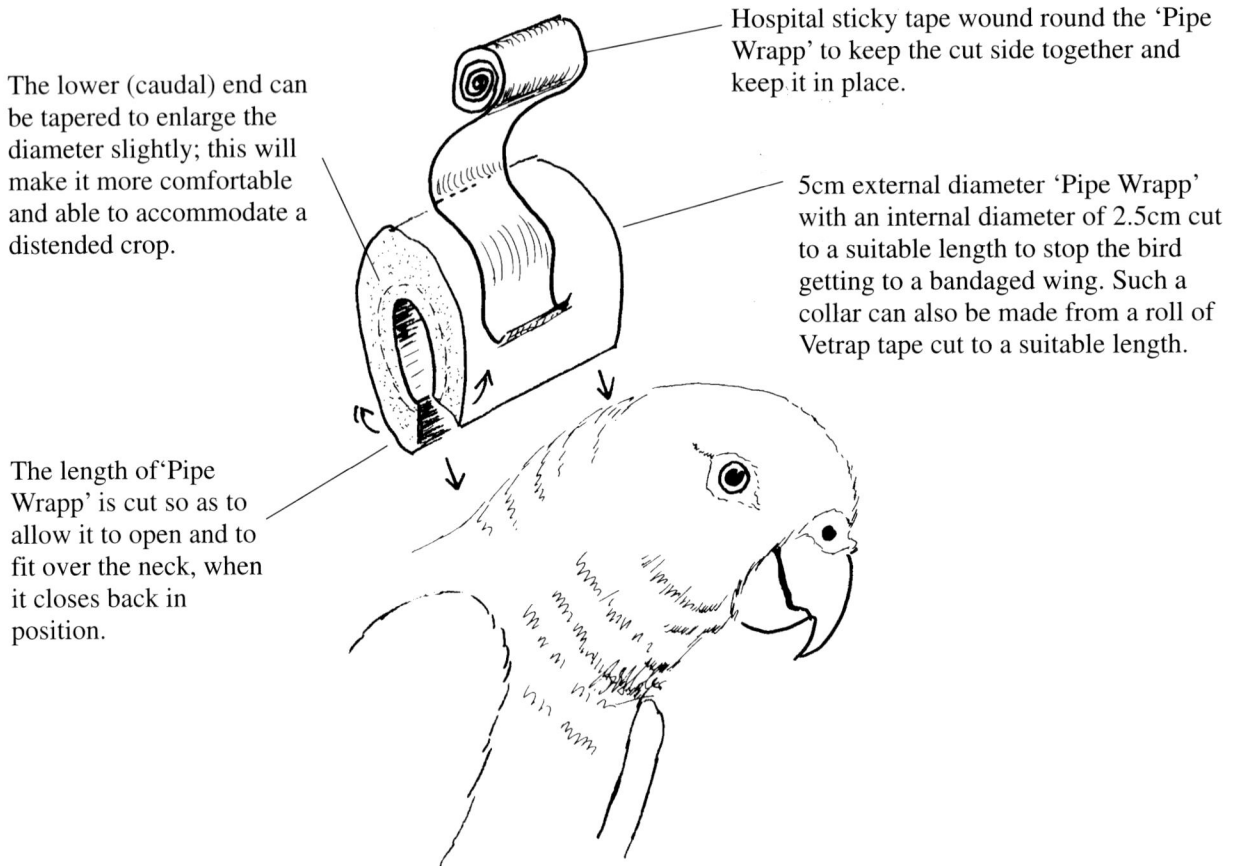

*Figure 14.4: Method of forming a restraining collar from commercial DIY 'Pipe Wrapp' or
domestic pipe insulating expanded polyurethane.*

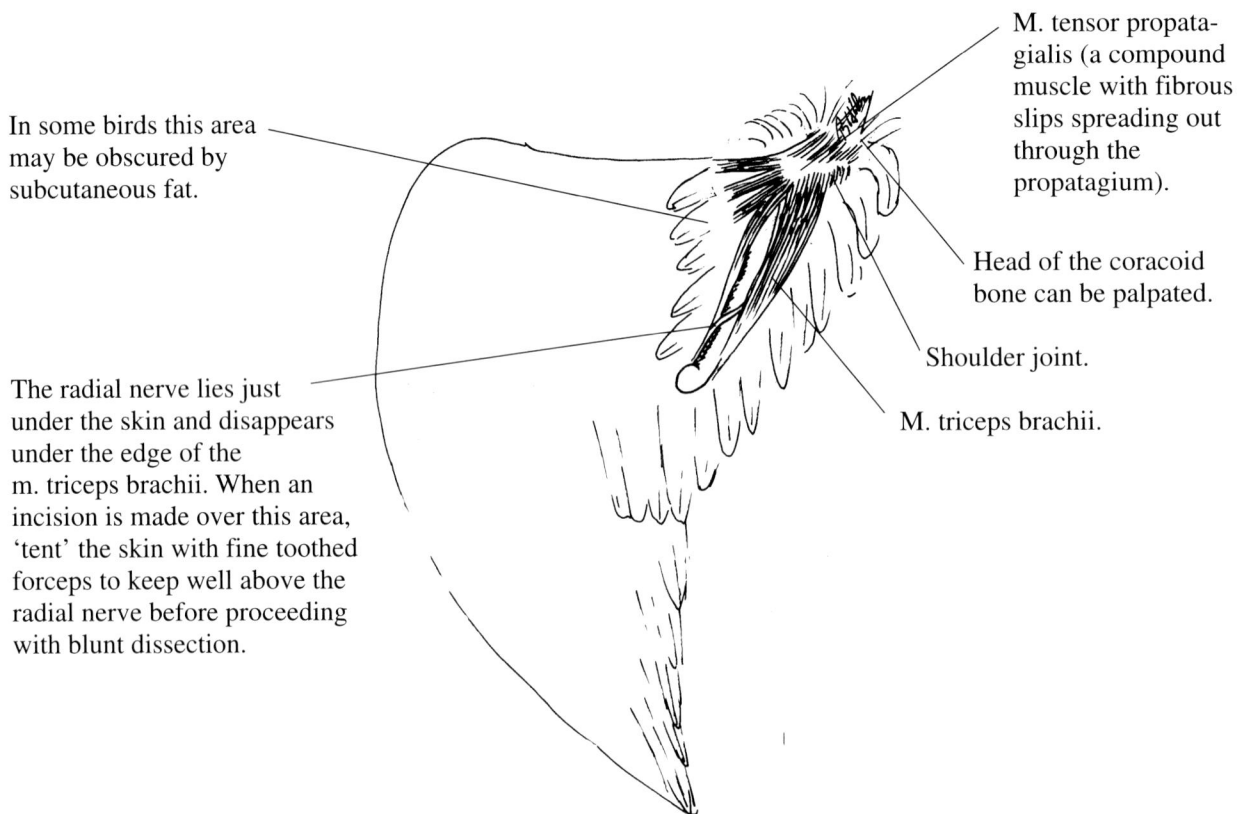

M. tensor propata-
gialis (a compound
muscle with fibrous
slips spreading out
through the
propatagium).

In some birds this area
may be obscured by
subcutaneous fat.

Head of the coracoid
bone can be palpated.

Shoulder joint.

The radial nerve lies just
under the skin and disappears
under the edge of the
m. triceps brachii. When an
incision is made over this area,
'tent' the skin with fine toothed
forceps to keep well above the
radial nerve before proceeding
with blunt dissection.

M. triceps brachii.

*Figure 14.5.1: The surgical approach to the humerus from the dorsal aspect after plucking of the covert feathers and wetting the
area with alcohol. The immediate subcutaneous anatomy may be obscured by fat or by haemorrhage into the tissues.*

The pin should emerge ventral to the pectoral crest on the lateral side of the expanded humeral head, well away from the shoulder joint.

Head of the humerus.

— Coracoid.

— Foramen triosseum.

— Scapula.

Tendon of m. supra coracoideus.

Radial nerve is **gently** pushed below the operation site.

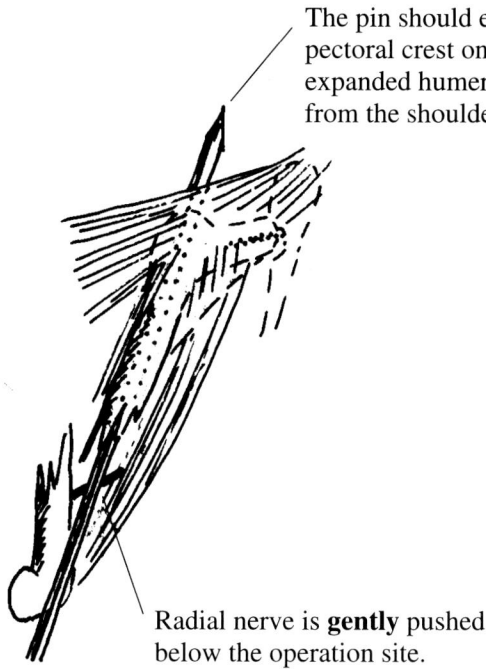

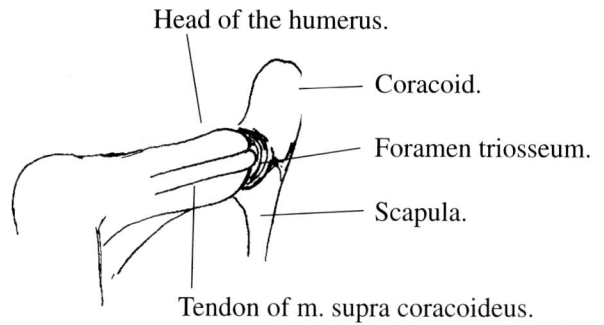

Figure 14.5.3: Enlarged view of the shoulder joint.

Figure 14.5.2: Surgical approach for intramedullary pinning or the shuttle technique.

Stem from a 1ml or 2ml syringe can be trimmed to the correct shape with scissors.

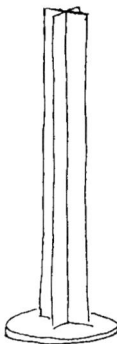

Figure 14.6.1: Shuttle pinning technique, stage 1.

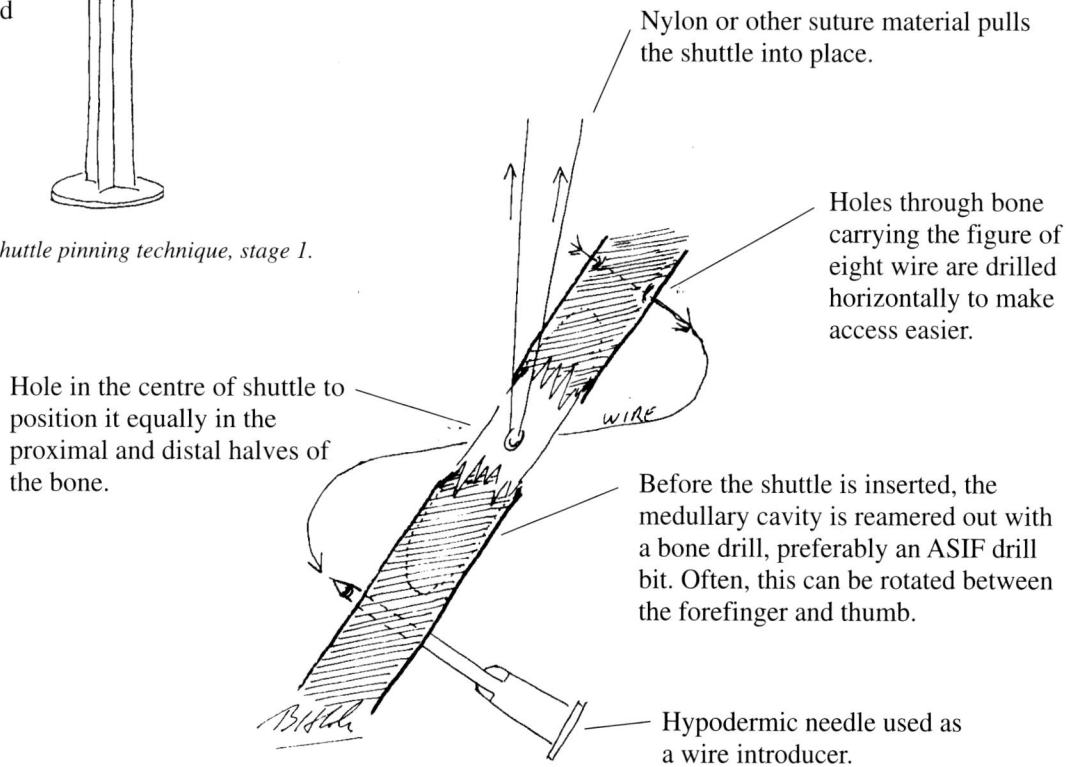

Nylon or other suture material pulls the shuttle into place.

Holes through bone carrying the figure of eight wire are drilled horizontally to make access easier.

Hole in the centre of shuttle to position it equally in the proximal and distal halves of the bone.

Before the shuttle is inserted, the medullary cavity is reamed out with a bone drill, preferably an ASIF drill bit. Often, this can be rotated between the forefinger and thumb.

Hypodermic needle used as a wire introducer.

Figure 14.6.2: Shuttle pinning technique, stage 2.

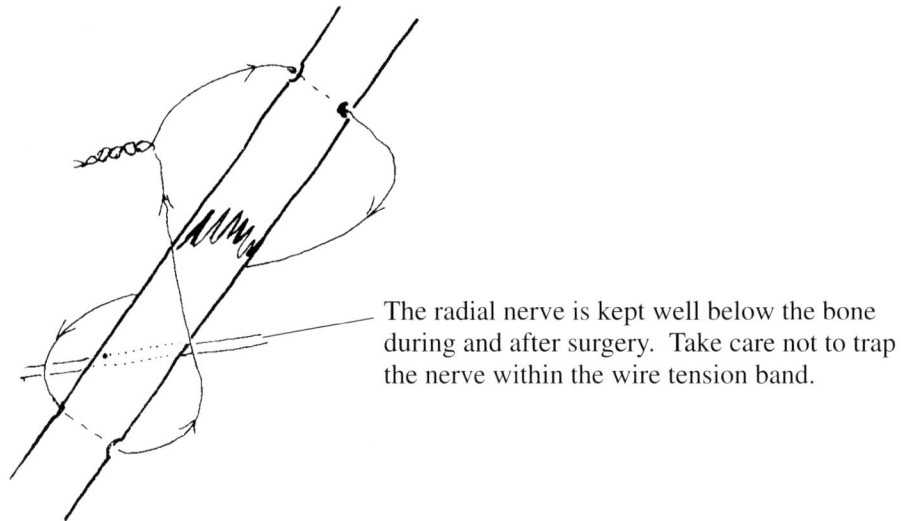

The radial nerve is kept well below the bone during and after surgery. Take care not to trap the nerve within the wire tension band.

Figure 14.6.3: Shuttle pinning technique, stage 3.

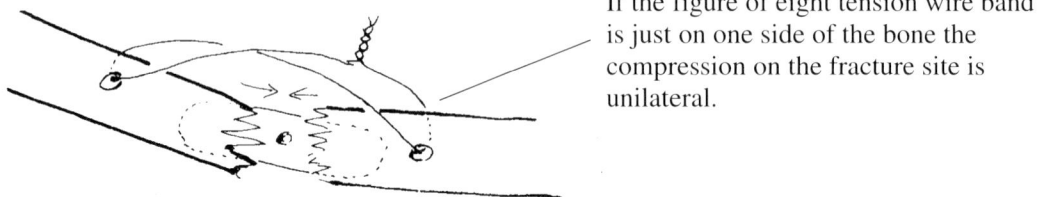

If the figure of eight tension wire band is just on one side of the bone the compression on the fracture site is unilateral.

Figure 14.6.4: Shuttle pinning technique, stage 4.

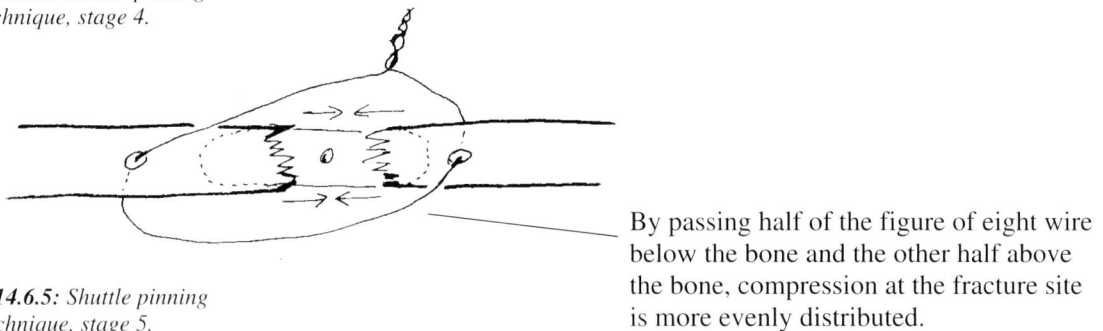

Figure 14.6.5: Shuttle pinning technique, stage 5.

By passing half of the figure of eight wire below the bone and the other half above the bone, compression at the fracture site is more evenly distributed.

rest is necessary, birds start to move the wing 24-48 hours after surgery. The main disadvantage of the method is its complexity.

Use of Kirschner-Emer Wires
This method can be used to treat fractures of the humerus. The technique is illustrated in Figures 14.7.1 and 14.7.2. The wires can be inserted percutaneously, but it is usually necessary to open the fracture site to free and align the bone fragments. A hand chuck can be used for inserting the pins, but various small model makers' cordless electric drills or a cordless screwdriver with a hexagonal shank fitting can also be used. They can be held in a sterilised plastic sleeve placed over the whole tool.

Impaction Pinning
This method has been described by Harrison (1990).

To some extent the method combines the technique of intramedullary pinning with that of Kirschner-Emer wiring (see Figure 14.8). This method also gives compression at the fracture site.

Luxation of the Elbow Joint
The elbow is not well protected by surrounding muscle. Once the humeral condyles have become dislocated from the articular surfaces of the radius and ulna they are difficult to reposition. Any surgery directly on the joint usually results in ankylosis. However, a method of repositioning the humerus, radius and ulna and then stabilising the joint was described for a number of raptor species by Martin *et al* (1993). Forbes (personal communication) has subsequently modified the technique for use in several psittacine species.

Repositioning is attempted under deep anaesthesia so that complete muscle relaxation is achieved. The

The smallest diameter KE wires consistent with the size of the individual bird are used and they should be placed at angles as far apart as possible. They should be inserted from the dorsal surface so as to emerge ventrally, otherwise the wing cannot be bandaged in the folded position.

Note that the ventral surface has the brachial artery and vein running approximately below the course of the radial nerve on the dorsal surface.

Sufficient space should be left between the bone and the external bar so that the wires can be cut when the bar is removed.

Plastic tube stiffened with an internal KE wire is made rigidly adherent to the KE wires by filling with acrylic or epoxy resin glue (Araldyte).

Alternatively, a length of Hexcelite thermoplastic casting tape can be folded over the ends of the wires to anchor them to the external bar.

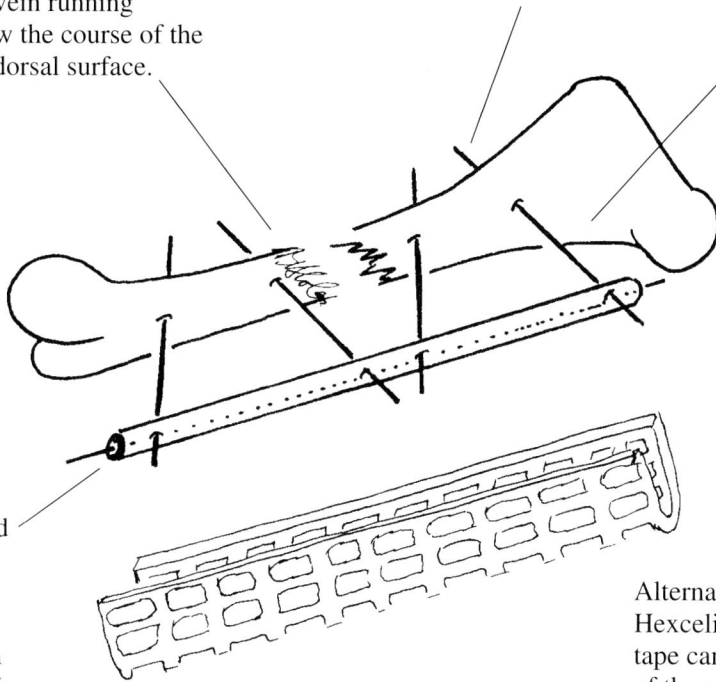

Figure 14.7.1: *Methods of internal fixation of the fractured humerus using Kirschner-Emer (KE) wires stabilised by different methods.*

External stabilising bar.

KE wires bent at a right angle to hold nylon tie.

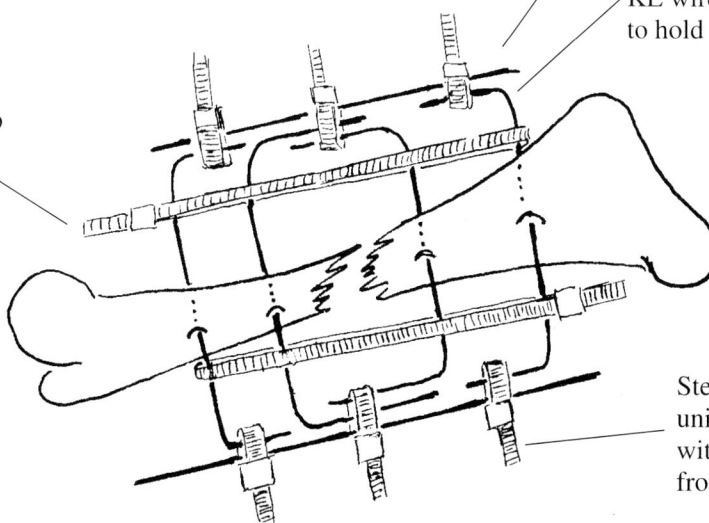

When tied, these nylon wire ties help to compress the fracture site.

Sterilised nylon 'wire ties', universal strap like nylon ties, with a box racket available from DIY stores.

Figure 14.7.2: *Method described by Howard (1992).*

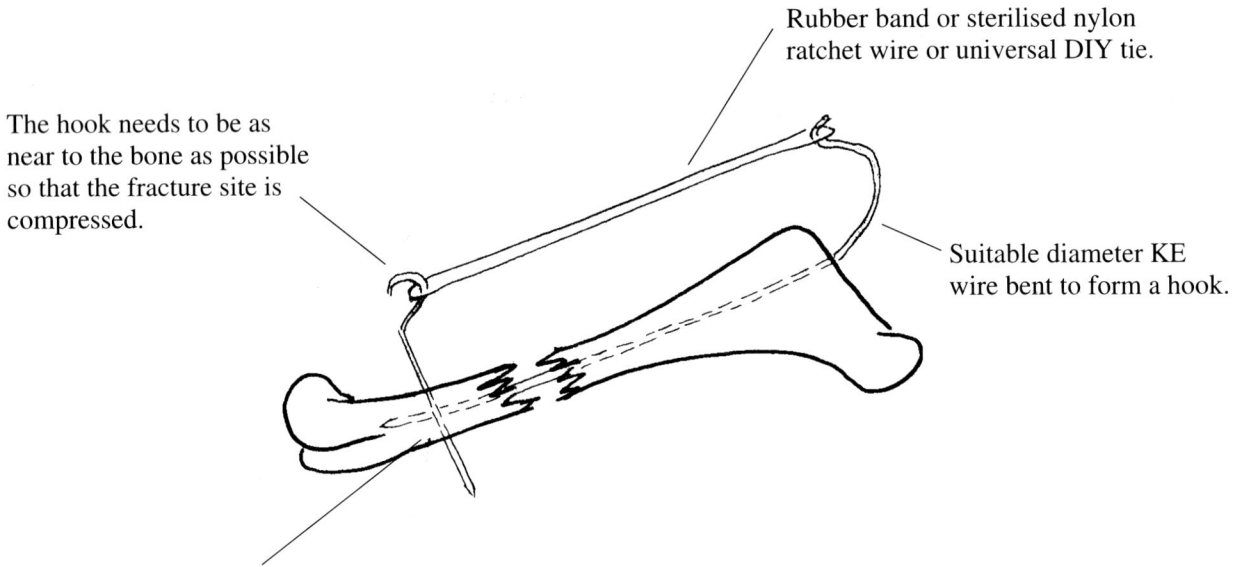

The hook needs to be as near to the bone as possible so that the fracture site is compressed.

Rubber band or sterilised nylon ratchet wire or universal DIY tie.

Suitable diameter KE wire bent to form a hook.

Note that the KE wires have to pass each other in the medullary cavity and therefore must be of a consistently small diameter.

Figure 14.8: The author's comments on the Harrison (1990) modification of the Doyle impaction technique.

distal humerus is grasped with one hand whilst the other hand holds the radius and ulna. The joint is flexed and the radius and ulna are rotated clockwise applying pressure to the proximal radius so that the head of the radius is forced into alignment with the dorsal humeral condyle. If successful the joint will be felt to 'pop' into place as the elbow is slowly extended. After repositioning the bones the joint is stabilised by placing two small Kirschner wires or, alternatively, two suitable size hypodermic needles through the distal diaphysis of the humerus and two more through the proximal diaphysis of the ulna. The joint is held in flexion and the dorsal ends of the Kirschner wires are stabilised with two fixator bars (see Figure 14.9). The fixator bars are made of plastic tubing filled with

'Technovit' (Kulzer and Company) or dental acrylic so that the whole structure is set rigid. The stabilising brace is left in place for about 10 days after which gentle exercise is encouraged.

Fractures of the Radius and Ulna

If only one or other of these bones is fractured the undamaged bone will form an adequate splint for its partner, providing the fracture site is stabilised by bandaging the wing in the folded position (see Figure 14.3). If both radius and ulna are fractured the ulna, which in birds is the more robust of the two bones, will require either internal or external fixation. When the fractured segments are displaced there is a danger that the segments of both radius and ulna will become involved

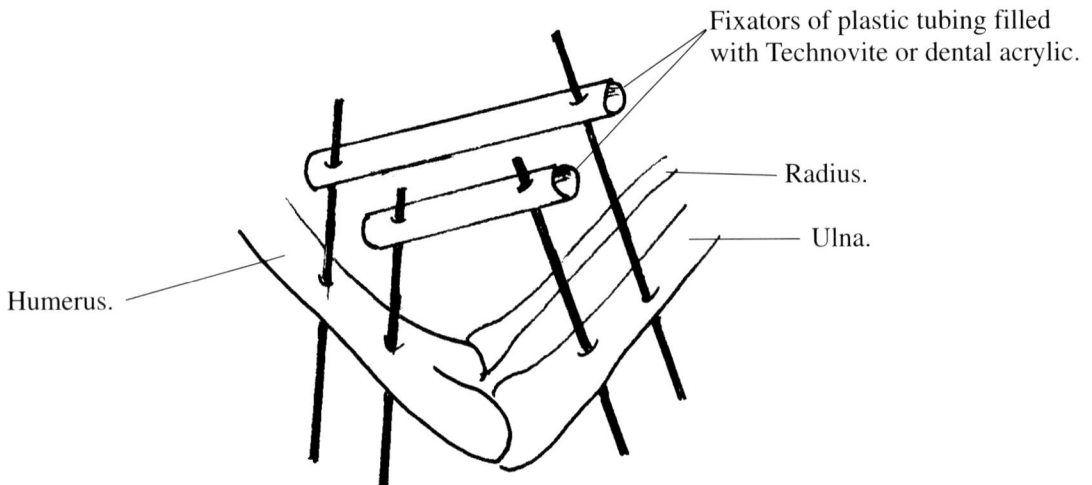

Fixators of plastic tubing filled with Technovite or dental acrylic.

Radius.

Ulna.

Humerus.

Figure 14.9: Method of stabilising the repositioned luxated elbow joint.

in the same callus, resulting in synostosis. This will prevent the normal action of the two bones sliding longitudinally in relation to each other when the wing is flexing and extending during flight. If synostosis has occurred, partial ostectomy of either the radius or ulna may restore flexion and extension of the wing so that it is held in the normal position, sometimes even allowing flight (Rupiper, 1993; Tanzella, 1993).

Various methods of dealing with fractures of the radius and ulna have been devised. All require bandaging of the wing in the folded position after surgery.

External Splinting
This method has been described by Coles (1985) (see Figure 14.10). To be successful the external splint needs to be applied within 24 hours of the injury before permanent muscle contraction and reorganisation of the tissues has taken place.

Rush Pinning
Use of a thin rush-type pin fashioned from a Kirschner wire and first inserted into the longest fracture segment. Great care is needed during insertion not to split the bone (see Figure 14.11).

Use of Kirschner-Emer Wires
Redig (1986) described this method in combination with a thin polypropylene (industrial welding) rod inserted into the medullary cavity of the ulna and a strip of Hexcelite wrapped around the external ends of the Kirschner-Emer wires to act as a fixator. The polypropylene rod helps to stabilise the wires.

Use of an Intramedullary Pin with a Threaded End
This can be inserted into the medullary cavity of the fractured ulna percutaneously at the level of the fifth or sixth secondary flight feather.

Sutures are tied firmly after all have been placed to bring the splint well down covering the fracture.

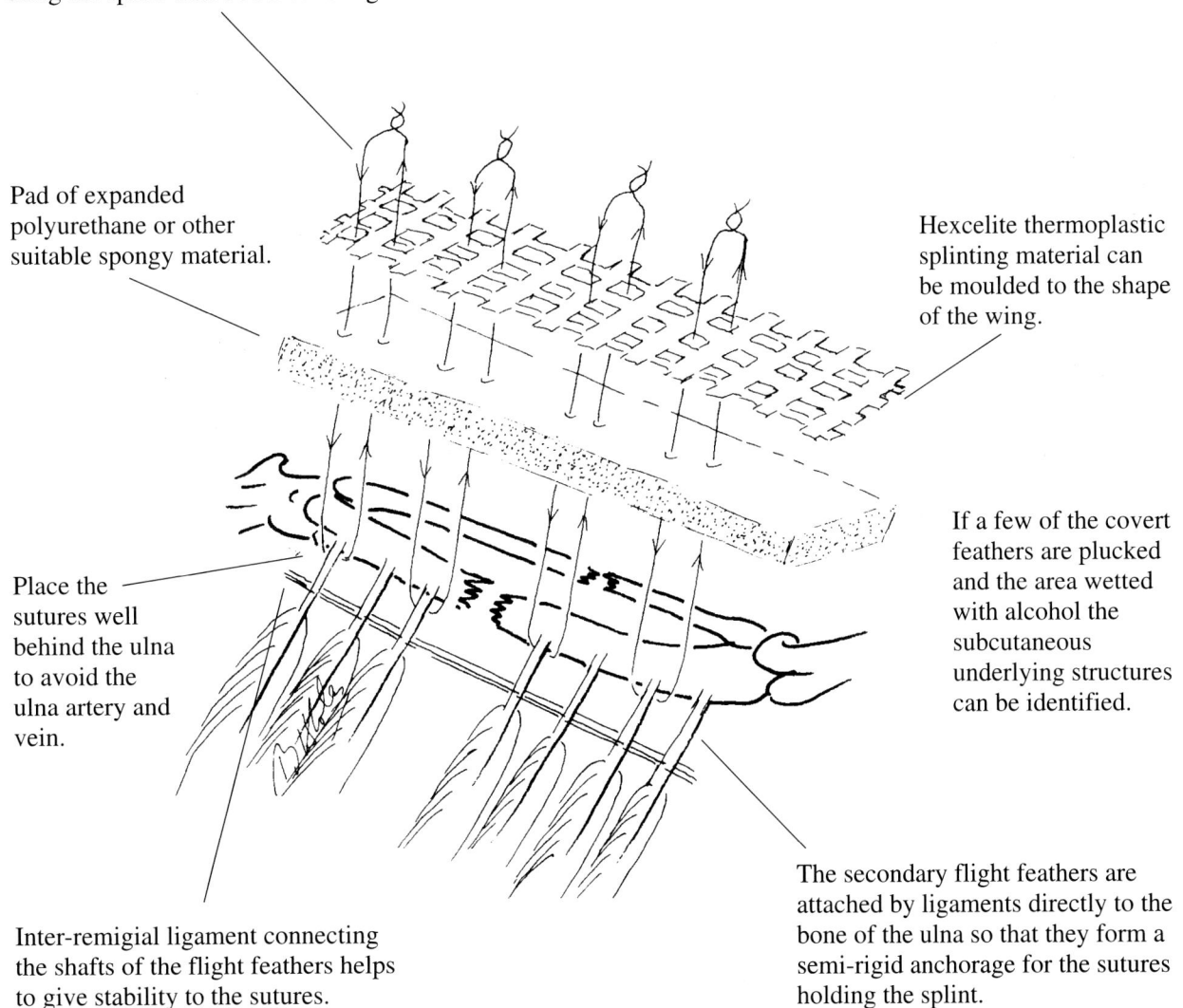

Pad of expanded polyurethane or other suitable spongy material.

Hexcelite thermoplastic splinting material can be moulded to the shape of the wing.

Place the sutures well behind the ulna to avoid the ulna artery and vein.

If a few of the covert feathers are plucked and the area wetted with alcohol the subcutaneous underlying structures can be identified.

Inter-remigial ligament connecting the shafts of the flight feathers helps to give stability to the sutures.

The secondary flight feathers are attached by ligaments directly to the bone of the ulna so that they form a semi-rigid anchorage for the sutures holding the splint.

Figure 14.10: Exploded diagram to illustrate the author's method of applying an external splint when both radius and ulna are fractured.

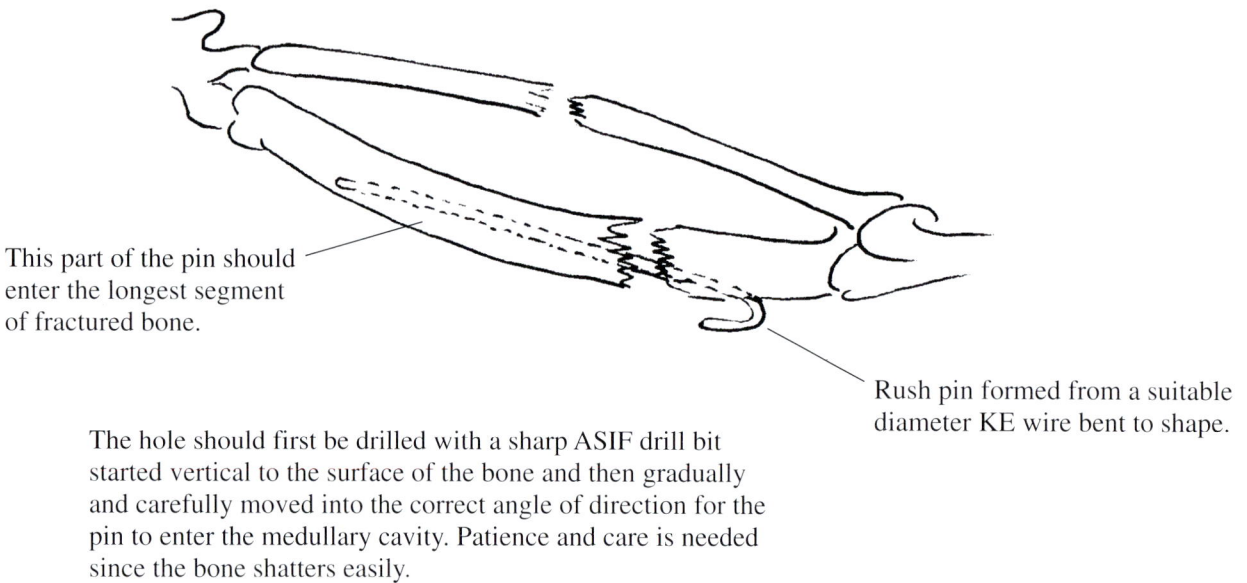

This part of the pin should enter the longest segment of fractured bone.

Rush pin formed from a suitable diameter KE wire bent to shape.

The hole should first be drilled with a sharp ASIF drill bit started vertical to the surface of the bone and then gradually and carefully moved into the correct angle of direction for the pin to enter the medullary cavity. Patience and care is needed since the bone shatters easily.

Figure 14.11: Modified rush pinning of the fractured ulna.

Fractures of the Carpus, Metacarpus or Digits

In all psittacines, with the possible exception of the very largest macaws, fractures of any of these bones are best treated with bandaging using Vetrap self-adhesive bandage. If necessary the bandage can be reinforced by coating it with a layer of acrylic resin.

NEOPLASIA OF THE WING

Neoplasia can occur in any part of the wing. Fibromata, chondromata or rhabdomyomata can occur together with their more malignant counterparts, eg. fibrosarcomata etc. (see Figure 14.12). Where practical and not limited by the size of the bird, biopsy samples should be taken to reach an accurate diagnosis. Scraping the surface of ulcerated tissue for cytological staining may help. It is often difficult to distinguish between the presence of a granuloma caused by self-inflicted damage and a true neoplasm. Commonly, all these lesions will require amputation of the wing proximal to the affected area.

However, in the author's experience, two types of neoplasm seem to be particularly common in psittacines:

● Haemangiomata, which can become haemangiosarcomata, have been reported in African Greys. These tumours arise from the vascular endothelium and usually involve a feather follicle. They are commonly spherical in shape and darkly pigmented, and can be mistaken for feather follicles. If their presence is suspected it would be wise in this particular instance not to try and take a biopsy, but to attempt removal. Haemangiomata bleed profusely and a tourniquet

Figure 14.12: Budgerigar with a fibrosarcoma over the metacarpal/digital region.

proximal to the lesion should be applied before surgery is carried out. Ideally, radiosurgery should be used.

● Xanthomas seem to be particularly common in cockatiels and budgerigars. They are not true neoplasms; they occur as diffuse thickenings of the skin forming yellow coloured plaques of tissue. The lesions may involve most of the skin overlying the radius and ulna. Xanthomas are difficult to remove because the tissue is friable and vascular. All the remaining feathers must be plucked. The surgeon should try carefully to reduce the bulk of the lesions by slicing off as much as possible. Harrison (1990) suggested using the fine wire electrode of a radiosurgical instrument for this purpose. This method also helps to control haemorrhage, which is a considerable nuisance when operating on these lesions. The area should be bandaged after surgery. The author likes to use a thin sheet of hydrophilic dressing, eg. Granuflex (Squibb), for this purpose, whilst Harrison advised covering the area with acrylic. Whichever method is used, healing is slow.

FEATHER CYSTS

Feather cysts are occasionally seen involving the feathers of the wing and they may be mistaken for neoplasia. They are dealt with elsewhere in this manual (see Chapter 11).

'ANGEL WING'

This condition may occur in budgerigars, macaws and conures. It is called 'angel wing' because the primary feathers become permanently rotated outwards and upwards so that they protrude from the normal contour of the wing even when in the resting position (see Figure 14.13). The condition results from a growth defect causing a partial luxation of the carpometacarpal joints. Amputation is usually the only course of action. However, a technique has been described by Yeisey (1993) for the surgical correction of this (valgus) rotational carpal deformity in waterfowl and it may be applicable for larger psittacine species. This method involves osteotomy of the large (third) metacarpal bone, then placing an intramedullary pin *in situ* and rotating the distal part of the wing into the correct position. The wing is kept bandaged for 4-6 weeks until there is radiographic evidence of a bridging callus. The pin is removed when there is complete bony union. An Elizabethan collar may be required during the period of convalescence.

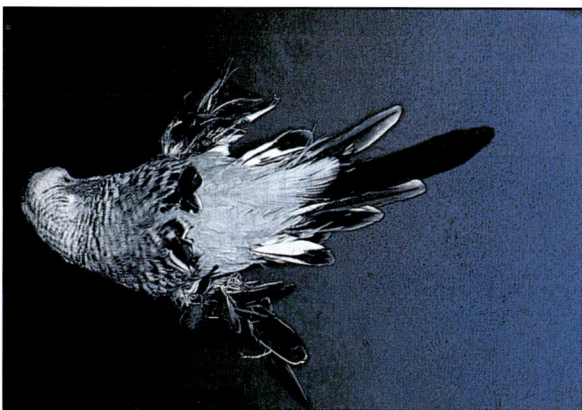

Figure 14.13: *'Angel wing' in a budgerigar.*

VITAMIN E/SELENIUM DEFICIENCY AND MUSCULAR DYSTROPHY OF COCKATIELS (AND OTHER PSITTACINES)

This condition was reported first by Harrison and Harrison (1986b) and again by Bennett (1994).

Affected birds show varying signs of paresis or paralysis of the muscles of the wings, legs or mouth. The wing may be dropped or held abnormally flexed and adducted depending on which group of muscles is affected. Usually, the condition is bilateral. In mild cases the owner will report a gradual inability of the bird to fly, even though the bird is not obese and appears otherwise quite healthy. Many cases respond dramatically to a single injection of vitamin E. *Giardia* spp. infection of the gastrointestinal tract may be a predisposing factor affecting the absorption of vitamin E. The author has found that needle biopsies of the pectoral muscles or serum creatinine phosphokinase (CK) levels are not particularly helpful.

INJURY TO THE PROPATAGIUM

This complex structure, composed of dorsal and ventral layers of dermis between which is sandwiched a meshwork of collagen and elastic fibres, runs from the shoulder to the carpal joint and fills in the angle of wing between the humerus and the radius and ulna. When the wing is extended the anterior section of this structure forms the leading edge of the wing's aerofoil section. Just beneath this leading edge is a strong ligament (the *ligamentum propatagiale*) the two ends of which are collagenous, but the central section of which is composed of elastic tissue, the *pars elastica*.

It is not uncommon for this area of the wing to sustain collision damage during flight. This injury has been described by Coles (1985). Because of the proximity of an artery and vein, haemorrhage can be profuse. Pressure bandaging is often required to control the haemorrhage. If the bandage is left on too long granulation and fibrosis may take place. This may result in scarring of the protopatagium which can lead to contraction of the *ligamentum protopatagiale* and loss of full extension of the wing. This may not be very important in a pet bird spending most of its life in a cage, but will severely disable any bird which is expected to fly normally. The anatomy, physiology and repair of this structure has been reviewed by Brown and Klemm (1990). Diagnosis of this condition may only be made if the bird is anaesthetised, otherwise the injury can be easily missed.

REFERENCES

Bennett RA (1994) Neuropathies. In: *Avian Medicine: Principles and Application.* Eds BW Ritchie, GJ Harrison and LR Harrison. Wingers, Lake Worth.

Brown RE and Klemm RD (1990) Surgical anatomy of the propatagium. In: *Proceedings of the Association of Avian Veterinarians Annual Conference 1990.* AAV, Lake Worth.

Coles BH (1985) *Avian Medicine and Surgery.* Blackwell Scientific Publications Oxford.

Harrison GJ (1990) Anesthesia and common surgical

procedures. In: *Proceedings of the Association of Avian Veterinarians Annual Conference 1990*. AAV, Lake Worth.

Harrison GJ and Harrison LR (1986a) Management procedures. In: *Clinical Avian Medicine and Surgery, including Aviculture*. Eds GJ Harrison and LR Harrison. WB Saunders, Philadelphia.

Harrison GJ and Harrison LR (1986b) Nutritional diseases. In: *Clinical Avian Medicine and Surgery, including Aviculture*. Eds GJ Harrison and LR Harrison. WB Saunders, Philadelphia.

Howard DJ (1992) Sterilised nylon wire ties. *Journal of the Association of Avian Veterinarians* **6(4)**, 203.

Martin HD, Bruecker KA, Herrick DD and Scherpelz J (1993) Elbow luxations in raptors: a review of eight cases. In: *Raptor Biomedicine*. Eds PT Redig, JE Cooper, JD Remple and DB Hunter. University of Minnesota Press, Minneapolis.

Mangili G (1971) Unilateral patagiectomy: a new method of preventing flight in birds. *International Zoo Yearbook* **11**, 252.

Royal College of Veterinary Surgeons (1993) *Guide to Professional Conduct*. RCVS, London.

Redig PT (1986) Basic orthopedic surgical techniques. In: *Clinical Avian Medicine and Surgery, including Aviculture*. Eds GJ Harrison and LR Harrison. WB Saunders, Philadelphia.

Robinson P (1975) Unilateral patagiectomy: a technique for deflighting large birds. *Veterinary Medicine/Small Animal Clinician* **70(2)**, 143.

Rupiper DJ (1993) Radial ostectomy in a Barn Owl. *Journal of the Association of Avian Veterinarians* **7(3)**, 160.

Seidel B (1991) Methods of flight prevention in birds. In: *Proceedings of the Association of Avian Veterinarians European Conference, Vienna, 1991*. AAV, Lake Worth.

Tanzella DT (1993) Ulna ostectomy in a Pale-headed Rosella (*Platycercus adscitus*) with multiple injuries. *Journal of the Association of Avian Veterinarians* **7(3)**, 153.

Tom C and Norbet K (1991) Treatment of fractures in wild birds: indication and possibilities. In: *Proceedings of the Association of Avian Veterinarians European Conference, Vienna, 1991*. AAV, Lake Worth.

Yeisey CL (1993) Surgical correction of valgus carpal deformities in waterfowl. In: *Proceedings of the Association of Avian Veterinarians Annual Conference 1993*. AAV, Lake Worth.

CHAPTER FIFTEEN

Respiratory Problems

Neil A Forbes

INTRODUCTION

Successful treatment of respiratory diseases is directly related to the speed at which an owner notices a problem and presents the bird to the clinician, who in turn makes a specific diagnosis and instigates appropriate therapy. In view of the inactivity of many pet psittacines, birds may often not be presented until severe dyspnoea is already present. It is important that a full clinical history is taken before the patient is examined. Information regarding the source of the bird, type of housing, diet, date of entry of last bird to the collection and any recent medical history of other members of the group, should be collected and considered. The correct diagnosis and treatment of avian respiratory disease is dependent on a full understanding of the anatomy and physiology of the avian respiratory system, which differs greatly from that of mammals. There is no diaphragm (its action is replaced by the intercostal and abdominal musculature) but there is a fixed lung, supplied with a constant unidirectional supply of air by the caudal air sacs, which act as bellows. At rest, respiratory effort should not be noticeable and the mouth should remain closed. Normal resting respiratory rates are listed in Table 15.1.

Respiratory disease commonly causes excessive chest movement, nasal discharge, head or tail bobbing (frequently with open mouth rather than nasal breathing), abduction of the wings from the body, neck stretching, coughing, alteration of voice or, on occasions, vomition. Birds should be observed for all these signs prior to handling. The presenting signs are determined by the cause and the site of the pathology.

In order for the correct treatment to be given the site and aetiology of the disease must be accurately determined. The major causes of respiratory disease in psittacines are listed in Table 15.2.

It is necessary to differentiate between infections of

Table 15.1. Normal resting respiratory rates.

Weight of bird	Respiratory rate/min
100g	40-52
200g	35-50
300g	30-45
400g	25-30
500g	20-30
1000g	15-20

Source of data : Harrison and Ritchie (1994).

Table 15.2. Major causes of respiratory disease in psittacines.

Bacterial (typically Gram-negative) *Klebsiella* spp., *Pasteurella* spp., *Pseudomonas* spp., *Bordetella* spp., *Salmonella* spp., *Haemophilus* spp., *Mycobacterium avium, Chlamydia psittaci,* plus others.	**Viral** Avipox, adenovirus, influenza, infectious bronchitis virus, paramyxovirus, laryngotracheitis virus.
Fungal *Aspergillus* spp., *Candida* spp., *Cryptococcus* spp.	**Parasitic** Tracheal mites, eg. *Sternstoma* sp. Gape worms, eg. *Syngamus* spp. Air sac worms, eg. *Serratospiculum* spp.

Table 15.2. Continued.

Protozoal	Nutritional
Sarcocystis spp., *Trichomonas* spp., *Crytosporidium* spp.	Vitamin A deficiency, iodine deficiency (goitre), obesity.
Toxic	**Metabolic/neoplasia/abdominal masses**
Teflon, creasote, tobacco, carbon monoxide, amonia, aerosols, plus others.	
Ruptured air sac	**Foreign bodies/aspiration pneumonia**

the upper respiratory tract (URT), including the nares and sinuses, and infections of the lower respiratory tract (LRT), including the trachea, lungs and air sacs (see Table 15.3).

URT infection in psittacines is frequently associated with malnutrition, in particular hypovitaminosis A (see Chapter 3). Characteristically, these birds have been fed principally on a diet of sunflower seed. Correct diagnosis and therapy cannot be carried out without a thorough examination of the affected area. Respiratory signs (either URT or LRT) are one of the commonest presenting signs of chlamydiosis (psittacosis). This infection should be ruled out prior to potential exposure of staff and other in-patients. The author uses the 'Clearview' (Unipath) test, which is performed on a faecal swab or a swab from any infective site, eg. air sac, liver, spleen or trachea. The test is an ELISA test, although it is not an accurate test for screening healthy birds in view of the intermittent shedding of *Chlamydia psittaci*. However, in sick birds (who are typically shedding) it is an invaluable test. The test is highly sensitive but not entirely specific, and gives rise to a significant number of false positives. However, the test has the great advantage that it can be used for instant in-house diagnosis.

For correct diagnosis of respiratory disease the bird should be anaesthetised and the respiratory system examined thoroughly. Birds should be masked down with isoflurane (see Chapter 6). Tracheal swabs should be taken and endoscopy performed, if required, prior to intubation. The cere, nares, operculum, nasal chambers, infraorbital sinuses and diverticluae, and choana should all be assessed (see Figure 15.1).

DISEASES OF THE UPPER RESPIRATORY TRACT

Nares

The external appearance of the nares is often indicative of the type of URT condition being presented. Hypovitaminosis A, as well as excessive dry heat, predisposes to URT infections. Hypovitaminosis A often presents with nasal, choanal, lingual or sublingual (often involving the salivary glands) sterile abscessation. Hypovitaminosis A causes squamous cell metaplasia

and hyperkeratosis, which results in these pathological changes.

Rhinoliths are frequently present (see Figure 15.2); these are typically related to hypovitaminosis A or to bacterial, mycoplasmal, chlamydial, fungal or viral infections. Severe infections with avian pox or *Cnemidocoptes* spp. (see Chapter 12), or mycotic, bacterial or mycoplasmal infections can all lead to marked proliferation of the cere with resultant occlusion of the nares. The centre of the nares is occupied by the operculum, which is a hard, but vascular, fibrous raised structure; it should be dry, smooth and shiny. Exudate often concentrates around the operculum, thus blocking the nares. The exudate should be removed with a fine blunt point, eg. endodontic paper points, prior to the cause of the exudate being treated. The nasal cavity is divided into two halves, each being made up of three segments (concha).

Figure 15.2: *Severe rhinolith in an African Grey.*

Sinuses

The sinuses are entered from the middle and caudal concha. Significantly, the entry points into the sinuses are at rostral level. Infection may enter the sinuses from the nasal concha. Infection, together with cellular debris and mucoid secretion produced within the sinuses, fills and extends the sinuses with fluid (see Figure 15.3). In view of the level of the entry points, the resulting mucoid fluid is often unable to drain away. The lack of drainage, together with the resultant

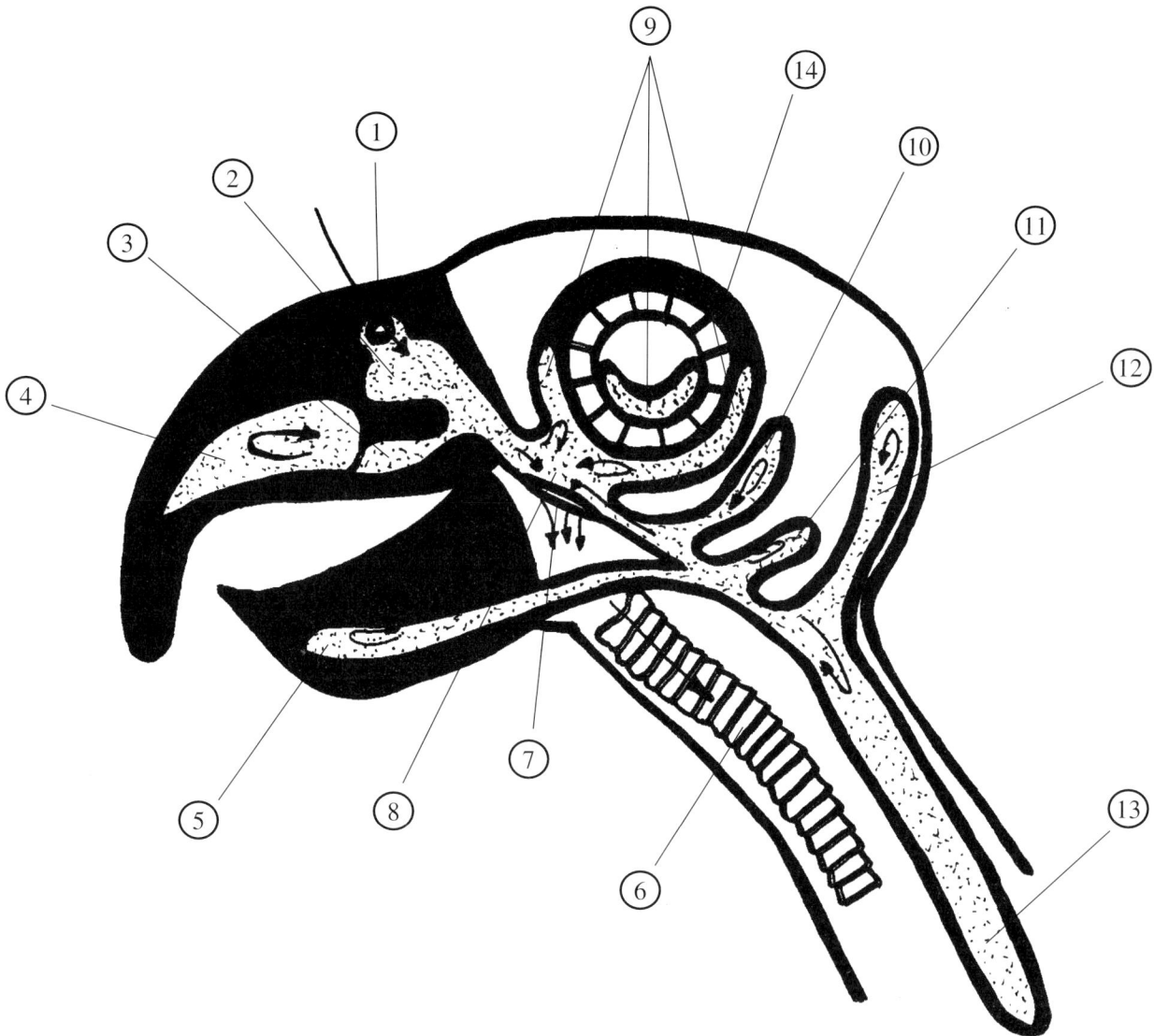

Figure 15.1: Diagram of the avian upper respiratory tract (typical Amazon).

IS = Infraorbital sinus

1	Nares	8	Suborbital chamber of IS.
2	Preorbital diverticulum of IS.	9	Infraorbital diverticulum of IS
3	Maxillary chamber of IS.	10	Posterior orbital diverticulum of IS.
4	Rostral diverticulum of IS.	11	Preauditory diverticulum of IS.
5	Mandibular diverticulum of IS.	12	Cranial portion of cervicocephalic air sac.
6	Trachea	13	Cervical portion of cervicocephalic air sac
7	Choana	14	Scleral ossicles.

reservoir effect of the accumulation of infected debris, has previously rendered sinus infections difficult to treat. The interconnection of the nasal chambers and sinuses of either side, together with the multiple ramifications of the infraorbital sinus, mean that if the sinuses becomes infected, many of the surrounding structures of the head may also become affected (see Figure 15.1). Therefore, sinusitis may be indicated by a persistent unilateral or bilateral ocular discharge. The amount of tissue destruction is dependent on the lytic properties of the pathogen involved, or is a consequence of pressure necrosis caused by the production of inspissated caseous material.

Diagnosis

The presence of URT infection is rarely difficult to demonstrate. Visual inspection, scrapes, rhinoscopy

Table 15.3. Differentiation between URT and LRT infection.

Upper respiratory tract infection	Lower respiratory tract infection
Open mouthed breathing.	Change of voice, dyspnoea, tail bobbing.
Nasal plugging, discharge, sneezing.	Inspiratory/expiratory difficulty, coughing.
Periorbital swelling, epiphora, head shaking.	Exercise intolerance.
Dyspnoea, exercise intolerance, yawning.	Inappetence/vomition.
Neck stretching, inflamed cere.	

sinus flushing, aspiration, choanal swabs and radiography should all be used where relevant. Choanal swabs or sinus aspirates should always be used in preference to direct swabs from the nares. Cytology should be performed on all samples collected (see Chapter 5). The normal flora of the choana should be predominantly Gram-positive, eg. *Lactobacillus* spp., *Streptococcus* spp. and *Micrococcus* spp., with less than 5% Gram-negative, only occasional budding yeasts (Tully and Harrison, 1994) and no fungal hyphae. Culture and sensitivity testing for significant pathogens should be carried out. Fungal infections are frequently found in the psittacine URT: *Aspergillus* spp. frequently, *Candida* spp. infrequently (Tsai *et al*, 1992). Normal cytology of the nasal and infraorbital sinuses reveals occasional non-cornified squamous epithelial cells with low levels of extracellular bacteria and debris (Campbell, 1994). Cytological evidence of sinusitis is denoted by the presence of inflammatory cells in the aspirate. If bacterial infection is present, septic, heterophilic or mixed cell inflammation will be evident. Mycotic infections will typically be demonstrated by mixed cell or macrophagic inflammation with the presence of fungal hyphae or spores. Mycoplasmal organisms have been frequently implicated in URT infection, although authenticated cases are rare. This may be due to the difficulty in culturing

Figure 15.3: Sinusitis and conjunctivitis in a Blue-fronted Amazon.

these organisms. Mycoplasmal infections respond well to tetracyclines, erythromycin, tylosin, spectinomycin or enrofloxacin.

Adenovirus, herpesvirus (similar to the laryngotracheitis virus of poultry) and reovirus have been implicated in chronic respiratory disease (Gerlach, 1994), but are rare in the UK. Diagnosis is by exclusion of other aetiologies and virus isolation from tracheal swabs or washes.

Treatment

If hypovitaminosis A is likely, the diet should be improved and parental vitamin A administered (30,000 IU/kg once/week). Parental therapy may be required for bacterial organisms such as *Pseudomonas* spp. However, sinus flushing or intrasinus injection of antibiotics is invariably essential. Prior to culture and sensitivity results being available, the author favours sinus flushing with enrofloxacin (0.75ml of 5% Injection in 20ml of saline/kg bodyweight). The bird should be held upside down allowing the more distant diverticulae of the sinuses to be penetrated. The syringe nozzle (without a needle) is held tight against the nares (the mouth should not be held closed) and the total contents of the syringe evacuated at force through the nasal chambers. This treatment is continued daily for a minimum of ten days. The technique is simple and may be easily demonstrated for the owner to carry out at home. Parenteral antibiotics may be given at the same time.

Candida spp., *Aspergillus* spp., *Trichomonas* spp., *Mycoplasma* spp. and *Chlamydia psittaci* may be present. These organisms should be tested for and treated as necessary. Table 15.4 shows some effective therapeutic agents.

When debriding oral or nasal abscesses, care should be taken to avoid causing haemorrhage. Chemical agents (silver nitrate or ferric sulphate) or electrosurgical equipment should be available. Trephination of sinuses should only be performed as a last resort; very few cases fail to respond to sinus flushing as described earlier. If nasal aspergillomata occur, the author favours the placement of an indwelling catheter following identification of the affected site. Therapy is continued with parental and topical medication (see later for aspergillosis therapy).

DISEASES OF THE LOWER RESPIRATORY TRACT

The lower respiratory tract comprises the trachea, bronchi, lungs and air sacs.

Trachea and Primary Bronchi

Diseases of the trachea and primary bronchi are several and varied. Differential diagnosis of these diseases provides one of the most important and potentially rewarding challenges of avian practice. Clinical signs will include loss or change of voice, coughing, rasping or rattling inspiration and/or expiration and dyspnoea. The trachea commences at the rima glottis, which is the slit-like opening positioned in the posterior segment of the tongue at the rostral end of the trachea, and obscured from sight in most conscious psittacines by the large fleshy tongue. The glottis is not protected by a soft palate, but has an efficient closing system, which operates whenever the bird swallows. The vocal apparatus is located at the bifurcation of the primary bronchi (syrinx) within the thorax, and not at the larynx as in mammals. The avian trachea differs in two main respects from mammals. Firstly, the tracheal rings are complete and secondly, the tracheal diameter is comparatively larger. The position of the syrinx is similar in all avian species, although the shape differs greatly. This makes radiological interpretation of syringeal pathology difficult in some species. A collection of radiographic normals for each species is useful.

Diagnosis

Clinical diseases affecting the trachea and primary bronchi include parasitic, bacterial (occasionally viral) and fungal infections, nutritional disorders, toxicity problems or consequences of foreign bodies. It is crucial that a specific diagnosis is made prior to instigation of therapy. Diagnostic tests for LRT disease should include cytology, faecal examination, haematology, biochemistry, endoscopy and/or radiography. If the bird is to be intubated, tracheal swabs and endoscopy should be performed first. Both these procedures will require general anaesthesia.

Tracheal washes may be carried out by one of two methods. If the bird is severely dyspnoeic, the bird should be anaesthetised and an air sac breathing tube placed in the caudal abdominal air sac. A sterile endotracheal tube is placed in the trachea and a plastic respiratory (or male dog urinary) catheter passed down the tube. The catheter is passed to the level of the syrinx (just caudal to the thoracic inlet) and sterile saline (0.5-1ml/kg bodyweight) is introduced and then withdrawn. Alternatively, an 18-22G plastic intravenous catheter is introduced through the skin and into the trachea in the caudal cervical area; the catheter is advanced to the level of the syrinx. The latter method may occasionally be carried out in a conscious bird. The bird is maintained parallel to the floor and the sample aspirated. The author favours the former method as tracheal endoscopy would routinely be carried out in all cases. The tracheal aspirate in a normal bird should have a low cellular content with minimal macrophages or inflammatory cells. An increase in heterophils, macrophages or other inflammatory cells is clinically significant. In bacterial conditions, bacterial phagocytosis will be evident, whereas in fungal infections there are characteristic thick septate hyphae that branch at 45° (Campbell, 1994).

Radiography may reveal the presence of an aspergilloma at the syrinx. However, careful and experienced interpretation is required in view of the interspecies variation of normal shape and size of the syrinx.

There is no substitute for endoscopy when investigating cases of LRT disease. Endoscopy allows visualisation of tracheal parasites, the degree of inflammation, the presence of hyperaemia or excessive

Table 15.4. Treatment of URT infections.

Organism	Therapeutic agent
Bacteria	Effective antibiotics.
Candida spp.	Nystatin/itraconazole.
Chlamydia psittaci	Doxycycline/enrofloxacin.
Mycoplasma spp.	Tylosin/lincocin/spectinomycin/enrofloxacin/erythromycin.
Aspergillus spp.	Amphoteracin B + itraconazole/flucytosine + enilconazole.
Cnemidocoptes spp.	Ivermectin.

mucoid secretions, and the collection of aspirates. Most importantly, endoscopy gives full visualisation of the proximal primary bronchi.

Aetiological Factors Involved in LRT Disease

Nutrition
See earlier.

Mycoses
Aspergillus spp. are the commonest fungal pathogens of psittacines; the organism is ubiquitous in nature, and the disease is difficult to treat. (Respiratory infection involving *Candida* spp. does occur on occasions, although it is generally secondary to an enteric *Candida* spp. infection.) Aspergillosis is commonest in African Greys, Amazons and cockatoos. Birds that are immune-suppressed, imported, stressed or malnourished, or that have been housed in dirty accommodation, frequently in the proximity of rotting vegetable matter (Forbes, 1991), or who are fed seed that was stored before it was fully dry, are the most susceptible. Where susceptible species have been in a potentially contaminated or stressful situation, prophylactic therapy is justifiable (Forbes, 1992). Every effort should be made to ensure that environmental *A. fumigatus* loading, as well as the level of stress, is minimised. Particular attention should be given to the quality of the seed and nuts, as well as the nest material supplied.

Infection may be localised, as in mycotic tracheitis (see Figure 15.4) (signified by a change or loss of voice and/or a rasping inspiratory noise) and some air sac forms (where one or more aspergillomata form), or it may be multifocal. Mycotic granulomata may be found within the nasal cavities, oropharynx, glottis, syrinx, lungs or air sacs. Multifocal cases tend to be more commonly associated with poor husbandry; the rate of pathogenesis and deterioration in these cases is faster. Clinical signs will vary greatly and will be dependent on the site and extent of the lesions. Change or loss of voice is highly suggestive of the syringeal form; other signs will include tracheal haemorrhage, weight loss, general malaise, loss of appetite and vomition, polydipsia and polyuria, a drooped wing or, in advanced cases, severe dyspnoea. Aspergillosis is not transmissible between birds.

Parasites
Syngamus trachea infection is relatively uncommon in psittacines. It is most commonly seen in ground dwelling species. Infection usually occurs from eating transport hosts, eg. infected slugs, snails, earthworms or other invertebrates, although direct bird to bird infection can occur. Passage via earthworms renders the parasite more infective to the main host (Morgan and Clapham, 1934). After ingestion the larvae can pass via the bloodstream into the lungs within six hours, and from there travel into the trachea.

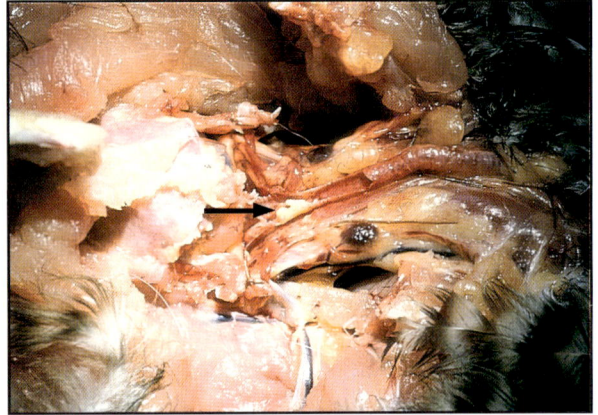

Figure 15.4: *Avian trachea with syringeal obstruction caused by an aspergilloma.*

The prepatent period is 17-21 days.

Bacteria
These are generally Gram-negative. The commonest respiratory bacterial pathogens isolated are *Klebsiella pneumonia, Pseudomonas aeroginosa* and *Pasteurella multocida*. Other organisms, such as *Yersinia pseudotuberculosis, Eshericia coli, Streptococcus* spp. and *Staphyloccocus* spp., have all been isolated on occasions. Although the clinical signs are similar to those seen with parasitic infections, a mucopurulent exudate may be visualised within the trachea, or the trachea may be excessively erythematous with copious mucoid discharge. If bacterial infection is suspected, aspirates or tracheal swabs or washes should be taken, impressions smears examined and culture and sensitivity testing performed.

Aspiration pneumonia
This occurs most frequently following inexperienced use of a crop feed tube, hand feeding of neonates or following anaesthesia (if the crop was not empty and the bird was not intubated). Although it is appreciated, particularly with small birds, that prolonged starvation prior to anaesthesia is potentially dangerous, it is now accepted by most workers that a limited time without food is advantageous (see Chapter 6). Birds which are known to have food in their crop, or where there is proximal gastrointestinal tract pathology, should be intubated in order to prevent the risk of aspiration.

Treatment of aspiration pneumonia is with antibiotics and anti-inflammatory therapy systemically, and by nebulisation.

Treatment
The importance of an accurate and specific diagnosis is realised when assessing the therapy and progress of a respiratory case. Treatment of *Syngamus trachea* involves the use of an anthelmintic, eg. fenbendazole (20mg/kg - should not be used during a moult as it may cause abnormalities of feather growth) or ivermectin (200mcg/kg s/c, p/o or topically). Two

doses of either drug should be given at 10 day intervals. A consequence of anthelmintic therapy is that a quantity of worms (the females being up to 2cm in length) will be killed in the trachea and primary bronchi. This may lead to foreign body pneumonia or tracheal obstruction. Hence, the clinical signs may not be alleviated (for up to six weeks), despite the fact that the primary pathogen has been treated effectively. Birds should be maintained on parenteral or droplet (nebulisation) therapy for the duration of the clinical signs. The commoner pathogens, together with advised treatments, are listed in Table 15.5.

METHODS OF MEDICATION

Nebulisation

Nebulisation has been traditionally thought of as being complicated and requiring expensive equipment. However, it is now within the financial reach of any veterinary practice. Small, mass-produced nebulisers are now readily availible. Nebulisation is typically used for 15-20 minutes, 4-5 times daily. If particle size as low as 0.5 microns can be achieved, medication can reach the lung and parts of the air sac system. Drugs such as amphotericin B, gentamicin, amikacin, polymixin B and tylosin have been shown to be poorly absorbed from the respiratory system. However, they are highly effective at a local level without the risk of toxic systemic effects. This method of medication can be carried out easily without any stress and without any need to handle the patient. This can be of great benefit in sick, dyspnoeic birds. An additional benefit of medication by nebulisation is that the humidity of the birds immediate environment is raised. Suitable drugs and dilutions for nebulisation are listed in Table 15.6.

Intratracheal

General anaesthesia is generally required to carry out this technique because of the large fleshy tongue which obstructs the rima glottis in most psittacine species. The author uses a therapeutic dose of any of the agents listed in Table 15.6. If the volume of fluid can be restricted to 0.5ml/kg bodyweight, no respiratory embarrassment will be caused. However, nebulisation remains the route of choice as no general anaesthetic is required.

SURGICAL CONDITIONS OF THE TRACHEA AND PRIMARY BRONCHI

Traumatic injuries to the trachea occur occasionally. Punctures, lacerations or avulsions of the trachea may occur. The primary treatment is to maintain a respiratory airway; this is often best achieved by placing an abdominal air sac breathing tube (see Chapter 6). Following this, reconstructive surgery can be attempted.

The commonest form of tracheal surgery which is requested is the devoicing of noisy birds (screamers/ screechers). This procedure is considered by the Royal College of Veterinary Surgeons to be an unnecessary mutilation. Therefore, it is an unethical procedure and may not be carried out under any circumstances by a veterinary surgeon in the UK.

Placement of an Abdominal Air Sac Breathing Tube

Acute airway obstruction in birds is typically caused by the formation of a syringeal aspergilloma or the presence of a tracheal foreign body. The former condition is common, and is initially characterised by alteration to, or loss of, the bird's voice. Time is critical; from the onset of signs, complete respiratory obstruction may occur within 10-15 days. Birds with acute LRT dyspnoea must be examined endoscopically as an emergency procedure. Prior to endoscopy or

Table 15.5. Therapy for some common pathogens of the LRT.

Pathogen	Medication	Route and duration
Sarcocystis spp.	Pyrimethamine.	Give with sulphonamides for 21 days p/o.
Syngamus spp.	Fenbendazole or ivermectin. + antibiosis.	P/o - repeat in 10 days. P/o, s/c or percutaneous - repeat in 10 days. Parenteral/tracheal/ nebulisation - up to six weeks.
Bacterial	Antibiosis.	Parenteral +/- tracheal or nebulisation.
Fungal	Amphoteracin. Flucytosine. Itraconazole. Enilconazole.	I/v (+ fluids) and/or tracheal or nebulisation. P/o. P/o. Tracheal or nebulisation.
Chlamydia psittacci	Enrofloxacin. Doxycycline.	I/m or p/o. I/m or p/o.

Table 15.6. Drugs used in treatment by nebulisation.

Drug	Dosage
Amphotericin B *	100mg in 15ml saline.
Chloramphenicol succinate	200mg in 15ml saline.
Erythromycin	200mg in 10ml saline.
Gentamicin *	50mg in 10ml saline.
Polymyxin B *	333,000iu in 5ml of saline.
Spectinomycin	200mg in 15ml saline.
Sulphadimethoxine	200mg in 15 ml saline.
Tylosin *	100mg in10ml saline or 1g in 50ml DMSO.
Amikacin *	50mg in 10ml saline.
Enrofloxacin	100mg in 10ml saline.
Doxycycline	200mg in 15ml saline.

* Poorly absorbed from the respiratory epithelium.
All these drugs can also be used by the intratracheal route (see later).

surgery, an abdominal air sac breathing tube must be placed (see Figure 15.5). A number of different sites have been recommended; each varies in ease of placement and effectiveness (full details may be found in Chapter 6).

Surgical Treatment of Syringeal Aspergillomata

Having placed an air sac breathing tube, the trachea may be operated upon more safely. Some authors describe retraction and transection (usually through 75% of the circumference) of the trachea to gain access to the syringeal region. However, this author favours the per-glottis approach. A 2.7mm rigid endoscope and a 'cut off' male dog catheter are passed simultaneously through the glottis and down the trachea. The aspergilloma is easily visualised on one or both sides of the syrinx. By careful placement of the bird, the bulk or all of the lesion can be removed by a rotational cutting motion with the prepared catheter, whilst simultaneously applying suction using a 60ml syringe. Segments of aspergilloma are sucked up or impaled within or on the end of the catheter, and can be recovered. If the aspergilloma cannot be recovered it may, as a last resort, be pushed down a primary bronchus, from where it will emerge on the ventral aspect of the lung, in the thoracic air sac. It may be either recovered from this new position or treated *in situ*. This latter technique is not an ideal solution, but at least the life threatening obstruction has been removed. Following surgical removal or debulking of an aspergilloma, long-term medical treatment is essential to prevent recrudescence and to eliminate any infection elsewhere in the lung or air sacs (see later).

MEDICAL TREATMENT OF FUNGAL INFECTIONS

In order for an antifungal drug to be effective, the organism must be susceptible to that drug at concentrations achievable at the site of infection. Most importantly, the drug must be able to penetrate to the centre of the infection. Furthermore, the antifungal drug must not be toxic to the patient at the level and duration of treatment that is required to eliminate the infection. It has been reported that the azole compounds do not reach adequate minimum inhibitory concentrations within the first 3-5 days of therapy (Flammer, 1993), although this point is refuted by the manufacturer of itraconazole and other azole group agents. In view of this, amphotericin B (1.5mg/kg tid i/v for 3-5 days) is recommended. Because of the potentially nephrotoxic properties of amphoteracin B, 15ml/kg of fluids should be given intravenously with each dose. There are several different medical treatment regimes that have been reported. The method preferred by the author is a combination of surgical removal or debulking of any identifiable lesion, followed by topical (intratracheal) enilconazole (0.5ml of 1:10 dilution per kg), concurrently with amphotericin B for 3-5 days, as well as either itraconazole (10mg/kg bid p/o) or flucytosine (250mg/

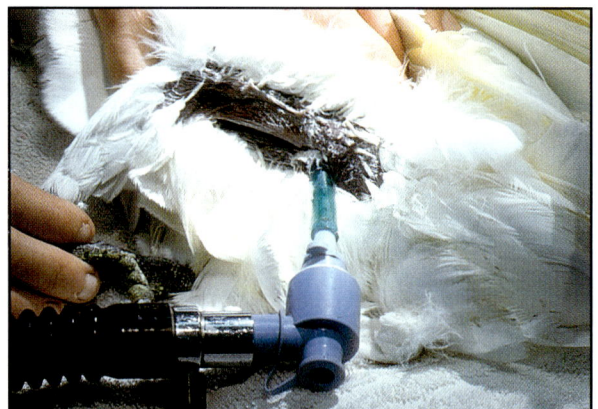

Figure 15.5: *Air sac breathing tube placed in the caudal abdominal air sac of a cockatoo.*

kg bid p/o). Topical treatment is maintained for two weeks, and parenteral treatment for two months following visual disappearance of any lesion.

LOWER RESPIRATORY DISEASE

Air Sacculitits

Most species of bird have at least four paired air sacs and one non-paired air sac. Inspired air passes down the trachea, through the lung via the intrapulmonary primary bronchi and through the neopulmonic parabronchi to the caudal air sacs (see Figure 15.6). The neopulmonic part of the lung possesses a highly efficient and active scavenging system. Any inspired particulate matter should be removed at this point. The caudal air sacs comprise the paired abdominal and caudal thoracic air sacs. No gaseous absorption occurs within the air sacs, they simply act as a bellows system. Oxygen absorption occurs in the paleopulmonic parabronchi during inspiration and expiration (see Figures 15.6, 15.7) (see Chapter 6 for a more detailed description of respiratory anatomy and physiology). Bacterial air sacculitis does occur, although it is rare in comparison with fungal or chlamydial air sacculitis. Fungal infections are by far the commonest condition of the air sacs. It must be appreciated that air sac disease rarely causes respiratory signs until the bird is *in extremis*. The severity of signs caused by air sacculitis does not relate to the severity of the pathology.

Aspergillosis of the air sacs most commonly affects the caudal air sacs. As the caudal air sacs are the first part of the air sac system into which air enters, particulate matter, eg. fungal spores, is most likely to precipitate here. Furthermore, it is the first part of the respiratory system into which the air has entered where there is not a scavenging system for the control of particulate or infectious particles. As the air sacs surround the digestive system, cases typically present with lethargy, inappetence or vomiting, and with dramatic loss of condition. Affected birds do not usually show any respiratory signs.

Diagnosis

Diagnosis is made on high quality lateral and dorsoventral radiographs, followed by endoscopy. The value of endoscopy cannot be overemphasised. All parts of the lower respiratory system, from the trachea and lungs to the air sacs, can be readily visualised. In addition, samples (of air sac tissue and lung) can be taken for culture, impression smear, or histopathology. It is imperative that the clinician has the use of an endoscope and is familiar with all approaches (Brearley *et al*, 1991; Taylor, 1994). Practising approaches on cadavers is invaluable, although interspecies variations in anatomy should not be forgotten.

Treatment

Unless an aspergilloma is detected very early, drug therapy alone is unlikely to be effective because of the thick, leathery, caseous encapsulation. In these cases, surgical removal should be attempted. Surgery of air sac aspergillomata is heroic, but is often the only possible chance of survival. Surgery usually involves midline and paracostal incisions on one or both sides.

Pneumonia

Pneumonia is a relatively uncommon condition in psittacines compared with other diseases of the respiratory system. The commoner causes of pneumonia are listed in Table 15.7.

Subcutaneous Emphysema

It is not uncommon for a rupture to occur in the wall

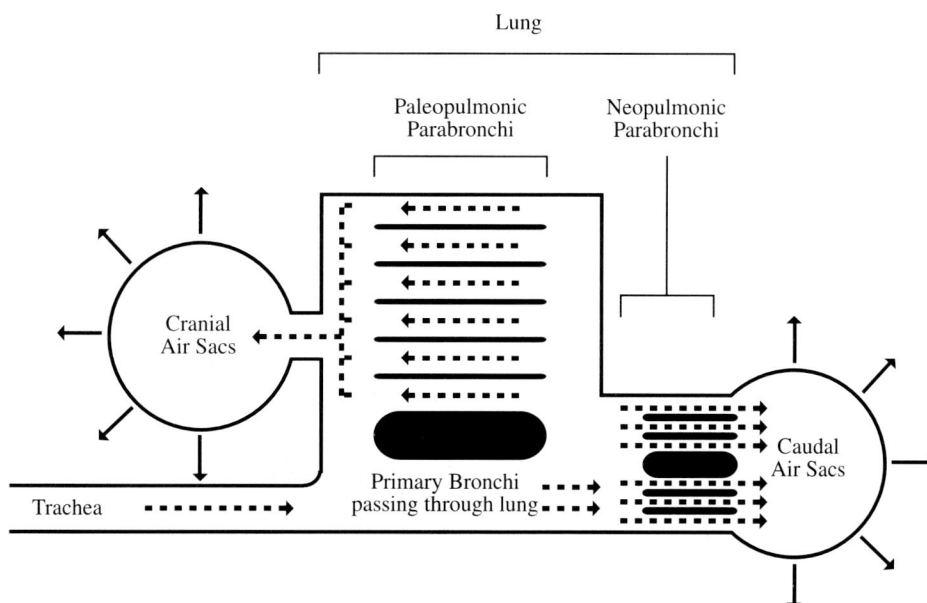

Figure 15.6: *Schematic diagram of the LRT during inspiration (after Fedde, 1993).*

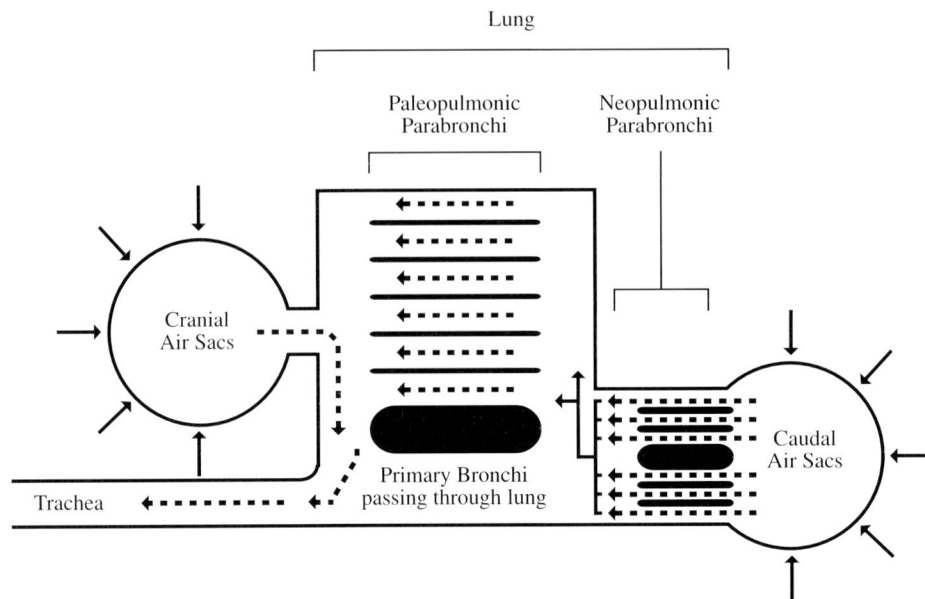

Figure 15.7: Schematic diagram of the LRT during expiration (after Fedde, 1993).

of a cervical, clavicular or other air sac. Any air sac rupture causes large volumes of localised or generalised subcutaneous emphysema. In such cases, electrosurgery or cautery should be used to burn a 3-5mm long incision in the cutis. This will continue to allow the subcutaneous air to escape, enabling the internal rupture to heal. The external incision will heal within a short period. In persistent cases, a sialastic tube may be sutured into the skin wound in order to maintain patency, giving a longer period for healing of the defect in the air sac wall.

Clavicular Air Sac Disease

Although this is rare, the presenting signs may be misleading. Typically, the bird is presented with a unilateral wing droop in the absence of any evident wing pathology. Radiographs will often reveal an increased radiodensity of the clavicular air sac on the affected side. This condition can be caused by foreign body penetration or aspergillosis.

NON-RESPIRATORY CAUSES OF RESPIRATORY SIGNS

A number of non-respiratory diseases which may present with respiratory signs are listed in Table 15.8.

REFERENCES

Brearley MJ, Cooper JE and Sullivan M (1991) *A Colour Atlas of Small Animal Endoscopy.* Wolfe, London.

Table 15.7. Common causes of pneumonia in psittacines.

Cause	Comments
Aspiration	Relatively common in handfed neonates.
Bacterial	Rare; diagnose and treat as for bacterial tracheitis.
Mycotic	Multifocal pneumonic aspergillosis is typically associated with a highly spore-ridden environment/food; typically, these lead to acute death. Treat as for any fungal infection.
Sarcocystis spp.	Coccidian parasite which causes haemorrhagic interstitial pneumonia or peracute death.
Toxic	eg.Teflon, commonly seen as peracute death due to pulmonary oedema.
Neoplastic	Rare; biopsy via caudal thoracic air sac.

Table 15.8. Non-respiratory diseases presenting with respiratory signs.

Cause	Comments
Ascites	Liver or kidney disease, neoplasia or any other space occupying lesion producing ascites.
Abdominal haemorrhage	Iatrogenic post-surgery, trauma, neoplasia or coagulation defect.
Malnutrition	General weakness/anaemia (+ other causes of anaemia).
Obesity	Causes space occupying lesions/hepatic disease leading to anaemia.
Goitre/trauma	Pressure on trachea or damage to integrity of trachea. This condition is common in budgerigars; birds present with a 'click' on inspiration and often have an altered voice. The condition occurs due to an iodine deficient diet, typically arising due to feeding low grade seed mixes, which leads to hypothyroidism. Treatment is by addition of Lugol's iodine (1 part Lugol's to 14 parts water - add one drop of this to 30ml of drinking water daily for three weeks). Increase dietary iodine content (better quality boxed seed, ground oyster shell or cod liver oil).
Heart failure	Due to ascites or inefficiency of circulation.
Herpes/reo/paramyxo/ adenoviruses	All cause viraemia which may present with respiratory signs.
Egg peritonitis or other causes of peritonitis	Due to effect on coelomic cavity as a whole.

Campbell TW (1994) Cytology. In: *Avian Medicine: Principles and Application.* Eds BW Ritchie, GJ Harrison and LR Harrison. Wingers, Lake Worth.

Fedde MR (1993) Structure and function of the avian respiratory system. In: *Avian Medicine and Surgery: Core Topics.* Association of Avian Veterinarians, Lake Worth.

Flammer K (1993) An overview of antifungal therapy in birds. In: *Proceedings of the Association of Avian Veterinarians Annual Conference 1993.* AAV, Lake Worth.

Forbes NA (1991) Aspergillosis. *Veterinary Record* **128**, 263.

Forbes NA (1992) Diagnosis of avian aspergillosis and treatment with itraconazole. *Veterinary Record* **130**, 519.

Gerlach H (1994) Viruses. In: *Avian Medicine: Principles and Application.* Eds BW Ritchie, GJ Harrison and LR Harrison. Wingers, Lake Worth.

Harrison GJ and Ritchie BW (1994) Making distinctions in physical examination. In: *Avian Medicine: Principles and Application.* Eds BW Ritchie, GJ Harrison and LR Harrison. Wingers, Lake Worth.

Morgan DO and Clapham PA (1934) Some observations on gapeworm in poultry and game birds. *Journal of Helminthology* **12**, 267.

Taylor M (1994) Endoscopic examination and biopsy techniques. In: *Avian Medicine: Principles and Application.* Eds BW Ritchie, GJ Harrison and LR Harrison. Wingers, Lake Worth.

Tsai SS, Park JH, Hirai K and Itakura C (1992) Aspergillosis and candidiasis in psittacine and passeriforme birds with particular reference to nasal lesions. *Avian Pathology* **21**, 699.

Tully NT and Harrison GJ (1994) Pneumonology. In: *Avian Medicine: Principles and Application.* Eds BW Ritchie, GJ Harrison and LR Harrison. Wingers, Lake Worth.

CHAPTER SIXTEEN

Polydipsia and Polyuria

Anne P McLoughlin

INTRODUCTION

Polyuria is an increase in the production of liquid urine. Care must be taken to distinguish this condition from diarrhoea, which is a fluid faecal component of the droppings, often with normal urates (see Figures 16.1, 16.2). Polyuria and diarrhoea frequently occur simultaneously. Polyuria is one of the most frequent presenting clinical signs and is associated with a wide variety of diseases. Many polyuric birds exhibit a compensatory polydipsia, although in some cases the polyuria may be secondary to the polydipsia, eg. diabetes mellitus or diabetes insipidus.

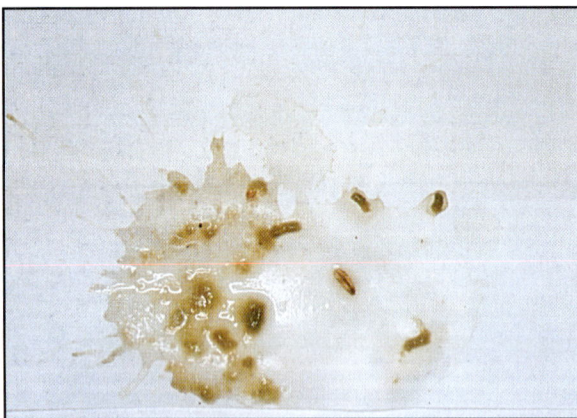

Figure 16.1: Polyuria with normal tube-shaped faeces (African Grey).

Figure 16.2: Polyuria with soft, unformed faeces (Amazon).

PHYSIOLOGY OF NITROGENOUS WASTE EXCRETION IN BIRDS

Birds, like reptiles, are uricotelic, excreting nitrogenous waste products mainly in the form of uric acid and urates (Sykes, 1971; King and McLelland, 1984). Uric acid is formed by the liver as an end-product of protein metabolism (see Figure 16.3).

Urea is produced only in small amounts as a by-product of detoxification pathways in the kidney and, to a lesser extent, the liver, but is not involved in uric acid synthesis (see Figure 16.4).

Uric acid and urates normally account for more than 60% of the urinary nitrogen, the remainder being excreted in the form of ammonia and urea (Sykes, 1971; Farner, 1982).

Urine Production

Both urine and urates in birds are formed by a combination of glomerular filtration, tubular excretion and tubular resorption. Urinary water is derived solely from the glomerular filtrate (Farner, 1982), the glomerular filtration rate ranging from 1.7-4.6ml/kg/min (Ringer, 1986). In the normal bird at least 90% of the original glomerular filtrate is reabsorbed by the tubules. During diuresis in some birds, as little as 6% of filtered water may be reabsorbed, resulting in polyuria.

Glucose is normally completely reabsorbed (Lumeij, 1994a), while absorption of sodium chloride and bicarbonate is variable and depends upon the diet, health status and state of hydration of the bird. Uric acid is excreted mainly by active excretion in the renal tubules, but partly by glomerular filtration. Uric acid and the salts arising from it (urates) form colloidal solutions at tubular concentrations of up to 3%. This allows transport through the tubules and collecting ducts without precipitation which would result in obstruction. In the ureter the urate component becomes thick and stringy, and mucus is produced to lubricate the movement of the precipitated urates down the ureter (King and McLelland, 1984). If the epithelium of the proximal renal tubules is damaged by disease, excretion of urates is reduced and the blood levels of uric acid rise. In graniverous birds, if the blood level exceeds a certain threshold ($600\mu mol/l$), recrystallisation

Amino acids
(deamination)   Dietary
glycine   Oxaloacetic
acid

Glutamic acid   Ammonia   Aspartic acid

PURINE ◄———— Nucleic acid
synthesis

Hypoxanthine

Xanthine

URIC ACID

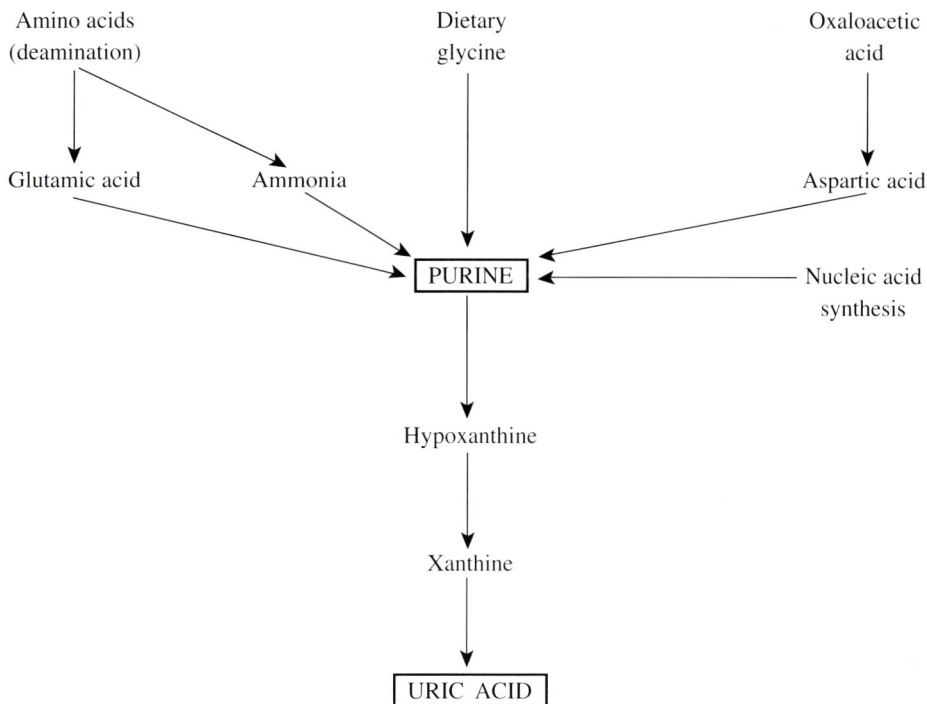

Figure 16.3: Production (metabolism) of uric acid in the avian liver (after Boorman and Lewis, 1971).

takes place producing solid deposits (tophi) of uric acid in joints (articular gout) and/or parenchymatous abdominal organs (visceral gout).

The semi-solid urine which leaves the ureter and enters the cloaca is then admixed with faecal material and moved by retroperistalis into the rectum and colon where further reabsorption occurs (Lumeij, 1994a). Cloacal reabsorption of water and solutes, including some urates, is important, particularly in times of water deprivation, as it enables further concentration of the urine and more efficient water conservation.

Normal urates appear as white or cream coloured semi-solids. Normal urine is a clear liquid, composed of water, colloidal uric acid and various solutes. It is usually excreted in small quantities with faeces and urates (see Figure 16.5).

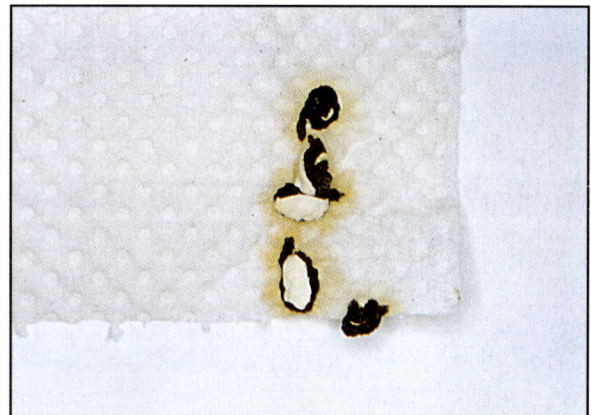

AETIOLOGY OF POLYURIA

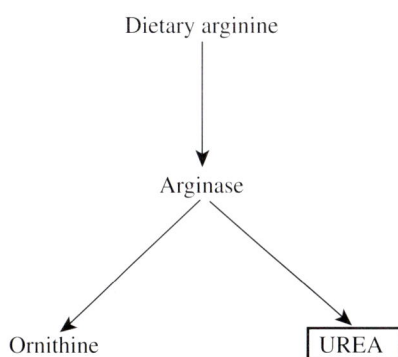

Dietary arginine

Arginase

Ornithine   UREA

Figure 16.4: Production (metabolism) of urea (occurs in the kidney and to a lesser extent the liver).

Figure 16.5: Normal faeces, urates and urine (cockatiel).

It is important to distinguish normal physiological polyuria from pathological polyuria. In the absence of any other clinical signs, a thorough clinical history will help to determine whether any of the following factors are contributing to polyuria.

Stress

Stress increases plasma cortisol levels which causes a transient hyperglycaemia. This is often manifested as polyuria and is commonly seen in birds transported to the surgery. Droppings passed by the bird in transit frequently show increased liquid content. Birds should be presented for examination in a cage which has not been cleaned for 24 hours. Hospitalisation may be necessary for more accurate assessment, particularly if the bird is not usually caged alone or if the cage has been cleaned prior to presentation.

Diet

A diet with a high water content will result in increased water content of the droppings. This is not true polyuria as much of the water is derived from the intestinal tract. This may be noted in adult psittacines fed large quantities of fruit or vegetable matter, or in young birds being handfed a semi-liquid formula, such as Milupa baby food.

Acute malnutrition, a poor quality diet or hypoproteinaemia may also result in polyuria due to the release of large quantities of body water by catabolism (Sayle, 1986). It is important to recognise that an abrupt change in diet often results in a reduction of food intake and, therefore, a polyuria.

Egg Laying

The water content of the droppings increases prior to the onset of egg laying in hens. Osteoclastic activity induced by parathyroid hormone results in demineralisation of medullary bone. Calcium is deposited in the egg yolk and shell and excess phosphate is excreted via the kidneys resulting in a primary phosphate diuresis (Lumeij, 1994b). The hen's water intake also increases at this time. This is partly in response to the diuresis, but primarily to compensate for addition of watery fluids to the albumen by the uterine glands.

An eggbound bird that has had the egg removed by manipulation may pass a clear uterine fluid that can be mistaken for urine (Sayle, 1986).

Psychogenic Origins

Recently weaned birds and some adults may develop psychogenic polydipsia and subsequent polyuria.

Iatrogenic

Many drugs are excreted through the kidneys and may result in polyuria. In the majority of cases this is due to an increase in uric acid production or water transport rather than true renal damage, eg. frusemide, progestagens such as megestrol acetate and medroxyprogesterone acetate, or delmadinone acetate. Allopurinol, which may be used as a treatment for gout, induces an osmotic diuresis by increasing the excretion of soluble urates. It is important that there is an adequate water intake in birds treated with these preparations.

The aminoglycoside antibiotics, eg. amikacin, gentamicin, etc., are nephrotoxic and should be used with caution, and not in dehydrated patients (Flammer, 1994). Low dose regimes and short-term treatment usually cause a reversible polyuria and polydipsia that ceases shortly after therapy is withdrawn, leaving little permanent renal damage. High doses may cause renal necrosis or death of the bird. Additional fluids should always be administered concurrently with these drugs.

PATHOLOGICAL CAUSES OF POLYURIA

Polyuria can be a feature of almost all diseases of psittacines. Most diseases of birds are pansystemic and may affect protein metabolism in the liver and water absorption by the kidney. One of the major clinical signs of 'sick bird syndrome' is anorexia, which results in the release of large quantities of body water as a result of catabolism. Possible causes of polyuria and polyurates are listed in Tables 16.1 and 16.2.

Table 16.1. Differential diagnosis of polyuria based on history and other clinical signs.

History/signs	Differential
Polyuric bird, no other clinical signs.	Stress. Diet with high water content. Psychogenic (especially recently weaned birds, and cockatoos). Food allergy. Diabetes mellitus. Pseudodiabetes. Calcium deficiency. Chronic chlamydiosis. Early hepatic or renal disease.
Non-specific signs of ill health (ruffled, lethargic, anorexic).	Renal disease (toxic, infectious, neoplastic, metabolic). Liver disease. Septicaemia. Viral infection. Diabetes mellitus. Toxins (lead, salt). Neoplasia.

Table 16.1. Continued.

History/signs	Differential
Diarrhoea.	Enteritis. Chlamydiosis. Pacheco's disease (herpesvirus).
Lameness.	Gout (mainly budgerigars). Renal neoplasia (mainly budgerigars). Acute nephritis.
Concurrent or previous drug use.	Overdose (especially aminoglycosides and corticosteroids).
Post i/v fluids.	Normal.
Neurological signs.	Hypocalcaemia (especially African Greys) - secondary to hepatopathy. Lead poisoning.
Change in colour of urine and/or urates (yellow, pea green) (see Figure 16.6).	Liver disease. Viruses (herpesvirus, adenovirus, psittacine beak and feather disease). Chlamydiosis. Vitamins, other pigments. *Salmonella* spp. and other bacteria. Pancreatitis.
Scant faeces (see Figure 16.7).	Infectious disease of the liver. Chlamydiosis. Anorexia.
Egg laying female.	Hypercalcaemia (normal). Egg related peritonitis. Metritis.
Blood in the urine (see Figure 16.8).	Acute haemorrhagic syndrome of Amazons. Lead poisoning. Coagulopathy. Cloacal papillomata.

Table 16.2. Differential diagnosis of polyurates.

Clinical/signs	Differential diagnosis
Reduced amount of faeces.	Excess dietary protein. Grit impaction. Obstruction, eg. cloacal calculi, gut torsion. Eggbinding. Infectious diseases. Other causes of anorexia. Water deprivation. Toxins.
Change in colour of urates.	Liver damage. Vitamin overdose. Bacterial infections.

Table 16.2. Continued.

Clinical/signs	Differential diagnosis
Reddish urates.	Acute haemorrhagic syndrome of Amazons. Lead poisoning. Other toxins. Any other cause of acute haemolysis.

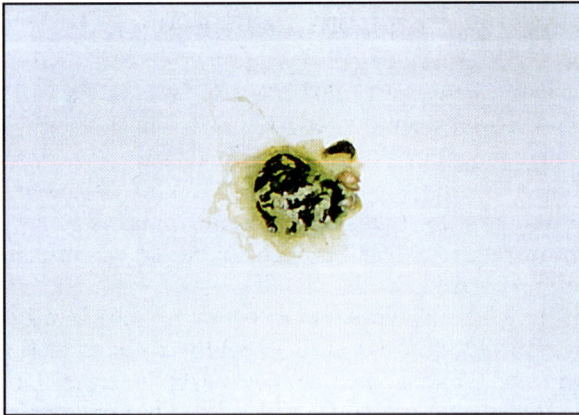

Figure 16.6: Normal faeces - green stained urates (macaw).

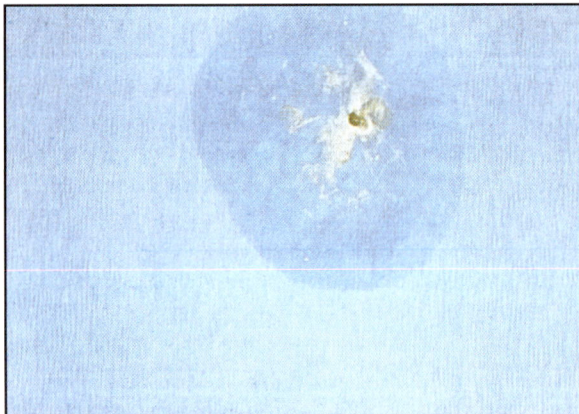

Figure 16.7: Polyuria - scant faeces (Hahn's Macaw).

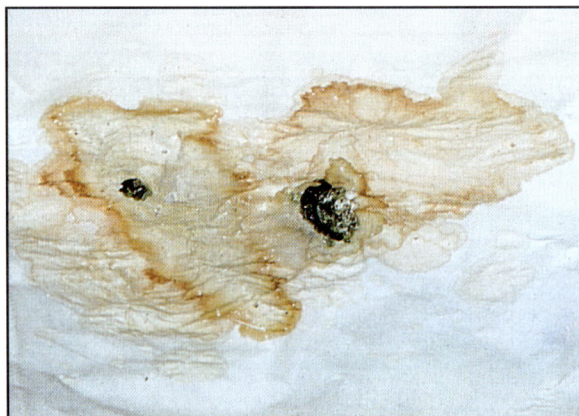

Figure 16.8: Haematuria (possibly acute haemorrhagic syndrome of Amazons).

Renal Disease

Although primary renal disease is difficult to diagnose in pet birds, secondary renal disease is frequently a component of multisystemic illness. Cooper and Lawton (1988) included the following in their main causes of renal disease: infectious, parasitic (rare), nutritional/metabolic, traumatic, neoplastic, toxic, uncertain.

Acute nephritis is almost impossible to diagnose *ante mortem* as the disease course is so rapid. The causes are usually infectious, eg. *Escherichia coli* septicaemia or purulent pyelonephritis, or toxic, eg. iatrogenic, salt poisoning from salty snacks, zinc poisoning from galvanised wire, aflatoxicosis from fungal contamination of food, lead poisoning or antifreeze consumption (Brugere-Picoux and Brugere, 1987). Birds in acute renal failure are usually oliguric or anuric (Lumeij, 1994a).

Chronic nephritis may be toxic, infectious or metabolic in origin. Rosskopf and Woerpel (1988) reported that kidney infections were common in caged birds, possibly because of the close proximity of the intestinal tract, resulting in contamination of any urine which happens to reflux from the cloaca. Haematogenous infection may arise directly as a result of venous drainage from the intestinal tract through the kidney (renal portal system).

A high protein intake may contribute to renal disease, causing interstitial nephritis and degenerative changes in the tubules and Bowman's capsules. Vitamin A deficiency causes squamous cell metaplasia of renal tubular epithelium and a reduction in resorptive capacity. Hypervitaminosis D or elevated dietary calcium may lead to calcinosis of the renal parenchyma. This should not be confused with urolithiasis, which is the most prevalent renal disorder of laying hens and can cause post-renal renal failure (Lumeij, 1994a). Renal tumours are relatively common in psittacines, particularly budgerigars. Tumours may be primary, eg. renal adenocarcinoma, or secondary, eg. lymphoma. Renal cysts have been reported (Hasholt and Petrak, 1982).

Many of the changes associated with chronic renal disease are of uncertain origin and may be sequelae to earlier infectious, parasitic or nutritional disease. There is also some evidence for allergic diseases of the kidney (Cooper and Lawton, 1988). Chronic chlamydial infection or other chronic disease may produce high levels of circulating immunoglobulin. This may lead to glomerulonephritis as a result of deposition of antigen:antibody complexes in the renal tubules (Lawton, unpublished data).

Liver Disease

Many psittacine diseases involve the liver. Infectious disease probably accounts for most cases in clinical practice. The more common causes are enteric bacteria, *Yersinia* spp., *Chlamydia psittaci*, herpesvirus (Pacheco's disease), reovirus and papovavirus.

Toxic causes of hepatic disease include aflatoxicosis and lead poisoning. The major metabolic cause of liver disease is fatty infiltration of hepatocytes in birds fed a high fat (usually seed) diet. Haemochromatosis (iron storage disease), although most commonly seen in toucans and mynahs, has been reported in Psittaciformes (Lumeij, 1994c). Liver neoplasia may be primary, eg. hepatocellular carcinoma, or secondary, eg. lymphoma, renal carcinoma.

Diabetes Mellitus

The pathophysiology of diabetes mellitus in psittacines remains unclear but differs considerably from that seen in mammals (Lumeij, 1994b). It is considered that glucagon is the major glucose-regulating hormone in granivorous birds. It is strongly catabolic, stimulating lipolysis, gluconeogenesis and glycogenolysis, and thus resulting in a marked and rapid hyperglycaemia. Diabetes is relatively common in pet birds, particularly cockatiels and budgerigars, and may result from excess glucagon secretion rather than from insulin deficiency. Diabetes has also been associated with pituitary tumours, egg-related pancreatitis, pancreatic tumours, peritonitis, renal tumours and deposition of fat within the liver cells (or hepatocytes). Diabetic birds have a profound polydipsia, causing a secondary polyuria. Polyphagia is often present and there is significant weight loss due to the strongly catabolic effects of glucagon.

Nutritional Secondary Hyperparathyroidism

This is a common problem of caged birds resulting from a reduction in blood calcium levels of birds fed large quantities of oil bearing seeds, eg. sunflower, safflower, or other foods deficient in calcium. An idiopathic hypocalcaemia syndrome is also seen in African Greys. Low plasma calcium levels (below 2.0 mmol/l) (Lawton, personal communication) stimulate the parathyroid glands to release an increased amount of parathormone. Parathormone stimulates calcium reabsorption by the kidney and urinary loss of phosphorus. The phosphaturia causes polyuria (Lumeij, 1994b). Long-term oxytetracycline treatment may also cause hypocalcaemia and secondary hyperparathyroidism.

CLINICAL ASSESSMENT OF THE POLYURIC BIRD

History

Initially, the origin of the bird, length of ownership, exposure to other birds, housing arrangements, diet, recent changes in food or water consumption, changes in behaviour, access to toxins (particularly lead) and previous treatment, if appropriate, should be established.

Observation and Physical Examination

Observation and examination of the sick bird are discussed elsewhere in this manual (see Chapter 4). Physical examination must be carried out thoroughly and systematically and should include gross examination of the droppings. Most polyuric birds will show non-specific signs of ill health, but in some cases more specific signs may give an indication as to the nature of the disease.

The physical condition of the bird is indicated by the ratio of muscle to bone and fat in the area of the sternum. Well rounded muscles indicate an acute condition, whereas muscle atrophy is suggestive of chronic disease. Obesity may be accompanied by fat deposition in the liver, kidneys or coelomic cavity.

Abdominal distension may suggest heart disease, liver or kidney disease, reproductive problems, neoplasia, ascites or obesity. Birds with abdominal distension may already be dyspnoeic (see Chapter 15) and care must be taken when palpating the abdomen. When ascites is secondary to heart disease, liver disease or egg peritonitis, it is possible to rupture the abdominal membranes, forcing fluid into the air sacs and causing rapid death (Harrison and Ritchie, 1994). Aspiration of ascitic fluid by abdominocentesis may aid the diagnosis. If liver disease is suspected, radiographs should be taken to ascertain the extent of the liver margin. Abdominocentesis is then carried out using a 21-25G needle inserted in the midline just below the caudal margin of the keel and directed towards the right side of the abdomen to avoid puncturing the ventriculus (Degernes, 1991). Removal of large volumes of fluid may result in hypoproteinaemia or hypovolaemic shock.

In birds weighing over 100g, cloacal examination can be performed (Cooper and Lawton, 1988). A lubricated gloved finger is inserted through the vent and moved dorsally in the cloaca to palpate the caudal border of the kidney. Any swelling, pain or asymmetry may be indicative of renal disease.

Neurological signs may be associated with pituitary tumours in budgerigars, causing a Cushing-like disease syndrome with polyuria and polydipsia. Particularly in budgerigars, renal tumours may result in hindlimb paralysis as a result of pressure on the sciatic nerve. The affected leg is usually non-weight bearing and is held in an abnormal position.

Skin elasticity can be used to assess the degree of dehydration (Harrison and Ritchie, 1994). In birds the skin of the neck and abdomen provide the most effective sites for assessment. Turgor of the wing veins also correlates with hydration. A plump and relatively turgid wing vein is usually associated with normal serum protein and haematocrit. Collapsed wing veins may suggest shock, dehydration, hypoproteinaemia or anaemia.

FURTHER DIAGNOSTIC TESTS

Urinalysis (after Lumeij, 1994a)

If the droppings are collected onto a non-porous surface, such as polythene film or greaseproof paper, the urine and urates can be aspirated with a needle and syringe. A commercial urinalysis 'dipstick' (Multistix, Ames) can be used. However, it is difficult to test the pure fluid portion of the dropping without contamination by faeces, and the presence of uric acid may affect the dipstick reactions.

The most important use of urinalysis is to detect the presence of active kidney disease long before the damage is severe enough to be detected by a rise in blood uric acid (Rosskopf and Woerpel, 1988).

Colour

Normal birds produce only a small quantity of urine and a variable quantity of urates. Normal urine colour ranges from clear to various shades of yellow, orange, light green and greenish white. The urates should be pure white, pale yellow or light beige. Normal variation in colour results from variation in specific gravity, the colour of the bird's plasma, the amount of faeces mixed with the urinary fraction and the administration of water soluble vitamins, eg. supplementation with B-complex vitamins produces yellow urine.

Liver disease, including chlamydiosis, often results in yellow-green coloured urine and mustard coloured urates, because of increased excretion of biliverdin. Lead poisoning and other causes of haemolysis may produce haemaglobinuria, resulting in mahogany coloured urine and urates.

Specific Gravity

The normal range is 1.005-1.020. In polyuric birds, values range from 1.002-1.033. The specific gravity varies with the state of hydration (Woerpel *et al*, 1987).

pH

The normal range is 5.5-6.9 (Lumeij, 1994a). Low pH is associated with acidosis which may occur in conjunction with dehydration.

Protein

Traces of protein are found in 90% of urine samples due to excretion of mucoproteins and glycoproteins in the distal portion of the nephrons. Protein levels are often normal in early cases of kidney infection (Rosskopf and Woerpel, 1988). Severe, persistent proteinuria (> +2) may be seen with degenerative nephropathies or glomerulonephritis owing to increased glomerular permeability.

Glucose

Normal urine often contains traces of glucose. Higher levels are commonly detected as a result of faecal contamination of the urine sample within the cloaca. The renal threshold for glucose varies between species. Cockatoos and Amazons may show glucosuria with blood glucose levels as low as 15mmol/l, while the renal threshold in cockatiels is 19.4mmol/l or higher (Woerpel *et al*, 1987). A diagnosis of diabetes mellitus should not be made on the basis of urinalysis alone.

Ketones

Ketonuria has been reported in severely diabetic birds (Woerpel *et al*, 1987) or birds with ketoacidosis resulting from catabolic processes associated with severe hepatitis. Liver disease results in hypoglycaemia, mobilisation of fat for energy and subsequent formation of ketones.

Blood

A positive reading for blood in the urine does not automatically indicate haematuria. The blood may also originate from the intestines, reproductive tract or cloaca. A sudden onset of watery orange-red urine is seen in cases of acute haemorrhagic syndrome of Amazons (Galvin, 1983). Severe intravascular haemolysis results in excretion of haemoglobin by the kidney. The pathogenesis of acute haemorrhagic syndrome is unclear, but is thought to be associated with toxin ingestion (Gould, 1992). True haematuria is seen in birds with lead poisoning, coagulopathies and some cases of liver disease or septicaemia. It is also possible that the red colouration of urine from birds with lead poisoning is caused by high levels of porphyrins (Lumeij, 1994a).

Casts

Normal birds do not produce urine casts (Rosskopf and Woerpel, 1988). Casts are commonly seen in birds with kidney disease. All polyuric birds should be examined for casts, as their presence is a valuable tool in the diagnosis of subclinical renal disease. They may be present while biochemistry results are still normal. Rosskopf and Woerpel (1988) described three main types of urine casts:
● Cellular casts (containing epithelial cells, erythrocytes from renal haemorrhage, leucocytes and bacterial casts from renal infection).
● Granular casts (coarsely or finely granular depending on the degree of degeneration).
● 'Haemoglobin' casts (seen as a result of tubule leakage in disease states with breakdown of red cells and

kidney damage, or as an aftermath of kidney disease as the kidneys heal). A transition from cellular or granular casts to 'haemoglobin' casts is frequently seen in birds recovering from kidney disease.

Crystals
Normal avian urine contains many amorphous crystals.

Bacteria
Gram-positive bacilli and cocci are commonly found due to faecal contamination of a urine sample and may be of no consequence.

Haematology
Examination of blood smears and cell counts using a haemocytometer are of limited use in the investigation of the polyuric bird. Stress may cause an increase in the white blood cell (WBC) count. WBC counts of greater than 11 x 10^9/l can be suggestive of inflammatory processes, but many birds (particularly Amazons) with chronic disease exhibit apparently normal WBC counts (Woerpel *et al*, 1987). Very low WBC counts are often associated with viral diseases, eg. psittacine beak and feather disease, but can also result from overwhelming infection, viraemia or toxaemia (causing bone marrow suppression).

The haematocrit is a simple test. Values higher than 0.6 may reflect dehydration. Values below 0.4 may be associated with acute or chronic disease, eg. chlamydiosis, septicaemia, neoplasia, egg peritonitis, heavy metal toxicity or malnutrition.

Biochemistry
Lithium heparin is the anticoagulant of choice for avian blood chemistry, including glucose determinations. Collection and processing of avian blood samples is discussed elsewhere in this manual (see Chapter 5). Table 16.3 refers to the interpretation of biochemistry results using either wet or dry chemistry methods. Although the albumin:globulin (A:G) ratio is a valuable diagnostic test in birds, albumin values determined with dry chemistry methods, eg. Kodak Ektachem or the bromocresol dye binding method (BCG), are unreliable in birds and hence give an unreliable A:G ratio. Plasma protein electrophoresis is the method of choice for determining albumin concentration (Lumeij, 1993).

It should also be borne in mind that plasma uric acid, urea and creatinine levels will only be elevated when renal function is below 30% of its capacity.

ADDITIONAL DIAGNOSTIC TESTS

Chlamydia psittaci
Faecal or serological tests for chlamydiosis are indicated if concurrent liver disease is suspected.

Bile Acids
This is a useful liver function test in psittacine birds (Fudge and Reavill, 1991; Gould, 1992). Normal Amazons have post-prandial values of less than 36μmol/l (Gould, 1992), although it is better to carry out the test after a 3-4 hour fast. Birds with liver pathology usually have significant two to five-fold increases. Chronic liver disease resulting in cirrhosis may lead to reduced production of bile acids and a subsequent decrease in plasma levels of bile acids (Hochleithner, 1994).

Table 16.3. Blood biochemistry - interpretation of results with relevance to the polyuric bird. (Tests carried out at 37°C using standard methodology.)

Blood parameter	Clinical findings	Possible causes
Plasma colour.	Icterus (rare).	Liver disease (eg. chlamydiosis). Acute haemolysis.
	Lipaemia (may cause elevated protein values).	High fat diet. Liver disease. Neoplasia.
Total protein.	Hyperproteinaemia (>50g/l).	Dehydration. Chronic disease (increased globulins). Shock. Lipaemia.
	Hypoproteinaemia (<25g/l - usually low albumin).	Malnutrition. Malabsorption. Anorexia. Hepatic disease. Renal disease.

Table 16.3. Continued

Blood parameter	Clinical findings	Possible causes
Glucose.	Hyperglycaemia (>20mmol/l) (normal levels 11-18mmol/l).	Stress. Diabetes mellitus. Renal adenocarcinoma. Fatty liver/obesity. Egg yolk peritonitis (transient).
	Hyperglycaemia (< 11mmol/l).	Anorexia. Malnutrition. Hepatopathy. Septicaemia. Endocrinopathy. Insulin overdosage.
Calcium (bound to serum proteins so affected by serum protein levels).	Hypercalcaemia (> 3mmol/l).	Egg laying. Excess vitamin D_3. Metastatic tumours. Renal disease. Recent change to high calcium diet (more than seven days ago).
	Hypocalcaemia (< 1.8mmol/l).	Nutritional secondary hyperparathyroidism. Idiopathic hypocalcaemia (African Greys). Renal failure. Long-term oxytetracycline therapy.
Phosphorus.	> 1.94mmol/l.	Renal disease. Nutritional secondary hyperparathyroidism.
Aspartate aminotransferase.	> 230u/l.	Stress. Iatrogenic (antibiosis and corticorsteroids). Many multisystem diseases. Septicaemia. Liver disease (toxic, infections, traumatic, neoplastic).
Lactate dehydrogenase.	> 450u/l.	Non-specific - trauma, neoplasia, liver disease. Muscle damage, eg. i/m injection.
Alkaline phosphatase (not a reliable test for liver disease).	> 320u/l.	Nutritional secondary hyperparathyroidism. Corticosteroid usage. Liver disease.
Creatinine phosphokinase.	> 900u/l.	Septicaemia. Hepatic disease. Chlamydiosis. Lead poisoning. Vitamin E/selenium deficiency. Neuropathies.

Table 16.3. Continued

Blood parameter	Clinical findings	Possible causes
Blood urea (not a useful test for renal function).	> 4.0mmol/l	Dehydration. Renal disease (trauma, gout, toxins, failure). Ureteral obstructions. Some liver diseases.
	< 0.3mmol/l.	Liver disease.
Uric acid (only useful test for renal function).	> 500μmol/l.	Primary or secondary renal disease. Severe dehydration. Starvation.
Creatinine (questionable value in evaluating kidney function).	> 60μmol/l.	Diet high in animal protein. Primary renal disease. Egg yolk peritonitis. Septicaemia.
Cholesterol.	> 5.0mmol/l	Obesity. Hypothyroidism. Bile duct obstruction. Fatty liver and kidney syndrome.
	< 2.0mmol/l.	Liver disease. Malnutrition.

(after Hawkey and Gulland, 1988; Hochleithner, 1994)

Glucose Tolerance Test

A diagnosis of diabetes mellitus cannot be made on the basis of a single raised blood glucose level. It should also be noted that the blood glucose level will be artificially high after administration of corticosteroids. To carry out a glucose tolerance test, the bird is starved for 2-3 hours and a blood sample taken to measure the fasting blood glucose level. Glucose is then administered orally at a dose of 2g/kg bodyweight. Blood samples are taken 10 minutes and 1.5 hours after administration. The truly diabetic bird is unable to alter its blood sugar level after administration of glucose (Woerpel *et al*, 1987).

Radiography

Plain lateral and dorsoventral radiographs may demonstrate enlargement of a kidney, hepatomegaly or displacement of other organs. Contrast radiography can also be used. Barium can be administered orally or *per cloacam*. Water soluble iodine-based contrast medium (Urografin, Schering) may be given intravenously into the brachial vein at a dose of 800mg/kg. For examination of the kidney, radiography is carried out 30-60 seconds later. The principles of radiography of psittacines are discussed in Chapter 7.

Ultrasonography

Although the value of ultrasonography in birds is limited due to the reflection of ultrasound waves by the gases in the air sacs, in the presence of ascites it may be possible to identify pathological changes in the liver, heart and urogenital system (Krautwald-Junghanns *et al*, 1991; Enders *et al*, 1993).

Laparoscopy/Laparotomy

Laparoscopy is an excellent aid to diagnosis of liver and renal disease using the site and technique described for surgical sexing (Taylor, 1994). Laparotomy should only be used if laparoscopy is unsuitable or unavailable, or if surgery is contemplated.

Biopsy

Liver or kidney biopsy may be indicated when additional information is required for diagnosis and treatment of hepatic or renal disease. Blind biopsy is not advisable because of the risk of damage to the abdominal air sacs or other organs. Biopsies can be taken by laparoscopy or at laparotomy (Kollias, 1984; Taylor, 1994).

TREATMENT OF THE POLYURIC BIRD

Supportive care including warmth, fluid therapy and nutritional support is essential before a specific diagnosis is made (Quesenberry and Hillyer, 1994).

Lactated Ringer's (Hartmann's) solution warmed to

38-39°C should be administered either subcutaneously, intravenously, intraosseous or by crop tube. As dehydration is usually accompanied by acidosis, bicarbonate can be administered at a dose of 1mEq/kg at 15-30 minute intervals to a maximum of 4mEq. With severe cases of metabolic acidosis, 5% dextrose is contraindicated as it is a strong acidifying agent. Dextrose should be diluted with equal amounts of lactated Ringer's to make a 2.5% dextrose solution.

Antibiotics are indicated in all cases, as debilitated patients are susceptible to invasion by enteric organisms through the portal system into the liver. Care must be taken in the use of potentially toxic chemotherapeutic agents in birds with impaired renal function. Many chronic liver cases respond well to treatment with doxycycline (Fudge, 1993).

Vitamin supplementation is essential as many psittacine diseases are due primarily to malnutrition. Vitamin A deficiency results in squamous cell metaplasia of the renal tubular endothelium. Vitamin E is important in reduction of free radicals and maintenance of hepatic cell membranes (Murphy, 1992). Daily supplementation with vitamin B complex is advisable in anorexic or anaemic birds (Quesenberry and Hillyer, 1994). In cases where liver pathology is present, vitamins are not stored as they would be normally.

Lactulose syrup is indicated for patients with liver disease (Ritchie and Harrison, 1994). It reduces the toxic potential of elevated blood ammonia resulting from liver dysfunction and acts as an osmotic retardant to the absorption of potential toxins from the gastrointestinal tract. The bacterial degradation of lactulose also acidifies the intestinal contents, providing a more suitable environment for proliferation of normal bacterial flora. The recommended dose is 0.2-0.4ml/kg given orally every eight hours (Gould, 1992). Medication can be continued for several weeks, but the dose should be reduced if diarrhoea develops.

Anabolic steroids, eg. nandrolone (5mg/kg), may be of value in the treatment of hepatic or renal disease (Lawton, personal communication).

Malley (personal communication) recommends the use of Spirulina Algae-Feast (Lanes of Brighton) as a protein and vitamin supplement in birds with liver disease. One tablet is mixed in 10ml water, and the suspension is given by crop tube at a dose of approximately 1ml/kg. The dose is repeated every time the bird is given oral fluid therapy.

Uraemic birds may develop secondary generalised visceral gout as a result of deposition of tophi in body tissues. Allopurinol lowers uric acid levels. Prolonged use of allopurinol may result in further kidney damage and other side effects. The preferred route of administration is via the drinking water (Ritchie and Harrison, 1994). A 100mg tablet should be crushed in 10ml water, and up to 1ml of the diluted suspension added to 30ml drinking water. In severe cases of gout, allopurinol should be used in conjunction with colchicine (0.04mg/kg bid). This agent also has antigout activity and may be indicated in some cases of hepatic fibrosis (Ritchie and Harrison, 1994).

Response to non-specific therapy is suggested by increased appetite and activity, weight gain and normalisation of the bird's biochemical parameters. Lack of clinical improvement indicates the necessity for further investigation. Where it is possible to make an accurate diagnosis, supportive care can be supplemented with specific therapy.

Treatment of herpesvirus infection of the liver (Pacheco's disease) may be attempted with either the oral or intravenous form of acyclovir (80mg/kg orally every eight hours for seven days, or 50-200mg/100ml drinking water) (Gould, 1992).

Lipotrophics, such as methionine, choline or inositol, may help 'fatty liver syndrome' (Fudge, 1993).

Lead poisoning is treated with chelation therapy using sodium calciumedetate (10-40mg/kg i/m bid for up to five days) (Dumonceaux and Harrison, 1994).

Traditionally, diabetes mellitus in mammals is treated by injections of insulin. This treatment is only palliative in birds and is not always effective in eliminating the hyperglycaemia as the diabetes is primarily caused by glucagon excess. However, it seems to prevent severe weight loss, and there are several case reports of successful treatment. An intermediate acting insulin, eg. NPH U40 (40 units/ml), should be diluted in lactated Ringer's solution to form a 10% solution of insulin (4 units/ml) for larger birds and a 1% solution (0.4 units/ml) for smaller birds. **NB.** Once diluted the insulin is not stable and cannot be stored. The insulin dose required varies for each individual bird; smaller birds need more insulin per gram of bodyweight compared with larger birds. Reported dosages range from 0.067-3.33units/kg. The dose should start low and be increased as needed on the basis of clinical signs and glucose test results. Twice daily administration of insulin provides better hyperglycaemic control. Birds on insulin treatment should be allowed free access to food to prevent hypoglycaemia developing.

If calcium deficiency is diagnosed, the imbalance should initially be treated with 10% calcium gluconate (10-20ml/kg given as a single i/m injection). Follow-up treatment involves dietary supplementation with calcium and vitamin D_3, eg. Nutrobal (Vetark), and a fundamental alteration of the diet so that it contains a lower percentage of seeds.

Dietary manipulation is useful in the treatment of hepatic and renal disease. Birds with liver disease should be fed a well balanced, low fat diet, free from hepatotoxins such as mouldy foods or peanuts. Seeds should be eliminated from the diet if possible. In birds with fatty degeneration of the liver, dietary fat content should be reduced and exercise encouraged. Birds with renal disease should be offered a low protein diet, with calories in the form of fat or carbohydrate, eg. millet seed or vegetable matter. Feeding large quantities of fruit and vegetables promotes diuresis. Polyuria usually continues for a variable length of time after other clinical and biochemical evidence of kidney disease has resolved, probably due to the reduction in absorptive capacity of swollen and damaged renal tubules.

REFERENCES

Boorman KN and Lewis D (1971) Protein metabolism. In: *Physiology and Biochemistry of the Domestic Fowl*. Eds DJ Bell and BM Freeman. Academic Press, London.

Brugere-Picoux J and Brugere H (1987) Metabolic diseases. In: *Companion Bird Medicine*. Ed EW Burr. Iowa State University Press, Ames.

Cooper JE and Lawton MPC (1988) The urogenital system. In: *Manual of Parrots, Budgerigars and Other Psittacine Birds*. Ed CJ Price. BSAVA, Cheltenham.

Degernes LA (1991) A clinical approach to ascites in pet birds. In: *Proceedings of the Association of Avian Veterinarians Annual Conference 1991*. AAV, Lake Worth.

Dumonceaux G and Harrison GJ (1994) Toxins. In: *Avian Medicine: Principles and Application*. Eds BW Ritchie, GJ Harrison and LR Harrison. Wingers, Lake Worth.

Enders F, Krautwald-Junghanns M-E and Duhr D (1993) Sonographic evaluation of liver disease in birds. In: *Proceedings of the Association of Avian Veterinarians European Conference, Utrecht, 1993*. AAV, Lake Worth.

Farner DS (1982) Some physiological attributes of small birds. In: *Diseases of Cage and Aviary Birds*. 2nd Edn. Ed ML Petrak. Lea and Febiger, Philadelphia.

Flammer K (1994) Antimicrobial therapy. In: *Avian Medicine: Principles and Application*. Eds BW Ritchie, GJ Harrison and LR Harrison. Wingers, Lake Worth.

Fudge AM (1993) Diagnosis and management of avian liver disease. In: *Proceedings of the Association of Avian Veterinarians European Conference, Utrecht, 1993*. AAV, Lake Worth.

Fudge AM and Reavill DR (1991) Plasma bile acids recommended for sick birds. *Journal of the Association of Avian Veterinarians* **6(2)**, 90.

Galvin C (1983) Acute hemorrhagic syndrome of birds. In: *Current Veterinary Therapy VIII*. Ed RW Kirk. WB Saunders, Philadelphia.

Gould WJ (1992) Liver disease in psittacines. In: *Current Veterinary Therapy XI*. Eds RW Kirk and JD Bonagura. WB Saunders, Philadelphia.

Harrison GJ and Ritchie BW (1994) Making distinctions in the physical examination. In: *Avian Medicine: Principles and Application*. Eds BW Ritchie, GJ Harrison and LR Harrison. Wingers, Lake Worth.

Hasholt J and Petrak ML (1982) Diseases of the urinary system. In: *Diseases of Cage and Aviary Birds*. 2nd Edn. Ed ML Petrak. Lea and Febiger, Philadelphia.

Hawkey C and Gulland F (1988) Clinical haematology. In: *Manual of Parrots, Budgerigars and Other Psittacine Birds*. Ed CJ Price. BSAVA, Cheltenham.

Hochleithner M (1994) Biochemistries. In: *Avian Medicine: Principles and Application*. Eds BW Ritchie, GJ Harrison and LR Harrison. Wingers, Lake Worth.

King AS and McLelland J (1984) *Birds: Their Structure and Function*. Baillière Tindall, London.

Kollias GV (1984) Liver biopsy techniques in avian clinical practice. In: *Veterinary Clinics of North America: Caged Bird Medicine* **14(2)**, 287.

Krautwald-Junghanns M-E, Riedel U and Neumann W (1991) Diagnostic use of ultrasonography in birds. In: *Proceedings of the Association of Avian Veterinarians Annual Conference 1991*. AAV, Lake Worth.

Lumeij JT (1993) Avian plasma chemistry in health and disease. In: *Proceedings of the Association of Avian Veterinarians Annual Conference 1993*. AAV, Lake Worth.

Lumeij JT (1994a) Nephrology. In: *Avian Medicine: Principles and Application*. Eds BW Ritchie, GJ Harrison and LR Harrison. Wingers, Lake Worth.

Lumeij JT (1994b) Endocrinology. In: *Avian Medicine: Principles and Application*. Eds BW Ritchie, GJ Harrison and LR Harrison. Wingers, Lake Worth.

Lumeij JT (1994c) Hepatology. In: *Avian Medicine: Principles and Application*. Eds BW Ritchie, GJ Harrison and LR Harrison. Wingers, Lake Worth.

Murphy J (1992) Psittacine fatty liver syndrome. In: *Proceedings of the Association of Avian Veterinarians Annual Conference 1992*. AAV, Lake Worth.

Quesenberry KE and Hillyer EV (1994) Supportive care and emergency therapy. In. *Avian Medicine: Principles and Application*. Eds BW Ritchie, GJ Harrison and LR Harrison. Wingers, Lake Worth.

Ringer RK (1986) Selected physiology for the avian practitioner. In: *Clinical Avian Medicine and Surgery, including Aviculture*. Eds GJ Harrison and LR Harrison. WB Saunders, Philadelphia.

Ritchie BW and Harrison GJ (1994) Formulary. In: *Avian Medicine: Principles and Application*. Eds BW Ritchie, GJ Harrison and LR Harrison. Wingers, Lake Worth.

Rosskopf WJ and Woerpel RW (1988) Kidney disease in a Military macaw, a Yellow-naped Amazon, and an Umbrella cockatoo. In: *Proceedings of the Association of Avian Veterinarians Annual*

Conference 1988. AAV, Lake Worth.

Sayle RK (1986) Evaluation of droppings. In: *Clinical Avian Medicine and Surgery, including Aviculture.* Eds GJ Harrison and LR Harrison. WB Saunders, Philadelphia.

Sykes AH (1971) Formation and composition of urine. In: *Physiology and Biochemistry of the Domestic Fowl.* Eds DJ Bell and BM Freeman. Academic Press, London.

Taylor M (1994) Endoscopy examination and biopsy techniques. In: *Avian Medicine: Principles and Application.* Eds BW Ritchie, GJ Harrison and LR Harrison. Wingers, Lake Worth.

Woerpel RW, Rosskopf WJ and Monahan-Brennan M (1987) Clinical pathology and laboratory diagnostic tools. In: *Companion Bird Medicine.* Ed EW Burr. Iowa State University Press, Ames.

CHAPTER SEVENTEEN

Diarrhoea and Vomiting

Christopher J Hall

INTRODUCTION

Diarrhoea and vomiting (regurgitation) are two of the most common presenting clinical signs of avian disease. However, diarrhoea is less frequent than polyuria as a cause of 'loose droppings'. In polyuria there is an increased amount of clear or opaque urine (see Chapter 16); the faecal component of the dropping retains its shape (although it may be reduced in volume or even absent). Diarrhoea can only be said to occur if there is a loss of shape and form of the faecal component (Sayle, 1986).

BASIC ANATOMY AND PHYSIOLOGY OF THE DIGESTIVE TRACT

The anatomy of the psittacine tract is shown in Figure 17.1. Psittacines lack a soft palate so the oral cavity and pharynx form one common cavity, the oropharynx, which is lined with stratified squamous epithelium. Salivary glands are found over the palatine folds, the base of the tongue and the pharynx; these produce primarily mucus. Food passes from the oropharynx into the oesophagus, which is thin walled and distensible and courses down the right side of the neck into the crop.

The crop is a dilatation of the oesophagus located cranial to the thoracic inlet. It is strongly attached to the underlying skin and is placed transversely across the neck. Food enters on the right side but leaves in the midline. Food can be stored in the crop, but little chemical digestion occurs here apart from that caused by salivary juices. From the crop, food passes into the glandular portion of the stomach (proventriculus); it is here that hydrochloric acid and pepsin are secreted. The food then passes into the ventriculus (gizzard). The wall of this organ consists of a large volume of smooth muscle and it is lined by a koilin layer (this is stained green as a result of regurgitation of bile pigments from the duodenum). Powerful asymmetrical contractions of this organ crush the food; proteolysis occurs here at a low pH. Grit is not essential for digestion in psittacines since muscular contraction in the ventriculus is sufficient to crush food. Sick birds may gorge themselves on grit and impact the ventriculus;

this can be fatal. Crushed oyster shell is preferable to grit for small psittacines as it supplies a source of calcium and is less likely to cause impaction (as it is absorbed with time).

Food leaves through the pylorus and passes into the duodenum; the pancreas is contained in mesentery in a loop of this organ. Pancreatic secretions contain amylase, lipase and proteases. There is no lacteal system of absorption as is found in mammals, only a well developed capillary system. The remainder of the small intestine is composed of coils of jejunum and ileum located largely on the right side of the abdomen. This leads into the large intestine. Psittacines have no caecae.

The liver consists of right and left lobes joined at the midline. The gall-bladder is absent in most psittacines; instead, each lobe empties bile directly into the duodenum. Birds, unlike mammals, lack bilirubin reductase so they excrete biliverdin directly into bile. Biliverdin is the major bile pigment and causes the green discoloration of urates in birds with liver disease. There is no commercial assay available for biliverdin in avian plasma. Bile acids are synthesised in the liver, released into the small intestine, reabsorbed and transported back to the liver by portal circulation (enterohepatic circulation). Malfunction of the liver or enterohepatic circulation results in increased bile acid levels in the plasma, and this can be measured.

End products of digestion pass from the rectum into the cloaca and are excreted together with the renal excretions.

ASSESSMENT OF PSITTACINE FAECES

Normal Droppings
Normal psittacine dropping is illustrated in Figure 17.2.

Normal Variables
● Species variation: lorikeets produce a liquid, sticky dropping as a result of the nectar component of their diet.
● Dietary: ingestion of large amounts of fruit produces a softer faecal component. Pelleted diets, eg. Nutri-Berries (Lafebers), may give the faecal element a brown colour; carrots may produce a reddish tinge.

Right　　　　　　　　　　　　　　　　　　**Left**

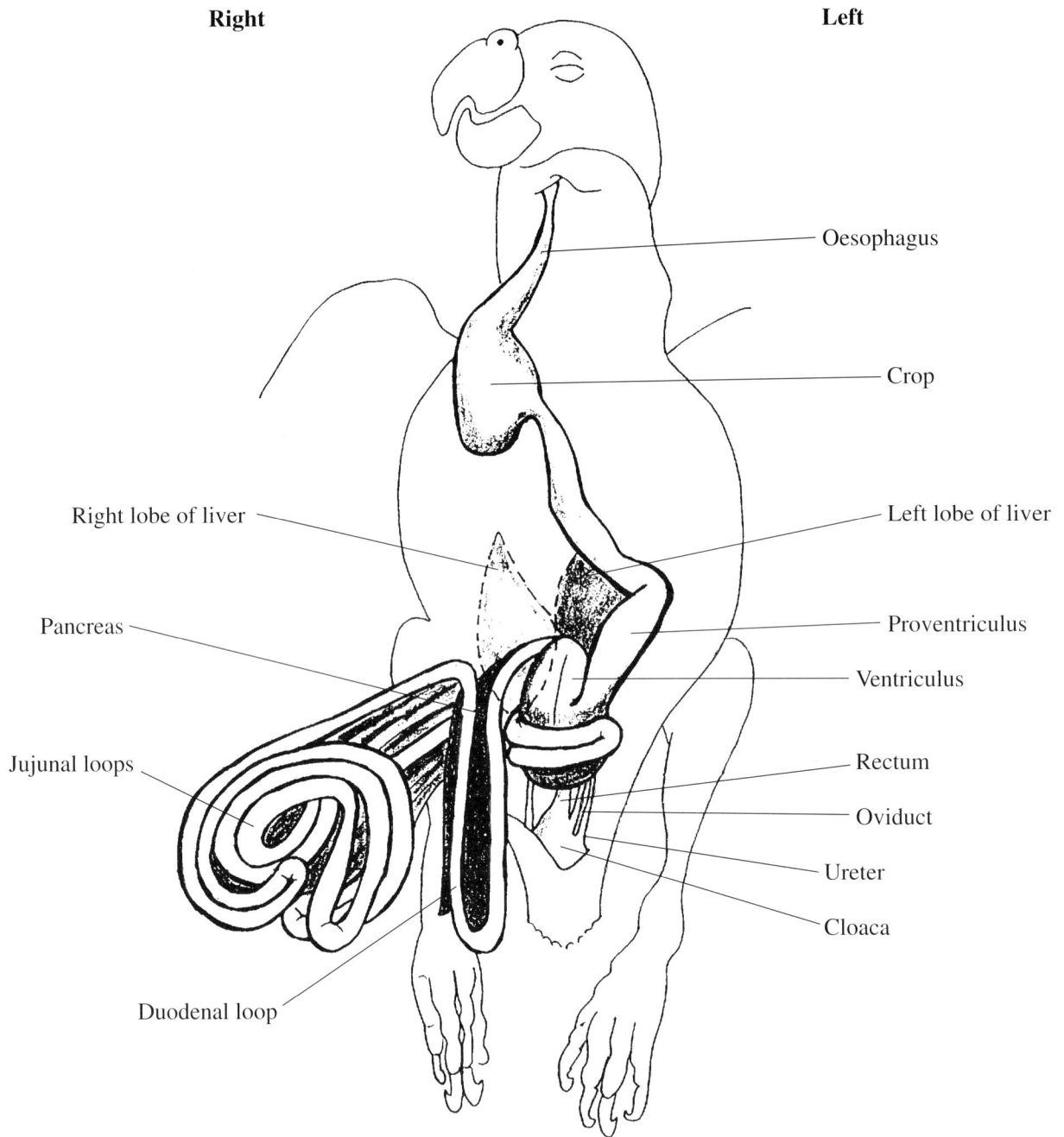

Oesophagus

Crop

Right lobe of liver

Left lobe of liver

Pancreas

Proventriculus

Ventriculus

Jujunal loops

Rectum

Oviduct

Ureter

Duodenal loop

Cloaca

Figure 17.1: Psittacine alimentary tract.

Neonates on hand-rearing diets may produce a softer, more voluminous stool.

● Stress, eg. travel to and examination at the surgery: often produces a looser, bubble-filled dropping with a higher urate content than usual (the clinician should examine a sample produced prior to the visit).

● Egg laying: prior to egg laying or during incubation a looser, large volume stool may be produced as a result of distension of the cloaca and hypercalcaemia. Lack of physical exercise during brooding may also cause this effect.

● **NB: polyuria is not diarrhoea.** Polyuria is an abnormal increase in the liquid urine component,

independent of the faecal component which retains its shape.

Abnormal Droppings

Lime green or mustard coloured faeces are often associated with hepatic disease and impaired excretion of bilverdin (Bayer and McDonald, 1981). Aetiologies could be chlamydiosis (green staining of urates also occurs), viral or acute bacterial infections, or toxicities. Brown or haemorrhagic faeces may indicate a primary enteritis (possibly with renal involvement). Frank haemorrhage in the faeces is usually associated with coagulopathies, liver disorders,

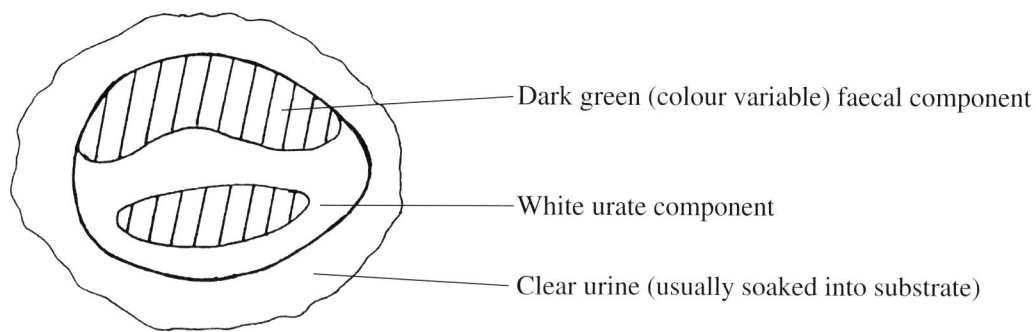

Dark green (colour variable) faecal component

White urate component

Clear urine (usually soaked into substrate)

Figure 17.2: Normal psittacine dropping.

enteric disease, poisoning (lead poisoning in Amazons), acute haemorrhagic syndrome as in conures and Amazons or, most commonly, cloacal papillomata. A lumpy consistency to the faeces may indicate pancreatitis, proventriculitis or ventriculitis, as well as intestinal disease. The presence of undigested seeds in the dropping may indicate psittacine proventricular dilatation syndrome (PPDS), also known as macaw wasting syndrome, or pancreatic disorders.

Diagnostic Tests

All birds with diarrhoea should be screened for chlamydiosis, especially in view of the zoonotic potential of this disease. A fresh faecal sample should be placed in an airtight container, double wrapped, clearly marked Pathological Specimen and sent to the Psittacosis Department at the Central Veterinary Laboratory, New Haw, Addlestone, Surrey, England KT15 3NB. Polymerase chain reaction (PCR) tests will demonstrate the presence of chlamydial DNA. This may also be followed by a complement fixation test (CFT). The sample should be sent before medication is given, since drugs such as tetracyclines and quinolones will stop the shedding of chlamydial antigen and give a false negative result. Barrier nursing and isolation should be carried out on birds giving a positive result.

Microscopical Faecal Examination

Direct faecal smears should be examined under low power magnification in 10% KOH solution to reveal undigested food. A wet smear in saline should be examined for parasites, particularly protozoa. Certain protozoa, such as *Giardia* spp., survive for only a short time in the faeces, so examination of a wet smear should be performed within minutes of the dropping being passed. Examination of serial samples may be necessary. A faecal flotation test should then be performed (the author prefers to use a saturated sugar solution). This is less effective in avian samples than in other species as some ova fail to float, but it does result in less debris obscuring the ova. Reference should be made to Table 17.1 for interpretation of the findings.

BACTERIAL DIARRHOEA

Diarrhoea caused by bacterial infection should be regarded as a symptom of systemic infection. Table 17.2 lists some of the more significant bacterial pathogens. It is possible, but rare, for bacterial enteritis to occur without involvement of other organ systems. Bacterial septicaemia will often result in diarrhoea, often in conjunction with crop stasis and/or regurgitation (see later). An example of bacterial septicaemia is shown in Figure 17.4.

Diagnosis

Gram Stain

This should be a routine part of any clinical investigation of a bird with diarrhoea. Although in itself it may not be diagnostic, it does point the clinician towards further areas of investigation which will establish a diagnosis. Abnormal Gram stain should be accompanied by bacterial culture and sensitivity tests to determine appropriate antibiotic usage.

Faecal samples can be swabbed directly from the floor of the cage with a sterile cotton bud or swab and smeared onto a recently cleaned slide in as thin a layer as possible. Alternatively, a swab can be taken directly from the cloaca (although this will lead to some contamination of the smear with urates). In the latter case the swab should be moistened with sterile saline and gently rotated round the wall of the cloaca. In birds of less than 100g bodyweight a urethral swab should be used (this can then be placed in transport medium after the smear is made, ready for culture). The owner should be warned that the bird may pass a blood tinged dropping after a cloacal swab. This is normal.

In a normal bird there should be 100-200 organisms per field (oil immersion at x100 objective lens). The ratio of Gram-positive rods to Gram-positive cocci should be between 4:1 and 3:2. It is normal to see 1-3 *Candida* spp. per field (these appear as black round bodies considerably larger than the bacteria; smaller bodies may be seen budding off them). Large numbers of Gram-negative rods or filamentous Gram-positive

Table 17.1. Intestinal parasites of psittacines.

Parasite	Frequency	Clinical signs	Diagnosis	Treatment
Protozoa *Giardia* spp. 9-14μm motile 	Relatively common in budgerigars and cockatiels. Also imported birds.	Often no clinical signs. Intermittent diarrhoea. Faeces may be greasy and mucoid. Can be associated with feather picking.	Serial examination of very fresh samples essential. May show with carbol fuchsin stains of air dried smears.	Metronidazole (10-30mg/kg p/o bid for 10 days). Dimetridazole (50mg/kg p/o bid for 10 days).
Coccidia spp., *Eimeria* spp. 20 by 20μm 	Occasionally in budgerigars and lorikeets.	Diarrhoea sometimes haemorrhagic. Weight loss.	Wet mount and faecal flotation. Trophozoites in intestinal mucosa at *post mortem*.	Sulpha drugs, eg. Microquinox, (C-Vet Livestock Products) (1.5ml/litre water; three days on, two days off, three days on, two days off, then a final three days on).
Helminths Ascarids 40 by 65μm (see Figure 17.3) 	Common in aviary birds on natural flooring, especially parakeets. Rare in pet birds. Beware in recent purchases or birds in outside flights.	Sometimes none; otherwise weight loss, intermittent diarrhoea.	Wet mount or faecal flotation.	Fenbendazole (100mg/kg p/o by crop tube - repeat after three weeks). Do not use during period of active feather growth.
Capillaria 25 by 50μm 	As above.	More likely to cause diarrhoea.	As above.	Ivermectin (200mcg/kg i/m - repeat after three weeks). Levamisole (dilute 1:40 with drinking water; sweeten with sucrose; withhold water for 12 hours beforehand. Repeat after three weeks). Less effective than individual dosing. Risk of toxicity.
Spiruids 30 by 20μm 	Rare. Indirect life cycle.	Wasting and death.	As above. Usually a *post-mortem* diagnosis. Swellings or nodules on mucosa of proventriculus and ventriculus.	Ivermectin may be effective.
Cestodes 75 by 90μm 	Uncommon except in imported psittacines.	May see diarrhoea; otherwise weight loss only.	Proglottids in faeces; serial samples required.	Praziquantel (10mg/kg p/o or 7.5mg/kg i/m - repeat after three weeks).

Figure 17.3: Roundworms in the intestines of a Splendid Parakeet.

Figure 17.4: E. coli septicaemia in a Blue-fronted Amazon. Note the abscesses in the liver and kidney. Presenting signs were diarrhoea, regurgitation and anorexia. (Photo courtesy Mrs R Freyer-Hall)

bacteria, or increased numbers of Candida organisms or white blood cells, or very large numbers of Gram-positive rods indicate an abnormality. Abnormal stains should be followed up with culture and sensitivity testing of a faecal swab. A complete absence of bacteria or less than 30 bacteria per oil immersion field indicates overtreatment with antibiotics (Gram stain can be used as an indicator of the need for probiotics). If the Gram stain shows large numbers of bacteria but nothing is obtained on culture, this indicates the need for specialist incubation techniques, such as anaerobic culture or the use of enrichment media (for example, for Salmonella spp. culture). Pathogenic organisms which require special conditions or nutrients include Campylobacter spp., Yersinia spp. and Mycoplasma spp. L-forms of bacteria may also require specialist culture techniques.

Acid Fast Stain

This should be undertaken where mycobacterial infection is suspected. A negative result does not indicate absence of infection as organisms may be shed intermittently. Acid fast bacteria appear bright red on a blue background.

Culture and Sensitivity Testing

Lactobacillus spp., Corynebacterium spp., Bacillus spp. and Streptococcus spp. are considered to be normal inhabitants of the psittacine digestive tract. One should not necessarily assume that if a significant bacterial pathogen is found it is the sole cause of disease; it may simply be secondary infection in a bird which is already positive for another condition, eg. chlamydiosis or polyomavirus.

Treatment

Supportive therapy is crucial to successful treatment (see Chapter 9). Aggressive fluid therapy using oral, subcutaneous, intravenous or intraosseus fluids (according to stage of dehydration) is essential, as is tube feeding of anorexic birds. Antibiotics should be selected on the basis of sensitivity tests but, while awaiting results, a broad-spectrum, clinically proven

drug should be used, eg. enrofloxacin (5-15mg/kg i/m bid). Carbenicillin (200mg/kg i/m bid) is also useful. Piperacillin (150mg/kg i/m or i/v bid) is also effective and can be used in conjunction with amikacin (10-20mg/kg i/m bid). If anaerobic infection is suspected, dimetridazole (50mg/kg p/o or 5mg/kg i/m bid) can be given. For individual birds, medication of drinking water is not advised due to variable intake and palatability problems. Enrofloxacin is available for the flock situation, however (see Table 17.2). In cases of bacterial septicaemia, treatment by injection is preferable to oral dosing, since achieving high tissue levels rapidly will increase success rates.

Kaolin (2ml/kg p/o tid) will give symptomatic relief and may aid in the absorption of toxins. The use of probiotics, eg. Avipro (Vetark) or Enterodex (Vetex), is strongly advised for the treatment of diarrhoea. Most probiotics contain a Lactobacillus spp. which adheres to the gastrointestinal epithelium, thus reducing the adherence of pathogenic bacteria. Many Lactobacillus spp. produce lactic acid, possibly inhibiting the activities of acid sensitive bacteria. The use of probiotics for 7-10 days after cessation of antibiotic therapy will help recolonise the gut flora. They can

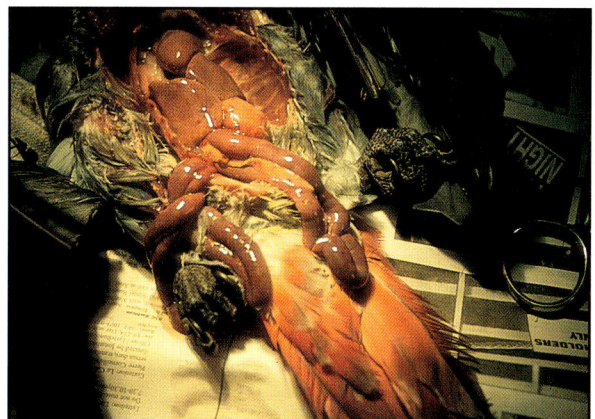

Figure 17.5: Necrotic enteritis in an African Grey following clostridial infection. Note the discolouration of the intestines. (Photo courtesy Mrs R Freyer-Hall)

Table 17.2. Bacterial diarrhoea/septicaemia.

Genus	Mode of transmission	Frequency	Comments
Gram-negative bacteria			
Escherichia coli	Oral route, occasionally aerogenic.	Very common.	In small numbers, this can be a normal inhabitant of the gastrointestinal tract. Large numbers in faecal Gram stain are significant.
Klebsiella spp.	Probably oral.	Common.	Diarrhoea generally associated with nephritis or hepatitis rather than localised gut infection. Very resistant to antibiotics.
Pasteurella multocida	Rodents and wild birds important vectors for indirect transmission.	Uncommon in caged pet birds. More frequent in the aviary situation.	Diarrhoea in acute phase only. Advise covered aviaries and rodent control if an outbreak occurs.
Pseudomonas spp. and *Aeromonas* spp.	Oral infection, especially contaminated drinking supplies, eg. poorly maintained water filters and moisturising systems of incubators, or uncovered header tanks.	Uncommon.	Catarrhal to haemorrhagic enteritis. Highly resistant to antibiotics (sensitivity tests essential). Amikacin (15-20mg/kg i/m bid for 10 days) or carbenicillin (200mg/kg i/m bid for 10 days). Advisable to give additional fluid therapy when using amikacin. Very resistant to disinfectants.
Salmonella spp.	Oral route, carriers common among survivors.	Common in imported birds and in some aviary situations (wild bird contamination).	Prognosis very poor, unresponsive to treatment, may produce carriers only. In a flock situation, apramycin (50g/100 litres drinking water over five days) may be effective. Also enrofloxacin (200mg/litre for 10 days).
Yersinia spp.	Oral. Feral birds and rodents frequently carriers.	Common.	Acute form causes diarrhoea and death. Chronic disease leads to wasting. Most likely a *post-mortem* diagnosis. Unresponsive to treatment.

Table 17.2. Continued.

Genus	Mode of transmission	Frequency	Comments
Acid fast bacteria *Mycobacterium* spp.	Alimentary. Arthropods may act as mechanical vectors.	*M. avium* common in some collections. *M. tuberculosis* rare - when occurs often due to infection of the bird by owner. More commonly cutaneous rather than enteric or hepatic infection.	*M.tuberculosis*: euthanasia. *M.avium*: enrofloxacin (15mg/kg bid for 7-10 days) with ethambutol (20mg/kg bid) and clofoxamine (1.5mg/kg sid) with cycloserine (5mg/kg bid) (Rosskopf *et al*, 1991). Use until acid fast stain negative. Follow up monitoring required. Zoonotic implications should be considered.
Gram-positive bacteria *Clostridium perfringens*	Ingestion of spores.	Rare.	Acute diarrhoea, which may be haemorrhagic, or death. Diagnose at *post mortem* (see Figure 17.5) and by detection of B toxin. Treatment in an outbreak is with lincomycin (100mg/kg bid for seven days). May be prevented by vaccination.
Campylobacter spp.	Oral.	Uncommon.	Diarrhoea secondary to hepatitis (see later). Treatment: erythromycin (10-20mg/kg p/o bid for 10 days) or tylosin (40mg/kg i/m bid for 10 days).

also be used at the same time as antibiotics to reduce iatrogenic diarrhoea. Patients on long-term antibiotic therapy may benefit from antifungal therapy to prevent secondary candidiasis, eg. nystatin (300,000iu/kg [3ml/kg] p/o bid). Steroids for the treatment of endotoxaemia should only be used as a last resort. Where indicated, dexamethasone (2-4mg/kg i/m or 1-2mg/kg i/v) can be given.

MEGABACTERIOSIS IN BUDGERIGARS

Megabacteriosis has been reported as a cause of diarrhoea (and vomiting) in budgerigars (Baker, 1992). Many birds will show diarrhoea ranging in colour from black to light khaki. A Gram stain of faeces may show 'megabacteria'; these are Gram-positive bacteria,

45µm long by 3-4µm wide (scrapings from the proventriculus at *post mortem* are more likely to be positive). At *post mortem* the crop may be distended with fluid and there is enlargement of the proventricular/ventricular junction.The disease causes a rise in the pH of the proventriculus and, therefore, loss of digestive ability. Treatment is by acidifying the drinking water to pH2 (although this decreases palatability) and feeding soft food (Pennycott, 1992). Other treatments include the use of amphotericin B (1ml/kg bid by gavage for 10 days) or as medicated drinking water (1g/litre) for the same period. Ketoconazole given in water (833mg/litre) is also considered to be effective.

PANCREATITIS

Pancreatitis can be a cause of diarrhoea in psittacines

but is difficult to diagnose. Certain infectious agents, eg. herpesvirus or adenovirus, can cause pancreatic lesions, or they may occur following complications due to peritonitis or excessive fat in the diet. Lymphoplasmocytic infiltration of the organ may occur and the condition can be associated with diabetes mellitus (Clipsham, 1991). The diagnosis of this condition is most likely to be at necropsy. *Ante-mortem* signs include passing of undigested food. Serum amylase levels may rise in a proportion of cases; hypoalbuminaemia also occurs. Supplementation of the diet with pancreatic enzymes may help. The underlying diabetes, if present, should be treated (see Chapter 16).

PROVENTRICULITIS

Proventriculitis has been documented as a result of *Candida* spp. and/or *Megabacterium* spp. infections in larger psittacines (Anderson, 1993). Clinical signs may include anorexia with or without diarrhoea, passing undigested food and vomiting. Faecal and choanal Gram stains are likely to be normal and diagnosis seems to be possible only on cytology samples taken during endoscopic examination of the proventriculus. Treatment is with ketoconazole (10mg/kg p/o bid) and the use of probiotics.

GASTRIC NEOPLASIA

Neoplasms of the proventriculus and ventriculus have been well documented (Lintner *et al*, 1992). Clinical signs include diarrhoea (may be haemorrhagic), anaemia, hypoproteinaemia, passing of whole seeds and unilateral or bilateral paralysis. Adenomata, haemangiosarcomata, carcinomata and adenocarcinomata have all been reported. Diagnosis is on contrast radiography and endoscopy, but is most likely to be on necropsy. Surgical excision could be attempted if an early diagnosis is made. Renal, gonadal and other abdominal tumours may cause similar signs.

REGURGITATION

Regurgitation may be due to systemic disease (with or without diarrhoea) or due to localised crop disorders.

Methods of Investigation

Haematology/Biochemistry (see later)

Physical Examination
An impacted crop will feel enlarged and firm on palpation. If the crop is dilated and atonic it may indicate an obstruction distal to the crop, eg. in the proventriculus or ventriculus. Crop atony can result from bacterial, fungal, protozoal or viral infection, or be secondary to a crop burn or heavy metal poison.

This can be localised or systemic. An empty crop is abnormal unless the bird has had no access to food. In small birds, wetting the crop skin with spirit and transilluminating the area (preferably with a cold light source) will allow better visualisation.

Crop Washes
A speculum (an auroscope for birds larger than a conure; a paper clip for birds of cockatiel size and smaller) allows the passage of a crop tube (endotracheal tubing for larger birds; intravenous drip tubing for medium sized birds; Jackson's cat catheter for budgerigars). Alternatively, a metal crop tube can be used (care must be taken not to damage the crop wall or the beak, which may be weakened in birds with chronic liver disease, for example). The bird's head and neck should be extended, the tube passed and the neck palpated; if the crop tube is correctly placed it will be felt lateral to the trachea on the right side. Sterile saline is passed into the crop (approximately 1ml for a budgerigar; 15ml/kg for larger parrots) and then withdrawn. The fluid is examined directly under the microscope as a wet mount for motile protozoa (*Trichomonas* spp.), and then a Gram or Diff Quick stain is performed for the presence of bacteria or *Candida* spp. (although a lactophenol stain may give a clearer result). A Diff Quick stain can be used for cytology: a normal aspirate should show cornified squamous epithelial cells, occasional *Candida* spp. buds, debris and plant fibres. A Gram stain should show primarily Gram-positive cocci with a few small to medium sized rods. The presence of heterophils/ macrophages (inflammatory cells), protozoa, excessive numbers of yeasts, large numbers of Gram-negative bacteria or only one type of Gram-positive bacteria is suggestive of infection. The aspirate can also be cultured.

Insufflation with Air or Saline and Direct Visualisation by Endoscopy
This procedure will reveal foreign bodies and evidence of infection, and is also useful for taking biopsy samples.

Radiographic Examination Using Contrast Medium
Barium solution (25%) is used (see Table 17.3 for volumes). The first radiograph is taken immediately, subsequent radiographs at 10-30 minute intervals. Contrast should enter the proventriculus within 15 minutes (Evans, 1981). Total transit time through the whole gut should be less than three hours. Air can be used for a double contrast study of the crop.

Differential Diagnosis

Courtship Behaviour
This is seen particularly in hand-reared psittacines re-

gurgitating for their owners, and single budgerigars and cockatiels regurgitating to mirrors and toys (see Chapter 11).

Crop Impaction

This may cause non-productive attempts at regurgitation. The condition is usually seen in young handfed birds, particularly where the hand rearing mix is too cold, too low in fibre or fed in too large quantities (Eamens, 1989). Affected birds may show an interest in food but make no attempt to eat. The contents of the crop can be softened with vegetable or mineral oil, or flushed with saline and the bird tipped upside down to empty the crop (ideally the bird should first be anaesthetised with isoflurane and intubated). However, there is a danger of aspiration pneumonia with this method and ingluviotomy is probably the treatment of choice. This normally requires general anaesthesia in adults (although this may not be needed in young birds). A soft feeding tube is placed in the crop to maintain the patency of the oesophagus and crop prior to surgery. The bird is placed in dorsal recumbency and a skin incision made on the right side of the crop, which is dissected bluntly from surrounding tissue. An incision is made into the crop, which can then be emptied. The skin and crop should be sutured as separate layers. The crop is closed with a continuous inverting pattern (4/0 absorbable) using an atraumatic needle. The skin can be closed with simple interrupted sutures (3/0 absorbable). The two incisions should be offset. Food and water should be witheld as long as possible after surgery, depending on the size of the bird (up to a maximum of 12 hours). Postoperative antibiosis should be given.

Crop Inflammation (Ingluvitis)

This is usually caused by infectious agents: bacteria, fungi (especially *Candida* spp.) or protozoa (*Trichomonas* spp.). The crop becomes flaccid and filled with mucoid material, and feathers around the crop become pasted (look for pasting on top of the head in budgerigars). Polydipsia may occur. Candidiasis is more likely in young psittacines. Predisposing factors are hypovitaminosis A and antibiotic overuse, eg. long-term tetracycline or doxycycline therapy for chlamydiosis. Candidiasis can be treated with nystatin (300,000iu/kg [3ml/kg] p/o tid). Itraconazole (10mg/kg p/o bid) can be used in refractory cases. This drug may be toxic in African Greys and cause appetite depression in other species.

Trichomoniasis is very common in budgerigars, but also occurs in larger psittacines. Examination of the crop may show white caseous nodules or even large necrotic areas which can be palpated in the oesophagus and crop. Systemic infections, which can be fatal, and respiratory infections also occur. Clinical signs are more severe in young birds. Anorexia, weight loss and general malaise are seen in addition to

regurgitation. Foul smelling fluid may accumulate in the crop and exude from the mouth.

Diagnosis is by crop wash and examination of a wet mount. Motile trichomonads may be seen, although repeat samples may be needed. Culture is possible. Treatment is with metronidazole (50mg/kg p/o every 12 hours on three occasions). Overdosage can lead to nervous signs, even death. Prevention in flocks is by medicating the drinking water with dimetridazole (2g/litre for seven days) before the breeding season.

Crop Neoplasia

This is rare. Leiomyosarcomata are described in budgerigars (Gilmore and Petrak, 1982).

Capillariasis

This is rare, but occasionally affects the oral cavity as well as the gut. Diagnosis is on the presence of bi-operculated eggs in a crop wash (Campbell, 1993) (see Table 17.1 for treatment).

Sour Crop

'Sour crop' involves inflammation and ulceration of the crop accompanied by fermentation of the contents. It is common in young psittacines and may follow feeding of spoiled food, irregular feeding, vitamin and protein deficiencies, or regurgitation of proventricular contents into the crop. The crop contents become more acidic (normal pH4.5-7) due to excessive lactate production. The resultant vomiting and diarrhoea leads to malnutrition, dehydration and death. The condition is treated by emptying the crop several times a day and giving a broad-spectrum antibiotic, eg. amoxycillin trihydrate (150mg/kg p/o bid), and antacids, eg. sodium bicarbonate. A liquid diet should be given every two hours for 1-3 days followed by a semi-solid diet for five days, then back on to normal food. Specific treatment for infectious agents should be undertaken. Metaclopropamide (0.5mg/kg i/m) can be very useful.

Ingluvioliths

Crop calculi have been recorded in psittacines (Batwell, 1978) but are rare. Diagnosis is on ingluviotomy followed by removal. Budgerigars and cockatiels are most likely to be affected.

Crop Burns (see also Chapter 18)

These may be small or extensive. They commonly occur in neonates where the hand rearing food is microwaved and not subsequently mixed properly, resulting in 'hot spots'. Acute, severe cases may be fatal as a result of metabolic changes, sepsis and absorption of toxins from necrotic tissue. Initial treatment should be supportive and include shock, antibacterial and antifungal therapy (treat the fluid loss, infection and inanition). If oedema is severe, surgery should be delayed until necrosis occurs as this may be extensive. Less severe cases may simply present as 'sick bird syndrome' with lethargy, anorexia and fluffing. The feeding regime will need to be changed. Tubing directly into the proventriculus is advised to bypass the damaged tissue. The proventriculus holds a smaller volume than the crop so feeds need to be more frequent and of smaller volume. (The proventriculus is also less elastic than a healthy crop and can be ruptured or perforated more easily.) Burned tissue becomes necrotic (dry, dark and leathery) 3-5 days after the initial pale and oedematous stage. Ultimately, the necrotic tissue separates and a fistula may form.

Surgery consists of removing the devitalised tissue, but this may be challenging if extensive areas of the crop are involved. Endoscopic evaluation of the crop is advisable before commencing surgery. If possible the length of the crop should be preserved rather than performing a resection and anastomosis (strictures are more likely with the latter). A two-layer crop closure with a double inversion technique using 3/0-6/0 Vicryl is advised. A Penrose drain may be placed to allow postoperative drainage. If there is extensive tissue loss a rotating skin flap may be needed.

Systemic Factors Leading to Regurgitation

Septicaemia
See Diarrhoea (Table 17.2).

Drugs
Enrofloxacin and doxycycline, both orally or by intramuscular injection, may cause regurgitation. Itraconazole and naltrexone, which are used for behavioural disorders, can also cause regurgitation.

Papillomatosis
This is a viral disease (papillomavirus) most commonly seen in South American species (particularly imports), although all species can be susceptible. It is spread by close contact. Papillomata occur throughout the alimentary tract and can cause regurgitation and dysphagia if present in the crop or oropharynx (McDonald, 1988). Papillomata also occur in the cloaca where they can cause persistent straining, producing a dropping with the appearance of diarrhoea, as well as frank blood in the faeces. Prolapse of the cloaca (requiring surgical intervention) is a common sequela to straining and it may be possible to visualise the papillomata (alternatively, manual eversion of the cloaca under anaesthesia may extrude the papillomata). Confirmation of the disease is on histopathology. Treatment is supportive only. Surgical removal of individual papillomata is possible with diathermy, cryosurgery or laser (Greenwood, 1993). Repeated daily applications of silver nitrate may reduce the size of lesions. Antibiotics should be used to control secondary infections. Cyclical spontaneous remissions occur. Affected birds show a higher incidence of bile and pancreatic carcinomata later in life (Graham, 1994).

Autogenous vaccines may be helpful.

Psittacine Proventricular Dilatation Syndrome (PPDS)
This syndrome, formerly known as 'macaw wasting disease', was first recorded in 1977. It is a fatal and contagious disease of unknown aetiology, but suspected to be viral; it affects a wide variety of psittacine species (see Figure 17.6). Symptoms include regurgitation, passing of whole undigested seeds (also seen in pancreatitis, some forms of enteritis and food allergies) and weight loss. Secondary infections are common. Tentative diagnosis is on barium contrast radiography, confirmed on proventriculus wall biopsy and histopathology. Doses and passage time for barium from crop to proventriculus are given in Table 17.3.

There may be an increase in soft food intake in affected birds and reversion to juvenile behaviour. Abnormal radiographs show increased transit time, a proventriculus outside the liver parameters (dorsoventral view) and folding of the proventriculus over the ventriculus. In some cases the proventriculus may enlarge dramatically. An increase in creatinine kinase (CK) in association with this condition has been reported. The normal range for CK in psittacines is between 100-400µmol/l; in PPDS, values may rise to 800µmol/l (this is not pathognomonic); elevated CK values will occur in other neuropathies, muscle wasting or soft tissue injuries. Definitive diagnosis in the live bird is on proventricular biopsy (see Figure 17.7). This is a specialist procedure and cases should be referred as the patient is a poor anaesthetic risk and the absence of the sealing peritoneum present in mammals makes fatal leakage from the proventricular incision possible. Alternatively, biopsies can be taken from the ventricular wall (partial thickness biopsies leaving the koilin layer unpenetrated). This is safer but may give false negatives. Doolen (1994) suggested that a full thickness biopsy of the crop wall may be diagnostic in most cases. At *post mortem*, samples

Figure 17.6: *Proventricular dilatation syndrome in an Eclectus Parrot. This was subsequently confirmed by histopathology. Note the massively enlarged proventriculus. (Photo courtesy Mrs R Freyer-Hall)*

Table 17.3. Doses and passage times for barium contrast radiography.

Species	Barium dose	Passage time from crop to proventriculus
Conures	3-4mls	20 minutes
Amazons and small cockatoos	7-8mls	25 minutes
Macaws and large cockatoos	12-15mls	30 minutes

(Adapted from Bond *et al*, 1993).

should be taken from the proventricular and ventricular wall, the epicardium and brain tissue. Histology reveals lymphocytic and plasmocytic infiltration of nerve ganglia. Affected cases must be isolated. Treatment is supportive only: crop tubing and provision of soft food may increase survival time. A pharyngostomy tube, endoscopically guided into the proventriculus and sutured to the neck, makes repeated feeding easier. There have been reports of remission of symptoms following long-term nursing with this technique (Malley, 1991). The incubation period is unknown if, indeed, there is an incubation period (Degernes *et al*, 1991).

LIVER DISORDERS

Liver disorders are a common cause of vomiting and/or diarrhoea in psittacines. Other clinical signs include polydipsia/polyuria, yellow to green urates, ascites and neurological signs. Icterus is rare in psittacines; jaundiced serum is more likely to be due to the presence of carotene pigments.

Pigment changes in feathers - for example, black streaking in Amazons - may be seen, as may abnormal moulting and overgrowth of beak and nails (chronic cases). Dyspnoea is common due to ascites or hepatomegaly. Occasionally, an enlarged liver may be palpated (this must not be confused with the ventriculus). Coagulopathies also occur. These should not be confused with other causes of liver disorders such as lead poisoning (see Figure 17.8) or conure bleeding syndrome.

Diagnosis

Biochemistry
The following biochemical parameters can be used for diagnosing liver disease:
● Aspartate aminotransferase (AST) - fairly liver specific, indicates active hepatocellular damage. However, elevated values may occur with muscle damage.
● Lactate dehydrogenase (LDH) - not as useful as AST (non-specific) and it disappears rapidly from plasma (Lumeij, 1993). Specific for liver disease if LDH is raised but creatine kinase (CK) is normal.
● Glutamate dehydrogenase (GLDH) - elevated values are specific for extensive liver cell necrosis only (as in Pacheco's disease). Located within the mitochondrium of liver cells.
● Gamma glutamyl transferase (GGT) may rise in liver disease, but is not as specific as AST. A rise in this enzyme may be associated with cholestatic liver disease.
● Bile pigments - in birds the major bile pigment is biliverdin; therefore, bilverdinuria may be seen in cases of liver disease (urates stained bright yellow or green - yellow stained urates may also be seen following injection of B vitamins). Plasma bile acid concentrations (PBACs) are a reflection of the clearing capacity of the liver; they are raised in liver disease. At present PBACs remain the single most useful test for liver disease. Psittacines have no gall bladder so significant rises in post-prandial bile acid concentrations do not occur.

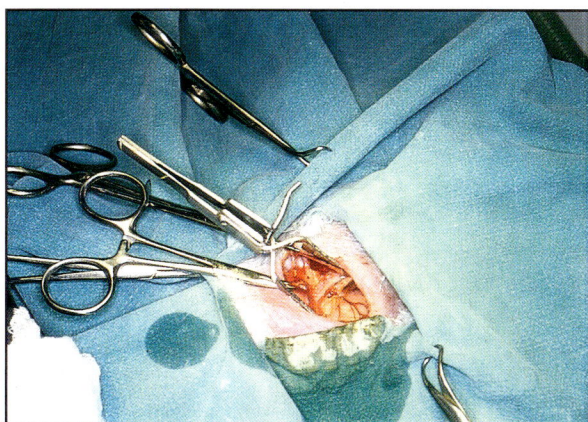

Figure 17.7: Proventricular biopsy in an African Grey. Histopathology confirmed PPDS. (Photo courtesy Mrs R Freyer-Hall)

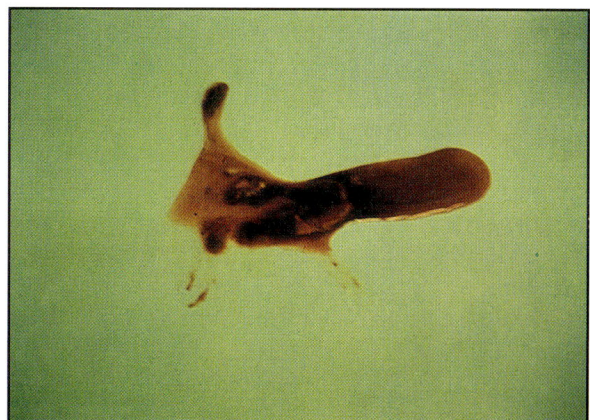

Figure 17.8: Haemorrhagic diarrhoea in an Amazon with lead poisoning. (Photo courtesy Mrs R Freyer-Hall)

Table 17.4. Causes of liver disease.

Cause	Comments
Bacterial	Gram-negative infections, *Yersinia* spp., mycobacterial infections, *Campylobacter* spp. infection.
Chlamydial	Acute and chronic (see Chapter 22).
Viral	Herpesvirus (Pacheco's), poxvirus, polyomavirus, rheovirus, inclusion body hepatitis (aviadenovirus).
Toxic	Hypervitaminosis A (incidence unknown, but usually iatrogenic). Mycotoxins/aflatoxins. Heavy metal poisoning, eg. lead.
Metabolic	Related to obesity, high fat diets (sunflower seeds), following persistent egg laying and/or egg yolk peritonitis. Diabetes mellitus.
Endocrine	Hypothyroidism, diabetes mellitus.

● Cholesterol levels may rise in association with fatty liver syndrome, but also in non-specific liver disease.

● Low T_4 levels may indicate hypothyroidism. This is a very useful test, considered by some authors to be essential.

● Fibrinogen is an indicator of inflammation and infection in birds (EDTA sample).

● Total protein (TP) levels may decrease with hepatic disorders, renal disease, poor nutrition, stress, injury, blood loss or any non-responsive chronic disease. It is believed that hepatic disorders will produce a decrease in serum albumen and hence a decrease in the albumen:globulin ratio. However, an increase in TP with a decrease in the albumen:globulin ratio may occur with egg peritonitis or chronic infectious diseases such as chlamydiosis, aspergillosis or tuberculosis. Elevated TP with a normal albumen:globulin ratio will be seen in dehydration. Severe hypoalbuminaemia caused by glomerular or hepatic damage may cause ascites and peripheral oedema of the feet and legs.

● Low blood glucose levels may be seen in hepatopathy (but are also seen in inanition, malnourishment, septicaemia and endocrinopathies). Hyperglycaemia occurs in diabetes mellitus (common in budgerigars, often resulting in hepatic fibrosis).

Repeated plasma chemistries are recommended when evaluating liver disease to prevent misinterpretation of results. Normal values are shown in Tables 17.5 and 17.6.

Haematology
Essential for completing the diagnostic work-up (see Chapter 5).

Radiography
Indicated if AST levels and PBACs are elevated. Hepatomegaly indicates liver damage (see Chapter 7), as does an increase in radiographic density.

Biopsy
Definitive diagnosis is on liver biopsy (see Chapter 4); this is indicated if bile acid concentrations remain persistently high, if AST levels continue rising despite treatment, or in the event of radiographic abnormalities. Caution should be exercised in birds which show prolonged bleeding times at blood collection and also in those patients with ascites (enter just caudal to the carina to avoid penetrating the air sacs and asphyxiating the bird with its own ascitic fluid).

Treatment
Fluid therapy is essential (see Chapter 9). Patients with liver damage are unlikely to feed on their own; crop tubing is essential. High fat and high protein levels must be avoided. The author favours fruit and vegetable based baby foods such as Millupa. Birds under treatment should be fed every three hours. If patients are regurgitating or have crop stasis, crop feeding with a mixture of amino acids and electrolytes, eg. Duphalyte (Solvay-Duphar Veterinary) is advisable (40ml/kg every five hours). Fermentation in the crop can be a problem with Millupa, but Duphalyte will not ferment. Reanymyl (Virbac) should not be used in cases of liver damage: it is possible that the high fat content of the diet may exacerbate the liver disorder.

Lactulose (Duphulac, Solvay-Duphar Veterinary) (0.2-0.4ml/kg tid by crop tube) helps by removing toxins osmotically via the large intestine; it also reduces diarrhoea by bulking the faeces (although excessive

Table 17.5. Normal biochemical data for psittacines.
(Lynx reference data reproduced by kind permission of the Zoological Society of London).

Variable	Units	Blue and Gold Macaw Range	Sulphur-crested Cockatoo Range	Number of birds sampled
Total protein	g/l	26-36	33-35	3
Albumin	g/l	12-18	14-18	3
Globulin	g/l	14-19	15-20	3
Alkaline phosphatase	u/l	188-413	34-159	3
Alanine transaminase	u/l	10-58	30-92	3
Gamma glutamyl transferase	u/l	0-10	0-9	3
Aspartate amino transaminase	u/l	219-270	152-153	3

Table 17.6. Blood chemistry values for psittacines.

Variable	Units	African Grey	Amazon	Cockatoo	Macaw	Number sampled
AST	u/l	54-155	57-194	52-203	58-206	> 90
GGT	u/l	1-3.8	1-10	2-5	< 1.5	> 99
LDH	u/l	147-384	46-208	203-442	66-166	> 96
CPK	u/l	123-875	45-565	34-204	61-531	> 90
Bile acids	umol/l	18-71	19-144	23-70	25-71	> 103
TP	g/l	32-44	33-50	35-44	33-53	> 97
A:G ratio		1.4:4.7	2.6:7.0	1.5:4.3	1.4:3.9	> 97

After Lumeij and Overduin (1990).

amounts can cause diarrhoea).

Isogel Granules (Charwell Pharmaceuticals) help to reduce the fluid loss in diarrhoea and appear to help clinically with toxin-induced liver damage, eg. aflatoxin toxicity.

Antibiotics, eg. enrofloxacin (5-15mg/kg i/m bid), should be used where Gram-negative infections are suspected. Doxycycline (100mg/kg i/m every five days) should be used where chlamydial infection is suspected (chlamydial infection is one of the commonest causes of liver damage; suspect if AST levels are high with any combination of leucocytosis/monocytosis/heterophilia). Muscle necrosis can occur with this drug. Some practitioners use doxycycline routinely in cases of liver damage of unknown cause as chronic *Chlamydia psittaci* carriers will give a negative PCR test and show no rise in CFT antibodies. Ideally, blood samples should be taken before intramuscular injections are given as AST levels may be raised by muscle necrosis following injection.

Corticosteroids should only be used if indicated on biopsy. They may be given in non-infectious hepatitis, autoimmune disorders and also as part of a chemotherapeutic regime for hepatomata (in conjunction with vincristine and chlorambucil). They must be used conservatively and in conjunction with antibiotics to prevent secondary infection. Dexamethasone (2-4mg/kg i/m or 1-2mg/kg i/v sid) or prednisolone (2mg/kg p/o bid) can be given. Intravenous administration is preferable to the intramuscular route; intramuscular injections may raise AST levels for up to five days post-injection, thus producing a steroid induced hepatopathy (Finnegan *et al*, 1993). Corticosteroids have been used successfully in mycotoxicosis to limit the formation of fibrosis.

Multivitamin preparations containing not more than 100,000 IU of vitamin A and 10,000 IU of vitamin D_3 per ml (depending on nutritional history) are useful as supportive therapy (0.1-0.2ml/300g once weekly).

Vitamin K (1mg/kg i/m once daily for five days or until clotting returns to normal) should be given if coagulopathies result from liver damage.

Colchicine (0.04mg/kg) may be useful in halting the progression of hepatic fibrosis (end-stage liver) (Fudge, 1993). Side-effects can include gastrointestinal signs and muscular weakness (Hoeffer, 1991).

Biotin, choline and methionine supplementation are indicated in cases of fatty liver infiltration.

Ascitic fluid should not be removed from birds with liver disease as this will deplete stores of protein. The use of frusemide (dose to effect) should be considered as an alternative (note the low therapeutic index, particularly in Lorridae).

Pacheco's Disease

The causative agent of Pacheco's disease is a herpesvirus which produces an acute disease. Symptoms may include anorexia, ruffled feathers (sick bird syndrome), diarrhoea with yellow discoloration of the faeces (liver involvement), regurgitation and, occasionally, nervous signs. In the UK it is largely seen in imported birds (especially from large holding stations with no all in/all out policy) so its incidence is decreasing. Virus is shed in the faeces. Infection is by nasal and/or oral routes. The incubation period is short, probably 3-7 days. Mortality may reach 80-90% in quarantined birds and in pet shops where the hygiene is poor. Birds, particularly conures, can be asymptomatic carriers and may release the virus when stressed, eg. by a change of environment. Control is by (strict) quarantine of newly arrived birds (at least six weeks), reduced stocking rates and strict disinfection. The use of sentinel birds is also advised. A vaccine is available in the USA but, due to vaccination reactions, it is only used on birds at risk. The virus is easily transmitted by fomites, including man. Acyclovir (80mg/kg tid by gavage) has been shown to reduce mortality in an outbreak.

The virus causes liver necrosis and at *post mortem* there may be well defined necrotic foci in the liver (a rise in GLDH occurs *ante mortem*). Haematoxylin and eosin stained sections of liver show these foci, but diagnosis depends on demonstrating the presence of basophilic and eosinophilic inclusion bodies.

Chlamydiosis

Chlamydiosis tends to cause a perihepatitis in the acute form or liver cirrhosis (fibrosis) in the chronic form. Smears from the liver and spleen can be stained with modified Ziehl-Neelsen stain to demonstrate the elementary bodies (however, this has been superseded by the PCR test). Smears or biopsy from the air sacs or pericardial sacs are more likely to give positive results. False negative results may occur in birds with latent infection. Other lesions which can occur in a liver affected by chlamydiosis include bile duct hyperplasia, bile stasis and portal fibrosis. However, irregularly shaped foci of coagulation necrosis do occur occasionally (Graham, 1994).

REFERENCES

Anderson NL (1993) *Candida/Megabacterium* proventriculitis in a Lesser Sulphur-crested Cockatoo. *Journal of the Association of Avian Veterinarians* **7(4)**, 197.

Baker JR (1992) Megabacteriosis in exhibition budgerigars. *Veterinary Record* **12-14**, 131.

Batwell R (1978) Crop lithiasis in a budgerigar. *Australian Veterinary Journal* **54**, 452.

Bayer EV and McDonald SE (1981) Psittacosis in pet birds. *California Veterinary Journal* **4(6)**,17.

Bond MW, Downs D and Wolf S (1993) Screening for psittacine proventricular dilatation syndrome. In: *Proceedings of the Association of Avian Veterinarians Annual Conference 1993*. AAV, Lake Worth.

Campbell TW (1993) Disorders of the avian crop. *Exotic Animal Medicine in Practice* **1**, 201

Clipsham R (1991) Introduction to psittacine pediatrics. *Veterinary Clinics of North America* **21**, 1381.

Degernes L, Flammer K and Fisher P (1991) Proventricular dilatation syndrome in a Green-winged Macaw. In: *Proceedings of the Association of Avian Veterinarians Annual Conference 1991*. AAV, Lake Worth.

Doolen M (1994) Crop biopsy - a low risk diagnosis for neuropathic dilatation. In: *Proceedings of the Association of Avian Veterinarians Annual Conference 1994*. AAV, Lake Worth.

Eamens GJ (1989) Zoonoses and other human diseases associated with cage birds. In: *Proceedings No 55: Refresher Course on Cage and Aviary Birds*. Ed TG Hungerford. Postgraduate Committee in Veterinary Science, Sydney.

Evans SM (1981) Avian radiographic diagnosis. *Compendium on Continuing Education for the Practicing Veterinarian* **3(7)**, 660.

Finnegan M, Kaufman GE and Murphy JR (1993) Preliminary evaluation of the effects of dexamethasone on serum hepatic enzymes, glucose and total protein in Red-tailed Hawks. In: *Raptor Biomedicine*. Eds PT Redig, JE Cooper, JD Remple and DB Hunter. University of Minnesota Press, Minneapolis

Fudge AM and Hoeffer HL (1994) Bile acid testing in psittacine birds. *Seminars in Avian and Exotic Pet Medicine* **3(1)**, 35.

Fudge AM (1993) Diagnosis and management of avian liver disease. In: *Proceedings of the Association of Avian Veterinarians European Conference, Utrecht, 1993*. AAV, Lake Worth.

Greenwood AG (1993) Laser surgery of psittacine internal papillomata. In: *Proceedings of the Association of Avian Veterinarians European Conference, Utrecht, 1993*. AAV, Lake Worth.

Gilmore CE and Petrak ML (1982) Neoplasms in pet birds. In: *Diseases of Cage and Aviary Birds*. Ed M Petrak. Lea and Febiger, Philadelphia.

Graham DL (1994) A color atlas of chlamydiosis. *Seminars in Avian and Exotic Medicine* **2(4)**, 188

Hoeffer H (1991) Hepatic fibrosis and colchicine therapy. *Journal of the Association of Avian Veterinarians* **5(4)**, 193.

Lintner M, Merryman M and Rae MA (1992) Gastric

neoplasia in caged birds. In: *Proceedings of the Association of Avian Veterinarians Annual Conference 1992*. AAV, Lake Worth.

Lumeij JT (1993) Avian plasma chemistry in health and disease. In: *Proceedings of the Association of Avian Veterinarians European Conference, Utrecht, 1993*. AAV, Lake Worth.

Lumeij JT and Overduin L (1990) Plasma chemistry values in Psittaciformes. *Journal of Avian Pathology* **19**, 235.

Malley DM (1991) Case study of a Moluccan Cockatoo with proventricular dilatation. In: *Proceedings of the Association of Avian Veterinarians European Conference, Vienna, 1991*. AAV, Lake Worth.

McDonald SE (1988) Clinical experiences with cloacal papillomas. In: *Proceedings of the Association of Avian Veterinarians Annual Conference 1988*. AAV, Lake Worth.

Pennycott TW (1992) *Psittivets Proceedings*. Janssen Animal Health, London.

Rosskopf WJ, Woerpel RJ and Asterino R (1991) Successful treatment of avian tuberculosis in pet psittacines. In: *Proceedings of the Association of Avian Veterinarians Annual Conference 1991*. AAV, Lake Worth.

Sayle RK (1986) Evaluation of droppings. In: *Clinical Avian Medicine and Surgery, including Aviculture*. Eds GJ Harrison and LR Harrison. WB Saunders, Philadelphia.

CHAPTER EIGHTEEN

Trauma

Greg N Simpson

INTRODUCTION

Traumatic injuries are among the commonest clinical conditions encountered by veterinary surgeons working with psittacines. Birds in their aviaries may be disturbed by storms, dogs, cats or other predators, causing them to injure themselves by flying into stationary objects. Other injuries include bite wounds from predators or cage mates, burns, electrocution, self-trauma, neonates injured by their parents defending their nest and iatrogenic injuries caused during handling. Traumatised birds are often presented in critical, life threatening condition and prompt, appropriate, emergency therapy is essential (see Chapter 9). Practical avian emergency care should include a brief physical examination; detailed investigations can be left until the patient is stabilised (see Chapter 4).

INITIAL CLINICAL EXAMINATION AND TREATMENT

Vital conditions, such as obstruction of the airway or haemorrhage, should be assessed and counteracted immediately. Bite wounds of the head area, eg. premaxilla, commonly lead to extensive haemorrhage, and this may result in blood clot formation in the upper respiratory tract. This is particularly dangerous if the glottis or trachea are affected. In the latter case the bird should be immediately anaesthetised and intubated, or an air sac tube placed (see Chapter 6), and the source of the haemorrhage controlled.

Haemostasis must be achieved as a matter of urgency. Blood volumes in most healthy birds are between 6-13% of the body mass (higher in smaller species) (Cooper and Eley, 1979) and therefore any blood loss from a small bird may be crucial.

Birds commonly damage developing feathers ('blood' or 'pin' feathers) and haemorrhage from the exposed axial artery may be significant. Haemostasis can be encouraged by the client applying digital pressure, flour or, if available, alum, potassium permanganate, silver nitrate or even 'superglue'.

In psittacines with bleeding broken blood feathers the quick should be removed. This may compromise future feather growth, but it does help in the immediate control of haemorrhage. Traumatic injuries to the beak or feet generally result in greater tissue damage, and haemostasis can often only be achieved through ligation or cauterising of damaged vessels.

Haemorrhage within the oral cavity may be difficult to control unless the bird is anaesthetised to facilitate haemostatic techniques. Peripheral blood circulation is poor in shocked patients, even when blood loss has been minimal. Intravenous (Bond *et al*, 1993) or intraosseus (Quesenberry and Hillyer, 1994) fluid therapy (see Chapter 4) is far more efficacious than intramuscular or subcutaneous fluids. The correct use of intravenous and intraosseus fluid therapy has greatly improved the clinical management of injured and sick avian patients (Huff, 1993). Bolus intravenous or intraosseus therapy is indicated if the patient is presented in a state of metabolic acidosis. All birds presented suffering from shock, disease or haemorrhage are likely to be suffering from metabolic acidosis (Redig, 1984). Lactated Ringer's (Hartmann's) solution is appropriate. The use of concentrated dextrose solution is contraindicated as it has a strong acidifying effect (Redig, 1984). If the bird is emaciated, calorific requirements can be provided by adding 5% or 10% glucose diluted to a 2.5% solution with Ringer's solution. Further details of fluid therapy can be found in Chapter 9.

Anaemic patients are best treated with iron dextran and/or gelatin plasma expanders, eg. Haemaccel (Hoechst) or Gelofusine (Consolidated Chemicals). Haemopoesis in avian species is naturally rapid. Birds suffering acute blood loss should receive plasma expander with or without parenteral iron dextran. Transfusion is only thought to be of value if the haematocrit is <20%, in which case an homologous transfusion should be given (Boss *et al*, 1990). Although transfused cell life span may be only 24 hours, this may assist in the initial critical phase.

Vitamin K_1 (0.2-2.5mg/kg i/m) should be given if a blood clotting abnormality is suspected. Clotting defects may be associated with sulphonamide medication. A routine broad-spectrum antibiotic, eg. amoxicillin, should be included in the initial therapy for any trauma case.

WOUND MANAGEMENT AND TREATMENT

Appropriate management of traumatic injuries reduces complications and wound healing time. A thorough and complete understanding of wound healing is important. The three recognised phases of wound healing are inflammation, collagen formation and maturation.

Inflammatory Phase

The inflammatory phase is characterised by initial vasodilatation, infiltration by polymorphonuclear leucocytes and monocytes which phagocytose any necrotic tissue or bacteria, and finally fibroblast proliferation. This initial phase lasts 36-98 hours.

Collagen Phase

Collagen fibres deposited by the fibroblasts aggregate during the collagen phase and capillaries migrate into the wound. Wound contraction occurs and epithelial cells proliferate and cover the wound surface.

Maturation Phase

The final maturation phase may last for several months whilst the weak mesh of collagen fibres is replaced with stronger thicker collagen fibres (Degernes, 1989, 1994).

Three important considerations in wound management are cleaning, closing and covering. These procedures are best carried out with the patient anaesthetised (see Chapter 6). The wound is prepared by plucking some of the surrounding feathers to expose a 2cm circumference of skin. The wound should be irrigated gently using warm sterile saline to remove all surface contaminants. In cases where bacterial infections are likely, the wound should be lavaged with 1% povidone-iodine in sterile saline. Swabs for bacterial culture and sensitivity should be taken in all cases. Necrotic material should be removed prior to flushing; this procedure may need to be repeated after a few days.

The principles of treating open, severely contaminated wounds which have large amounts of necrotic tissue are similar to those employed in mammals (Bojrab, 1981). Wet-to-dry bandaging (warm, saline-soaked gauze swabs) techniques are used in the first 3-4 days, with daily changes to encourage debridement and removal of necrotic tissue. Following this, hydroactive dressings, eg. Biodress (C-Vet), are applied to encourage epithelialisation and wound contraction whilst at the same time preventing excessive desiccation of tissues. These dressings are left in place for three days. Hydroactive dressings may be kept in place by sutures or by covering them with self-adhesive bandages or conforming stretch stockinette (Degernes, 1989). Paraffin impregnated gauze, although readily available and cheap, may lead to extensive oiling of the plumage; its use should be avoided. Primary wound closure using absorbable suture materials and swaged, atraumatic, tapered needles is advisable in fresh, uncomplicated, uncontaminated wounds.

Wounds along the sternum or on the carpal regions are slow healing. Good results can be achieved by suturing an occlusive dressing, eg. Granuflex (Squibb), over the wound to encourage granulation and to protect the area from further trauma or pressure necrosis. These dressings assist in immobilising the wound during the healing phase (Degernes and Redig, 1993).

A variety of topical medicines can be used beneficially. Bacitracin, neomycin and polymyxin may be used in combination and will provide a wide spectrum of antibiosis. Preparation H (Whitehall Laboratories), a live yeast cell derivative, is an ointment known to promote epithelialisation (Swaim and Lee, 1987).

SPECIFIC TRAUMATIC INJURIES

Some basic principles for routine emergency management (REM) of traumatised psittacines are given in Table 18.1.

Concussion

Concussed birds may be found on the floor of the aviary. They may exhibit depression, ataxia, head tilt, circling, or paresis of a wing or leg. Aniscoria or delayed pupillary light reflex may be evident and, if excited, birds may convulse.

Treatment

Birds should be maintained in a cool, dark, quiet environment. Steroids, eg. dexamethasone (2-4mg/kg i/m bid) should be given by injection. Fluid therapy is required both initially (to rehydrate the patient) and later if a bird is not able to drink. Excessive rehydration should be avoided as this can lead to cerebral oedema. Prognosis of concussed cases is difficult; if there is no improvement within 48 hours, the prognosis is poor. However, if vital signs are stable and both fluid and nutritional supplementation can be maintained, treatment may be continued for up to five days.

Bite Wounds

Bite wounds, if caused by other psitaccines, are commonly on the head. REM is required. If bite wounds are caused by predators, the injuries are commonly of the crushing and tearing type; the latter causes extensive bruising and tissue damage. Such wounds typically contain large volumes of highly pathogenic bacteria from the predator's teeth or beak. Sepsis is a major complication and steps should be taken to counteract this. Standard principles as discussed earlier should be followed.

Lacerations and Abrasions

REM. Specific management is determined by the size,

Table 18.1. Routine emergency management (REM) of traumatised patients.

Letter	Heading	Action
A	Airway	Check airways are unobstructed. Provide oxygen via face mask, endotracheal tube or air sac tube.
B	Bleeding	Achieve immediate haemostasis.
C	Circulation	Counteract shock by bolus intravenous or interosseous infusion of 10% glucose saline solution plus Haemaccel (Hoechst). Bolus volume = 1% bodyweight.
D	Drugs	Analeptics: doxapram (5-10mg/kg i/v or i/m, once). Analgesics: flunixin megulmine (1-10mg/kg i/v or i/m); 　　　　　　ketoprofen (2-10mg/kg i/m); 　　　　　　buprenorphine (0.01-0.05mg/kg i/m). Shock:　　fluid therapy +/- dexamethasone (2mg/kg i/v or i/m; sid, bid or tid). Antibiosis: broad spectrum, eg. long-acting amoxycillin (150mg/kg i/m sid).
E	Environment	Hospitalise in warm (30°C), quiet, dimly lit, humidified environment for 36-48 hours.

location and level of wound contamination.

Fractures
REM. Dressings and bandages are required to maintain fractured limbs in their natural anatomical position prior to comprehensive therapy (see Chapters 13 and 14).

Feather, Toenail and Beak Injuries
Significant haemorrhage may occur. The owner should be advised to apply direct digital pressure to the area after flooding it with a saturated salt solution or flour (see earlier - Initial Clinical Examination and Treatment). REM prior to veterinary care.

Ring or Band Injuries
These injuries occur all too commonly, especially with split identification rings where one end becomes bent and digs into the leg. Swelling of the leg may occur if too small a ring has been fitted, or if a normal sized ring is present but there has been a build-up of dry skin or scale beneath the ring. In each case the blood supply to the limb distal to the ring is occluded. Wherever possible rings should be removed and replaced with electronic microchips (for identification and sex information) prior to problems arising.

Self-Mutilation
This may manifest as chewing of toes, wings, etc. The first action is to control haemorrhage, then to prevent further immediate damage. Depending on the species involved this may entail applying a neck collar (tube) or Elizabethan collar (see Chapter 11).

Electrocution and Burns
REM. Apply appropriate (non-oil based) topical antibiotics. Burns are most frequently encountered when free flying pet birds land in hot cooking oil. The oily substances can be removed by washing, rinsing and drying the bird repeatedly, or using baby powder on birds that will not tolerate being bathed. Feathers should be gently removed from an area of some 1cm around any lesion to facilitate application of medication and allow aeration. Frequent application of cool water or saline is advantageous. A smear should be taken from the burnt surface (Gram stain) to check for existing infection. If infection is not present a hydroactive dressing will prevent excessive desiccation of the tissues (Perry, 1987).

Oil
Small numbers of birds, either free living or free flying household pets, become contaminated with oils. The initial effect on the bird is shock and hypothermia (due to loss of the thermal insulating effect of the feathers). Once the bird is stabilised, it should be bathed in warm water containing a commercial green detergent, eg. Fairy Liquid. Such washings may need to be repeated. In the interim the bird should receive fluid therapy, be kept in a hospital cage at 30°C and receive enteric binding compounds, eg. activated charcoal, to counter any effects of ingestion of oil during attempted preening.

Crop Burns (see also Chapter 17)
These are typically caused by poorly mixed, microwave heated food administered to handfed neonates. The feed does not appear to cause discomfort at the time, but the injury is demonstrated by an area of thickened, erythematous skin overlying the crop some hours or days later. If the area is feathered the burn may not be apparent until the skin sloughs and a crop fistula

occurs. Although the latter appears alarming to the owner, monitoring of the patient is all that is required initially. Extra care must be taken to ensure that adequate food and water is still received by the neonate. Once the wound has settled, all necrotic tissue has sloughed and infection has been controlled, the fistula may be repaired using a two layer approach. General anaesthesia is not always required to repair crop wounds in very young neonates. An oesophageal tube is placed to aid identification of the oesophageal borders. Blunt dissection using haemostats is used to separate the skin from the underlying oesophagus and crop. With the wound adequately exposed, the necrotic tissue is carefully debrided. Care must be taken not to damage the cervical, oesophageal or tracheal nerves or blood vessels. The wound is sutured with 4/0-6/0 vicryl (Ethicon) in an inverting, simple, interrupted suture pattern. Systemic, broad-spectrum antibiotics should be used for 3-5 days.

A more dangerous situation arises if the crop wall necrotises but the skin does not, or if the crop wall is iatrogenically lacerated during crop tubing. Either situation will lead to a subcuticular build-up of fermenting food in the cervical region, which can lead to acute toxaemia, septicaemia and death. This injury may be confused with crop emptying disorders and a definitive diagnosis can be made on palpation, transillumination, insufflation and endoscopy. The patient must be stabilised (see Chapter 9) before reparative surgery is performed.

Trauma in Neonates

Common, but often preventable. Large psittacines often bite and traumatise their young while defending their nests. Nestboxes with sliding doors to separate the adults from their young should be used. Then, if a parent needs be caught or a chick examined, this may be done without risk of the chicks being injured. Injured chicks require treatment for hypothermia, dehydration, hypoglycaemia and shock. They may also require prophylactic antibiotics and therapy for any other specific injuries.

Chronic Pedal Trauma or Pressure

Very many caged or aviary birds are supplied with totally unsuitable perching material. The perches may be too small or too smooth. Pressure necrosis or infection may well arise on the plantar aspect (see Chapter 13).

REFERENCES

Bond MW, Down D and Wolf S (1993) Intravenous catheter therapy. In: *Proceedings of the Association of Avian Veterinarians Annual Conference 1993*. AAV, Lake Worth.

Bojrab MJ (1981) *A Handbook on Veterinary Wound Management*. Kendall, Massachusetts.

Boss JH, Todd B, Tell LH, Ramsey EC and Fowler ME (1990) Treatment of anemic birds with iron dextran therapy: homologous and heterologous transfusions. In: *Proceedings of the Association of Avian Veterinarians Annual Conference 1990*. AAV, Lake Worth.

Cooper JE and Eley JT (1979) *First Aid and Care of Wild Birds*. David and Charles, Vermont.

Degernes LA (1989) Wound management in the avian patient. *Journal of the Association of Avian Veterinarians* 3, 130.

Degernes LA (1994) Trauma medicine. In: *Avian Medicine: Principles and Application*. Eds BW Ritchie, GJ Harrison and LR Harrison. Wingers, Lake Worth.

Degernes LA and Redig PT (1993) Soft tissue wound management in avian patients. In: *Raptor Biomedicine*. Eds PT Redig, JE Cooper, JD Remple and DB Hunter. University of Minnesota Press, Minneapolis.

Huff DG (1993) Avian fluid therapy and nutritional therapeutics. *Seminars in Avian and Exotic Pet Medicine* 2, 1.

Perry RA (1987) Avian dermatology. In: *Companion Bird Medicine*. Ed EW Burr. Iowa State University Press, Ames.

Quesenberry KE and Hillyer EV (1994) Supportive care and emergency therapy. In: *Avian Medicine: Principles and Application*. Eds BW Ritchie, GJ Harrison and LR Harrison. Wingers, Lake Worth.

Redig PT (1984) Fluid therapy and acid base balance in critically ill avian patients. In: *Proceedings of the Association of Avian Veterinarians Annual Conference 1984*. AAV, Lake Worth.

Swaim SF and Lee AH (1987) Topical wound medications: a review. *Journal of the American Veterinary Medical Association* 190, 1588.

CHAPTER NINETEEN

Fits, Incoordination and Coma

Neil A Forbes

INTRODUCTION

The approach to psittacines with neurological problems is a challenge. Neurological diseases may be primary or secondary, and they may affect the central or peripheral nervous system. The presenting signs of central nervous system disease may be seizures, convulsions, depression, ataxia, paresis, paralysis, tremors, circling, head tilt, nystagmus, torticollis, visual defects or behavioural abnormalities. Peripheral nervous disease may present with paresis, paralysis, ataxia, tremors, weakness or self-mutilation (see Chapters 13 and 14). Nursing and support care of the patient is essential in all cases (see Chapter 9). Certain routine therapies may be required in the initial stages, prior to the availability of investigative results.

NEUROLOGICAL EXAMINATION

A thorough history is essential. Important factors to be considered include:
- Age.
- Duration of ownership.
- Aviary/cage/free flight.
- Single or multiple bird household.
- Any new or in-contact birds.
- Duration and rate of progression of signs.
- Diet.
- History of trauma.
- History of potential exposure to toxins.

The bird itself should be examined in order to try and localise the site of the lesion. The bird's mental status should be assessed. Is it as bright, alert, talkative or aggressive as usual? Is it hyperaesthetic?

Aetiology
Not all CNS diseases are caused by a discrete lesion. However, in cases where a lesion is present, delineation of the site of the lesion may be useful. Assessment of cranial nerve function will help evaluate the extent of any CNS lesions, if present. If a single cranial nerve is affected the lesion is more likely to be localised; several affected nerves suggest widespread damage (Bennett, 1994). Tables 19.1 and 19.2 give a guide to possible aetiologies.

Table 19.1. Cranial nerve assessment.

Sense or clinical sign	Clinical alterations indicating cranial nerve damage as shown in the column on the right	Affected cranial nerve(s)
Olfaction.	Test response to noxious substances, eg. bitter aloes. Any change in appetite.	I
Sight.	Central loss of vision in the absence of ocular lesions.	II
Menace response.	If lost, indicative of possible defect.	II, VII
Pupillary light reflex.	If lost, indicative of possible defect.	II, III
Eye movements.	Require coordination of cerebellum and brain stem as well as III, IV, V and VIII.	III, IV, V, VIII
Facial sensation.	Totally supplied by V. (Motor function is affected by VII.)	V

Table 19.1. Continued.

Sense or clinical sign	Clinical alterations indicating cranial nerve damage as shown in the column on the right	Affected cranial nerve(s)
Eye blink.	Lost with defects of V and VII.	V, VII
Head tilt or deafness.	A number of possible causes, including VIII.	VIII
Tongue movement, swallow and appetite.	If defective may indicate defect of IX, X, XI and XII (or pathological conditions affecting the tongue itself).	IX, X, XI, XII
Tongue.	Deviation to one side.	XII

Table 19.2. Peripheral/central lesions.

Reflex	Indication
Pain perception in wing present.	Peripheral nerve and cervical cord intact.
Wing withdrawal reflex present.	Peripheral nerve intact.
Weakness or knuckling of legs or feet.	Upper or lower neuron or peripheral (sciatic n.) defect.
Leg withdrawal reflex present but not exaggerated.	Peripheral nerve function intact.
Vent reflex present.	Local peripheral nerve function intact.
Head normal; wing, leg, cloacal dysfunction.	Cervical spinal cord lesion present.
Weakness in wings and legs, but withdrawal reflex present in each.	Indicates cervical spinal cord lesion or toxicity.
Wings normal, legs and vent affected.	Thoracolumbar spinal lesion.
Loss of deep pain perception.	Likely total cord dysfunction, poor prognosis.

NEUROLOGICAL CONDITIONS

There are many causes of neuropathies in psittacines (see Table 19.3). Much can be learnt from the history and a thorough clinical examination. However, further tests must be carried out immediately and initial therapy instigated.

DIAGNOSIS

Fits, seizures and convulsions can not only be visually dramatic, but also potentially fatal for the patient. Therefore, immediate control of fitting using diazepam (0.3-1.0mg/kg i/v or i/m, dose to effect) or isoflurane (pending tests) may be indicated even before a full clinical history has been taken. For African Greys, in which hypocalcaemia is particularly common, blood sampling and calcium supplementation should be considered prior to anaesthesia, in view of the risk of anaesthetising severely hypocalcaemic birds. Following history taking and clinical examination, blood samples should be taken for haematology and routine biochemistry profile. Even if this does not lead to a definitive diagnosis, it should eliminate some causes and may give some positive indications. Radiography should be carried out to check for enteric lead or, if suspected, cranial or spinal trauma. Serum should be taken for heavy metal analysis and chlamydial and/or viral serology.

Table 19.3. Neuropathies of psittacines.

Neuropathy	Cause and comments	Signs and diagnosis	Therapy
METABOLIC			
Hypocalcaemia	Very common (especially African Greys; may be secondary to virus infection affecting the parathyroids). Poor Ca:P dietary ratio, eg. sunflower based diet; lack of UV light or deficiency in dietary vitamin D_3 can be significant. Kidney or parathyroid abnormalities and infectious agents have been implicated. Oxytetracycline medication can precipitate onset of clinical signs by chelation of calcium (Ca:P:D_3 metabolism is complex - see Chapter 3.)	Fits, convulsions, tremors, weakness, long bone defects in neonates. Blood calcium <2.0mmol/l.	Diazepam (0.3-1.0mg/ kg i/v or i/m - dose to effect) to control CNS signs. Calcium borogluconate 10% (1-5ml/kg slow i/v or s/c). Improve diet. Calcium plus vitamin D_3 supplementation, eg. Nutrobal (Vetark).
Hepatic encephalopathy	Any severe hepatic disease.	Depression, ataxia. Signs peak shortly after eating. Raised blood ammonia and liver enzymes on biochemistry. Endoscopy, biopsy.	Treat liver disease, reduce dietary undigestible protein (see Chapter 17).
Hypoglycaemia	Starvation, liver failure, infection, endocrine disorders.	Lethargy, weakness, seizures. Blood glucose < half normal value for species.	50% glucose solution (1ml/kg i/v). Treat the underlying cause.
TOXIC			
Heavy metals	One of the most frequent causes of fitting in psittacines. Lead is the commonest (many possible sources in most houses - old paint, curtain weights, roofing felt, old metal toys, plumbing or electricians clips, solder on old cages), followed by zinc (usually from faulty galvanising of new cages). Never believe a client who states lead poisoning is impossible: they may be wrong. Always check. Lead poisoning must be suspected in any bird showing neurological signs.	Lethargy, weakness of legs, ataxia, paresis, any nervous signs. Green faeces, anaemia. Caused by acute ingestion or chronic inhalation (car exhaust). Diagnose by radiography (beware fact that the metal particle may already be passed by the time of presentation) or blood sample.	Chelation therapy, eg. sodium calciumedetate, (10-40mg/kg i/m bid) or D-penicillamine (55mg/kg bid p/o). Aid clearance of particulate lead from the gut with $MgSO_4$, peanut butter or liquid paraffin. Ingluviotomy and ventricular flushing if required.
Pesticides	After pest spraying inside (accidental exposure) or crop spraying outside (drift of toxic agent).	Diagnose on clinical signs and history. Blood assay is possible.	See below for differentiation between toxin groups.

Table 19.3. Continued.

Neuropathy	Cause and comments	Signs and diagnosis	Therapy
Pesticides (Continued)	Acetylcholinesterase inhibitors, eg. carbamates, malathion, dichlorvos (acetylcholinesterase inhibition slowly reverses).	Acute onset, many different nervous signs.	Sedation, nursing. Atropine (0.1mg/kg i/v or i/m every 3-4 hours) or pralidoxime chloride (2-PAM) (10-40mg/kg) (Ritchie and Harrison, 1994). 2-PAM is non-proprietary. Contact National Poisons Bureau for availablity. No specific antidote.
	Organophosphates (irreversible acetylcholinesterase inhibition).	Delayed 1-3 weeks. Weakness, ataxia, paresis.	No specific antidote.
Dimetridazole and metronidazole	Overdosage of treatment for giardiasis, trichomoniasis, histomoniasis (typically when given in water in hot weather, especially if nursing).	Convulsions, wing beating, opisthotonous.	Diazepam, fluid therapy, nursing.
NUTRITIONAL DEFICIENCIES Vitamin E and selenium	Acute nutritional deficiency in neonates or chronic nutritional deficiency in adults. Causes encephalomalacia. Nervous signs may be accompanied by muscular dystrophy or exudative diathesis.	Ataxia, weakness, straddle legs, head tilt, tremors. Diagnose by clinical signs, blood test, response to therapy or at *post mortem* and on histopathology.	Parental vitamin E plus selenium (0.05-0.1mg/kg, repeat after 7-14 days); continue with oral supplementation. If therapy not started early, bird may fail to respond due to nerve damage.
Thiamine (vitamin B_1)	Not very common, but supplement all CNS cases.	Opisthotonous (star gazing), ataxia, paresis. Respond very rapidly to therapy (less than three hours).	Thiamine (1-2mg/day i/v, i/m or p/o) plus continued supplementation.
Riboflavin (vitamin B_2)	Chicks (7-20 days old) most commonly affected.	Curled toe, paralysis, weakness.	B complex injection (to give 0.05mg/kg weekly i/v or i/m).
Pyridoxine (vitamin B_6)	Uncommon.	Nervous jerky walk, flapping wings, convulsions.	B complex injection (to give 1-2mg/kg weekly i/v or i/m).
Calcium/vitamin D_3	See earlier (Metabolic Causes).		

Table 19.3. Continued.

Neuropathy	Cause and comments	Signs and diagnosis	Therapy
TRAUMA Central nervous system	Common.	Any clinical signs. Diagnose on history, examination and radiography.	Dexamethasone (2mg/kg i/m sid or bid). Manitol (0.5mg/kg daily by slow i/v injection); frusemide (1-2mg/kg sid or bid). Nursing.
Spinal	Common.	Clinical signs vary with respect to site of lesion.	Dexamethasone (2mg/kg i/m sid or bid), rest, decompression, acupuncture.
Peripheral	Rare.	After any fracture, brachial/pelvic nerve avulsion.	Dexamethasone (2mg/kg i/m sid or bid), rest, support. Rarely successful.
	(See Chapter 20.)	Horner's syndrome.	Antibiotics and anti-inflammatories.
		Eggbinding leading to pressure on sciatic nerve.	Egg removal. 10% calcium borogluconate (1-5ml/kg slow i/v), oxytocin (0.1-1.0 units i/m once), dinoprost (0.02-0.1mg/kg intracloacal or i/m), heat.
Neoplasia	Central, eg. pituitary. Rare.	Magnetic resonance imaging (MRI) or computed tomography (CT) scan.	Grave prognosis. If neoplasia, usually no effective therapy.
	Peripheral (renal, gonadal). Common, especially budgerigars - bird with one leg held out posteriorly.	Renal tumours/infection - pressure on sciatic nerve. Contrast radiography.	Guarded prognosis. Surgery may be attempted.
INFECTIONS Fungal	Secondary cerebral aspergillosis. In lumbar (pneumatic) vertebrae.	Ataxia, opisthotonous (CNS). Bilateral leg paralysis. Diagnose on serology, clinical signs or *post mortem* and histopathology.	Antifungal therapy (see Chapter 15).

Table 19.3. Continued.

Neuropathy	Cause and comments	Signs and diagnosis	Therapy
Bacterial	*Listeria* spp., *Mycobacteria* spp. granuloma or abscessation of pre-auditory infraorbital sinus.	Haematology, CT scan, aspiration.	Non-steroidal anti-inflammatories. Antibiosis.
	Nephritis - bacterial or any other cause. (Commonest cause of unilateral leg weakness or paralysis.)	Diagnose on radiography; may be raised uric acid levels.	Intensive fluid therapy. Allopurinol (10mg/ 30ml of drinking water).
Viral (Some viral diseases are evident on clinical signs alone; most require serology or, more commonly, histopathology to confirm a diagnosis.)	Paramyxovirus.	Signs vary with respect to species and virus strain. Sudden death. Depression, ataxia, torticollis, head tremors, leg/wing paresis, opisthotonous.	Nursing, vaccination (if available) of in-contacts. Euthanasia of infected birds in flock outbreaks. Disinfection. Per-oxygen compound disinfectants, eg. Virkon (Animalcare) (1g/l), may be used in water supplies to reduce enteric virus levels.
	Newcastle disease.	Similar to above.	
	Polyomavirus (budgerigar fledgling diseases).	Tremors of head, neck and limbs; ataxia.	
	Reovirus.	Ataxia, depression, anorexia, paresis. Diagnose on clinical signs, *post mortem* and histopathology.	
	Togaviridae.	Encephalitis, any nervous signs. Diagnose on histopathology of CNS.	
	Mareks (herpesvirus).	Peripheral nerve dysfunction, splay or straddle legs; sciatic nerve may appear swollen at *post mortem.*	
	Psittacine proventricular dilation syndrome (macaw wasting disease).	Anorexia, depression, vomition, undigested food in faeces (see Chapter 17).	
Chlamydial	Rarely causes nervous signs.	Flaccid paralysis. Diagnose on serology or polymerase chain reaction (PCR) test.	Doxycycline or enrofloxacin (see Chapter 22).

Table 19.3. Continued.

Neuropathy	Cause and comments	Signs and diagnosis	Therapy
Parasitic	*Toxoplasma* spp. (Patton, 1993).	Blindness, head tilt, head jerking, circling, conjunctivitis, paralysis, death. Diagnose on serology or *post mortem* and histopathology.	Pyrimethamine (0.5mg/kg p/o bid for 30 days).
	Filaroides spp. (infection by ingestion of insect intermediate hosts).	Torticollis, ataxia. Diagnose on blood smear.	Ivermectin (200mcg/kg) /benzimidazole, eg. fenbendazole (20mg/kg p/o - repeat after 10 days) - do not use whilst feathers are actively growing.
	Sarcocystis spp. (spread by insect transport hosts). Commonest in first year birds (Bicknese, 1993).	Weakness of wings and legs, dyspnoea, posterior paresis. Sudden death. Diagnose on blood smear or histopathology at *post mortem*.	Pyrimethamine (0.5mg/kg p/o bid for 30 days) and trimethoprim/sulphadiazine (30mg/kg i/m bid for 14 days). Control insects.
MISCELLANEOUS Congenital CNS defects	Rare. Must differentiate from acute vitamin deficiency. Hypogenesis, eg. cerebellar, occasionally seen. Commoner in Lutino colourations.	Exclusion of other causes.	Euthanasia.
Idiopathic epilepsy	When all else has been excluded. Reported in Red-lored Amazons (Rosskopf *et al*, 1985).	Seizures. Diagnose on elimination of other causes together with clinical signs.	Diazepam (0.3-1.0mg/kg i/v or i/m - dose to effect) short term; phenobarbitone (4.5-6.0mg/kg p/o bid) long term.
Otitis	Bacterial, yeast, neoplastic, parasitic.	Head tilt, aural discharge.	Symptomatic.
Circulatory	Cerebral vascular accidents ('strokes'). Fat embolism (especially during egg laying).	Seizures, paralysis.	Symptomatic. Nursing.
Increased intracranial pressure	Rare. Several causes - hydrocephalus, neoplasia, haemorrhage, jugular stasis, atherosclerosis (Shivaprasad, 1993).	Seizures, paralysis, lethargy, head pressing.	Symptomatic.

EMERGENCY THERAPY

Fitting or convulsing should be controlled in all patients (diazepam, 0.3-1.0mg/kg i/v or i/m). B complex vitamins (3mg/kg thiamine i/m) should always be given. Anti-inflammatory agents (steroids if infection can be excluded; if not, non-steroidal), fluid therapy (slowly in cases of suspected cerebral oedema), calcium and antibiosis should also be considered (see Chapter 9). The history and patient type may well indicate other interim therapies, eg. vitamin E/selenium in neonates and cockatiels. The patient should receive general nursing and support depending on its condition, eg. moderate heat (15.5-21°C), reduced stimulation (dark and quiet) and maintainance of an airway. Treatment can be altered or augmented once a definitive diagnosis has been made.

REFERENCES

Bennett RA (1994) Neurology. In: *Avian Medicine: Principles and Application.* Eds BW Ritchie, GJ Harrison and LR Harrison. Wingers, Lake Worth.

Bicknese EJ (1993) Review of avian sarcocystosis. In: *Proceedings of the Association of Avian Veterinarians Annual Conference 1993.* AAV, Lake Worth.

Patton SP (1993) An overview of avian coccidia. In: *Proceedings of the Association of Avian Veterinarians Annual Conference 1993.* AAV, Lake Worth.

Ritchie BW and Harrison GJ (1994) Formulary. In: *Avian Medicine: Principles and Application.* Eds BW Ritchie, GJ Harrison and LR Harrison. Wingers, Lake Worth.

Rosskopf WJ, Woerpel RW and Lane R (1985) Epilepsy in Red-lored Amazons *(Amazona autumnalis).* In: *Proceedings of the Association of Avian Veterinarians Annual Conference 1985.* AAV, Lake Worth.

Shivaprasad HL (1993) Diseases of the nervous system in pet birds: a review and report of disease rarely documented. In: *Proceedings of the Association of Avian Veterinarians Annual Conference 1993.* AAV, Lake Worth.

CHAPTER TWENTY

Breeding Problems

John E Cooper

INTRODUCTION

The captive propagation of psittacines is now a well developed art and science (see Chapter 2) (Stoodley and Stoodley, 1983). It plays an important part in reducing the pressure on wild populations and the need to import psittacines in large numbers. Captive breeding techniques are also increasingly being applied to programmes for the conservation and management of wild (free-living) populations. Anything that has an adverse effect on breeding is, therefore, of importance.

The main groups of breeding problems in psittacines can be listed on the basis of their presenting clinical features. They are as follows:
● Reproductive disease in adult (breeding) birds.
● Failure to produce eggs or production of eggs of low fertility.
● Poor quality or abnormal eggs.
● Poor hatchability (parent-incubated and/or artificially-incubated).
● Poor chick survival (see Chapter 21).
● Overproduction of eggs, both physiological and induced, eg. double clutching.
● Incorrect environment or management.

Before discussing these groups it is important to consider some general points that are relevant to breeding problems. All clients who breed birds should be encouraged to keep full breeding records, including identification of pairs, dates, numbers and success or failure of all eggs produced. If failed, at what stage did the failure occur? The aim should be to achieve an 85-90% hatchability rate of fertile eggs.

APPROACH TO THE CASE

● Take as full a history as possible. Any one aspect of management may be relevant to breeding, as may other factors, eg. ambient temperature. Obtain copies of the owner's records and supplement these with answers to questions of your own. Consider producing a questionnaire, which the client can complete **before** you examine the bird(s) or investigate the problem.
● Whenever possible visit the owner's premises. Important information may be missed if this is not done. When a visit is impossible, obtain photographs or drawings of the premises since these may help in detecting management problems.
● Observe all the birds carefully and carry out a thorough clinical examination of birds that are associated with a breeding problem. Remember that apparently incidental or minor clinical signs or lesions may be relevant, eg. a painful lesion on a digit could prevent copulation.
● Be prepared to combine examination of birds with appropriate clinical and laboratory investigations, eg. laparoscopy, semen evaluation, hormonal assays, examination of eggs.
● Do not overlook the value of examination of eggs, eggshells, incubators, nestboxes and equipment. All non-hatched eggs should be fully examined as soon as possible after the point of failure. Regular candling will assist in determining failure at an early stage. Environmental monitoring may be necessary and this may necessitate consulting colleagues or other people with relevant experience.
● Keep careful records of all you do and endeavour to retain information in an easily retrievable form. When analysing data do so in various ways (for example, plot egg production against a range of variables including temperature, relative humidity, staff absences, etc.), if necessary with the assistance of a statistician.
● Familiarise yourself with relevant literature, ranging from veterinary textbooks to avicultural publications. Do a literature search. The Royal College of Veterinary Surgeons (RCVS) Wellcome Library (or comparable institutions in other countries) can assist with this.

The groups of breeding problems will now be discussed in turn.

REPRODUCTIVE DISEASE IN ADULT (BREEDING) BIRDS

The most important causes of reproductive disease in psittacines are:
● Egg peritonitis.
● Oviductitis, salpingitis.

- Cloacitis.
- Ovariitis/ovarian neoplasia.
- Eggbinding.
- Ruptured genital tract.
- Prolapse of oviduct.

While some conditions, eg. eggbinding, produce characteristic clinical signs, others such as egg peritonitis may be associated with non-specific features or cause sudden death. Early diagnosis is often hampered by the fact that many breeding birds are kept in exten-

sive aviaries with secluded nestboxes, and handling them for examination may be difficult or even deleterious. It is good practice to examine birds clinically before the breeding season and also whenever they have to be caught or handled for other reasons. On each occasion, faeces, blood and other samples can be collected and examined in the laboratory. Aviaries and nestboxes should be designed to facilitate regular examination at all stages of the breeding season.

The salient features of the above diseases are given in Table 20.1.

Table 20.1. Reproductive diseases of psittacines.

Disease	Aetiology	Clinical diagnosis	Treatment	Control	Comments
Egg peritonitis and ectopic egg production.	Multifactorial: infectious, traumatic, nutritional (obesity), physical or mental, climatic.	Clinical findings - bird unwell, abdominal discomfort, anorexia, vomiting, dyspnoea. Haematology - leucocytosis. Radiography. Laparoscopy.	I/v fluid therapy. Systemic antibiotics. Irrigation of coelomic cavity with warm sterile isotonic saline. Supportive care. Long-term antibiosis may be necessary. Salpingohysterectomy - may present practical difficulties due to adhesions.	Avoid obesity. Minimise trauma and stress during ovulation. Monitor laying birds carefully. Good diet.	See Keymer (1980), Joyner (1994) and Rosskopf and Woerpel (1987).
Oviductitis, salpingitis.	Infectious, sometimes following trauma to reproductive tract or infections of respiratory system.	Clinical findings as above, or production of abnormal eggs. Irregular inter-egg intervals. Repeated straining and prolapse of oviduct. Endoscopy.	Systemic and topical antibiotics. Supportive care. Surgery may be necessary.	None specific. Monitor laying birds carefully.	See Joyner (1994) and Blackmore and Cooper (1982).
Cloacitis.	Infectious, often following abrasion or other trauma, cloacal calculus, cloacal viral papillomata, dehydration or prolonged recumbency, eg. nesting.	Clinical findings - soiled vent, abnormal droppings, blood in droppings, apparent 'prolapse'. Endoscopy. Digital examination.	Attention to predisposing factors. Removal of calculus or polyps (for details of treatment of cloacal viral papillomata see Chapter 10). Topical and systemic antibiotics.	Attention to cloacal wounds. Adequate hydration.	See Joyner (1994).
Ovariitis (oophoritis).	Infectious - ascending or blood-borne.	Clinical findings - bird unwell, abdominal discomfort. Endoscopy. Radiography.	Systemic antibiotics may help.	None specific. Monitor laying birds carefully.	See Keymer (1980).

Table 20.1. Continued.

Disease	Aetiology	Clinical diagnosis	Treatment	Control	Comments
Ovarian or oviduct neoplasia.	Unknown. Possibly viral (cf. Galiformes).	Clinical findings variable. Tumour may be palpable or present clinically via a prolapsed oviduct. May be visible on endoscopy or radiography. Biopsy. Ultrasound.	Surgery - removal of ovary or oviduct or both (or localised tumour).	None specific.	See Keymer (1980) and Calnek et al (1991).
Eggbinding.	Fatigue. Oversized or malpositioned egg. Oviduct damage. Hypocalcaemia. Low environmental temperature. Inclement weather. Disturbance or interruption of laying hen.	Clinical findings - bird unwell, may strain, swollen abdomen, often off legs. Egg visible on radiographs.	Increase temperature to 30°C. Increase relative humidity. Lubrication. Calcium (1-5ml of 10% solution slowly i/v) and oxytocin (0.1-1 units/kg i/m once). Surgery or draining of egg (ovocentesis). Joyner (1994) recommended i/m or topical prostaglandin, eg. dinoprost (0.02-0.1mg/kg), or arginine vasotocin (0.01-1.0mg/kg).	Good nutrition (but not overweight). Maintain laying birds at warm temperature and monitor carefully.	See Joyner (1994) and Rosskopf and Woerpel (1985).
Ruptured genital tract.	External trauma or straining. Secondary to infection or oviduct impaction, or iatrogenic in attempted treatment of eggbinding.	Clinical findings. Endoscopy (per cloacam) or laparoscopy.	Surgery - suturing or removal. Antibiotics as necessary.	None specific.	See Blackmore and Cooper (1982).
Prolapse of oviduct.	Follows egg laying, dystocia or intraoviductal adhesions.	Clinical findings. Prolapsed tissue visible. Bird may peck at tissue or show discomfort.	Keep tissues moist. Return prolapse, suture if necessary. Consider laparotomy and oviductpexy to abdominal wall; if not careful an intussusception may persist in the replaced oviduct, leading to necrosis, peritonitis and death.	Monitor laying birds carefully.	See Rosskopf and Woerpel (1989).

FAILURE TO PRODUCE EGGS/EGGS OF LOW FERTILITY

A number of the conditions described under the previous heading can be the cause of this group of problems, but in addition the following questions need to be asked:

- Are the supposed 'breeding pair' of the same species or sub-species?
- Is it possible that the 'pair' have not been sexed correctly and are either both males or both females?
- Are the two birds sexually mature?
- Even if the birds are of the correct species, correct sex and sexually mature, are the pair compatible?
- Do they show signs of abnormal aggression, or is there excessive dominance by one or the other?
- Is either bird so imprinted on humans that normal avian relationships are unlikely?
- Is one or other bird incapable of full copulation because of (for example) a wing or leg injury?

These questions can usually be fairly easily answered and, sometimes, appropriate action taken or advice given. More difficult are those cases where an endocrinological disturbance - for example, an over-production or underproduction of a particular hormone - is suspected, in which case the following investigations may be necessary:

- Hormonal assays on blood or faeces (where available).
- Semen evaluation (see later).
- Laparoscopic examination (and possibly biopsy) of gonads.

Semen Evaluation

Although the production of fertile eggs is the best indicator of sperm viability, semen may be collected from imprinted birds by voluntary donation or from other birds by manual milking under sedation or anaesthesia. Examination of semen samples can aid in the assessment of fertility and reproductive diseases.

Figure 20.1: *Eggs of a macaw showing disparity in size. This is not unusual and is generally associated with immaturity of the laying bird. However, infections and nutritional disease can also be a cause of disparity in egg size.*

Normal sperm varies from light milk to cream in consistency. Normal volumes and concentrations of ejaculate vary from 3.5-13µl and 9.5-11.3 x 10^{12}/ml in budgerigars (Samour *et al*, 1986) to 50-100µl and 9-10 x 10^6/ml in larger psittacines (Brock, 1991). Normal ejaculate volumes will not be achieved reliably if samples are not donated voluntarily. Study of sperm motility (by the hanging drop method or direct wet preparation) and sperm concentration may assist in the prediction of fertility. Motility is estimated as a percentage of sperms moving in a forward direction. Sperm morphological abnormalities and live-dead counts may be calculated in eosin-nigrosin stained slides made from fresh samples.

POOR QUALITY OR ABNORMAL EGGS

These can be the result of a reproductive disease in adult birds, eg. oviductitis, but other generalised infections may also be the cause (see Figure 20.1). Nutritional deficiencies - for example, calcium deficiency in the hen, total lack of ultraviolet light or absence of active vitamin D_3 in the diet - can also be responsible (see Chapter 3), and metabolic disease, eg. renal or hepatic failure, must also be considered. Soft-shelled eggs are sometimes laid. The cause is usually either a calcium deficiency or an oviductal abnormality affecting shell gland activity.

Certain types of poisoning and environmental factors, eg. high temperature, may, in addition, result in eggs of poor quality or abnormal shape, size or consistency.

POOR HATCHABILITY

As mentioned earlier, the aim should be to achieve 85-90% hatchability of fertile eggs. There are many reasons why apparently normal, fertile eggs fail to hatch. Those common to both parent-incubated and artificially-incubated eggs are:

- Nutritional deficiencies in the hen.
- Poisoning.
- Infection.

Parent-incubated eggs may not hatch because one or both adult birds do not incubate properly (either due to direct parental neglect or disturbance by, for example, rats, cats or humans), or because the nest/nestbox is inadequate and, therefore, draughty or damp.

Artificially-incubated eggs, on the other hand, are subject to incubation faults and also to damage during handling and candling.

Investigation and diagnosis of poor hatchability necessitate laboratory examination of the eggs (see later) and investigation, including swabbing for bacteriology and mycology, of the nestboxes and incubation equipment. A review of findings in 'dead in shell' poultry, much of it relevant to other birds, can be found in Horrox (1993). Table 20.2 (after Joyner, 1994) summarises causes of death or abnormality in psittacine embryos.

The incubation period of some psittacine species is given below:

Budgerigars	18 days
Cockatiels	21 days
African Greys	26 - 28 days
Amazons	24 - 28 days
Macaws	24 - 28 days
Cockatoos	24 - 30 days

OVERPRODUCTION OF EGGS

Although bird keepers, especially serious aviculturists, are usually preoccupied with **increasing** egg production, sometimes the converse is a problem and a female bird becomes a 'chronic egg layer'. In psittacines this is seen particularly often in single pet cockatiels, which may lay up to 15-20 eggs per month.

Treatment of overproduction of eggs has been attempted in various ways including reducing the length and intensity of light, lowering the temperature, changing the bird's environment, reducing protein in the diet, salpingohysterectomy and chemotherapy. Insofar as the last of these is concerned, a number of hormones have been tried. Medroxyprogesterone is the agent used most commonly. The dose is in relation to the size of the bird (see Table 20.3). Side effects with this agent include lethargy, obesity, polydipsia, polyuria and hepatic lipidosis. Recently, long-acting GnRH (gonadotrophin releasing hormone) agonists have shown some promise.

Salpingohysterectomy is an effective and safe method of control of overproduction of eggs. The ovary need not be removed. Hens should, if possible, be stopped from egg laying prior to surgery. This should be achieved by moving the bird to new accommodation and reducing day length. The surgical approach is by a left coeliotomy. The oviduct is identified as a white convoluted structure in a dorsal position in the abdominal cavity. Surgical removal is accomplished easily, with appropriate haemostasis where necessary. The ovary is left *in situ* and it will not give rise to future clinical problems.

In addition to attempting to 'cure' chronic egg layers the veterinary surgeon should give advice regarding the general health of the affected hen. Repeated egg laying will reduce calcium stores and can cause demineralisation of long bones and reduction in weight and condition. Dietary supplements, including hand feeding, will help to counter this problem.

EXAMINATION OF EGGS

As outlined earlier, examination of eggs can often provide useful information about breeding problems.

Techniques for egg examination have been

Table 20.2. Causes of death or abnormality in psittacine embryos (listed in approximate order of importance).

Stage of incubation	Causes
First third of incubation.	● Intermittent start of incubation. ● Poor storage of eggs. Eggs which are to be artificially incubated throughout should be collected as soon after laying as possible. They can be stored at 55°C (for not more than two weeks) with the air cell at the top. ● Poor handling of eggs, eg. sudden jarring. ● High temperature or other incubator fault. ● Damaged eggs. ● Transovarian infections. ● Infection of eggs immediately post laying as the egg cools. ● Nutritional deficiencies in the hen. ● Developmental abnormalities (some genetic). ● Poisons.
Second third of incubation.	● Nutritional deficiencies in the hen (especially of vitamins and minerals). ● Infectious disease - bacterial, fungal, possibly viral. ● Incubator faults (including improper turning).
Last third of incubation.	● Incubator faults (including hatching procedure). ● Malpositioning of embryo (NB. some malpositions are not lethal). ● Infectious disease. ● Developmental abnormalities.

Table 20.3. Dose rates of medroxyprogesterone for treatment of overproduction of eggs.

Weight of bird	Dose of medroxyprogesterone
Up to 150g	0.05mg/g
151 - 300g	0.04mg/g
301 - 700g	0.03mg/g
over 701g	0.025mg/g

published elsewhere (Cooper, 1993) and are summarised in Figure 20.2. Careful records are essential. Interpretation of findings often requires careful correlation with clinical history and the results of any other investigations.

Candling of Eggs

Candling is a standard husbandry technique which involves transillumination of eggs so that fertility can be monitored. Eggs should be candled first at 6-7 days. The importance of candling is that it allows removal of cracked, infected or non-viable eggs. In addition it allows early detection of failed development. Assessment of the stage of egg failure greatly facilitates determination of the cause of the failure. All 'dead in shells', irrespective of the stage of failure, should be investigated fully.

Egg Weighing

Eggs should lose 12-13% of their start weight by the time of pipping (pipping usually commences 36-48 hours before hatching). A sample of eggs from each

Figure 20.2: Examination of psittacine eggs.

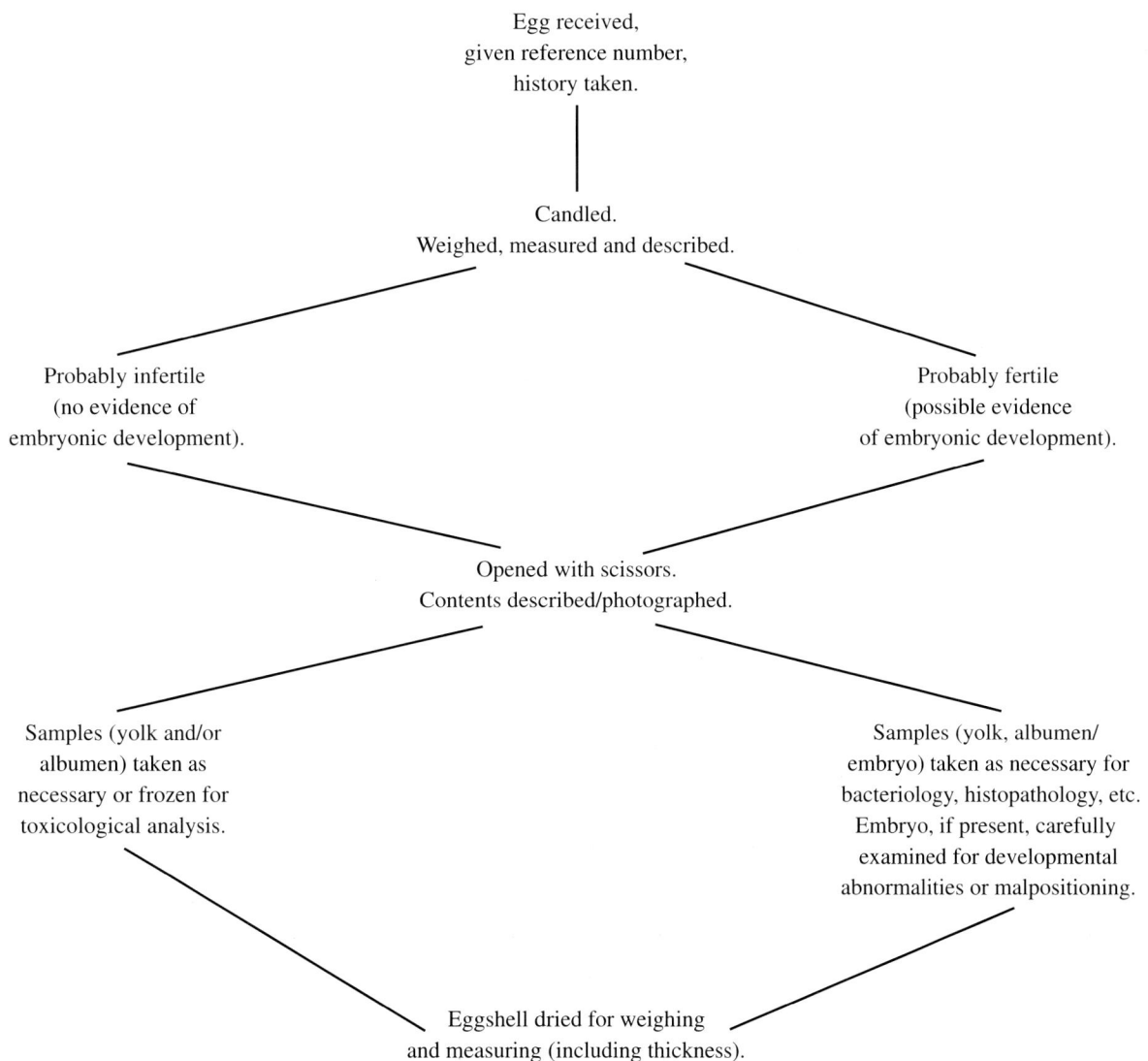

batch should be weighed to check that the humidity levels are correct. There can be problems when incubating eggs of different size or shell porosity in the same incubator; each will require different humidity control.

INVESTIGATION OF INCUBATION TECHNIQUES

This can be a complicated and time-consuming procedure, but it provides valuable information. Useful advice can often be obtained from colleagues who work with poultry or game birds.

Some basic rules are:

● Do a test run of the incubator and map the temperature/relative humidity/air flow at intervals and at different points in the incubator. Are the eggs being turned? Is the forced-ventilation working properly? Is the electricity source reliable?

● Investigate and observe incubator technique. For example: how are eggs handled; is the candler too hot or the eggs kept on too long; are there vibrations or other disturbances that may be adversely affecting incubation; is the incubator fumigated (correctly) before use?

● Take samples (moistened swabs and/or 'settle plates') for bacteriological and mycological examination.

CONCLUSIONS

Breeding problems in psittacines can be difficult to diagnose and difficult to treat. A sound knowledge of normal breeding and incubation (see Chapter 2) is an essential prerequisite to investigation. A systematic approach to the problems is always needed. Good records are essential. Determining the stage (time) of incubation failure will greatly assist in making a specific diagnosis of the cause. Changes to management may be necessary in addition to specific treatment.

REFERENCES

Blackmore DK and Cooper JE (1982) Diseases of the reproductive system. In: *Diseases of Cage and Aviary Birds.* Ed ML Petrak. Lea and Febiger, Philadelphia.

Brock MS (1991) Semen collection and artificial insemination in the Hispanolian Parrot *(Amazona venralis). Journal of Zoo and Wildlife Medicine* **22(1)**, 107.

Calnek BW, Barnes HJ, Beard CW, Reid WM and Yoder HW (1991) Eds. *Diseases of Poultry.* 9th Edn. Wolfe, London.

Cooper JE (1993) Pathological studies on eggs and embryos. In: *Raptor Biomedicine.* Eds PT Redig, JE Cooper, JD Remple and DB Hunter. University of Minnesota Press, Minneapolis.

Horrox NE (1993) The hatchery and hatching of eggs. In: *The Health of Poultry.* Ed M Pattison. Longman, Harlow.

Joyner KL (1994) Theriogenology. In: *Avian Medicine: Principles and Application.* Eds BW Ritchie, GJ Harrison and LR Harrison. Wingers, Lake Worth.

Keymer IF (1980) Disorders of the female avian reproductive system. *Avian Pathology* **9**, 405.

Rosskopf WJ and Woerpel RW (1985) Eggbinding in caged and aviary birds. *Modern Veterinary Practice* **65**, 437.

Rosskopf WJ and Woerpel RW (1987) Pet avian obstetrics. In: *Proceedings of the Association of Avian Veterinarians Annual Conference 1987.* AAV, Lake Worth.

Rosskopf WJ and Woerpel RW (1989) Cloacal conditions in pet birds with a cloacapexy update. In: *Proceedings of the Association of Avian Veterinarians Annual Conference 1989.* AAV, Lake Worth.

Samour JH, Baggott GK, Williams G, Bailey IT and Watson PF (1986) Seminal plasma concentration in budgerigars *(Melopsittacus undulatus). Comparative Biochemistry and Physiology* **84(4)**, 735.

CHAPTER TWENTY ONE

Neonate Husbandry and Problems

Peter W Scott and John Stoodley

Neonatal psittacines may be parent reared or hand reared.

PARENT REARING

It is important to note the date of laying of eggs so that their progress can be monitored and the date of hatch anticipated. When feasible, inspection of eggs should be carried out on alternate days. Cracked eggs may be repaired using a minimal amount of clear nail varnish. Obviously infected eggs should be removed.

During this period most cock birds become aggressive and may prevent hens from leaving the nestbox. Sometimes, they perceive a threat and kill their mates and their chicks. This is a particular problem with cockatoos.

On hatching, it is important to make sure that the parents have access to fruit and vegetables and some soft food, such as one of the commercial egg foods, eg. EMP (Donald Cooke, Rotherham), which often help stimulate the parents to feed their offspring.

Generally, chicks should not be interfered with. Some very experienced breeders will take chicks from a nest and place them in another nest - cross fostering - thus allowing the possibility of the original parents double clutching. This procedure is not to be recommended; without intimate knowledge of the birds and very careful selection of the foster parents, chicks may be killed. It is not a technique for amateur breeders.

HAND REARING

The fashion for hand rearing has satisfied a demand for nice, handleable birds. Sadly, the downside is that a number of malformed birds have been produced. Some, undoubtedly, would have been natural, congenital malformations and probably would have died in the nest or been killed by their parents. Poor diets and techniques have led to some of these problems.

Before taking chicks for hand rearing it is important to be aware of the demands that this will create. Specialist equipment and constant attention are needed. Hand-reared birds will command a premium price. However, if there is not a sufficient market for them a great deal of time and effort may be wasted. It can sometimes be necessary to take sluggish chicks away and 'feed them up' so that they can be returned to their parents vigorous and asking to be fed. Alternatively, they can be taken out, fed and returned to the nest. This is not a routine method of husbandry and should be carried out with caution; some parents will kill chicks which have been interfered with.

When hand rearing, the eggs may be taken as each one is laid or when the whole clutch has been laid. Many hand rearers prefer to take the chicks at 10-21 days of age when the parent bird has done most of the difficult work. Beyond this time it can be difficult to humanise and tame the bird. Birds may be sold described as 'EBHRST' - English Bred Hand Reared Soppy Tame.

There are various reasons for hand rearing:
● To prevent chicks being injured by parents.
● In some species to allow double clutching.
● Parent reared birds on a good diet may become too fat.
● Parents may not be any good at rearing.
● Disease problems.
● Chicks become better, more tractable pets.

Psittacine chicks are altricial (they have no feathers on hatching) and cannot thermoregulate efficiently. Newly hatched chicks should be held in a brooder at 33-37°C; outside aviary birds can be kept at the lower end of this range. Most can come down to 32°C by three weeks of age, although some small species may need to stay at a warmer temperature for longer. Hand rearers should alter the brooder temperature to suit the chick and not insist on a particular temperature. Single youngsters are more difficult to maintain than three or four kept together; a group of birds maintains body temperature more easily, supports each other and is more vigorous in feeding.

Care must to be taken to maintain relative humidity (RH), which needs to be in the region of 50-60%. Disinfectants, such as Ark-Klens (Vetark), can be used in the humidifier water to prevent bacterial and fungal growth. The exact requirements of chicks vary with the origin of the bird; lowland forest species will differ from upland forest species and lowland open terrain species.

The usual advice is to feed 4-8 times a day, between 6am and 10pm, depending on crop emptying time. By three weeks of age this can usually be reduced to three feeds per day. However, it is worth noting that Amazon chicks have been found in the wild with full crops at dawn, ie. they have been fed during the night. Normal crop emptying time is up to four hours. If this becomes longer, perhaps 6-7 hours, action is required - a fluid feed (electrolytes and high energy support) is usually enough to restore motility. Prolonged crop emptying time can occur if the brooder humidity is too low. Some breeders maintain young chicks in brooders which are virtually running with water, ie. a very high RH.

The recommended food temperature is 40.5-43°C. Some species, eg. conures, prefer cooler food (37-39°C). To allow for temperature variation in the food it is safer to aim for 40.5°C. Crop burns (see Chapters 17 and 18) are said to occur when food is fed at 43°C (presumably due to hot spots at much higher temperatures). Microwaves should be used very cautiously; they have a tendency to heat unevenly and produce hot spots within the food. It is safer to mix food using boiling (and boiled but cooled) water to produce the correct temperature.

It is important to use freshly made up wet food; storing wet food in the refrigerator is bad practice. *Escherichia coli* blooms can occur even after 30 minutes in the refrigerator.

Hand rearing mixes are discussed in Chapter 3. Very little scientific study has been done on the ideal constituency of hand rearing food, but in general, for the first 2-3 days, chicks should be fed a diet which is 93% water/6.7% solids, ie. like thick soup. After three days, when the chick has filled out a little and its intestinal tract has started working properly, the solids can be increased and the water reduced to 75%, ie. like yoghurt. This can be thickened still further after about three weeks. For the first four days chicks take approximately 25-28% of their bodyweight per day. From 5-12 days, as the food becomes more solid, this drops to approximately 15% of bodyweight, and will decrease a little further towards weaning.

To simulate some of the digestion which occurs within the crop of the parent bird, the use of a probiotic/ enzyme, eg. Avipro Paediatric (Vetark), blended into the food for at least the first 14-21 days is very valuable. This is particularly useful with some difficult species such as large cockatoos and macaws. Probiotics are also invaluable in reducing the incidence of enteritis, pathogenic bacterial overgrowth, septicaemia, and death in chicks 1-14 days old.

In most cases the chicks are fed until their crops are full. Care should be taken to ensure that the crop is emptying properly and that it is not overfilled. Overfilling the crop can cause poor emptying or result in a 'droopy crop'; this may need the equivalent of a 'bra' to give it support.

When hand rearing chicks it is important that their daily weight is recorded and a growth curve plotted. Birds should be weighed at the same time each day, before feeding, so that the crop contents are not included. As a general rule, psittacines should double their hatch weight by seven days old. Daily weight gain varies between species, but the percentage daily increase for many species in the first seven days is 17% (Eclectus Parrots are slower). Over the first three weeks this falls to 14%, ie. the weight gain percentage for most chicks is greatest in the first week of life. It is important to keep good records.

Weaning (with most psittacines) seems to be a process which happens naturally rather than needing to be taught. Allowing birds the opportunity to take food other than that fed by the hand rearer is the key to weaning. Once feathering is well progressed, soft fruit, orange and cut apple can be hung over the sides of the rearing container to tempt the birds to start taking an interest in feeding themselves. Once this starts, sections of corn on the cob also can be hung. At weaning (approximately 12 weeks of age for most species) all birds lose weight; macaws may lose 20% or more of their bodyweight, although usually one should expect 10-15%. This must be monitored. Birds seem to have an optimum time for weaning, which should not be missed, otherwise it can take months of persuasion.

RINGING

Captive-bred birds should ideally be close-rung. This is normally done within the first five days after hatching. When ringing, a little Vaseline or corn oil makes the task of slipping the ring over the toes and first joint easier.

PHYSICAL EXAMINATION OF NEONATES

Time spent observing the demeanour of a chick before the physical examination helps to minimise the amount of time spent handling the bird. If they are available, siblings should also be studied to compare behaviour, posture, activity and overall build, taking into account different hatching dates. When handling chicks, particular care must be taken if the crop is full. Normal movements of the smooth muscle wall should be noted (usually about 1-2 per minute). Chicks are temperature sensitive, so hands should be clean and warm, and the examination carried out in a warm room or under a heat lamp. Respiratory rates vary from 20-60 per minute depending, at least partially, on temperature and humidity. Respiratory movements in chicks are obvious in comparison with adults.

The skin should be warm, soft and pink (certain species have a normal yellowish cast), often with a slight dry flaking. Reddening suggests excessive heat, dehydration or septicaemia; pallor suggests excessive cooling, shock or general metabolic problems. It is an advantage to have observed normal chicks; Eclectus Parrots, for example, are normally quite red when compared with other species. Excessively flaky skin may be a consequence of low RH in the brooder. Feather growth should be checked for signs of abnormal growth, stunting or haemorrhage within the shafts. The crop should be palpated gently. The eyes usually open at 2-3 weeks of age in large psittacines, often earlier in smaller species. The skin covering the ears usually opens at the same time as the eyes open. The nares are normally open within 2-3 days of hatching. When the beak is examined, chicks usually demonstrate an alarmingly vigorous pumping action.

INFECTIOUS DISEASES

Virus Diseases

Polyomavirus - Budgerigar Fledgling Disease (BFD)
This disease is seen in a wide range of psittacines. The feather abnormalities seen in budgerigars are less common in other species. Baby birds usually die after showing signs of depression, crop slow-down, diarrhoea, subcutaneous haemorrhages, dyspnoea, paralysis or tremors; some birds show feather dystrophy. Problems are commonest at weaning. Polyomavirus may also kill adult birds. Experience suggests an incubation period of less than 14 days.

Transmission occurs via faeces, urine, crop secretions, respiratory secretions and feather dust, and through the egg. Chicks may hatch out carrying and shedding virus, yet have protective maternal antibodies which slow development of clinical signs.

Psittacine Beak and Feather Disease (PBFD) (see also Chapter 10)
PBFD is seen in a wide range of psittacines, normally in birds under three years of age, although it may occur at any age. The first clinical sign is the appearance of abnormal feathers. In young birds all feather tracts may be involved, whereas in older birds it depends on the stage of the moulting cycle. Feathers may break, bend, pinch off or retain sheath or blood within the shaft. In cockatoos and African Greys, loss of powder down feathers is often seen first, with affected birds developing shiny beaks because of the loss of powder. Chicks become depressed, regurgitate and usually die. Beak necrosis may be seen in some older individuals, particularly in cockatoos.

The minimum incubation period appears to be from 21-24 days before the development of feather lesions.

Transmission occurs via faeces, urine, respiratory secretions and feather dust, and through the egg.

Diagnosis of Polyomavirus Disease and PBFD
Polymerase chain reaction (PCR) tests developed by the research team at the University of Georgia are available for the detection of both polyomavirus and PBFD viral DNA by specific probes. These tests are far more accurate than viral culture or electron microscopy.

In Europe these tests are available from Vetgen Europe, PO Box 60, Winchester, SO23 9XN, who will supply collection tubes and the correct preservative.

Poxvirus
Poxvirus causes problems in Amazons, especially Blue-fronts. It is mainly a disease of imported birds. The commonest manifestation is papules and erosions around the unfeathered skin of the eyes, beak/skin margin and legs. A 'wet form' is seen in which necrotic yellow/brown plaques are seen in the mouth. These often interfere with eating and affected birds will lose condition.

Avian Serositis Virus
This condition has been reported in macaw chicks and (Indian) Ringneck Parakeets. Acute signs are seen, eg.

	Polyomavirus	Psittacine beak and feather disease
Viraemia	Not consistently viraemic.	All infected birds remain viraemic, but at a low level if immunosuppressed.
Diagnosis	Cloacal swab. Environmental factors. Faeces.	Blood is an ideal testing medium. Require two drops of blood. Feather pulp or environmental swabs. Feather pulp is essential in suspect cases.
	ALL SAMPLES COLLECTED INTO DNA PRESERVATIVE. Post-mortem samples can also be collected.	
Monitoring	The USA experience suggests testing twice a year, before and after the breeding season.	Test all new stock and any progeny. Test new birds, especially when babies have been purchased through pet shops.

intestinal stasis, dyspnoea, ascites and death. Hepatomegaly and fluid filled lungs are the major *post-mortem* findings. A togavirus is believed to be the cause.

Prevention of Virus Disease Outbreaks

● Hygiene. Polyomavirus and PBFD virus are non-enveloped. They are quite stable in the environment, especially when protected by organic material. Various disinfectants have been examined for efficacy; benzalkonium chloride has a good effect and is a very valuable cleanser. For this reason a two-stage disinfection is recommended; a benzalkonium chloride wash initially, eg. Ark-Klens (Vetark), followed by a more specifically antiviral disinfectant, eg. Tamodine-E (Vetark) or Virkon (Antec).
● Test all new birds.
● Three months quarantine of all new birds whilst tests are carried out is advisable. A six week period (to exceed the probable incubation period of chlamydiosis) should be the minimum.
● Avoid contact between birds or bird handlers from different collections.
● Keep visitors out of nurseries; adult birds are more resistant. Do not allow other bird keepers to handle your birds.
● Use a hand wash/disinfectant, eg. Amprotect Hand Rinse (Vetark), in the bird nursery between batches of birds and between incubators.
● Do not mix neonates from different sources.
● Do not take birds to, or purchase from, bird shows.
● Vaccines.

Bacterial Diseases

On hatching, chicks are considered sterile and so must establish a normal bacterial flora. Within hours, bacteria start to colonise the bird's crop and intestinal tract. Bacteria are present on and in food ingredients or, in the parent reared bird, can come from the parent's crop. The hand reared chick is at special risk of becoming colonised by inappropriate bacteria. A survey in the USA showed all seeds carried *Enterobacter* spp., with 20% carrying *Pseudomonas* spp. or *Escherichia coli*; *Klebsiella pneumoniae* was found in 5% of the seeds. Fresh sunflower seed is no better; surprisingly, this has a higher bacterial count than seed stored for 3-6 months, probably due to moisture levels. Establishing the correct bacterial flora in baby birds is important in avoiding the establishment of pathogenic bacteria in the crop and intestinal tract.

Normal intestines are primarily populated with Gram-positive bacteria (dominated by *Lactobacillus* spp. and *Streptococcus* spp.). Many hand rearers use probiotics to help colonise the chick's intestine. The aim is to flood the intestine with bacteria thereby producing acidic conditions which are inhospitable to unwanted *E. coli*, *Salmonella* spp., etc. Permanent colonisation with probiotic-derived bacteria is prob-

ably unnecessary and may be undesirable; normal bacteria will become established as other birds are encountered. Care should be taken in mixing probiotics with milk-based hand rearing diets; fermentation may occur and cause colic. In addition to providing bacteria to colonise the chick's gut, the parents also predigest the food to a degree by regurgitating enzymes from the proventriculus into the crop; this may be part of the reason why parent reared birds can become too fat. Avipro Paediatric (Vetark) is formulated to provide both the bacteria and the enzymes which the parent bird normally provides.

NON-INFECTIOUS DISEASES

Constricted Toe Syndrome

Eclectus Parrots in particular (also to a lesser degree African Greys and macaws) seem prone to the formation of a constricting ring around a toe. This leads to dry gangrene and loss of the portion distal to the constriction. Histopathology shows only keratin accumulation. The aetiology is uncertain, but increasing the humidity in the nestbox or brooder by spraying the substrate appears to reduce the incidence.

Early cases can be treated by making four shallow cuts through the constriction 90° apart (see Figure 21.1). A light dressing can be applied for 24 hours.

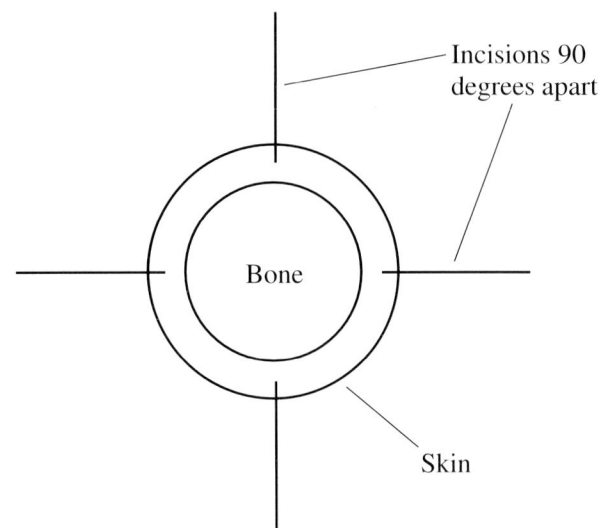

Figure 21.1: Incision sites for treatment of constricted toe syndrome.

Beak Abnormalities

A range of abnormalities is seen. The commonest are deviations to one side or another, so called 'scissor beak'. Deviations to the right are commonest and, strangely, these are much more common in hens.

Corrective techniques have been described by Clipsham (1990). These generally use a combination of light-cured dental materials (Triad, Dentsply International Inc, York, Pennsylvania 17405-0872, USA) and the specialist cyano-repair materials supplied by

Ellman International (UK) Ltd, 16 Rye Hill Court, Lodge Farm, Northampton NN5 7EU.

Congenital or Developmental (Growth) Problems

These are not uncommon and include splay legs, scoliosis and lordosis, opisthotonus or joint deviations. Occasionally, 'miniature' birds develop; the long-term survival of these is poor. As chicks, these 'miniature' birds often appear to have excessively large eyes and feather up slower than normal.

Whilst it was once nonsense to suggest inbreeding as a cause of congenital or developmental (growth) problems because most birds were wild caught, increasingly, brother/sister or parent/offspring matings are carried out. Unscrupulous breeders will sell related birds as unrelated. This can be confirmed only by DNA fingerprinting.

Crop Burns (see also Chapters 17 and 18)

Following burning, a degree of crop slow-down usually occurs initially. Over the following weeks the crop wall and skin slowly necrose and slough, leaving a fistula which requires surgical excision and repair. It is important to allow the lesion to progress as this allows the chick to maximise weight and the exact limits of the lesion to be defined prior to surgical correction.

Crop Emptying Problems

The crop should normally empty within four hours; if crop emptying is longer than four hours, dehydration should be suspected. Ensure that the RH is 50-65% or higher. Chicks which have become seriously dehydrated should be rehydrated over two hours using Avipro (Vetark) solution by mouth (5-10% bodyweight, ie. 5-10ml/100g). Lactulose syrup (one drop in food to achieve half a drop per chick) should also be given; this tends to lower the pH and encourages fluid to remain in the intestinal lumen. Chicks which have become very depressed require support/feed using Critical Care Formula (Vetark), possibly for a few days.

Lactobacillus spp./enzymes, eg. Avipro Paediatric (Vetark), can be given to encourage digestion once the chicks are back on normal feeding.

A crop aspirate should be examined for *Megabacterium* sp., *Candida* spp., etc.

Nystatin suspension is effective in treating *Candida* spp. infections (50,000-100,000iu are usually given, irrespective of bodyweight). The drug is not absorbed so toxicity is not a problem. The suspension seems also to have a direct gut sedative effect in much the same as might occur with kaolin.

Crop Foreign Bodies

An ingluviotomy is necessary to remove most foreign bodies. Sometimes, in young chicks, forceps can be inserted *per os* and the foreign body manipulated into the forceps using fingers outside the skin. The commonest foreign bodies are short pieces of rubber tubing which have been used on syringes for feeding. This technique is popular with some hand rearers who, because they deal with a lot of chicks, want a quick method. A modification of this is known as 'power feeding'.

In very young chicks (up to 10 days of age) it may be preferable to carry out ingluviotomy without anaesthetic. This is usually easy and quick and avoids the risks associated with general anaesthesia.

Impaction

Usually, grit or bedding are the offending items. Affected birds become anorexic and dull and may vomit. If untreated they will die. Surgery on these birds is to be avoided whenever possible.

A medical technique described by Clipsham (1992) involved rehydration parenterally, tubing with dioctyl sodium sulfosuccinate and digestive enzymes, followed by metaclopramide (0.5mg/kg) (despite its normal contraindication in cases of bowel obstruction) and liquid paraffin (mineral oil). Barium sulphate (1-1.5ml/100g) was given by gavage tube 30-60 minutes later. Hydration is important during this procedure because barium sulphate is hygroscopic and the patient is often already dehydrated.

Proventriculotomy carries a poor prognosis in chicks.

Metabolic Bone Disease (MBD)

By far the commonest species affected by MBD is the African Grey. Partly this appears to stem from an innately poor control and absorption of calcium. This is compounded by their dietary habit of becoming addicted to specific foods which are extremely difficult to supplement. Part of the aetiology is the rapid growth often seen in captivity. Psittacine chicks often have no access to direct sunlight and so activated vitamin D_3 supplements are required. Common lesions include folding (green-stick) fractures of the distal tibiotarsus and bowing or fractures of the distal femur. Simple folding fractures can often be corrected. Generally, the best results follow surgery (osteotomy and intramedullary pinning using double pointed Kirchner wires) rather than external support. Correction of the diet by use of nutritional supplements, eg. Nutrobal (Vetark), is also required. Some cases with bilateral bowing can be helped by suspension of the bird in a sling.

Some severely affected individuals have spinal and wing abnormalities. Generally, however, leg problems manifest first due to weight bearing. Parental trauma can in some cases produce very similar lesions.

ANAESTHESIA OF NEONATES

The only anaesthetic agent which can be recommended

is isoflurane administered by face-mask (see Chapter 6). Complex surgery or beak repair will require the bird to be intubated; a Bethune T-piece and home-made endotracheal tubes made from cat catheters can be used. One supplier (Cook Veterinary Products, 6 Such Close, Letchworth, Herts SG6 1JF) is now prepared to manufacture soft endotracheal tubes in suitable sizes. To maintain adequate oxygenation of tissues in the neonate, a lighter plane of anaesthesia is preferred to avoid any depression.

Maintaining body temperature is essential, especially in poorly feathered neonates. Heat pads under a sheet of Vetbed are ideal as a substrate. For surgery expected to take more than 10 minutes, glucose levels need to be supplemented by the use of dextrose saline (2.5% dextrose and half-strength saline). Blood loss can be critical so electrosurgery is invaluable; the Ellman Surgitron and bipolar forceps are well tried and proven in avian work.

REFERENCES AND FURTHER READING

Clipsham R (1990) Surgical correction of beaks. *Proceedings of the Association of Avian Veterinarians Annual Conference 1990*. AAV, Lake Worth.

Clipsham R (1992) Non-infectious diseases of pediatric psittacines. In: *Seminars in Avian and Exotic Pet Medicine. Vol. 1, No.1*. Ed AM Fudge. WB Saunders, Philadelphia.

Fudge AM (1992) Ed *Seminars in Avian and Exotic Pet Medicine. Vol. 1, No. 1*. WB Saunders, Philadelphia.

Fudge AM (1993) Ed *Seminars in Avian and Exotic Pet Medicine. Vol. 2, No. 3*. WB Saunders, Philadelphia.

CHAPTER TWENTY TWO

Miscellaneous

Neil A Forbes and Martin P C Lawton

INTRODUCTION

There are a number of conditions that do not fall readily into the format of the other chapter headings within this manual. This may be due to their multifactorial nature - for example, chlamydiosis, which could quite easily have been put in any chapter due to its wide effects on the bird or its potential as a zoonosis - or simply that it is not possible to place them elsewhere. The result is a miscellany of conditions and topics which are unrelated but could not be left out of this manual.

CHLAMYDIOSIS

Chlamydiosis (psittacosis) is caused by an intracellular infection of *Chlamydia psittaci*. Infected birds are frequently asymptomatic carriers and only shed the organism intermittently. The infection is not only highly infectious and potentially fatal to psittacines, but is also a potential serious human pathogen (zoonosis) which may, on rare occasions, be fatal.

Although diagnosis of the condition is generally simple in an aviary or an individual sick bird, identification of the asymptomatic intermittent shedder may prove difficult. Asymptomatic carriers are likely to undergo some form of stress or immune suppression during their life, eg. transport, concurrent disease, sale or entering a breeding scheme, after which time (often 2-45 days later) they may shed infective particles whilst either remaining clinically normal or demonstrating one or more of the clinical signs of chlamydiosis. Infective particles may endanger other birds within the same air space, or humans who enter the area.

Clinical Signs

The presenting clinical signs vary with respect to the biotype of *C. psittaci* involved (Brown and Newman, 1992), with any one or more of the clinical signs listed below being considered as suspicious of possible infection and indicating the need for further testing. Clinical signs of avian chlamydiosis include:
- Conjunctivitis or other ocular discharge.
- Choanal inflammation.

- Diarrhoea (often green) or regurgitation.
- Any respiratory signs.
- Weight loss.
- Poor feather condition.
- Depression or anorexia.
- Generally fluffed up or 'sick bird' syndrome.
- Neurological signs, ataxia, flaccid paresis, etc.
- Reduced reproductive performance.
- Increased neonatal death rate.

Young birds under two years of age are considered more susceptible to the disease (Fudge, 1992) and will more commonly shed the organism once infected. Incubation periods for infection are stated as varying between 30-45 days and seven years in budgerigars (Storz, 1971; Tully, 1993). Most clinical signs can be caused by, or associated with, chlamydiosis.

Diagnosis

Diagnosis of chlamydiosis can be a considerable challenge; the methods listed in Table 22.1 may be employed. In the authors' experience, if all patients presented with any of the above clinical signs are tested, 50-70% of the cases will be positive for chlamydiosis.

A number of specific *Chlamydia* spp. tests are available for use or adaptation as a screening aid for the identification of possible psittacine chlamydiosis. Those available in the UK are listed in Table 22.2, with the relevant merits or drawbacks of each method being described .

Treatment

The initial decision must be whether the birds should be treated or destroyed. If infected birds are part of a group of individually low value birds being sold from a pet shop, the cost effectiveness and risk of persistent infection in some individuals is likely to render euthanasia the 'treatment' of choice. The risk of zoonosis (see later and Chapter 23), latent infection and recrudescence must be explained fully to the owner. When dealing with a collection of birds, it is not realistic to expect total elimination of the organism from all birds (Gerlach, 1994).

Group therapy may be carried out effectively by

Table 22.1. Diagnostic methods for chlamydiosis.

Method	Comment
Clinical signs.	As listed earlier, but diagnosis must be confirmed. Reliance on clinical signs only for diagnosis is not possible.
Routine haematology.	Leucocytosis, typically >40x10^9/l. This is indicative of a chronic infection and should always be followed by other investigations.
Liver enzymes.	Variable increase in non-specific liver enzymes (SGOT, LDH, plasma bile acids). This is an indication of liver damage which is usually present in cases of chlamydiosis, as well as with other disease. Further investigation is always required.
Radiography.	Splenomegaly, hepatomegaly, air sacculitis, etc. should always be considered as suspicious of possible chlamydiosis.
Specific serology, or faecal or tissue enzyme linked immunosorbant assay (ELISA), or polymerase chain reaction (PCR) test.	Several tests available (see later for comparison). The ELISA tests may be over-sensitive and not sufficiently specific while the PCR test is more reliable if antigen is present. These tests will not identify carriers which are not shedding.
Post mortem (see Chapter 8).	Splenomegaly, hepatomegaly. Modified Ziehl-Neelsen (MZN) on spleen impression smears, looking for the inclusion bodies. Beware zoonosis.

Table 22.2. Specific *Chlamydia* spp. tests for use in birds in the UK.

Method	Comment
Culture.	Requires a special transport media. Must use fresh non-desiccated faeces; it is a sensitive method and able to detect even small numbers of viable organisms. Culture is carried out on cell lines; it requires three passages and takes at least two weeks to obtain a result.
ELISA.	ELISA tests look for the presence of antigen in either faeces or tissues (at *post mortem* or air sac smear *ante mortem*). A number of human chlamydial tests are available for laboratory or in-house use, eg. Clearview Test (Unipath). Such tests require a significant number of elementary bodies (130 for Clearview) (Gerlach, 1994) to be present in the tissue or faeces for a positive result to be obtained. This test can give false positives by cross reactions with some bacterial contaminants. All positives should be confirmed by PCR (see later). As the disease is characterised by intermittent shedding of the organism, the chances of detecting a positive case are increased by collecting and pooling faeces over a three day period and testing as a single sample. However, such tests are invaluable when used on sick clinical cases which are likely to be shedding, and where an immediate result is required prior to therapy or hospitalisation.
Serology.	Several methods are available; all require two samples, three weeks apart. These tests look for a rising titre of antibodies because of the chlamydial infection. The major advantage is that shedding of the organism at the time of collection is not required. The disadvantage is the requirement for two samples, and hence a delay in receiving a final result. A number of different test techniques are available, with varying sensitivity and specificity; the laboratory should be consulted for current details. Antibody detection does not necessarily indicate present infection, just previous exposure. It can be used for long-term monitoring for potential recrudescence in previously treated cases.
PCR test.	A single sample (blood, tissue or faeces) may be tested by PCR. This test detects circulating (blood) or excreted (faecal) chlamydial protein; however, only very low levels of antigen are required (less than are required for a positive ELISA test). The test is very specific and sensitive, but generally takes two weeks. False positives are not considered to occur.

in-feed medication using chlortetracycline, doxycycline or enrofloxacin. Birds kept individually, as well as those refusing to take medicated food, may be treated using oral, intramuscular or subcutaneous administration of doxycycline or enrofloxacin.

Chlortetracycline has a short half-life. Minimum inhibitory concentrations (MIC) cannot be achieved in drinking water and it must be given incorporated into the only source of food. Most species require inclusion at 1% (1,000ppm). Such food may be a medicated compounded pellet or soft mix. Calcium can interfere with intestinal chlortetracycline uptake, therefore the administration of grit in the diet should be ceased during medication. Some birds will refuse medicated diet; these must be given parenteral therapy. Birds who have previously been on a calcium deficient diet, and those actively egg laying, may suffer clinical hypocalcaemia during therapy. Breeding activity should be prevented during medication (Dorrestein, 1993). On occasions, bacterial or yeast enteric imbalances may occur during therapy. Therapy should be continued for a minimum of 45 days.

Doxycycline may be administered in food at 1,000ppm for 45 days, orally at 8-25mg/kg bid for 45 days, or by using long-acting doxycycline injections at 60-100mg/kg every 5-6 days for 45 days. One problem of the latter method is the very large volume of injection which needs to be given (up to 5ml/kg); with some drug preparations this can occasionally result in muscle necrosis. Doxycycline has less effects on the gut flora than chlortetracycline.

Enrofloxacin has been widely and effectively used in the control of chlamydiosis in recent years. It should be given at 10-15mg/kg p/o, i/m or s/c bid, or at a rate of 200mg/l in drinking water or 1,000ppm in food for a period of 21 days.

Although clinical signs will usually cease following therapy, there is no method of proving that there are no residual carriers or latency in previously affected birds. Veterinary surgeons should never guarantee that any bird is definitely clear of *Chlamydia* spp.; he or she can only state that it could not be detected at the time of testing. Regular routine screening of previously affected birds for the rest of their lives is recommended.

Zoonotic Risk
The clinician has a duty to clients, staff and him/herself to be aware of the potential zoonotic risk of chlamydiosis. All in-contact individuals should be warned of the potential risk, the clinical signs of the disease should be clearly explained to them (preferably in writing) and they should be advised to seek advice from their own physician. Under the Health and Safety Legislation (see Chapter 23) there is an obligation to inform and educate staff, to minimise the risk to which they might be exposed, and to monitor

their health. Failure to diagnose chlamydiosis in an affected bird, or to inform the owner of an affected bird of the zoonotic risk, could render the clinician liable to litigation. The main clinical signs of human chlamydiosis are:
- Headaches.
- Flu-like symptoms.
- Swollen lymph nodes.
- Non-productive cough.
- Pneumonia.
- Shortness of breath.
- Deranged liver enzyme levels.
- Mental confusion.
- Death (rare).

ENDOSCOPIC EXAMINATION AND BIOPSY

A good, rigid fibreoptic endoscope (or arthroscope) is an essential piece of equipment in a practice that undertakes avian examinations. Although an endoscope can be used for surgical sexing (see Sexual Differentiation later), the greatest benefit is in the examination of the body cavities. The anatomy of the bird, and in particular the system of air sacs, lends itself to examination with an endoscope, and this technique of examination is discussed in more depth elsewhere (Taylor, 1994). While viewing via the endoscope it is possible to take samples of the liver, lung, kidney or any other abnormal mass seen at the time of examination. There are a number of instruments available for collecting samples; the most useful are round cup forceps. Biopsy can be performed 'free hand' or by using instruments via a sheath attached to the endoscope for guided positioning of the biopsy forceps (Taylor, 1993). Until experience is gained, it is best to use a guide tract and pass the biopsy instrument adjacent to the endoscope so that the end of the instrument may be visualised and directed towards the lesion. Once experience has been gained, it is possible to introduce the instrument from an alternative site, distant from the endoscope, in order to obtain the best position for the biopsy. For organs such as the kidney, liver or lung, the use of haemaclips (Solvay Animal Health, USA) to staple off a small edge helps to control the small but possible risk of a fatal haemorrhage. Endoscopy and, if necessary, biopsy of the following can be performed.

Oral Cavity
The whole of the oropharynx can be easily examined. With a small dental mirror it is possible to see through the choana towards the nares.

Upper Intestinal Tract
An endoscope can be easily directed down the oesophagus and into the crop. The use of air or fluid to expand the crop greatly facilitates examination.

Doolen (1994) described a technique of crop biopsy to aid the diagnosis of proventricular dilatation syndrome (macaw wasting syndrome). Although this was performed via surgical incision, samples may also be obtained at the time of endoscopy. Crop biopsy has the advantage of being easy to perform and does not carry the risk of intra-abdominal leakage as can occur following surgery of the proventriculus. The distal oesophagus can also be entered and, depending on the size of the bird and the endoscope length and diameter, the proventriculus and occasionally the ventriculus can be examined.

Foreign bodies within the crop can be located and removed by endoscopy.

Respiratory System
Entry via the glottis allows visualisation of the trachea and syrinx. In larger birds the primary bronchi may also be examined. The lung tissue is usually examined via an abdominal approach (see later), at which point biopsies may be collected. The abdominal approach is also used for examination of the air sacs. Any abnormal lesion should always be sampled.

Abdomen
There are a number of approaches for examining the abdomen, depending on which organ is the main subject of the examination. The left lateral approach between the last and penultimate rib and into the caudal thoracic air sac is classically used for surgical sexing of birds, although it also allows examination of the intestinal tract, including the proventriculus and the left lung, together with part of the liver. The same approach can be used on the right side to examine the right kidney in more detail, together with the right lung and part of the liver. If a detailed examination of the liver is required, a midline approach is preferable. The bird is placed in dorsal recumbency and entry made directly caudal to the sternal notch. The heart can also be well visualised by this approach or by either of the lateral approaches.

Cloaca
The cloaca is best examined when insufflated with air or fluid. It is possible to enter the rectum and the oviduct, especially if the bird is egg laying.

ESCAPED BIRD

This is an all too common telephone query for avian practices. It is a very difficult problem to deal with, and there is no easy answer. The introduction of ketamine into fruit may be attempted, although for seed eating birds this is often of no help. This approach relies on the bird eating sufficient drugged food to sedate it and enable capture. Attempting to capture the bird in a net usually results in it flying further away. The placing of the bird's own cage outside with its favourite tit bit may lure it back, but this may require a great deal of patience. The eventual recapture of the bird often relies more on luck than actual technique.

EUTHANASIA

Euthanasia is always a difficult and emotional occasion for the owner, and often for the clinician. Irrespective of species, the clinician has a duty to perform this task in as quick, humane and stress-free method as possible, taking into account the patient, the owner and the experience and facilities available to the clinician. For the experienced clinician, intravenous (usually jugular) injection of barbiturate is a fast and humane method for any size of bird. Gaseous anaesthetic by mask, or via an anaesthetic chamber to facilitate handling, followed by intravenous barbiturate is often the method of choice for the less experienced clinician. If gaseous anaesthetic is not available and the clinician is not confident about performing intravenous administration, anaesthesia may be induced with an intramuscular agent such as ketamine (40-100mg/kg) prior to intravenous barbiturate. Cervical dislocation should not be attempted. Intracardiac injection is possible for budgerigars, although if any barbiturate is injected into the lungs, the bird will breath this out causing additional distress to the bird and the owner (if present).

FEATHER PLUCKING

Feather plucking is frequently a complicated, multifactorial problem, which may be refractory to therapy. The client should be counselled as to the severity of the problem, the cost of thorough investigation and the likelihood of a complete recovery.

A feather plucking bird can be identified by the presence of healthy head feathers and feather loss or mutilation in body areas accessible to the beak. Feather loss may be whole body or regional. The commonest species presented are African Greys, lovebirds and Amazons; however, many affected cockatiels are not presented because of their low value. Understanding the main causes of feather plucking is important (see Tables 22.3 and 22.4). Only when all the medical causes have been excluded and standard environmental changes have failed to lead to an improvement, can psychological causes be considered. A thorough investigation is required. Table 22.5 suggests a method of investigation. If medical causes are excluded and the bird fails to respond to the managemental treatment of a psychological cause, behavioural modifying drugs may be employed (see Chapter 11). It must be appreciated that there is no currently accepted 'cure all' medical agent.

Table 22.3. Medical causes of feather plucking (see also Chapter 10).

Condition	Comments
Allergies.	Some authors believe that birds may develop allergies which lead to plucking, although this is not authenticated as yet.
Chlamydiosis.	Chlamydial infection is a significant cause of feather plucking and should always be excluded as a potential cause.
Ectoparasites.	Ectoparasites are often considered to be the cause of feather plucking, but are rarely responsible; however, they must always be excluded. One of the most troublesome culprits is *Dermanyssus gallinae*, which will rarely be found on the bird during the day because of its habit of living in crevices in wood work in the aviary.
Endoparasites.	Endoparasites are frequently found associated with feather plucking. *Giardia* spp. are most frequently responsible, especially in cockatiels; however, roundworms and tapeworms can also be responsible.
Environment.	Tobacco smoke or too dry an environment can lead to poor quality feather growth, resulting in brittle feathers. Breakage of affected feathers may lead to plucking. In some cases, feather plucking commences annually when the central heating is turned on. Most psittacines are accustomed to life in a rain forest, where they would be rained on daily, therefore they will benefit from a light daily water spraying.
Infectious dermatitis/ folliculitis.	The cause and effect may be difficult to differentiate. Plucking may lead to infection, although it may have started because of infection. The skin should always be carefully examined; skin scrapes, cultures, impression smears or biopsies should be performed as necessary.
Malnutrition.	Malnutrition is the most significant cause in the majority of pet birds. If the bird's diet is inadequate, feather quality will be poor. The feathers will break or will irritate the bird, who will then attempt to remove them (see Chapter 3).
Metabolic	On occasions, metabolic disorders are responsible for feather plucking. Hypothyroidism disorders. (especially in cockatiels) diagnosis cannot be made on a single T_4 test; a thyroid stimulation test is required. Any form of hepatitis can lead to cutaneous pruritus and hence plucking. Chronic hypocalcaemia can lead to feather plucking.
Neoplasia.	Feather plucking will often occur over the site of a skin neoplasm. There is circumstantial evidence that the trauma of chronic feather plucking can lead to cutaneous neoplasia.
Polyomavirus.	Psittacine beak and feather disease (PBFD) should be excluded. A PCR test is now available (Vetgen Europe) and should be used if the signs are suggestive (see Chapter 10).

Table 22.4. Psychological causes of feather plucking (see also Chapter 11).

Condition	Comments
Attention seeking.	Many pet birds are bored; feather plucking can be a way of attracting their owner's attention. In such cases, once a bird starts plucking, it rapidly becomes a vicious circle. The more the owner scolds the bird, the more attention it is receiving and hence the happier it will be. Such birds tend to pluck predominately in their owner's presence.
Boredom.	Boredom or lack of routine is a very common cause of feather plucking. In comparison with a wild caught bird's natural life, life in a cage or a household, when owners are often absent for much of the day, may be similar to solitary confinement for a human.

Table 22.4. Continued.

Condition	Comments
Overcrowding.	Too many birds, social stress or too small an environment can lead to plucking. This can also occur where there are disputes between caged birds over territory rites. A dominant bird in a cage or aviary will sometimes pluck a subordinate bird in order to enforce his/her dominance.
Environmental change.	Birds thrive best when life is entertaining but routine; therefore, any recent change or a disorganised constantly changing household can lead to plucking.
Excessive preening.	This can start as normal preening and then become overexaggerated.
Excessive day length.	Birds whose day length (including artificial light) exceeds 12 hours may begin feather plucking.
Nest building.	Many species will pluck in order to line their nest prior to the nesting season. However, this behaviour will sometimes continue after the end of the nesting season. Frustrated courtship, towards another bird or the owner, can also lead to feather plucking.
Feather clipping.	A poorly or unevenly clipped wing can entice a bird to start feather plucking in an attempt to perform a neater job.
Trauma.	Birds which have had any traumatic injury or internal pain may pluck in an attempt to alleviate pain or irritation.

Table 22.5. Step by step diagnosis of the feather plucking bird.

Investigation	Comments
Dietary history.	A detailed history should include the type of diet and food items, the duration of feeding this diet, any selective feeding and the frequency of feeding.
History of clinical signs.	Record the length of time the clinical signs have been noted, the age of the bird when the problem first occurred, the site of plucking, the initial appearance and progression of the lesions, and any previous treatments.
History of a general nature.	Any changes in the household at the commencement of the problem; if plucking behaviour occurs at certain times of the day or in relation to the presence of humans; is there any vocalisation when plucking occurs. Ascertain if there are, or have been, any other birds in the house, and if so were they in the same room as the patient. If it is an aviary bird, examine other birds to see if they are affected. Quantify the length of daylight the bird is exposed to (including artificial light) and assess if this is excessive. Are any toys present in the cage and are they ever changed.
Examination of a fresh faecal sample.	A Gram stain should be prepared for assessing the ratio of Gram-positive and Gram-negative bacteria. The sample should also be checked for the presence of yeasts and protozoa. Carbol fuschin prepared slides should be examined for *Giardia* spp.; ELISA or PCR screening for chlamydiosis is advised.
A complete physical examination.	In particular, check for signs of chewing, discoloration and mutilation of feathers and tissues. Note any skin scale, debris, erythema, etc. Record the areas of feather loss for comparison on subsequent visits by making a diagram or taking photographs. Feathers should be examined grossly and microscopically.

Table 22.5. Continued.

Investigation	Comments
Examination for ectoparasites.	Both skin and feather scrapes should be taken for examination under a microscope for the presence of mites or eggs. Red mite (*Dermanyssus gallinae*) is diagnosed by placing a white cloth over the cage at night; when removed in the morning the inside will be covered with mites. This will need to be done by the owners at home.
Collection of skin samples.	Samples should be submitted for yeast, fungal and bacterial culture. Skin biopsy should be taken, including a feather follicle.
Blood sampling.	A complete haematological and biochemical profile should be established, including bile acids estimations. A thyroid stimulation test should be carried out where thought to be warranted. A sample should be submitted routinely to exclude PBFD.
Radiographic examination in some cases.	Radiography can be useful, especially where biochemistry suggests hepatic or renal damage, but high quality detail pictures in two planes will be required.

IDENTIFICATION

Methods of identification of psittacine birds are important. Permanent identification allows parentage to be recorded or confirmed, will act as a deterrent towards theft or allow recovery of a stolen bird, and will confirm the stated sex of an identified bird. Various methods of identification have been attempted. Tattooing is neither reliable nor permanent. Preferred methods are the use of steel split rings (not alloy), microchipping or DNA recording. Steel split rings can be removed, but with difficulty.

DNA Records

With the development of PCR tests and DNA probes, the permanent identification and parentage of a bird can be established from its DNA profile. This method requires a blood sample to be obtained and stored (Vetgen Europe will store samples). This is most easily performed at the time of collection and submission of a sample for sex determination (see later). For confirmation of the identification of a bird, a second sample must be taken and the DNA pattern compared to the first sample.

Microchip Identification

Microchips are transponders which react to a magnetic field (the reader) by giving a unique identification code. The microchip should be inserted within the caudal pectoral musculature, where it is difficult or impossible for lay persons to remove. The routine microchip identification of as many birds as possible is to be encouraged. Only when there is a significant likelihood that any stolen bird has been microchipped, such that the future resale potential is affected, will the theft of birds decline.

SEXUAL DIFFERENTIATION

Some psittacine species are sexually dimorphic. Male cockatiels over one year of age lose the horizontal bars on the ventral aspect of the tail coverts, whilst females retain them. Most sexually mature female budgerigars have a brown cere, whilst males are blue. However, many psittacine species have no sexual dimorphism. In contrast to many owners' beliefs, behaviour is of little indication, as two birds of the same sex will frequently behave as a pair. The only behaviour which can be taken as reliable proof of sex is the production of an egg by a female; it being fertile proves the mate to be a male. The current necessity of breeding rather than importing birds to supply the pet trade, coupled with the increasing successes in psittacine reproduction, means that many clinicians will be consulted on the subject of gender determination. The two options are surgical sexing or DNA probe blood testing.

DNA Probe Sexing

DNA probe sexing is possible on most psittacine species. It is readily available to members of the public as well as the profession through Vetgen Europe (PO Box 60, Winchester, Hampshire, SO23 9XN. Tel: 01962 880376). Blood samples are collected into DNA preservative (supplied by Vetgen) via venipuncture or short nail clipping. The sex of the bird is determined by use of a PCR test and a DNA probe. Testing takes on average two weeks, and a certificate of sex determination is supplied. Some breeders are put off by the delay, the perceived possibility of mixing samples and the cost, which might be greater than surgical sexing, particularly when numbers of birds are involved. Birds may be sex differentiated by this method at an early age, which may be of assistance in determining which method of rearing the bird is to be used.

Surgical Sexing

Surgical sexing involves the use of a quality rigid endoscope and a powerful fibreoptic light source. It should be carried out under general anaesthesia. The technique requires considerable initial training and practice in order that maximum safety and complete certainty of result can be assured. The procedure has the benefit of providing a simultaneous internal examination, when concurrent disease may be diagnosed, as well as assessment of sexual activity or maturity and an immediate determination of sex. The procedure is, however, invasive and hence carries the risk of contamination or accidental damage to internal organs (especially the liver if it is pathologically enlarged) and involves a general anaesthetic. For these reasons, some clinicians consider that where a safer method exists, ie. blood sampling, it is an unnecessary surgical procedure and should not ethically be carried out.

Method of Surgical Sexing

Endoscopy is contraindicated in ill or obese birds. The surgical approach is made from one of several potential sites on the bird's left side (see Chapter 4). The bird is anaesthetised and placed in right lateral recumbency with the wings extended dorsally. The sites most commonly used are between the last and penultimate rib, behind the last rib (with the leg pulled back) or behind the leg (with the leg pulled forward). Patients should have been starved for three hours. A small area of feathers may need to be removed, the skin prepared and a drape applied. Sterilisation of the endoscope prior to and between birds is very important. Following incision of the skin and blunt dissection through the muscle wall, a sheathed 2-4mm rigid endoscope is introduced. Entry is generally into the caudal thoracic or anterior abdominal air sac. The air sac walls are penetrated until the left gonad is visualised in its normal position between the adrenal gland and the cranial pole of the kidney. Although birds have paired testes, the right ovary is absent in most species. Even in young birds the ovary typically has a granular or roughened surface; in more mature birds the surface may be interspersed by developing follicles. In very young female birds the thick white band of the supporting ligament of the infundibulum is readily visible as it transverses the cranial division of the kidney; no similar structure is visible in male birds. Testicles are generally white, although in some species they are grey to black, eg. cockatoos; they have a completely smooth surface. When active, the testicle increases greatly in size and the surface is covered with small blood vessels. Whilst performing endoscopic sexual differentiation, a full internal examination should be undertaken. Gender differentiation is in itself futile if the bird is not to be individually identified (see earlier). All birds which are endoscoped should have some form of permanent identification.

SUDDEN DEATH

All cases of sudden death should be investigated fully. A *post-mortem* examination will be required in order to rule out possible causes and hopefully provide a diagnosis (see Chapter 8). Possible causes of sudden death are listed in Table 22.6. Although these problems are listed under sudden death, in many cases the early clinical signs may have been missed and corrective therapy may have been possible.

Table 22.6. Possible causes of sudden death.

Cause	Diagnosis and comments	Possible prevention
Arteriosclerosis.	Diagnosis is on *post mortem* and the changes to the major blood vessels caused by the build up of cholesterol and calcium deposits. This is usually associated with old age and excessive dietary cholesterol. Usually, death is associated with a cerebrovascular accident or heart failure. Where there is not sudden death, evidence of a stroke or heart failure may be seen.	Development of this condition may be suspected following the establishment of high cholesterol and triglyceride blood levels. Radiography may show the changes to the major blood vessels *ante mortem*. If the condition is diagnosed at an early stage, possible dietary control of fats and oils may help to reduce further degeneration of the vessels. The use of frusemide (0.5-1mg/kg sid or bid) may help in reducing the congestion associated with heart failure. Exercise is to be encouraged.

Table 22.6. Continued.

Cause	Diagnosis and comments	Possible prevention
Caffeine (tea/coffee/chocolate) toxicity.	Diagnosis is usually made on the history of having had caffeine prior to death.	The effect of caffeine depends on what was recently eaten and the state of health of the bird, and not just the amount consumed. There is no way of knowing if a small amount could cause an overdose, even if the bird has tolerated that amount previously. Very small amounts of caffeine in a sensitive individual may cause cardiac arrhythmias, vomiting and diarrhoea, or seizures and death. Suspected overdose should be treated with sedatives and the bird kept as quite as possible.
Clostridial infections.	*Clostridium perfingen* organisms are usually isolated from distended gastrointestinal tracts. There is often generalised vasculitis associated with a terminal toxaemia. There may also be evidence of a necrotising enteritis.	Antibiotic therapy can be attempted if this condition is diagnosed *ante mortem*; however, the toxaemia may still result in death. Clostridial infections are thought to be associated with high sugar diets, although some antibiotics can also predispose towards *Clostridium* spp. in the intestinal tract becoming opportunist pathogens. Thorough washing of sprouted seeds before feeding is important.
Dehydration.	*Post-mortem* examination will show the presence of uric acid crystals in the kidney lobules, ureters and possibly the liver and pericardium. Blood urea levels are usually elevated, as this analyte will only be increased in a dehydrated bird. If the dehydration was associated with renal failure consequent to nephritis, changes in the kidney associated with this condition may be seen.	The degree of dehydration can be assessed by testing skin elasticity, although the best way to assess dehydration is on blood urea assay. Urea levels will only be elevated when there is dehydration. This analyte may also be used for assessing the response to fluid therapy. Renal function may be estimated by blood uric acid and creatinine levels. When uric acid levels are above 500mmol/l it is advisable to use an antigout agent in addition to fluid therapy. Allopurinol (10mg/30ml drinking water) and colchine (0.04mg/kg bid) can both be used. Unless uric acid blood levels are kept low, irreversible visceral or articular gout may occur.
Eggbinding.	Eggbinding is a common problem in birds and may be associated with the presece of an over-large egg or hypocalcaemia. In cases of sudden death the egg will be found within the oviduct or cloaca. There may be concurrent egg peritonitis (see later).	Palpation of the abdomen of hens will allow detection of any egg except where it is still in the magnum (Cooper and Lawton, 1988). Usually the bird will be depressed, sitting low on the perch or even straining. The egg may be manually removed *per cloacam* or may require calcium and oxytocin or even salpingotomy (see Chapter 20).
Egg peritonitis.	Evidence of proteinaceous material will be found within the body cavity. There may be oviductitis. There may be concurrent eggbinding (see earlier).	This condition is caused when there is an escape of yolk material into the peritoneal cavity (Blackmore and Cooper, 1982). The clinical signs are usually those of sudden death, but a sick bird may be presented with a swollen abdomen. This is particularly a problem in budgerigars, cockatiels and lovebirds (Harrison *et al*, 1986). Drainage of the abdomen and treatment with antibiotics may help prevent death.
Electrocution.	There may be evidence of burns depending on the voltage and current, and the length of time exposed. Often there are very few obvious signs.	Prevention of contact with cables near cages.

Table 22.6. Continued.

Cause	Diagnosis and comments	Possible prevention
Head trauma.	There may be a history of having flown into a window, door or wall. There may be fractures of the skull or intracranial haemorrhage.	Providing the trauma is not too severe as to cause immediate death, treatment may be attempted (see Chapters 18 and 19).
Heavy metal toxicity.	Lead poisoning is seen more commonly in psittacines than would be expected. Birds can be exposed to lead from their old cages, stained glass windows, champagne tops, lead weights in curtains, or even from atmospheric lead associated with car fumes. Once the clinical signs develop, the course may be rapid and result in death (Lawton, 1995). *Post-mortem* examination may reveal traces of lead particles in the gizzard. Liver samples can be analysed for lead concentrations. Zinc poisoning (new wire disease) occurs occasionally when birds ingest galvanised metal. It is commonest immediately after birds are placed in a new cage or flight (see Chapter 19).	Lead poisoning should always be suspected in a fitting bird. Mild clinical signs include regurgitation and polyurea. Routine biochemistry will often show that there is both renal and hepatic damage. Access to the source of lead should be prevented. Where there is lead in the gizzard, gavage or surgery is indicated providing the bird is strong enough to survive the procedure. Supportive therapy will be required for the renal and hepatic damage. Fits should be controlled with diazepam (0.5-1mg/kg i/m tid). The use of binding chelating agents, such as sodium calciumedetate (35-40mg/kg i/m bid for five days), or penicillamine (55mg/kg p/o bid) may neutralise systemic lead.
Hypocalcaemia.	Findings associated with hypocalcaemia include eggbinding (see earlier), heart failure or convulsions. Diagnosis is on low blood levels. Radiographs may show concurrent signs of osteodystrophy, although it is possible for a bird to die of hypocalcaemia without having oesteodystrophy.	The majority of psittacines will tolerate a degree of hypocalcaemia. However, at times of stress, such as handling, underlying disease or egg production, clinical signs associated with hypocalcaemia may be seen. African Greys are particularly prone to hypocalcaemia and may have a higher requirement for dietary calcium than other birds. Hypocalcaemia may also be brought about indirectly by too little dietary D_3, too much phosphorus or too high a protein diet. Calcium and phosphorus blood assessment should form part of the routine examination of all psittacines. Treatment should always be aimed at improving the diet and, in particular, by the use of a suitable calcium and vitamin supplement. Where there is eggbinding or signs associated with fitting, the use of intramuscular calcium injections is indicated.
Intestinal blockage.	The blockage will be found at *post mortem*. It may be caused by foreign bodies or a very large infestation of intestinal parasites, especially in young birds.	The toys and objects to which birds have access should not be capable of being swallowed. Routine worming of aviary birds will prevent the build up of intestinal parasite burdens.
Renal failure.	See Dehydration (earlier).	

Table 22.6. Continued.

Cause	Diagnosis and comments	Possible prevention
Respiratory blockage.	Usually there is a blockage in the trachea or syrinx. Often the blockage is caused by a foreign body, such as a seed, or an aspergillosis granuloma.	Loss of voice should be suggestive of a foreign body or granuloma at the syrinx and endoscopy should be undertaken to investigate (see Chapter 15). The use of an air sac tube may prevent death from respiratory blockage (see Chapter 6).
Stress of handling.	Death while handling can occur in very small birds or those with respiratory embarrassment. Birds with hypocalcaemia may also die following handling.	Take care not to restrict the movement of the keel and the abdomen while handling the bird.
Teflon toxicity.	There will be a history of exposure to fumes from an overheated non-stick pan. *Post-mortem* examination shows the bright red/orange changes in the lung tissue. The bird may be several rooms away from the source of the toxic fumes.	There is often respiratory distress before death. If the bird is presented soon enough it is possible to attempt treatment with nebulisation, fluid therapy and corticosteroids.
Tick toxicity.	An *Ixodes* spp. tick may be found, particularly around the head of a bird which has suffered sudden death.	Birds in outside aviaries close to vegetation are at risk in tick areas (Forbes, 1993).

REFERENCES

Blackmore DK and Cooper JE (1982) Diseases of the reproductive system. In: *Diseases of Cage and Aviary Birds*. 2nd Edn. Ed ML Petrak. Lea and Febiger, Philadelphia.

Brown PA and Newman JA (1992) Diagnosis of avian chlamydiosis: questions, answers, questions. In: *Proceedings of the Association of Avian Veterinarians Annual Conference 1992*. AAV, Lake Worth.

Cooper JE and Lawton MPC (1988) The urogenital system. In: *Manual of Parrots, Budgerigars and Other Psittacine Birds*. Ed CJ Price. BSAVA, Cheltenham.

Dorrestein GM (1993) Avian chlamydiosis therapy. *Seminars in Avian and Exotic Pet Medicine* **2(1)**, 23.

Doolen M (1994) Crop biopsy - a low risk diagnosis for neuropathic gastric dilatation. In: *Proceedings of the Association of Avian Veterinarians Annual Conference 1994*. AAV, Lake Worth.

Forbes NA (1993) Pathogenicity of ticks on aviary birds. *Veterinary Record* **133(21)**, 532.

Fudge AM (1992) Clinical observations with avian chlamydial infections. In: *Proceedings of the Association of Avian Veterinarians Annual Conference 1992*. AAV, Lake Worth.

Gerlach H (1994) Chlamydia. In: *Avian Medicine: Principles and Application*. Eds BW Ritchie, GJ Harrison and LR Harrison. Wingers, Lake Worth.

Harrison GJ, Woerpel RW, Rosskopf WJ and Karpinski LG (1986) Symptomatic therapy and emergency medicine. In: *Clinical Avian Medicine and Surgery, including Aviculture*. Eds GJ Harrison and LR Harrison. WB Saunders, Philadelphia.

Lawton MPC (1995) Neurological problems of exotic species. In: *Manual of Small Animal Neurology*. 2nd Edn. Ed SJ Wheeler. BSAVA, Cheltenham.

Storz L (1971) *Chlamydia and Chlamydia Induced Diseases*. Charles C Thomas, Springfield.

Taylor M (1993) A new endoscopic system for the collection of diagnostic specimens in the bird. In: *Proceedings of the Association of Avian Veterinarians Annual Conference 1993*. AAV, Lake Worth.

Taylor M (1994) Endoscopic examination and biopsy techniques. In: *Avian Medicine: Principles and Application*. Eds BW Ritchie, GJ Harrison and LR Harrison. Wingers, Lake Worth.

Tully TN (1993) Clinical aspects of companion bird chlamydial infections. *Seminars in Avian and Exotic Pet Medicine* **2(4)**, 157.

CHAPTER TWENTY THREE

Zoonoses and Health Implications

John E Cooper and Margaret E Cooper

INTRODUCTION

Many zoonoses are transmissible from birds (Cooper, 1990) and a number of these can be associated with psittacines. Table 23.1 lists some important examples.

Control of zoonoses associated with psittacines is, in general terms, best achieved by:
● Ensuring that staff are aware of the potential dangers and how best to protect themselves and others. Employers should prepare a written list of all the potential dangers in handling and nursing psittacines and what action should be taken to minimise those risks. All members of staff, including any students, should read and sign these notes.
● Minimising contact with live or dead psittacines, their droppings (faeces/urates) or material that may have been contaminated by them.
● Practising strict hygiene when exposure is unavoidable.
● Arranging regular health checks for staff, including

immunisation against tuberculosis and other diseases where necessary.

In addition to infectious diseases, psittacines can present a risk to humans by causing:
● Physical damage with beak (especially), claws, and wings (see Chapter 4).
● Sensitisation to allergens in avian faeces, feathers, etc., eg. bird fancier's lung (see later).

CHLAMYDIOSIS

Chlamydiosis (psittacosis) will be discussed in most detail because it is known to members of the public, is associated in the minds of many with psittacines ('parrot fever'), is sometimes fatal in humans and is not infrequently the cause of litigation, insurance claims or complaints about professional conduct.

Important points that have to be remembered about

Table 23.1. Examples of zoonotic diseases associated with psittacines.

Disease	Causal organism	Means of spread	Effect on Host		Possible control measures	Comments
			Bird	**Human**		
Salmonellosis.	*Salmonella* spp.	Usually ingestion, occasionally other routes.	Varies from sub-clinical (non-apparent) to acute systemic disease.	Varies. Often gastrointestinal, sometimes fever.	Hygiene. Routine health checks.	Carriage is common in some species. See Cooper (1990).
Chlamydiosis (psittacosis or ornithosis) (see Chapter 22).	*Chlamydia psittaci.*	Usually inhalation, occasionally other routes.	Varies from sub-clinical to acute systemic disease.	Varies from sub-clinical to severe respiratory disease. Can be fatal.	Minimise contact. Hygiene. Routine health checks. Screening of in-patients. Safe *post-mortem* technique (see Chapter 8).	Can also be contracted from other (non-psittacine) species. See Wreghitt *et al* (1990).

Table 23.1. Continued.

Disease	Causal organism	Means of spread	Effect on Host		Possible control measures	Comments
			Bird	**Human**		
Yersiniosis (pseudotuberculosis).	*Yersinia pseudotubulosis* and *Y. enterocolitica.*	Usually ingestion.	Varies from sub-clinical to acute disease.	Alimentary signs.	Control rodents; minimise contamination of food by rodents or wild birds. Hygiene.	A wide range of animal hosts.
Tuberculosis (mycobacteriosis).	*Mycobacterium* spp.	Usually ingestion, occasionally other routes.	Varies from local lesions to systemic disease. Cutaneous lesions are commonly *M. tuberculosis,* whilst systemic lesions are commonly *M. avium.*	Varies from local lesions to extensive involvement of respiratory or alimentary tract.	Hygiene. Routine health checks.	Immunosuppressed individuals are particularly susceptible to mycobacteria, including atypical species.
Ectoparasite infestation.	Many species, especially *Dermanyssus gallinae.*	Contact.	Varies from sub-clinical to pruritus and anaemia.	Pruritus and skin lesions.	Hygiene. Routine health checks.	Some individuals seem more susceptible than others. See Haag (1988).

chlamydiosis, in addition to those mentioned earlier, are:

● Transmission to humans is primarily through inhalation of infected dust.

● Transmission is more likely when birds are unwell or stressed as they are likely to be shedding the causal organism. However, apparently healthy birds can carry *Chlamydia psittaci* asymptomatically for many years and can excrete the organism intermittently. Detailed information on chlamydiosis can be found in Chapter 22.

Although the diagnosis of chlamydiosis is not always easy, tests can be carried out on live birds in order to detect the organism. A full clinical 'work up' is essential (Tully, 1993). Affected birds can be treated and some will cease to excrete the organism. Others, however, may remain infected and culling may be necessary.

The veterinary surgeon must do all that is possible to protect his/her clients and staff, and the general public, from chlamydiosis. There are no hard-and-fast rules, but the following may help to reduce the risk of infection and attendant legal and professional difficulties:

● Inform all prospective purchasers of psittacines of the possible risks from chlamydiosis and other diseases.

● Encourage purchasers:
    ● To obtain their birds from good quality sources where screening for *C. psittaci* has been performed.
    ● To bring their new acquisitions for a veterinary examination, including screening for *C. psittaci.*
    ● To isolate (quarantine) all new birds for at least six weeks.

● Advise clients of the risk of latent infection and intermittent shedding. Prepare a client information sheet listing the signs of chlamydiosis in birds and in humans, and give a copy to all new owners. Advise clients to have all birds screened at least annually.

● Advise all members of staff in the practice, both veterinary and non-veterinary, of the particular hazards presented by psittacines and provide both verbal and written instructions as to how these dangers can

Table 23.2. Suggested protocol for practices dealing with psittacines.

Circumstances	Action to be taken
General.	Be wary of all psittacines, even if clinically healthy, and ensure that a veterinary surgeon is involved from the outset. Develop a good relationship with local medical colleagues. Staff with a history of ill-health, including allergy, should not work with psittacines.
Telephone calls from clients regarding sick psittacines.	Keep a note of any advice given. If clinical description or circumstances suggest that a zoonosis is possible, advise veterinary examination as soon as possible. Give initial advice to reduce risk to those in contact with the bird.
Psittacines being brought to the practice.	If an infectious disease is suspected or possible, make a specific appointment so that on arrival the bird can be examined promptly and isolated from other patients and clients. Advise on movement of bird, eg. avoid public transport, keep cage covered. If an infectious disease seems unlikely, a specific appointment is not essential, but is advisable. Make every effort to ensure that the bird does not spend an extended period of time in a crowded waiting room. Consider isolating the bird on arrival until examination can be carried out.
Examination of psittacines.	Must be performed by a veterinary surgeon with a minimum number of supporting staff who are familiar with the work and the risks involved. The examination room must be well ventilated, preferably with extractor fans, and easily cleaned and disinfected. Clean leather gloves, towels, rubber gloves, goggles and face masks should be available and always used when chlamydiosis is suspected. Protective clothing (coats) must be worn. Bites and scratches should be avoided, as should close contact with faeces, exudates or feather dust. Any injuries or incidents must be listed in the practice accident book.
Laboratory samples.	Take all samples hygienically, avoiding spillage or contamination of bottles. Use evacuated tubes, not syringes, for blood. Label all containers clearly and include the species' name. Process in-house samples with care, wearing protective clothing. The laboratory must be well ventilated and, if possible, the investigations performed under a hood or in a fume cabinet. Microscope slide preparations should all be mounted with cover slips. If hygienic and safe laboratory work is not possible in the practice, samples should be sent to an outside laboratory with adequate facilities for containment. Samples should be delivered by hand if possible: if the mail is used the Post Office Regulations must be followed. All samples must be properly wrapped, labelled and packaged before posting (a copy of the specific requirements can be obtained from the Post Office).
Hospitalisation of psittacines.	Ensure that the bird is in a well ventilated room or its own isolation chamber. All sick psittacines should be considered chlamydiosis positive until proved to the contrary (see Chapter 22). Keeping the bird in an isolation chamber is essential if chlamydiosis is suspected. Care should be taken that parrots are kept in parrot-proof cages, ie. ones with metal bars and lockable doors. Escaped parrots can be a danger to themselves and to members of staff. Parrot cages must not be left adjacent to electric wires or other items on which they might chew. This can endanger the birds and/or put the health of members of staff at risk. Only suitably trained and experienced members of staff should tend and clean the bird and they must wear protective clothing (see Chapter 4 for safe handling techniques). Faeces, bedding and other waste material must be properly wrapped, and incinerated as clinical waste. Local Health and Safety Executive (HSE) rules should be posted outside the avian hospitalisation area.
Nebulisation.	Although this is an invaluable technique in the treatment of psittacines, consideration should be given to minimise the risk of inhalation of unnecessary therapeutic agents by members of staff (see Figure 23.1).

Table 23.2. Continued.

Circumstances	Action to be taken
Discharge of psittacine patients.	Only discharge when you are confident that the bird does not present an unacceptable risk to its owner or others. Explain the situation to the owner and provide a written report. A veterinary surgeon must authorise discharge.
Post-mortem examination (see Chapter 8).	Send psittacines to a Veterinary Investigation Centre (VIC) or other suitably equipped laboratory. Wrap and despatch the carcase as outlined earlier (see Laboratory Samples). Only perform a *post-mortem* examination in the practice if the facilities are suitable (Gresham, in press). Eggs can be examined in the practice laboratory, but follow the precautions outlined above.

best be minimised. This is a legal requirement in many countries, eg. The Control of Substances Hazardous to Health Regulations (COSHH) 1988 (UK), Occupational Safety and Health Administration (OSHA) (USA), etc. A suggested protocol covering all types of danger is given in Table 23.2 and referred to again at the end of this chapter.

The precautions listed will help to reduce the risk from other infectious agents as well as from *C. psittaci*, but in specified cases additional steps may be advisable. It is always prudent to put advice in writing and to keep a copy for future reference.

SENSITISATION TO ALLERGENS

'Bird-fancier's lung' (budgerigar-fancier's or pigeon-breeder's lung) is a form of extrinsic allergic alveolitis resulting from sensitisation to faeces, feathers or other products of birds. The clinical signs in affected persons are predominantly respiratory - dyspnoea, cough, intermittent pyrexia. The onset may be sudden or gradual. While corticosteroids and other chemotherapy may give temporary relief, the only long-term treatment is removal of the affected individual from the offending material to which he/she has become allergic. In veterinary practice, bird-fancier's lung can present problems if a member of staff is susceptible. If this is the case the following measures must be considered:
● The affected person should not as a general rule be permitted to deal with live or dead birds or their derivatives (feather, faeces, cages, etc.).
● On the rare occasions when contact with birds or their derivatives is inevitable, appropriate clothing must be available, including a safety helmet or filter mask.
● In rooms where live birds may be brought or examined, the risk of accidental exposure to allergens must be minimised by:
● Good ventilation, including at least 10 air changes per hour.
● High standards of hygiene, including vacuum

cleaning of surfaces immediately after the bird has left the premises.
● In rooms where live birds may be kept for observation or treatment, the door should be self-locking and airtight, ventilation and hygiene as above, and access to the room restricted to authorised persons. Ideally, the birds should be kept in isolation chambers, laminar flow cabinets or a similar containment facility (see Figure 23.1).
● In rooms where dead birds may be examined *post mortem*, precautions comparable to those mentioned above should apply and the necropsy should be performed in a safety cabinet.

In addition to these points all members of staff should be made aware of their colleagues' susceptibility to bird-associated allergy and the correct steps to take if an acute reaction occurs.

Brief mention should also be made of recent claims (Kohlmeier *et al*, 1992) that pet bird ownership is associated with an increased risk of developing lung cancer. The validity of the study has been questioned by a number of authors. Nevertheless, practitioners should be aware of this debate since they may be approached about the risk by clients or medical colleagues.

Useful contacts and addresses are to be found in *The Health and Safety at Work Directory 1994/95* published by Croner, Kingston-upon-Thames.

LEGISLATION

Legal requirements relating to matters discussed in this chapter will differ from country to country. The legislation described below is specific to the United Kingdom.

It must be assumed that any contact with psittacines can be hazardous to health, and this raises both legal and ethical issues.

In formulating a policy the veterinary surgeon has to consider a) him/herself, b) the staff in the practice, and c) his/her clients and other members of the public.

Figure 23.1: A macaw in a nebulising chamber being treated for a respiratory infection. The use of such a chamber will also help to protect staff from zoonoses and bird-associated allergens.

The responsibilities insofar as the veterinary practice is concerned are:
- Legal.
  - Under the criminal law:
  The Health and Safety at Work Act (HSWA) 1974. The Control of Substances Hazardous to Health (COSHH) Regulations 1988 (OSHA is the equivalent legislation in the USA) and subsequent regulations complying with European Union (EU) legislation or directives.
  - Under the civil law:
  Possible liability for negligence (including that of employees), breach of statutory duty, harm caused by non-domesticated animals (Animals Act 1971), etc. (Cooper, 1987).
- Moral.
  - Quite apart from any legal consequences, failure to protect staff, clients and members of the public is likely to bring the veterinary surgeon, the practice and the profession into disrepute.

Basic guidelines that will minimise the risk to humans of infectious disease, physical damage and sensitisation are as follows:
- Have a written, standard, in-house protocol for the reception, examination, treatment, hospitalisation and discharge of psittacines. Ensure that all staff members have a copy and that it is displayed prominently within the practice. From time-to-time discuss the protocol with staff and, where appropriate, make any necessary changes.
- Regularly check and review the practice's facilities and equipment. Gloves, nets, hospital cages and other items should be properly maintained, be sterilised or thoroughly disinfected between use, and be available at all times.
- Keep written records of all psittacines seen and of any incidents, however minor, that occur that might present, or increase the risk of, a threat to humans.

The two main pieces of legislation of relevance to this chapter, HSWA and COSHH and associated regulations, impose many responsibilities upon the veterinary surgeon and his/her staff. It is essential that all those working in the practice are aware of the main requirements of these statutes. A summary is given below:

Health and Safety at Work etc Act 1974
The purpose of this Act is to secure the health, safety and welfare of persons at work, and to protect others from risks to health and safety resulting from the activities of those at work.

The Act imposes general duties upon employers, employees and self-employed persons relating to safety and welfare at work. The employer has legal responsibilities, but so also have employees - in their case a) to take reasonable care for their own health and safety and any other person who may be affected by their acts or omissions at work, and b) to cooperate with the employer to enable him/her to perform any duty imposed by the Act.

It is important to note that all duties under this Act are imposed 'so far as is reasonably practicable'. This means that it is not an absolute duty to prevent any danger, but a matter of balancing the measure of the risk with other factors, such as feasibility and cost.

The Control of Substances Hazardous to Health Regulations 1988
The Regulations require risk assessments to be made whenever activities are undertaken in the workplace that may result in a health risk. This includes exposure to pathogens or animals that may be harbouring them.

It is also a requirement that the employer should provide health surveillance of employees where there is a probability that disease may arise from occupational exposure. This includes obtaining information about previous employment and sickness history, and keeping and regularly reviewing records of health status.

Further information about the above legislation is to be found in Cooper (1987), British Veterinary Association (1991), British Small Animal Veterinary Association (1993) and Royal College of Veterinary Surgeons (1994). Assistance over specific problems and explanatory literature can be obtained from the Health and Safety Executive Secretariat, General Enquiry Point, Rose Court, 2 Southwark Bridge, London SE1 9HS.

CONCLUSIONS

All aspects of avian practice can present hazards and the veterinary surgeon has a legal and moral responsibility to protect him/herself and others. Work with psittacines can be associated with special risks and an awareness of these - and how best to minimise them - is essential.

REFERENCES

British Small Animal Veterinary Association (1993) *Guide to Local Rules on Health and Safety.* BSAVA, Cheltenham.

British Veterinary Association (1991) *COSHH - BVA Guide to the Initial Assessment in Veterinary Practice.* BVA, London.

Cooper JE (1990) Birds and zoonoses. *Ibis* **132**, 181.

Cooper ME (1987) *An Introduction to Animal Law.* Academic Press, London.

Gresham ACJ (In press) Post-mortem examination of cage and aviary birds. *In Practice.*

Haag D (1988) Brutende strassentauben als ursache einer invasion von *Dermanyssus gallinae* (De Geer, 1778). *Der Praktische Schadlingsbekampfer* **8**, 180.

Kohlmeier L, Arminger G, Bartolomeycik S, Beuach B, Rehm J and Thamm M (1992) Pet birds as an independent risk factor for lung cancer: case-control study. *British Medical Journal* **305**, 986.

Royal College of Veterinary Surgeons (1994) *Legislation Affecting the Veterinary Profession in the United Kingdom.* RCVS, London.

Tully TN (1993) Clinical aspects of companion bird chlamydial infections. *Seminars in Avian and Exotic Pet Medicine* **2(4)**, 157.

Wreghitt TG, Barker CE, Treharne JO, Phipps JM, Robinson V and Buttery RB (1990) A study of human respiratory tract chlamydial infections in Cambridgeshire, 1986 - 88. *Epidemiology and Infection* **104**, 479.

APPENDIX - FORMULARY

This Appendix lists the generic drugs mentioned in this manual together with an example(s) of the trade name(s) and manufacturer(s) current at the time of publication*. In the case of drugs which are produced by several companies, eg. some of the antibiotics, the trade name and manufacturer favoured by the author is shown. The dosage(s) and route(s) of administration is the standard one for treatment of psittacines, but in some instances different doses are required for specific conditions and these can be found in the rel evant chapter(s).

The editors stress that this is not a comprehensive list of all the trade names and manufacturers of drugs mentioned in this manual.

* The trade names and/or manufacturers names shown in italics are for equivalent products which are available in North America. Some of the generics listed have the same trade name in North America as in the UK. The editors are grateful to Dr Michael Doolen DVM of the Avian and Exotic Animal Hospital, Oakhurst, New Jersey for providing this additional information.

Drug	Dosage(s) and route(s)	Comments
Antimicrobials		
Amikacin (Amikin, Bristol) *(Amiglyde, Aveco)*	10-20mg/kg i/v, i/m or s/c, bid or tid.	Must not be used in dehydrated patients.
Amoxycillin/clavulanic acid (Synulox Ready to Use Injection, Pfizer; Synulox Palatable Drops, Pfizer) *(Clavamox, SmithKline Beecham)*	30mg amoxycillin/5mg clavulanic acid (ie. 0.2ml Injection) per kg i/m; 100mg amoxycillin/30mg clavulanic acid (ie. 0.16ml Palatable Drops) per kg p/o bid.	
Amoxycillin	Short acting - 150mg/kg i/m qid. Long acting - 150mg/kg i/m sid; 150mg/kg p/o, bid or tid.	
Apramycin (Apralan Soluble Powder, Elanco *[SmithKline Beecham]*)	0.5g/litre water p/o.	
Carbenicillin (Pyopen, SmithKline Beecham) *(Geopen, Roerig)*	200mg/kg i/m or i/v, bid.	
Carnidazole (Spartrix, Janssen) *(Wildlife Laboratories)*	20-30mg/kg p/o once.	For treatment of trichomoniasis.
Chloramphenicol (Chloramphenicol, Willows Francis *[Parke-Davis; Fort Dodge]*; Intramycetin, Upjohn)	80mg/kg i/m, bid or tid; 50mg/kg p/o, tid or qid.	Use with care and only in cases of severe non-responsive bacterial septicaemia. Can cause anaemia. Can cause vomition when given p/o.
Clazuril (Appertex, Janssen)	7mg/kg p/o 3 days on, 2 days off, 3 days on.	Coccidiostat.
Clindamycin (Antirobe, Upjohn)	100mg/kg p/o sid.	Good for osteomyelitis. Must monitor hepatic and renal function.
Clofazimine (Lamprene, Ciba)	1.5mg/kg p/o sid.	Treatment of mycobacteriosis.

Drug	Dosage(s) and route(s)	Comments
Doxycycline (Vibravenos, Pfizer; Ronaxan, Rhône Mérieux) *(Henry Schein; Roerig)*	10mg/kg i/m sid, or 75-100mg/kg i/m every 5-7 days; 25-50mg/kg p/o bid.	Treat for 45 days for chlamydiosis. Some injectable doxycycline preparations can cause myositis.
Enrofloxacin (Baytril 2.5% or 5% Injection; 2.5% or 10% Oral Solution; Bayer) *(Baytril 2.27%, Haver/Diamond)*	5-15mg/kg i/m bid; 1-2ml of 10% solution/1litre drinking water.	Treat for 21 days for chlamydiosis, and use 15mg/kg or 2ml/litre.
Erythromycin (Erythrocin, Sanofi) *(Lextron)*	10-20mg/kg p/o bid; 500mg/4.5 litres drinking water.	
Ethambutol (Myambutol, Lederle)	15-20mg/kg p/o bid.	Treatment of mycobacteriosis.
Gentamicin (Gentacin, Nicholas) *(Butler; Schering-Plough)*	5-10mg/kg i/m tid for 5 days.	Can be nephrotoxic. Might be better to use amikacin.
Lincomycin (Lincocin, Upjohn)	100mg/kg i/m bid; 75mg/kg p/o bid.	
Lincomycin/spectinomycin (Linco-Spectin Soluble Powder, Upjohn)	0.125-0.25 teaspoonfuls per 568ml drinking water.	Water soluble treatment for enteritis and mycoplasmal sinusitis.
Metronidazole (Torgyl, Rhône Mérieux; Flagyl S Suspension, Rhône Poulenc Rorer) *(Flagyl, Searle)*	10-30mg/kg p/o bid for 10 days; 10mg/kg i/m sid.	Antiprotozoal.
Oxytetracycline (Terramycin, Pfizer) *(Liquimycin - LA200, Pfizer)*	50mg/kg i/m sid.	
Piperacillin (Pipril, Lederle) *(Pipracil, Lederle)*	100-200mg/kg i/v or i/m, bid or tid.	
Polymixin B (Polyfax, Cusi; Surolan, Janssen)	Topical treatment.	
Rifampicin (Rimactane, Ciba) *(Rifadin, Marion Merrell Dow)*	15mg/kg p/o bid.	
Spectinomycin (Spectam, Sanofi) *(Syntex)*	10-30mg/kg i/m, bid or tid.	
Streptomycin (Devomycin, Norbrook) *(Azimycin, Schering-Plough)*	10-30mg/kg i/m, bid or tid.	
Sulphaquinoxaline/pyrimethamine (Microquinox, Microbiologicals)	15ml/10 litres drinking water, 3 days on, 2 days off, 3 days on, 2 days off, 3 days on.	Coccidiostat.
Tobramycin (Nebcin, Lilly; Tobralax, Alcan)	2.5-10mg/kg i/m tid; can be given topically.	

Drug	Dosage(s) and route(s)	Comments
Trimethoprim/sulphonamide (Borgal, Hoechst; Duphatrim, Solvay Duphar; Cosumix Plus, Ciba) *(Bactrin, Roche)*	8mg/kg i/m bid; 20mg/kg p/o, bid or tid. Cosumix Plus should be given at rate of 1g/l drinking water daily for 5 days.	Cosumix Plus is a water soluble powder and is useful for providing sulphachlorpyradizine in the drinking water.
Tylosin (Tylan, Elanco) *(Butler)*	20-40mg/kg i/m tid; 2 teaspoonfuls per 4.5 litres drinking water.	
Antifungals		
Amphotericin B (Fungizone Injection; Fungilin Suspension; Squibb)	1.5mg/kg i/v tid for 3-5 days; 1ml/kg p/o bid for 3-5 days.	Nephrotoxic in dehydrated birds. Give 15ml fluids at same time to prevent nephrotoxicity.
Enilconazole (Imaverol, Janssen) *(Clinafarm, Sterwin)*	1:10-1:100 dilution. Intratracheal or topical.	Aspergillosis and candidiasis.
Flucytosine (Ancobon, Roche)	20-75mg/kg p/o bid for 21 days.	For systemic yeast/fungal infections.
Itraconazole (Sporanox, Janssen)	5-10mg/kg p/o bid for 3 weeks to 3 months.	Adverse reactions recorded in some species, especially African Grey.
Ketoconazole (Nizoral, Janssen)	10mg/kg p/o bid.	More hepatotoxic than itraconazole.
Nystatin (Nystan, Lagap Pharmaceuticals) *(Myco 20, Squibb)*	300,000iu/kg (ie. 3ml/kg) p/o bid for 10 days.	Gut activity only. If given via gavage, may be placed distal to lesion.
Anti-inflammatories and analgesics		
Buprenorphine (Vetergesic, Animalcare) *(Buprenex, Norwich Eaton)*	0.1mg/kg i/v or i/m, bid.	
Butorphanol (Torbugesic, Willows Francis) *(Torbutrol, Bristol Laboratories)*	3-4mg/kg i/v or p/o, tid.	
Carprofen (Zenecarp, C-Vet)	2-10mg/kg i/v, i/m or s/c, sid.	
Dexamethasone (Dectan, Hoechst; Azium, Schering-Plough)	1-2mg/kg i/v or 2-4mg/kg i/m, sid or bid.	
Flunixin meglumine (Finadyne, Schering-Plough) *(Banamine, Schering-Plough)*	1-10mg/kg i/m.	
Ketoprofen (Ketofen, Rhône Mérieux) *(Fort-Dodge/Aveco)*	2mg/kg i/m.	
Prednisolone (Prednicare, Animalcare) *(Solu-Delta-Cortef, Upjohn)*	2mg/kg p/o bid.	

Drug	**Dosage(s) and route(s)**	**Comments**
Parasiticides		
Cypermethrin (Dy-Sect, Deosan)	Spray.	
Fenbendazole (Panacur, Hoechst)	15mg/kg daily for 5 days; or 20-50mg/kg once and repeat after 10 days.	20-50mg/kg daily for 5 days for capillariasis. Do not use during moult.
High cis permethrin (Harkers' Louse Powder, Harkers)	Topical dusting.	
Ivermectin (Ivomec, MSD AgVet)	200mcg/kg i/m, s/c, p/o or percutaneous.	
Levamisole (Nilverm, Mallinckrodt) *(Lavasole, Pitman-Moore)*	Use 1:40 dilution of 7.5% solution: 20-50mg/kg (5-15ml/ 4.5 litres) for 1-3 days. 2-5mg/kg i/m or s/c, repeated every 10-14 days on 3 occasions as an immunostimulant.	Has a low therapeutic index, therefore beware use as a wormer.
Praziquantel (Droncit, Bayer) *(Haver/Diamond)*	9mg/kg i/m or 10-20mg/kg p/o. For tapeworms repeat after 10 days. For fluke give 10mg/kg i/m or s/c daily for 3 days, then p/o for 11 days.	
Pyrantel (Strongid, Pfizer)	4.5mg/kg p/o. For nematodes repeat after 10 days.	
Pyrethrin/piperonyl butoxide (Ridmite Powder, Johnson and Johnson)	Apply to plumage. Repeat after 10 days.	
Antiviral agent		
Acyclovir (Zovirax, Glaxo-Wellcome)	80mg/kg p/o tid for 7 days; or up to 240mg/kg in food.	May cause vomiting.
Anaesthetic agents		
Alphaxolone/alphadalone (Saffan, Mallinckrodt)	5-10mg/kg i/v or 36mg/kg i/m or i/p.	May cause a transient apnoea.
Atipamezole (Antisedan, Pfizer)	250-380mcg/kg i/m.	Used to reverse xylazine or medetomidine.
Halothane (Halothane, Rhône Mérieux; Fluothane, Mallinckrodt) *(Fort Dodge)*	Inhalation agent.	
Isoflurane (Isoflurane, Abbots Laboratories) *(Aerrane, Anaquest)*	Inhalation agent.	
Ketamine (Ketaset, Willows Francis *[Fort Dodge]*; Vetalar, Upjohn)	20-50mg/kg i/v, i/m or s/c.	

Drug	Dosage(s) and route(s)	Comments
Medetomidine (Domitor, Pfizer)	60-85mcg/kg i/m.	Use atipamezole to reverse.
Midazolam (Hypnovel, Roche) (*Versed, Roche*)	0.2mg/kg i/m or s/c.	For use in combination with ketamine.
Propofol (Rapinovet, Mallinckrodt) (*Diprivan, Stuart*)	1.33mg/kg i/v.	Too short a duration, therefore of no practical use.
Tiletamine/zolazepam (Telazol, Robins *[Fort Dodge]*)	5-10mg/kg i/m.	
Xylazine (Rompun, Bayer *[Miles]*; Virbaxyl, Virbac)	1-2.2mg/kg i/v or i/m.	
Behavioural modifiers Amitryptyline (Lentizol, Upjohn) (*Elavil, Stuart*)	1-5mg/kg p/o, sid or bid.	Behavioural modifier. Useful in some feather pluckers.
Clomipramine (Anafranil, Geigy *[Baker Cummings]*)	0.5-1mg/kg sid or bid.	
Delmadinone (Tardak, Syntex)	1mg/kg (0.02ml/kg) i/m or s/c, once.	
Diazepam (Valium, Roche)	0.5-1mg/kg iv or i/m, bid or tid; 2.5-4mg/kg p/o, tid, qid or as required.	Used parenterally as anti-axiotic or anti-fitting agent; orally for sedation.
Doxepin (Sinequan, Pfizer *[Roerig]*)	0.5-1mg/kg p/o bid.	Behavioural modifier. Useful in some feather pluckers.
Fluoxetine (Prozac, Dista)	0.4mg/kg p/o sid.	Antidepressant. Useful in some feather pluckers.
Haloperidol 2mg/ml solution (Dozic, RP Drugs) (*Haldol, Henry Schein*)	0.4mg/kg p/o sid.	For feather plucking.
Medroxyprogesterone (Promone-E, Upjohn)	5-50mg/kg i/m or s/c every 4-6 weeks: 150g bird - 0.05mg/g; 300-700g bird - 0.03mg/g; > 700g bird - 0.025mg/g.	Used for excessive egg production, especially in cockatiels. Can cause lethargy, inappetence, polydipsia and fatty liver syndrome.
Megestrol acetate (Ovarid, Mallinckrodt) (*Ovaban, Schering-Plough*)	2.5mg/kg sid for 7 days, then twice weekly.	
Naltrexone (Nalorex, Du Pont) (*Trexan, Du Pont*)	1.5mg/kg p/o bid.	An opioid antagonist used to prevent self-mutilation.
Phenobarbitone (*Phenobarbitol Poythress*)	0.003mg/g (ie. 3mg/kg) p/o bid.	Used in cases of feather plucking. May cause deep sedation and inability to perch.

Drug	Dosage(s) and route(s)	Comments
Miscellaneous		
Activated charcoal (Forgastrin, Arnolds) *(Toxiban, Vet-A-Mix)*	2-8g/kg p/o as required.	Toxin binding agent.
Allopurinol (Zyloric, Glaxo-Wellcome)	Dissolve one 100mg tablet in 10ml water - 1ml of diluted solution/30ml drinking water.	Replace with fresh solution 3-4 times daily.
Atropine	0.05mg/kg i/m or s/c, repeat hourly.	
Calcium borogluconate 20% (Calcibor CBG20, Arnolds)	0.5-1ml/kg i/v or i/m.	
Calcium gluconate (Sandocal, Sandoz) *(SmithKline Beecham, Fort Dodge)*	50-100mg/kg i/v slowly to effect; 5-10mg/kg i/m or s/c bid as required.	
Colchicine (Colbenemid, Merk *[Lilley]*)	0.04mg/kg p/o bid.	
Digoxin (Lanoxin, Glaxo-Wellcome) *(Cardoxin, Evsco)*	0.01-0.05mg/kg p/o bid.	
Dinoprost (Lutalyse, Upjohn)	0.02-0.1mg/kg i/m or *per cloacum*, once.	For eggbinding.
Doxapram (Dopram-V, Willows Francis *[Fort Dodge]*)	5-10mg/kg i/v or i/m, once.	Respiratory stimulant.
Electrolytes, vitamins, amino-acids, dextrose (Duphalyte, Solvay Duphar) *(Avipro, Vetark Animal Health)*	40ml/kg i/v slowly qid.	
Frusemide *(furosemide)* (Lasix, Hoechst)	0.15-2mg/kg i/m or s/c, sid or bid.	
Glucose 5% (Aquapharm No 6, Animalcare) *(Dextrose 5-50%, Fort Dodge, Butler)*	50mg/kg (1ml/kg) i/v slowly.	
Iron dextran (Vet Iron Injection, Animalcare) *(Butler, Lextron, Vedco)*	10mg/kg i/m, repeat 7-10 days as required.	
Kaolin (Kaogel, Upjohn) *(Koalin, Vet-A-Mix, Evsco)*	2ml/kg p/o, bid or tid.	
Lactated Ringers (Hartmann's) Solution (Aquapharm No 11, Animalcare)	10ml/kg/minute i/v or i/o.	Calculate fluid deficit from PCV. Give over 2 day period plus 50ml/kg/day. Give the calculated daily requirement in 4 equal volumes during the day.

Drug	Dosage(s) and route(s)	Comments
Lactulose (Duphalac, Solvay Duphar) *(Cephulac, Marion Merrell Dow)*	0.2-0.4ml/kg p/o tid.	
Iodine (Lugols)	2 parts iodine + 28 parts water - add 3 drops to 100ml drinking water.	For treatment of goitre in budgerigars.
Mannitol (Mannitol, Sandoz) *(Webster, Vedco)*	0.5mg/kg i/v slowly sid.	
Metoclopropramide (Emequell, Pfizer) *(Reglan, Robins)*	0.5mg/kg i/m, i/v or p/o, repeat every 8 hours as required.	Anti-emetic and stimulation of normal gut activity.
Oxytocin (Oxytocin S, Intervet; Oxytocin, Leo) *(Butler, Lextron, Vedco)*	0.01-0.1ml/kg i/m once.	For eggbinding. Give with calcium.
Penicillamine (Distamin, Dista) *(Cuprimine, Merk)*	50-55mg/kg p/o bid.	Chelating agent that binds copper, zinc, mercury and lead.
Pralidoxime (Mesylate, Ayerst) *(Protopam, Wyeth-Ayerst)*	100mg/kg, repeat once after 6 hours.	For treatment of organophosphate poisoning.
Pyrimethamine (Daraprim, Glaxo-Wellcome)	0.5mg/kg p/o bid.	For treating *Plasmodium* spp., *Sarcocystis* spp. and *Toxoplasma* spp.
Sodium Calciumedetate (Sodium Calciumedetate [Strong], Animalcare) *(Calcium Disodium Versenate, 3M Pharmaceuticals)*	20-40mg/kg i/v bid for 5 days.	Heavy metal chelating agent.
Thyroxine (Soloxine, Vet-2-Vet) *(Butler)*	20-100mcg/kg p/o bid (ie. 0.025 mg/100ml water) for 4 weeks).	Used to induce moult and treat hypothyroidism.
Testosterone (Androject, Intervet) *(Henry Schein, Upjohn)*	8mg/kg i/m weekly as required.	Use with great care. Usually contraindicated. May effect spermatogenesis.
Vitamins ADE	0.1-0.2ml (10-20,000iu)/300g i/m weekly as required.	
Vitamin B complex	To give 1-3mg thiamine/kg i/m every other day.	
Vitamin B_{12} (Cyano, Bimeda) *(Cyanocobalamin, Butler)*	250-500mcg/kg i/m weekly.	
Vitamin E (Dystosel, Intervet) *(Seletoc, Schering)*	0.06mg/kg i/m weekly.	
Vitamin K (Konakion, Roche) *(Butler, Phoenix, Vet-A-Mix)*	0.2-2.5mg/kg i/m daily as required.	

INDEX